NEW ROADS TO RICHES

In the Other Americas

by

EDWARD TOMLINSON

Charles Scribner's Sons · New York
Charles Scribner's Sons · Ltd · London
1940

CONTENTS

[v]

Contents

ILLUSTRATIONS

[vii]

Illustrations

NEW ROADS
TO RICHES

At last Americans are discovering one another. From Alaska to Cape Horn the peoples of the Western Hemisphere are becoming conscious of their peculiar relationships, the ties —material and spiritual—which, because of geography, science and circumstance, bind them together.

Before the World War burst upon mankind in 1914, interest, news, and travel in the American nations were all oriented East and West. A majority of the families in this country, Colombia, and Argentina alike, were linked either by blood or sentiment to the countries of Europe. Millions still are. In the speech of many there remains the trace of Old World accents.

Naturally, when the average citizen of the United States, Venezuela, or Chile thought of the world beyond the borders of his own immediate country, he thought of the homelands of his forebears. When he travelled abroad he wanted to return to the ancestral haunts. He wanted to see the cities, the cathedrals, art galleries, and libraries so often described by his grandparents that to him they had become treasured traditions.

He was anxious for information concerning the happenings, incidents, and changes in Europe. Consequently, his newspapers and periodicals, sensitive to the currents of thought and interest, enabled him to follow them. Foreign news and European news were synonymous.

Telegraphic and cable communications had been laid not between New York and Lima or Valparaiso, but between New York and London, and between Buenos Aires, Rome and Paris. And since the people of Virginia, Massachusetts, Chile and the other American countries alike wanted to travel to England, France, Spain, Italy and Germany, maritime accommodations had been organized to suit popular demand.

The swift luxurious greyhounds of the Atlantic never ventured out of Northern waters. Business men and diplomats of the United States going on missions to Santiago, Chile, or Buenos Aires, or those Brazilians and Argentines, who, upon occasion, found it necessary to visit New York, travelled first to Europe and then to their respective destinations.

Peruvians, or Chileans were much more familiar with the Champs Elysées, Piccadilly, Unter den Linden, the piazzas and plazas of Rome and Madrid, than they were with Broadway, Michigan Boulevard, or Pennsylvania Avenue.

Commerce also followed the beaten paths. Alabama and Carolina cotton fed the looms of Lancashire, while English woollen fabrics protected New Englanders from the wintry blasts. The countries of South America exchanged wheat, hides, copper and an amazing assortment of raw materials for British and Continental manufactures. And the styles of Bond Street constituted sartorial criterions for the *señores* of the Rio de la Plata.

For a time, even the Great War served to intensify these Old World connections. Never before had the people of our own and the Other Americas felt, thought, hoped and prayed so intensely in terms of Europe. Mothers and fathers in Manhattan and Missouri had sent their sons to the scarlet-stained fields of Armageddon, many of them never to return, while thousands of Germans, Italians, Frenchmen and Britons in

New Roads to Riches

Guatemala, Colombia, Chile and Argentina offered their all to the lands of their youth.

Paradoxically enough, the World War brought home to the thinking people of North and South America an appreciation of the mutual advantages which a freer, if not closer, relationship might produce, and a realization of their growing interdependence. But if this realization was more the result of necessity than of choice it was none the less a fact.

Overnight, European factories had been converted into forges for the fashioning of engines of destruction, or kept busy turning out clothing and equipment for the legions who manned them. No longer were there finished products to offer in the markets of the Americas.

The machinery of European credit, upon which South America had hitherto depended, no longer functioned. Every shilling, franc, mark or lira was needed at home. Except for munitions and staple foods, commerce between the United States and Europe declined. Business men on both continents began seeking other outlets for their surplus products, outlets which they presently found in neighboring countries.

Then came the event which removed the greatest single handicap to communication and transportation between the United States and its neighbors. The Panama Canal was opened to traffic, affording a new road to the riches in these Other Americas. By water, Chile, Perú and Ecuador were now within a few days, at most two weeks, of all Atlantic and New England ports, while San Francisco was more than a month nearer to Rio and Buenos Aires. Atlantic and Gulf steamers took Louisiana lumber or Virginia apples to the West coast and returned with Chilean nitrate, Peruvian copper and Colombian coffee. United States-South American trade grew profitable to all concerned.

Steamship service had begun to improve, an improvement which has continued ever since, until today fast, comfortable

and commodious liners ply between this country and all the
ports of South America.

Answering the demand for even speedier transportation for
mail and travellers over the vast distances which separate the
capitals and populous centers of the New World, thousands of
miles of regularly scheduled air lines were established. Today
an extensive and efficient system of airways has brought New
York and Bogotá, Chicago and Santiago, Chile, within but a
few days of each other. Giant fifteen to forty passenger airplanes or flying boats are ready to whisk mail, express and passengers to the remotest city in any republic to the south of us.

Meantime a network of cables supplemented by American-
owned telephone systems in several of the countries had connected all the cities of the hemisphere. More recently radio
has added another important link in the vast system of communication which has made practically every person in the
hemisphere a next-door neighbor of every one else.

Highway construction is not only the newest but the most
needed development in all of South America, particularly in
the countries of the northern and western half of the continent.
Until the last few years there have been practically no roads.
It was impossible to drive an automobile beyond the limits of
even some of the largest cities without sinking into mud or sand.
Except by airplane, an occasional narrow-gauge railway, or a
mule trail, important towns and communities within the same
countries were completely isolated from one another. By land
or sea some are still as far apart as Seattle and Alaska.

But this condition will not prevail much longer. Venezuelans
have already spanned several mountain ranges with the most
modern highways. As far back as eight years ago they had
already surveyed and graded the first border-to-border automobile road on the continent. And the highway campaign is
still in progress. The indefatigable and undefeatable Gonzalo
Mejia, of Medellín, Colombia, is arguing, agitating, working

New Roads to Riches

day and night to keep the government, the engineers, the automobile owners, enthusiastic about work on a highway from Bogotá to the Gulf of Darien. And he is making progress.

Perú takes the prize in highway construction. I have just travelled over one of the most amazing automobile roads in the world, from Lima on the shores of the Pacific, up through the historic Rimac Valley, and on over the backbone of the continent, through the snow fields of the cordillera and down to the edge of the steaming jungles of Amazonia, while a second such road is already nearing completion. In fact, the Pan-American highway—"from the Rio Grande to Patagonia"—is no longer a wishful dream.

All of which helps to deal a death blow to isolation and provincialism, the parents of suspicion and misunderstanding. Now that it is possible for citizens of Pittsburgh, Kansas City, Valparaiso, La Paz, Caracas and Quito to get accurate and almost instantaneous news about one another, and even to visit one another with the greatest speed, convenience and comfort, neither can continue a stranger to the other.

Each country may maintain its own mode of living, business methods, culture and religion, just as next-door neighbors in the same city or community may indulge their own individual tastes in architecture, landscaping and interior decorations, as well as attend different clubs and churches, and yet be the closest of friends.

Nor should the fact that business and commerce between most of these countries has enjoyed tremendous expansion during the past few years cause them to overlook the cultural contributions which each may make to the other. Today students from Bogotá, Lima, La Paz and Santiago are finding American colleges and universities much more adapted to their needs than any others in the world, while archæologists and anthropologists from the universities and museums of this country have been flocking southward to study the historical treasures of

New Roads to Riches

Perú and Bolivia. The remains of the Inca and pre-Inca civilizations excite the imaginations of scientists and college students alike.

North American authors and journalists are now turning out voluminous amounts of copy every week on South American subjects. Some of it, of course, is faulty and inaccurate. A great deal of it is based upon prejudiced or preconceived ideas. Most of it is the result of cursory investigation and observation, but nearly all of it is enthusiastic. Furthermore, it is no longer merely the glamorous-adventure-soldier-of-fortune type of the Richard Harding Davis and O. Henry schools. It attempts to be serious, to deal with social, political, and cultural matters.

Club women and schoolteachers who formerly spent their summer vacations in Europe are turning more and more to the countries closer home. Tourists who have frequented the Mediterranean are now going in unprecedented numbers to the Caribbean. For several years cruise ships have been weekly visitors to La Guaira, Cartagena and Panamá. The old Spanish Main has become the American Mediterranean, both in winter and in summer, while in the past two years, seasonal traffic to the Atlantic and Pacific coasts has been increasing steadily.

And although the professional tourist, the inveterate cruise passenger, excites the fancy of the caricaturists, and is frequently decried by sophisticates, he not only spends his money in hotels, restaurants, sightseeing buses, and curio shops, thereby giving employment and livelihood to countless people in the various countries and cities which he visits, but he helps to swell the South American consciousness back home. He sees not only the growing cities and the modern new developments, but the colorful marketplaces, the picturesque old houses and churches, the strange and fascinating tropical fruits, hears the haunting and rhythmic native music. When he returns home he talks about them to his neighbors and friends, who in turn are intrigued into making the same trip and bringing back stories of similar experiences. The governments of some of the South American republics take the tourist quite seriously. Touring Clubs are important national enterprises in every capital from Caracas to Santiago.

It is this growing interest and enthusiasm upon the part of the general public in all the countries which has facilitated the solution of many political disputes. Today there is a definite, insistent, and outspoken demand for non-interference in the internal affairs of their neighbors. Likewise South American cordiality and good feeling toward the United States have grown rapidly, at least among the intelligent classes. With due respect for the motives of Franklin D. Roosevelt, and to the genuine and unostentatious statesmanship of Secretary of State Cordell Hull, the policy of "the good neighbor" was not merely the result of their own high purposes, but a happy expression of the sentiment of growing numbers of their fellow countrymen.

There will continue to be doubts, fears, misunderstandings and clashes of interests, all the changing impulses known to human emotions. But as an eye-witness to developments and events in most of the southern Americas for more than fifteen years, I am convinced that the ties between them are becoming stronger and more enduring with every passing year.

Now, then, in the pages that follow I have not attempted to delve deeply into the current politics or the history of the countries concerned. Politics in some of them is such a transitory matter that today's picture might easily become an old-time daguerreotype before this sees the light of print. As for history, that should be written by a professional. However, enough about both has been included to lend color and flavor and to round out the general story.

Nor have I presumed to crowd all the South American countries into one volume, the well-known six-weeks-round-the-continent method. Not only are most of them amazing in area, but each is a paragon of diversity and individuality. Perhaps the five Andean countries, Venezuela, Colombia, Ecuador, Perú and Bolivia, together with Panamá have more in common than any others. Popularly known as the Bolivarian republics, their liberation from the mother country was the direct result of the military campaigns of the great Venezuelan patriot, Simón Bolívar. They were not only conquered and settled at about the same time, and largely by the same people, but the first European settlements on the continent were made in the territory from which they were carved. Anyway, for the present it is to this group that I shall confine myself.

Finally, I should like to say that much of the material contained in this book has appeared in articles in *Collier's*, *This Week*, *The Cosmopolitan*, *Country Home*, *The New York Herald Tribune*, *The American Newspapers, Inc.*, *The Rotarian* and *The New York Times*.

VENEZUELA

I

Land of the Liberator

IF THE Yankees of Massachusetts had not become angry enough to make tea in Boston Bay the Henry Cabot Lodges, the late and the present one, might never have become United States senators. Even Calvin Coolidge might have lived and died a country storekeeper or perhaps a provincial British constable in Vermont. It is just as easy to suppose that if pickles had been selling in Italy and along the coast of Spain and Portugal in 1499, there might not be a single American in the world today. Apparently it was due to a recession in this particular trade that the young Italian merchant, Amerigo Vespucci, shut up his shop, went out to see the world, and got a couple of continents named after him.

Of course, if it had not been for Amerigo's luck in meeting at the moment a Spanish explorer by the name of Alonso de Ojeda, things might have turned out differently. Alonso, who had previously accompanied Columbus on that persistent old mariner's third trip across the Atlantic, was now consumed with ambitions to discover something himself. Not only that but he had been impressed with the lands along the southern edge of the Caribbean, and was now about to sail forth for another look at them on his own. Whether he signed Vespucci on as just another roustabout, or to keep the records of the expedition, is not clear. At any rate the restless youth, like most of his successors

[3]

who have forsaken legitimate callings for the primrose path of adventure, wrote a book about his experiences.

This may not be the sole, but it is one of the principal, reasons our Southern neighbors never cease to resent, and perhaps rightfully, the possessive spirit of the Yankees for presuming to make exclusive use of the word "America."

"Indeed," says one proud and rhetorical Venezuelan, "you have no right to monopolize it. The valorous Vespucci wrote not about North America but about South America, indeed about the future Venezuela and Colombia. Moreover, Señor, if truth be repeated, it having been stated many times before, our claim rests not alone upon the facts set forth in the chronicles of Vespucci. There is also the Waldseemüller Map of 1507, perhaps the earliest map of the world. On that map the word America appeared upon the South American and not upon the North American continent."

These facts furnish as good a reason as any for selecting Venezuela as the place of departure in this journey of observation through the mountainous regions of the Other Americas. Looking southward from Yankeeland, Venezuela is the first of the Andean countries. In Colombia the mighty cordillera splits into three main ranges, one of which meanders more or less indifferently over into Venezuela, leaving in its course here and there tiny lakes, and pocketlike valleys. For more than half a thousand miles its northern wall skirts the shores of the Caribbean, rising sheer from the water's edge like a giant battlement warning all intruders against trespassing upon the treasured territory of this enormous country.

Superimpose upon the map of Venezuela all our fourteen states, whose shores are washed by the Atlantic, and there would still be room enough left for West Virginia. La Silla and Naiguata tower upward above the lazy old port of La Guaira more than 9000 feet, an impressive scene as your ship oozes out of the pale blue mist into the semicircular bay in the early morning.

[4]

Venezuela

Before the English put in a sea wall which penned off a small area of the Caribbean, just large enough for three or four ships to tie up at a time, vessels calling at La Guaira anchored out in the open ocean and bobbed up and down like corks on a fishing line. However, all of this is being changed. Work on an elaborate new port is already in progress, which is only one in a series of modern ports planned for the country's 1800 miles of coast line.

Whether because of a sudden burst of generosity, or with his tongue in his cheek, or out of pure pique over some acts of theirs which displeased him, the King of Spain once presented the Belzares family with the bulk of all Venezuela, provided they would go out, conquer, settle and develop it. Too busy with affairs at home to take a personal interest in such a useless piece of property, they sent Ambrosio de Alfinger, a gentleman of German origin, formerly known as Ambrose Ehinger, and a few men out to look over the situation. But the heathen Caribs and the Los Teques objected to Ambrosio's intrusion, so he did not tarry, but moved on westward toward Lake Maracaibo.

In fact, it was not until forty odd years after Vespucci's book that the Spaniards succeeded in staying on the other side of the mountains long enough to make a settlement. Even then they merely took by force the little Carib village of Caracas on the banks of the Apure River. Adding a few words to lend it the proper civilized, not to say Catholic dignity, they called it, "Santiago Leon de Caracas." Caracas served as a haven for the families of high officials on tour in the colonies. Even today Caracaños insist that the oldest families of the Venezuelan capital are descendants of early Spanish officials, and not of ordinary settlers.

For more than three hundred years a trip from La Guaira to Caracas, only seven miles straight across the mountains, was in the nature of an adventure until the English secured a concession for a railroad in order to connect their port and dock at La

New Roads to Riches

Guaira with the city of Caracas. For another twenty-five years this narrow-gauge line which winds around cliffs, through tunnels and over switchbacks, and which is said to have cost $200,-000 a mile, was the only communication between the Venezuelan capital and the outside world, until the old dictator, Juan Vicente Gomez, became too old and ailing to ride on horseback, took to automobiles, and became the first good-roads enthusiast in South America.

The highway from La Guaira to Caracas was the first piece of highway construction planned and completed by Gomez and one of the first all-concrete roads south of the Rio Grande, and probably the costliest. What is more, no South American road since shows more superb engineering, a compliment to the skill of the native Venezuelans who planned it and carried it to completion. It takes a running start from the docks in La Guaira, climbs upward in curves and curlicues along the precipitous cliffs, and leaps caverns for some twenty-three miles, before it rushes down into the main streets of the capital.

This remarkable road has put Caracas in the path of armies of tourists and sightseers who frequent the Caribbean both summer and winter. To the chauffeurs and taxi owners of Caracas a week without two or three cruise ships is a week to be struck from the calendar. Even the hundreds of families who go down to Macuto and its beach resort just outside of La Guaira for the week end hardly make up for the loss in revenue.

An enterprising lot the taxi men of La Guaira and Caracas. They join with the *gente bien* of the country not only in promoting travel but in advertising safety. At Buena Vista, on the brow of the mountain just before the road makes a last hairpin curve and disappears on the other side, the Chauffeurs' Union and the Rotary Club have erected a strange monument. They have piled the horrible wreck of an automobile on a great concrete block or pedestal and inscribed below it the usually unheeded injunction, "Go slower and live longer." But having already swallowed your heart several times as your car swings suddenly around a sharp curve at what you thought was ninety miles, but which the driver with one hand on the steering wheel and the other in the air as an aid to conversation, tried to explain was only ninety kilometers, an hour, the monument seems like the work of a sadist.

The Government too has gone in for education along the highways. Every few miles there are bold signs exhorting every one who passes to "Do Your Duty and Cure Yourself of Syphilis." Not to overlook any opportunity, the "Best-Friend-Won't-Tell-You" Pharmaceutical Company of St. Louis, Missouri, has plastered every bridge, rock and wall with the legend, "Listerine, the Perfect Prophylactic." In addition to these, garish billboards stare down at you from the rugged and verdant mountain tops, reminding you of the virtues of everything from rubber tires to aspirin.

Fortunately, just before the blatant persistency of modern commercialism becomes too unbearable, the car swings around another cliff and you look down upon Caracas, one of the few old cities of Caribbean South America that has not yet substituted drab, dull, corrugated iron roofing for that lovely old red Spanish tile, that fits so perfectly into the tropical scheme of things. And here, where bright scarlet bougainvillea climbs over walls and fences and tapering palms, apamate and other tall trees line streets and suburban roads, you may relax after a thrilling journey and enjoy the most delightful climate on all the South American continent.

It is a climate which even expatriate Yankees, long resident in Caracas, insist is the most equable in the world. Caracas has everything they will tell you—charm, an easy-going friendliness, but above all a climate. A Californian would not only feel at home here, but would envy the ability of natives and foreigners to describe the climate.

"Here in this little valley in the heart of the tropics," they say, "you find none of the climatic extremes. It is neither too hot nor too cold. It is neither too dry nor too wet. It rains neither too little nor too much. There are showers in May, June and November, and bright days and nights from Christmas to March and on into April."

On my last visit to Caracas I arrived late Saturday night in plenty of time for week-end activities. Sunday in the Venezuelan capital is far from being a day of rest. Contrary to Anglo-Saxon custom, it is a day of recreation. On Sunday the social swirl is at its height. First of all, church in the early morning, and again at eleven, when the streets are crowded with people. At that time old and young fulfill the tradition of their ancestors by withdrawing from the world for a brief moment in order that the spirit may not perish.

I joined an old friend for the eleven o'clock parade to the cathedral on the Plaza Bolívar. And parade it was, to the accompaniment of a symphony of bells and chimes. Devout old dowagers and elderly gentlemen in stately dignity alighted from their cars and hurried in. Dressy, if not dashing, dons lingered a moment on the steps to observe divine femininity, raven-eyed señoritas, wearing the latest creations of Paris, shyly conscious of the battery of admiring eyes. But presently the streets were empty and the city quiet except for the mellow strains of the organ, the shrill chant of the choir, and low voices repeating the old old story of the ages. Then the final words by the brilliant Monsignor Novarro, and again the streets were filled with laughter and gaiety.

From church we sped off to Paraiso—little Paris—there to see and be seen. High noon is the hour of the Sunday *paseo* in this dignified old suburb, filled with the old homes of the aristocracy. Scattered along its boulevards are statues of the great —Sucre, Bolívar and others. There is even a marvellous likeness of George Washington, a fit figure to stand in the city of Bolivar, the man who did for several of the Other Americas

[8]

Hacienda La Vega

Road from La Guaira to Caracas

what Washington did for ours. It stands in the most prominent position on the thoroughfare and at its base there is always a fresh wreath of flowers. Washington is not merely a name in Venezuela. He was the idol of Simón Bolívar, the George Washington of Venezuela, and he is a hero to the schoolboy of today.

As I watched the people of Caracas parade in state before the memorial of Washington in Paraiso, I thought of the humble statue of Bolívar in Central Park in New York. This memorial to the father of Venezuela doesn't fare so well. It stands on a secluded knoll, almost forgotten, except for an occasional visit from some Bolívar enthusiast, a dutiful Committee of the Pan-American Society of New York City, or a patriotic Venezuelan.

But getting back to the *paseo*, the main boulevard of Paraiso was jammed with shiny new cars. There were two lines moving in opposite directions, so that every one faced every one else. Round and round they drove. Every one seemed to know every one else. The men were continually tipping their hats, so continually there was a perpetual wig-wag of arms.

Caracas wouldn't be Venezuela without its *paseo*. Venezuelans wouldn't be Spanish Americans if they didn't pass each other in review at least once a week. In the days of General Gomez, when he spent an occasional Sunday in Caracas, he too would be found in the parade. Even in the late afternoon on weekdays he would visit the imposing Pabellon, or restaurant in Paraiso where hundreds gathered at teatime. It was considered smart by his followers and discreet by his enemies to have tea with "Benemerito General," as his friends affectionately referred to him.

Like the people of old Madrid the citizens of Venezuela still thrill to the sport of the mother country. The graceful matador in his silks and fine laces is still a popular idol. For now and then on Sunday, and more often, he continues to tease and tantalize El Toro. I suppose there have been more gala fights than the one I saw in Caracas that Sunday afternoon. But the crowd was very excited, even if the bulls were not overly ferocious. The matadors were not so famous, as wigglers of the cape go, but they were stunning to look at. Especially Saturio Torón, the tall Moor from Spain; and tiny Heriberto García, from old Mexico. What flashy fighters these; and what flashy tailoring they wore. The Moor was fitted out in pink jacket and breeches, purple lace collars and cuffs and stockings of deepest lavender. At least if these were not the exact colors, they were just as conspicuous, not to say exciting. The Mexican lad wore a complete ensemble of orange and gold—jacket with golden collar and cuffs, orange pants and stockings, and slippers with golden buckles. No bull, however raving, could have taken the spotlight from these gallant lads!

Señor Torón had the first go. He faced a somewhat frisky old roue of the range, who looked as though he bore in his heart an age-long hatred of the Spaniards and all their progeny. For a time it was a delightful encounter. Gyrating back and forth from side to side, the big Moor led his quarry on to the point of desperation. Once or twice he turned away for a moment, with mock indifference. Then just as he was poised on his tiptoes ready to jab the *banderillas* in the shoulders of the king of kine, something happened. Señor Torón lost his balance, and to his own amazement, was tossed high in the air. Ten thousand hearts stopped beating for a moment. Ten thousand people held their breath—waiting to witness the worst.

But this time luck was kind. Although somewhat embarrassed at suffering such indignity, and soiling his exquisite silks and laces, Torón retrieved his shattered dignity and again took his stand on the field of honor. *Banderillas* in hand, he rose on his tiptoes, threw out his chest, until his back was curved in, or, if you like, his chest curved out like a half moon, and waited for the charge. Like a flash it came, and once more Señor

Torón went up, then down, and then out—on a stretcher.

But no such misfortune befell the amazing little Mexican when he faced his partner. Both were as light on their feet as kittens. García careened back and forth, his cape wig-wagging in perfect rhythm. He was the poetry of motion and the master of his prey. From right to left they oscillated, until the bull turned away as if to say, "Well, what is this anyway!"

And then came the second act. Our little hero took his stand, raised his arms high with colorful *banderillas* in his hands. El Toro sniffed, and lunged forward, only to find himself decorated something after the manner of a porcupine, with fancy, beribboned arrows sticking in the back of his neck. A little more cape play, and then the *Mozo de Estoque* handed García something shiny—that slender rapierlike sword, the *estoque*, which dispatches its victim to the eternal grazing grounds. A bugle split the air, and the spectators leaned forward, eyes glued to man and beast. A pause—now—in the flash of an eye all was over, except the shouting. The multitude went mad. Hats were thrown into the ring. The band burst into "Los Banderilleros," the music of the bullfighter. García, like a hero returned from the field of victory, marched round and round the ring, bowing and waving, salvos of bravos ringing in his ears.

But if I had never been to Caracas before, and I had time to visit only two or three of its many points of interest, I would have no difficulty selecting them. I wouldn't go to the fashionable suburb of Paraiso to see the Sunday *paseo*, even though it would afford an opportunity to mingle with the aristocracy, as well as the privilege of feasting the eyes upon flocks of señoritas. I should even forego the bloodcurdling experience of the bullfight. I would pass up the old university, whose stormy career dates back to 1725. In the shadows of its aged walls I should probably pass sprouting lawyers, orators and poets enough to identify its classic atmosphere. Contrary to their custom a few years ago, when Gomez was in power, they would probably be engaged in heated argument about the world in general—socialism, capitalism and communism.

In the ornate old capital building across the way from the university I would spend a few minutes, just long enough to visit the Salón Eliptico, its great hall where national history has been spectacularly recorded by native artists. It is the dome of this hall that contains Martin Tovar y Tovar's historic painting of the battle of Carabobo. Tovar y Tovar was the most notable of all Venezuelan painters and the public buildings of Caracas are the scenes of his artistic triumphs. Perhaps, while in the mood for Tovar y Tovar, I would drop into the municipal Council Chamber, close by, and take a look at another of his glamorous portrayals of historic events, this time the signing of the act of Venezuelan independence.

But as quickly as possible I would find my way into Calle Sur Uno—South First Street—one of those ancient, narrow thoroughfares of the old Caracas. I would stop before a certain great door in a blank wall which I would have no difficulty in identifying, for over this door the flag of the nation always flutters in the breeze. To one side of it is a bronze plaque bearing the inscription, "Casa Natal," the birthplace. Casa Natal is the Mt. Vernon of Venezuela. Here Simón Bolívar looked upon the world for the first time.

In Casa Natal today you may read the life story of this remarkable man. Around its walls is the cycloramic story of another of Venezuela's foremost artists, Tito Salas, who ranks just after Tovar y Tovar. Salas was a strange and eccentric fellow who, before he began a picture, scrawled on the back of the canvas, "God protect me and St. Joseph assist me." In Casa Natal, Salas has recorded the outstanding events in the life of his hero, a life into which was packed enough romance, glamor, glory, pathos, disappointment, suffering, humiliation, seeming failure and immortal successes to fill a dozen careers.

Venezuela

Bolívar was the son of a rich father. He was an aristocrat of the colonies, cradled in luxury. As a child he had slaves to do his bidding, governesses and tutors to provide his every need. All the culture of hundreds of years of Spanish glory shone upon him. As a young man he travelled in Europe, played games with dukes and princes, visited His Holiness, the Pope. At twenty he fell desperately, insanely in love and married "the fairest of all earthly creatures," whom he worshipped until one year later when she died in his arms.

Then darkness descended. The world ended for the time being. The specter of insanity haunted him by night, the demon of suicide tempted him by day. Grief wracked him, body and soul. But eventually the clouds lifted, and he completely forgot self— for others. Life became something to give to humanity. He discovered other unhappy men all about him, men inexcusably oppressed. He witnessed the folly of kings, the cruelty of rulers, the injustice of governments, not only in the colonies of America, but in Spain itself and wherever he travelled on the Continent.

One day it all came to him. He was in Rome, the Rome of the Cæsars, the Rome of Nero, who, whether deservedly or not, is known as one of the most nefarious of oppressors, the Rome destined to become the stamping ground of Mussolini's Black-Shirted legions and the capital of a state in which there is probably more material progress and less spiritual and mental freedom than old Nero could ever have fancied in his most cruel moments. That day in the Eternal City Simón Bolívar climbed one of the seven hills, looked westward toward America— Venezuela—Colombia—Perú—and swore never to rest until the last puppet of the Spanish King was driven from the shores of the Americas forever.

And then began a crusade even more dramatic than that of our own George Washington, the North American titan who was the father of but one country. Simón Bolívar, as already indicated, became the father of five nations, Venezuela, Colombia, Ecuador, Perú and Bolivia. Colombia was the stage for his principal activities—in fact, Colombia, in the early days of independence, sprawled clear across the northwestern corner of the continent from the Orinoco Valley in the east down to the desert wastes of Perú, and from the frontiers of Costa Rica in Central America across the Andes and down into the Amazonian jungle, including the present republics of Panamá, Ecuador and Venezuela.

For years he rode in triumph up and down the Andes along the Caribbean and along the Pacific coast, leading armies, chasing viceroys, fashioning governments, and making diplomats and presidents out of captains and colonels. Lavish with himself, his spirit and his devotion to the cause of a new way of life for the unhappy but ungrateful colonists of Spain in the New World, this dashing, impetuous, incomparable son of one of the first families of colonial Spanish America finally fulfilled his pledge to conquer and drive the soldiers of his Spanish Majesty back to the Old World. He carved out the various nations and himself took over the republic of New Granada, the climax of his amazing career.

But just when he might have relaxed for the first time, and offered his sage wisdom and advice to the officials of the young nations, disease took hold of him, dissension grew up among his followers, and eventually he was actually hounded from office and from public favor. He came down from Bogotá on top of the Andes to Cartagena on the coast, only to find even more bickering and strife. Disappointed and ill, the cursed white terror creeping through his patrician body, he boarded a small ship and sailed out to sea hoping to go eventually to what was once his native city of Caracas. But the wish was not to be gratified. After stopping at Barranquilla for a few days' rest, he finally put in at Santa Marta.

I can imagine the scene. At Santa Marta the Andes reach the end of their Colombian journey, walk right out and disappear in the sea, one slender prong circling westward in a semicircle to make a quiet bay and harbor which shelters ships from the eternal trade winds. On that day the mountains lifted their tall white heads aloft as if in silent welcome to the unhappy arrival. He was greeted by a faithful friend who invited him to a little colonial cottage, known today as San Pedro Alejandrino, a little way out from the humid shores of the bay. There he went, to die in despair, humiliation and poverty and to be buried in a borrowed nightshirt.

The simple tragedy of his passing, the helplessness, the disappointment, the disillusionment, has in it all the emotional elements that make one of history's greatest dramas. The story has been told many, many times before, but it is worth repeating, as a continual reminder of the ungratefulness and perfidy of humankind, and the poor rewards a man may usually expect for his services to the public, especially while he lives.

It was already afternoon. The hot tropic sun beat down upon the world, a half-dozen faithful friends stood just outside the door. A French doctor and a young surgeon from a United States ship which lay in the harbor, were at the bedside. Bolívar looked up at the Frenchman and asked, "Doctor, what caused you to cross the Atlantic and settle here at Santa Marta?"

"I was seeking liberty," the doctor replied.

"Have you found it?" Bolívar asked.

"Yes, General, I have found it."

"Then," said Bolívar, "you have been more fortunate than I. I have not yet found liberty. But, Doctor, I do not grieve for myself. It is for the people. I wish for them complete liberty. They have been freed from an Old-World oppression, but now there is a new oppression—division, dissension. They dispute among themselves."

The sick man closed his eyes for a moment as if exhausted. But presently he again looked up and said to the doctor, "Please write down this message."

The doctor, with tears in his eyes, and his hand shaking with emotion, began to write as Bolívar dictated, "If my death—should unite them—I shall go to my grave—with a calm and contented mind."

Then after a long pause he spoke again, his words scarcely audible, "Yes, my grave. That is what they have presented me. But I am not bitter, I forgive them. If I could only know they were united, working together in harmony, then I should be happy in this last moment—but I have plowed the waters of the sea."

All this and more Tito Salas has recreated with his brush in Casa Natal in the city of Caracas. And, having read it, I would move on a few blocks uphill to the Pantheon, a graceful cathedral overlooking the city and the country beyond, the Westminster Abbey of Venezuela, where rest the country's illustrious dead. I would enter, and here amid the reverential stillness of this house of memories, I would stand in salute before the marble tomb of Simón Bolívar—The Liberator!

II
Fabulous Empire

IN CARACAS there is a stately old house looking out from a steep hillside. Extending its entire length is a terrace which in width suggests nothing so much as the boardwalk at Atlantic City. For a dozen years this house served as the home of the American Legation, before our diplomatic post in Venezuela was elevated to ambassadorial status. In the days when that hearty and generous host, George T. Summerlin, watched over Venezuelan-Yankee relations, it was the mecca of all strangers who hungered for congeniality, or thirsted for liquid inspiration. Here in the cool of the evening came not only members of the Yankee colony, but also of the British and French, visitors from Panamá, New York, Paris or Rio, almost any traveller passing through, and always more Venezuelans than foreigners. Even in those days Yankees and Venezuelans seemed to like one another, and the genial Minister, along with his whisky sours, and rum punches, helped to keep them on good terms.

It was there that I first met that deep-voiced giant, tall and wide of beam, William Tecumseh Sherman Doyle, whose name the Venezuelans are pleased to pronounce "Doilie." As a matter of fact it was at a stag dinner in his honor, preceding one of his rare trips out of the country. Some twenty male members of the American community having taken on highballs sufficient to mellow them into a state of raucous hilarity, sat down around a table groaning with roast pig, baked apples, dozens of other dishes and sauces, and gallons of red wine. Among the guests were Billy Phelps, the elder, who of late successfully and happily combines business with botany and other natural history subjects, Don C. Booker, famed as the twin convivial of Doyle, himself a character among the *Caracaños,* and many others.

As the pig and provender disappeared and the wine flowed they flung experiences back and forth across the table. They drank to the Minister, to Venezuela, to General Gomez, then in the calm afternoon of his dictatorial power, and to Doyle and his "brief absence."

"And brief absence it'll be," Doyle boomed back, his voice reverberating up and down the long dining room, with somewhat the resonance of a bull in a well.

"This will be my third visit to the United States in fifteen years."

Which seemed to surprise every one. For no one could have found a heartier welcome in his homeland. Doyle's career in the United States had been by no means a modest one. He started out as a newspaperman in New York, then went to Washington and essayed diplomacy, beginning as a clerk in the Department of State. Later Elihu Root took him on that triumphal and historic tour through South America. Back in Washington, he carried on, until Philander Knox came to plot the course of international affairs, when Doyle became an important adviser. He was a linguist, spoke French and Spanish. Gradually he took into hand our relations with the Other Americas, and served on several special missions to the southern republics.

But a tenant of another political complexion came to the White House and Doyle found it necessary to look for other worlds to conquer. One day he found himself in Venezuela and there he has been for many years—a powerful business figure, priest and guide to many of his compatriots—friend of Venezuela, and beloved by all.

Around midnight, when nearly every one else had gone,

Venezuela

Doyle and I stood by the stone railing of the terrace. Stars hung low in the clear heavens, like brilliant jewels dangling on transparent threads. The city was a sea of twinkling lights filling the valley below us.

"Down there," said Doyle, "is the future New York of the Caribbean, the metropolis of a fabulous empire, the capital of a country full of the riches the old Spaniards looked for but never found, riches of which Caracas is only the reflection. Come back in five years and you'll see."

As I thought the pig and wine had produced their proper and poetic effects, these remarks made no impression upon me at the time. But five years have passed. Two hundred thousand people had already taxed its housing capacity. But within the past two years twenty to thirty thousand more have caused it to overflow into half a dozen new suburbs. Few landmarks in the old part of the city have changed. But fields, farms and the grounds of old *haciendas* have given way to numerous subdivisions that look for all the world as if they had just been transported from Miami and Hollywood. No more houses in colonial style, with *patios* and grilled windows. Today it is bungalows and villas, with spacious gardens and grassy lawns.

Many people in the old part of the city have forsaken their stuffy colonial houses and moved out into the fresh air. Even Señora Herrera Uzlar, a descendant of the immortal General Ybarra, one of Bolívar's associates in independence days, has rented San Pablo, the marvellous old mansion which stands across the square from the Opera House and the Majestic Hotel. What a house, San Pablo! From the outside, just a giant wooden door in a blank wall. On the inside a thing of exquisite beauty, with several flower-filled *patios*. Originally it was imposing enough, but five years ago it was revamped to accommodate a big family of married sons and daughters who, in keeping with immemorial Spanish custom, brought their mates back to live in the big house.

[19]

New Roads to Riches

Each couple was provided with an apartment, or a series of several rooms, sufficiently separated from all the others to insure domestic privacy, but with access to the various drawing rooms, libraries and glass-enclosed conservatories. Each apartment was arranged, decorated and furnished in a different style, according to the individual tastes of its occupants, one of the Louis XVI period, another with a Moorish atmosphere, and still another in the Spanish colonial style. Yet all blended beautifully into the colonial atmosphere of the entire house. Now all the families have gone modern, moved out into the suburbs into individual houses or apartments.

With the passing of the dictatorship of General Gomez, thousands of people in Caracas have unsocked their money and put it to work in real estate developments. Hundreds of other old families who either could never stomach the Gomez regime, or whose views and activities Gomez would never tolerate, have come back from Paris, London and New York to enjoy the income from their properties and holdings. Even many who had forsaken the capital for their farms and ranches in the interior have returned to the city to live. And all have had to rebuild, rehouse and modernize their living conditions in keeping with the new age that came to pass while they were in exile, in retirement, or in eclipse.

Only five years ago the imposing country club stood in an isolated district of the countryside, several miles from the heart of the city. Today the intervening section is a succession of parks and new residential districts surrounded by wide, shady streets, white ways and broad boulevards. In this section Señor Arismendi, the Carl Fisher of Caracas, has just completed "Los Cāobos," a subdivision named for the forest of giant mahogany trees that stood in the park of an old estate.

Even Paraiso has had its face lifted. The great old mansions have been revamped and repainted. New streets have been cut through some of their spacious gardens and parks. The *Hippo-*

dromo, or race track, is completely surrounded by new homes. Small farms have been turned into recreation fields and playgrounds for the youth of the city. A new Olympic stadium has just been completed so that continental athletic tournaments may be invited to meet in the Venezuelan capital.

Beyond Paraiso is something new under the Venezuelan sun— Bella Vista. Sponsored by the Workmen's Bank of Caracas, it is a city of modern homes for workmen. Any man who labors with his hands may buy an ultra-modern house worth $3000 and pay for it in twenty years, in the best United-States-Federal-housing-for-workingmen manner, a bit a month, so to speak, until paid for. This innovation has thrilled the popular imagination and other projects are already in the making, or in prospect. Naturally the government has inspired or led the way in this particular field of development.

But I suspect the most unusual, if not the strangest, real-estate tax laws in the hemisphere have encouraged the building boom by private individuals. The tax laws covering city residential property are so simple and plain that even a layman can understand them. It appears that these laws were enacted for the purpose of helping the property owner instead of the legal profession. There are no Federal, that is, no national, or even state taxes on private real estate. Only the municipality may levy taxes on such properties.

If you own your house and live in it, you pay no taxes. If you rent your house to a tenant you pay a municipal tax equivalent to one half of one month's rent each year. That is to say, if, in the estimation of the municipal appraisers, with whom you have the right to discuss and argue the matter personally, and not through your lawyers, your property would rent for a hundred dollars a month, your tax to the city for one year is exactly fifty dollars.

Even the tax on a business enterprise is not exorbitant, and is also simply computed. For instance, in case of a bank, there

New Roads to Riches

are both a Federal and a municipal tax; the Federal Government collects a two per cent tax on net profits. Unless the bank makes money the Federal treasury receives nothing from it. A prominent bank capitalized at twelve million *bolivars* pays a flat municipal tax of twenty thousand *bolivars*, or about one sixth of one per cent. The *bolivar* is the monetary unit of Venezuela and is so called in honor of Simón Bolívar. At this writing it is worth thirty-one and a half cents in United States currency. In the case of banks there are, of course, certain stamp taxes on checks and other transactions, just as exist in this and many other countries, but they are so small as to be negligible.

José Marino is the proprietor of a small tailor shop and haberdashery. When I asked José what the taxes on such a business would be, he replied, "My entire stock is worth about thirty thousand *bolivars*. My total taxes this year amounted to three hundred *bolivars*."

Unfortunately, at the present time, such happy innovations are practically cancelled by the high cost of living. Rents are exorbitant, both on business and residential properties. Even when vacancies can be found, and no residence remains vacant overnight, a salaried foreigner, a bookkeeper, bank clerk, or engineer, with a salary of, say $250 gold per month cannot possibly make ends meet. His rent alone for a small five- or six-room house will average from $75 to $125 per month. Practically all American companies have added local differentials, as they call them, or additional salaries in *bolivars*, in order that their employees can meet this high cost of living. The rent now asked by Señora Herrera Uzlar for San Pablo is approximately $750 per month.

Hotel rates are correspondingly high and all hotels have waiting lists. When one is available in the Majestic Hotel, a room with bath in which tepid water is sometimes supplied, would cost from five to seven American dollars. In addition, or in spite of this, the guest, especially if he is a Yankee, must be willing to endure the frigid treatment of the management.

The prices of food in ordinary restaurants are even more exorbitant than hotel rates. A four-course luncheon for two, preceded by a rum cocktail, in any one of the two or three first-class restaurants in Caracas, will cost from eight to twelve dollars. The prices of luxuries are fantastic. A friend of mine paid six dollars for a two-pound tin of Blue Boar smoking tobacco. Boom prices, all of these, of course, in spite of high import taxes on all products not produced in the country, and still higher tariffs on products that must compete with local products.

"This situation," says a Caracas banker, "is due primarily to the shortage of labor. You see, because of the high wages paid by the oil companies, most of the small farmers and farm workers have left the countryside and gone to the oil fields. Therefore, production of food products within the country has fallen very low. This means that we have to import nearly everything we eat, a ridiculous situation in a country with as much land and with such rich soil as this. Add to this situation high import tariffs, which have long been too high, but which some politicians think will help to increase production. The argument is advanced by some of them that, when laborers come to realize that their high wages are practically cancelled by the high prices they are compelled to pay for the necessities of life, many of them will go back to their farms. Dubious reasoning, of course, but the minds of politicians are often filled with strange ideas."

The situation has been intensified not only by the tremendous influx of natives from the small towns of the interior, and the expatriates coming home from abroad, but by the increasing numbers of foreigners—oil operators and employees, salesmen and branch managers of foreign business and commercial enterprises, mining prospectors and concession hunters interested in the gold, diamonds and other potentialities of the wild Orinoco and Guayana country—who must be supplied and fed.

New Roads to Riches

The most uninhabited region of the Southeast, both the basin of the Orinoco and the mountainous country along the borders of British Guiana and Brazil, has long excited the imaginations of romantic explorers. But today it is becoming a South American Klondike, the lodestone of geologists and mining engineers from far and near. It was this region that inspired Doyle's remarks five years ago. "A fabulous Empire," he called it, "a country full of the riches which the old Spaniards looked for and never found, and of which Caracas is only the reflection."

Until recently this vast hinterland was so remote from Caracas and the populous centers of the nation, that it was altogether another world. To reach it was like going from the United States to Alaska. You took a steamer from La Guaira to the British island of Trinidad, then transferred to a river boat for the Orinoco and Ciudad Bolívar. That is, unless you preferred to assume the rôle of a true adventurer and ride, and occasionally swim, on the back of a mule across mountains, raging rivers and mosquito-infested jungles. Even this was possible only in the dry season.

Today the trip to Ciudad Bolívar, the river metropolis, may be made by automobile or bus over a highway which will eventually be surfaced with asphalt or concrete the entire distance. Or you may travel by airplane and arrive within a couple of hours. In the mountainous valleys south of Ciudad Bolívar, especially in the valley of the Rio Caroni, gold and diamonds were discovered several years ago. In 1932 Doctor Rafael Requeña, then secretary and physician to General Gomez, showed me a piece of ore, almost solid gold, the shape and size of an iron wedge which had been picked up along the bed of a trickling stream near the Guiana border. In the vaults of a New York bank I was recently shown a ten-pound piece of quartz which is ninety per cent gold. It had been picked up by an engineer in the upper Caroni Valley, near the base of the newly discovered mountain, Auyantipuy, called by local Indians, "The Mountain of the Devil."

Venezuela

"Rivers of gold," one geologist calls the tributaries of the Caroni, all of which splash down from Mt. Auyantipuy and rush on northward to the Orinoco, tumbling over countless precipices on the way. One of the falls on the Caroni, only 80 miles from Ciudad Bolívar, is three times higher than Niagara. Jimmy Angel, old time stunt and movie flyer, who helped to speed up the pulses of millions of fans in "Hell's Angels" and other late Hollywood thrillers, and since then pilot for Yankee mining companies, recently showed me a handful of diamonds which he says he gathered along one branch of the Caroni 200 miles south of Ciudad Bolívar.

On an aerial exploration junket over this region, Jimmy and his lovely golden-haired aviatrix wife, who shares all his adventures, landed their plane on the top of Mt. Auyantipuy. They even discovered what appears to be the highest of all waterfalls, which has been estimated at over 5000 feet. The water plunges down from the top of the 10,000-foot plateau on the top of the mountain into the fathomless depths of a gorge which looks as if the Maker of the Universe himself had become angry and slashed the mountain in half. While searching for vantage points from which to photograph this amazing spectacle they ran on to a trickling stream along the banks of which gold nuggets lay scattered around like so many pebbles on the seashore.

Other adventurers have also explored Mt. Auyantipuy. Billy Phelps, obeying his natural history impulses, has only recently returned from an expedition to this region sponsored by the American Geographical Society. And while the Phelps expedition was primarily interested in such æsthetic things as flowering plants and rare birds, its members were not unmindful of the locations of rivers and streams, the heights of mountains and possible landing fields for airplanes. Shorty Wilson of the Gulf Oil Company and others have also made aerial photographs of the entire area.

[25]

New Roads to Riches

In Caracas on the terrace of the Hotel Majestic an Englishman and an American, both grave and serious, not to say hardbitten, sat exchanging opinions between highballs.

"I tell you," said the Yankee, "that if we can get the government to agree to our proposition, we can produce enough gold up there to make the Klondike look sick. I have dipped up with my own hands gobs of sand that fairly glistened with gold. Every river and stream in the surrounding country will yield a fortune."

"Yes," said the Englishman, "quite. In forty years in Africa I have seen nothing to surpahss it. But the officials here seem to suspect every one. They act as if we might dip up the blahsted rivers and slip out of the country with them overnight. If they'd agree to any sort of a proposition so the region could be explored, opened up, Ciudad Bolívar would become another Johannesburg within a month. But, no, they say the government itself will do the exploiting. They say 'Venezuelan gold for the Venezuelans. No more exploitation by foreigners.' A fine mass of grahft that'll be."

Anyway, such are the stories and rumors that go the rounds in Caracas and eventually trickle out to the world. However, the representative of a Wall Street bank, while doing scout duty in Venezuela, told the President not to give his "country's riches away." Since then he has informed me, "most confidentially," that a syndicate of American interests is ready to put up the money for a complete scientific survey of the region. This syndicate, says he, is ready to join with the Venezuelan government in developing the entire region. And plans are already under way to build a railroad 250 miles long from Ciudad Bolívar, right out into the Caroni Valley, making easier the access and exploitation of the region.

But whether yellow metal will actually flow from the Caroni and the Mountain of the Devil or not, black gold is already flowing from wells all over the lower Orinoco Valley, or more properly, the Delta region. The stories told by explorers a few years ago, about oil bubbling up near the headwaters of the San Juan and the Rio Tigre and half a dozen other rivers of the Delta region, which spreads out like a fan from Ciudad Bolívar down to the Atlantic, have now come true. Not only are they true but the big companies, Yankee and British, are already pumping it up, pressing it through pipe lines, into tankers that worm their way down the jungle rivers into the sea and the markets of the world.

There are the Quiriquiri field and the Caripito refinery whose products are taken out by way of the San Juan River and the Gulf of Paria to Trinidad. Quiriquiri is the newest Yankee oil field and the first large-scale operation in eastern Venezuela. Caripito is already a thriving metropolis, and perhaps the most modern oil town in the world. It may be put down to the credit of the oil companies, no doubt spurred on to good works by their sad experiences in Mexico and other countries, that no expense has been spared to provide the workmen with all the comforts, conveniences and even luxuries of modern civilization. Workmen's houses even eclipse the modern homes of Bella Vista in Caracas. Peasants never before accustomed to anything but an adobe hut of four walls and a thatched roof now enjoy baths, electric lights, screens to protect them from the myriad insects of the tropics. There are not only hospitals for the workmen themselves, but playgrounds and schools for their children.

But these modern innovations do not faze the modern radical agitator, of whom fortunately there are not yet so many in Venezuela. Some of the inhabitants of Caripito, into whose ears the proper poison had been spilled, recently told government investigators, "No, the houses are terrible, they are too hot, because the company left the electric wires inside the walls. And the school? The company school, of course, cannot compare with our native schools." The native schools of this region usually being, at least until the present government's ambitious educational campaign, huts with dirt floors presided over by half-ignorant *peons* for two months a year. "And these playgrounds are all wrong—it is injurious for children to engage in violent exercises in the tropics."

Temblador, another field down near the Manamo River which likewise flows into the Gulf of Paria, will soon be opened up along with others scattered over the *sabanas* and jungles. Perhaps the most important, however, will be the fields back eastward in the mountains half way between Ciudad Bolívar and the Caribbean. Oil has already been discovered around Santa Ana but cannot be taken out until a pipe line and a highway are built down the mountains to the sea. The routes for both have already been surveyed, and satisfactory government permission for work to begin is expected at any time.

All of which suggests that within a few years the fabulous fields that surround and even occupy Lake Maracaibo in the western part of the republic, and which make Venezuela the second oil-producing country in the hemisphere, may have to yield the palm to the newer fields in the East.

And speaking of lakes, a few miles from Caripito, right in the middle of this eastern region of scattered and spouting geysers of oil, there is a lake of asphalt. Every one has heard of the famed "Pitch Lake" on the island of Trinidad. I have just read the observations of one of the world's renowned globe girdlers, as well as a prominent radio commentator on every subject from the night life of the Lamas of Tibet to the love life of the gypsy moth of New Jersey, who reminds us that "Trinidad's lake of asphalt is the only phenomenon of its kind in the world." I am sure, of course, he had no intention of misleading anybody, but unfortunately while the cruise ships all call at Trinidad none of them yet ply the San Juan and the Orinoco.

The Trinidad phenomenon is a marvel, of course, a lake of the pure, sticky, tarlike substance, a mile and a half wide. For fifty years pitch from this lake has been transported to every country and city in the British Empire without so much as leaving a dent in it. Seemingly the more they take out the more there is. But the asphalt lake of Bermudez in the Venezuelan Delta state of Monagas is quite as remarkable as the one in Trinidad. It covers a thousand acres, and is only one of several deposits in the republic.

Nor are the value and use of asphalt to be passed up lightly. This product alone, without the surrounding oil fields and the possible gold and diamond golcondas farther southward, might easily justify Doyle's "fabulous Empire." It is used not only for paving streets and roads, but also as a base for roofing and waterproofing, in various kinds of varnishes and as an inner lining for cold-storage plants. The decks of ships are calked with it and even shoe blacking contains asphalt.

Authorities on the subject have gone extensively into its history and romance. According to these erudite, if sometimes overly enthusiastic, gentlemen, it could easily be classed among the original seven wonders of the world. One of them boldly informs us that "it is as old as earth!" Another indulges his poetic fancy to the effect that "it was the cement that welded together the stones of the Tower of Babel, the pitch that calked the Ark from the waters of the flood. Even the pyramids are built on asphalt. It is found on the shores of the Dead Sea, and the Egyptians used it in the preservation of their illustrious dead. That it was effective can be judged from the mummies in the museums."

These references to the dead, to museums and mummies bring to mind the ghostly experience of José Calderon, tottering old peasant who spent most of his life as a cowboy in the *llano* country north of Ciudad Bolívar, and who now lives with his son in the outskirts of Caracas. José has seen with his own eyes "those strange lights," a phenomenon which has become a legend among many rural Venezuelans.

"Often, Señor," says José, "when I have been riding alone

in the quiet of the night I have seen them. Sometimes they were pale blue, and other times they were almost green, that deathly green, Señor, which gives one the most eerie feeling. Usually they hung like candles, suspended in mid-air for several moments, and then suddenly disappeared. Once one of them rose out of the ground, floated across my path, and again disappeared into the earth."

These lights, according to José, "are but the spirits of the ancient peoples who once inhabited all our country. Perhaps the souls of the brave Indian chieftains murdered by the white men in the early days of conquest. Yes, they return to protest to us for the cruel injustices done them."

Such mysterious gaseous flames have been seen in many isolated regions of the back country, in lonely river valleys, and even in the deserted fields of old *haciendas*, not only by the simple peasant folk, but by otherwise reliable people with strong nerves. But alas, along come the cold-blooded scientists, who so often deny us the pleasure and satisfaction of poetic fancy, and tell us that this Venezuelan phenomenon, this "will-o'-the-wisp," is only the indication of vast underground deposits of pitch, or, speaking in the proper scientific manner, "the gaseous flames of asphaltum."

III
The Road to Maracay

IF I HAD never drunk *café aguarapado* I would still think of Venezuelan coffee as about the most unpalatable caffeinic concoction with which I have ever been confronted in tropical South America. The coffee served me in most of the cafés and lunch stands and even better-class restaurants of Caracas, Valencia and other Venezuelan cities usually tastes as if it had been made out of a worm-eaten table leg, or an ancient buggy axle. But then cafés and lunch stands would hardly be the places to find *café aguarapado*, because into its making must go a great deal of culinary artistry, a measure of science, and a strong tradition. When I asked her to tell me the primary essential for making so delicious a beverage, one Venezuelan hostess replied, "A grandmother who made it long before you."

Speaking as a layman, I wish to pass the formula on to others who may feel as I do, that what this country needs is a good cup of coffee, whether it costs five or twenty-five cents. First make the *café*, the coffee. Make it out of healthy, well-cured beans, freshly roasted the day they are used, not the day before. And incidentally, instead of grinding them, pulverize them. The coffee bean is a mass of tiny cells each of which contains the most delicate chemicals and oils which go to make up flavor and aroma. The beans are roasted in order to

[31]

cook those precious properties, and then they should be pulverized in order thoroughly to expose them to water.

Another thing—as soon as they are exposed to air, evaporation sets in, so that if kept for several days, as is commonly the case in the general run of restaurants, hotels and many casually visited places called homes, there is nothing left but the rancid pulp of the bean.

Anyway, to complete the making of *café*, allow boiling water to be slowly dripped, not doused, through the freshly pulverized beans, and you have good coffee, but not *café aguarapado*. Of course, if you are already weary with the process, and you want to add sugar, hot half-and-half, or hot milk (but never thick cream!), even this mixture will tickle the palate and soothe the stomach no end. But if you wish the Venezuelan delicacy you must now prepare the *guarapo*, and to prepare *guarapo*, you must have *papelón*, a species of candied-brown sugar made from the juice of sugar cane. The cane juices are cooked until they sugar, enough syrup being left in it so that when it gets cold it is more like the hardest of rock candy than sugar. Break up a piece of *papelón*, pour water over it, put it on the stove and let it come to a slow boil, and you have *guarapo*, or glorified sweetened water. Mix piping *guarapo* with piping *café*, serve demi-tasse, and you have *café aguarapado*, which, if it were served you at La Vega, as it was to me, would be worth a trip to Venezuela.

Like *café aguarapado*, La Vega is a Venezuelan tradition, a lingering reminder of what was colonial Venezuela, a dignified old Spanish colonial house, set in a perfectly preserved garden and the whole surrounded by great fields of sugar cane. It is a one-story structure with enormous rooms, and a broad veranda with simple rounded columns on two sides. At La Vega generations of the same historic family have been born, reared, married, and from its quiet surroundings most of them have been buried.

[32]

Venezuela

Captain Garcí Gonzalez de Silva, one of those old conquerors of the valley of Caracas, received the land, thousands of acres of it, directly from the hands of King Philip II himself exactly thirteen years before the first families came to Jamestown, Virginia. Through the following two centuries it trickled on down from generation to generation until fifteen years before our own Boston Tea Party, when Maria Patronila de Tovar built the present house. Today it is the home of Señor Manuel V. Rodriguez Llamozas, likewise a gracious member of Captain de Silva's posterity. And it was he who served me *café aguarapado* on the broad veranda at La Vega. As we sipped it, we looked out over the cane fields, the mills and *trapiche,* the refinery, or cookery, where *papelón* is made.

La Vega is now much smaller than the original *hacienda,* having been reduced to 372 acres, due to the garish urban encroachments of Caracas. But it still follows the customs of its forebears. Under the direction of Señor Rodriguez, workmen still grow sugar cane, grind it, cook the juices and pour the *papelón* into the same iron moulds that have been in use for a hundred years. Generations of the same Negro peasants, cultivate, harvest and process the cane and work under the very same system that has obtained since Spanish colonial days, a system called *medianeiro,* which in this country would be called share-cropping. *Medianeiro* was introduced by the Spanish colonists, and it still exists not only at La Vega, but pretty generally throughout the country, especially in the sugar-cane industry.

The land is parcelled out to share-croppers, one *tablon* to a family, a *tablon* being equivalent to two acres. The owner furnishes the seed cane and the implements for cultivation. The family plants, cultivates and harvests the crop, giving one half to the owner and retaining the other half.

It was in 1932 that I first visited La Vega. As I left Caracas recently I drove by it again, and with the lingering aroma of

[33]

café aguarapado in my memory, if not my nostrils, took the road westward to Maracay, and the valley of Valencia. I wanted to see once again rural Venezuela, the long settled and cultivated countryside. For this road leads through the most highly developed and historic farming and ranching section of the republic. The ancient Caribs and Los Teques tramped the same route for hundreds of years before the palefaces arrived. In the early days of the conquerors it was the route for mule trains from the capital to the rich valley beyond. In the struggle for independence Bolívar and his various armies fought the Spaniards back and forth along almost every mile of it. Later a narrow wagon and buggy road was dug out of the sides of the hills to make possible travel by carriage and wagon between Caracas and the city of Valencia, as well as the rich *haciendas* surrounding it.

Eventually one of the remarkable railroads of the continent was constructed along the same route. Then, when Gomez discarded horses for automobiles, the present highway was laid and concreted for 125 miles all the way from the capital to Maracay. Later two roads were built from Maracay to Valencia, at the opposite end of Lake Valencia, one on either side of the lake. And still later Valencia was linked with Puerto Cabello, Venezuela's second, and probably her best, seaport, across the coastal range on the Caribbean.

Some idea of the enormous difficulties that had to be overcome in the construction of these roads may be gained when a speed-mad chauffeur whisks you almost straight up from La Guaira to Caracas. But this stretch of road is only a hint of what the Caracas-Maracay branch is like. The Caracas-Valencia railroad—which parallels it all the way to Valencia, as well as on down to Puerto Cabello—passes through eighty-six tunnels and crosses 230 bridges in approximately 175 miles.

Elsewhere even greater difficulties had to be overcome. An extremely mountainous country, some of the ranges are from

[34]

Venezuela

10,000 to 12,000 feet high, and yet as far back as ten years ago expert Venezuelan engineers had already blasted, dug and graded a road southwestward 700 miles from Valencia on over the Andean cordillera to the Colombian border. Today the road-building program is taking on new impetus. Within the past year and a half the Caracas-Maracay road has been widened, short curves lengthened and new bridges built. Soon every important town and populous center in the republic, except those of the far interior, will be connected with one another by the most modern highways.

From Caracas the route to Maracay leads among the tree-shaded streets of Paraiso, by Bella Vista and various *fincas*, or small farms, and *haciendas*, suburban villages and towns, and on through the passes and deep gorges of the mountains.

Several times I have made this trip, but this time I was lucky enough to travel with my old friend, José Antonio Calcaño Calcaño. "I added the second Calcaño," he says, "so that people wouldn't confuse me with my cousin, José Antonio Calcaño." Anyway, José is one of those astonishingly versatile people typical of the Other Americas. He is an artist, a scholar and thoroughly grounded in the lore of his country. He came from a family of musicians. Having heard so much music as a boy he decided to study medicine, but eventually gave it up and succumbed to the family tradition. He became a professor of music and an authority on the folk songs and dances of Venezuela.

Incidentally he was not only following a family bent, but a Venezuelan tradition as well. Surprisingly enough, many of the old families of the country have produced some remarkable musicians. There was Teresa Carreño, called by European critics the greatest woman pianist of all time, who for years thrilled audiences in Paris, Rome, Berlin and other continental capitals. She capivated both maestri and mere music lovers. The composer Reynaldo Hahn, now living in Paris, writes melodic descriptions of his native Venezuelan hills and valleys,

[35]

and we must not overlook Juan Lecuna, not to be confused with the Cuban Lecuona, who for the moment subjects music to diplomacy while filling the post of secretary in the Venezuelan Legation in Washington.

Like Juan Lecuna, José finally combined music with the foreign service. He was for some years a consul at St. Louis but later ended up as chief economist for the Ministry of Foreign Affairs at home. So on the road to Maracay our conversation varied between the *Joropo*, a Venezuelan species of Spanish fandango diluted with native Indian rhythms, economic developments of the republic, and history.

Four thousand feet up, at the summer resort of Los Teques, capital of the state of Miranda, named after the old patriot, we stopped for coffee which in me, after *café aguarapado*, produced a state of internal sadness. But when we resumed the trip my thoughts were no longer of my stomach. At the edge of town we began to climb swiftly, until we were on the very top of Venezuela. As we skirted the steep cliffs I gazed with mixed emotions down into the bottomless valleys and caverns. Then in the very next moment, as we scaled the top of some sharp ridge, I looked out upon layer after layer of mountains stretching away to the horizon like giant stair steps covered with pale green carpets. Occasionally it seemed as if half the world were spread out before us.

Hour after hour of this and then suddenly, as we swung around another cliff and entered another gap in the mountains, we could see far ahead and below the valley of Valencia with waving fields of sugar cane. As we began to descend the air was laden with the fragrance of coffee blossoms. For while the floor of the valley is utilized for the growing of sugar cane, the hillsides are covered with coffee bushes, carefully shaded by tall *bucare* trees which sport their own gorgeous red blossoms.

We paused for a little at the *hacienda* of the Vollmers near

Venezuela

El Consejo, for a drink of their Santa Teresa, the finest rum in all of Venezuela. A little farther along we came to La Victoria, where old Spanish colonial houses, with exquisitely grilled windows, line the narrow main streets. Just outside of La Victoria we stopped again to look at the great Hacienda Quebrado, or Hacienda on the Creek, with its Moorish marble palace, once the country home of Gonzalo Gomez, one of the countless progeny of the old General.

Strangely enough, an exception has been made of this magnificent estate. Practically all the properties of the Gomez family had been confiscated by the government, and most of them parcelled out in small tracts on long-term payment to the people who had worked on them in the days of the dictator. But not Hacienda Quebrado. Even the gatekeeper, the same, so he told us who guarded the entrance when the Gomez clan was still intact, insisted that "it is the *hacienda* of Gonzalo Gomez."

Although he is now camping conveniently in Curaçao, Gonzalo was popular with the peasants and working classes. He mixed and mingled with them, built an athletic park on his property and organized various kinds of modern sports. He had spent some time in the United States, and was an ardent baseball fan. The baseball diamond and grandstand at Hacienda Quebrado stands close by the highway, but at the moment is grown high in grass and weeds. Baseball seems to have departed with Gonzalo.

We swept along the winding valley to historic San Mateo. On a steep hill above the town is Casa Fuerte, where Commander Ricaurte, one of Bolívar's officers, became one of the greatest of all Venezuelan heroes. Even after the enemy had stormed the place and soldiers had crowded into it, he set fire to a pile of gunpowder, thus blowing them and himself into eternity, and his memory into immortality. At the foot of the hill just below Casa Fuerte is another historic landmark,

Ingenio Bolívar, the old sugar *hacienda* of the Liberator. *Ingenio*, incidentally, is the name for a small sugar refinery, as distinguished from a *trapiche* where *papelón* is made. It was the slaves of this plantation that Bolívar freed the moment he began his fight for independence.

As we left San Mateo the chauffeur's appetite asserted itself, and without so much as asking by our leave he drew up at a roadside café on the outskirts of the town. José suggested that we join him, and, realizing that to refuse would be to offend, I immediately squelched all thoughts of the questionable sanitary environment. And how glad I am now that I did! Otherwise I might never have been introduced to that delicious corn cake known as *arepa*, and *pabellon*, the national dish of Venezuela.

Take finely ground corn meal (the peasants make their own meal with a pestle and mortar, and I'm sure it's better), add salt, a little bacon grease, mix with water, roll into a ball the size of your fist and bake in an oven and serve hot with butter—that's *arepa*.

And *pabellon*? Four dishes in one, of which *carne frita* is the principal one. Literally *carne frita* is dried beef fried with peppers and other sauces. But before frying it the beef is torn into shreds. Pile a mound of plain steamed rice on your plate, cover it with *carne frita*. Then add black beans that have been boiled almost to a paste and seasoned with a pinch of sugar and a little grease, and surround the whole with pieces of fried plantain. Served this way it is à-la-the-people. At La Vega, it would probably not be mixed up. Anyway, a dish of *pabellon* and a couple of *arepas* constitute a formidable enemy to hunger, or they did on this occasion.

The territory along all this part of the road is, or was, Gomez country. Until his passing in 1937 *hacienda* after *hacienda* was the property of some member of the family or a satellite, and all of them showplaces. Some produced sugar cane, others coffee, while still others were cattle ranches. Dairy farms are still numerous all along the way and in front of every gate there are milk cans to be picked up by truck or bus and transported to the creamery at Maracay.

For rural beauty, as well as rural industriousness, not even the Shenandoah Valley surpasses this portion of the Valencia Valley. The road sweeps along in graceful curves by these *fincas* and *haciendas*, every foot of it perfectly kept and even swept once a day. Portions of the road are assigned to peasants living along the way who contract to keep it clear of trash and débris. Nearly every mile of the road from the mountains to Maracay is completely arbored with the giant *saman* trees. On the hottest day you may roll along with the top of your car down, and the only sunshine that reaches you are the few polka dots that manage to spill through the thick foliage above.

Just beyond Turmero, with its trim little plaza surrounded by houses and walls covered with bougainvillea, we stopped for a moment at the Saman de Guere, an ancient *saman* tree surrounded by a fence made of guns with fixed bayonets. It was under this tree that Bolívar used to pitch his tent when making his forays against the Spaniards up and down the valley. It is not only the Tree of War, hallowed by memories of the Liberator, but it is one of the oldest living things on the continent. Back in 1801 the great naturalist Humboldt said it was probably ten thousand years old.

And then Maracay, once a sleepy old colonial village which Gomez transformed into the trimmest, loveliest town in the country. Flower-filled plazas, with fountains and pagodas, and winding walks of colored tile, broad, spotless streets lined with white and yellow and pink Spanish colonial buildings. And then there is El Jardín, the most picturesque hotel I ever saw outside of a picture book. Sprawling over an area as large as two city blocks, it is of Moorish architecture, surrounding an enormous *patio* with swimming pools and playgrounds, open-air bars and dining pavilions. All rooms open onto broad galleries or porches overlooking the court.

To El Jardín in Gomez's time came all who had business or expected an audience with the dictator. In the evenings it was the gayest spot in Venezuela, jammed with high officials, diplomats, army officers, heads of oil companies and representatives of foreign business houses, a miniature League of Nations. In Maracay in those days were stationed the crack regiments of the army, the aviation corps and school, several troops of cavalry and the cavalry school. Each unit was provided with permanent barracks, enormous buildings of Spanish architecture, part of them fronting on the main plaza.

The bull ring in Caracas is second rate by the side of the one in Maracay. Gomez was particularly fond of this Old-World sport and in his last years had erected in Maracay an exact replica of the historic ring of Seville. In addition he provided the bulls and paid fancy fees to bring fighters from Spain, Mexico and elsewhere for several months during the year.

But without its creator Maracay is having a struggle to survive. Already it is slipping back to the even tenor of colonial times. Grass and weeds are growing in some of the little parks and plazas, and many of the sumptuous houses are now closed and boarded up. The walls and ceilings of El Jardín are splotched with mildew, and cockroaches, forced to retire to outlying buildings in the heyday of the dictatorship, have, as in the Majestic Hotel in Caracas, reformed their lines and moved to the attack once more.

But then in spite of a bustling agriculture and live-stock industry, and good roads, history and tradition are tremendous forces in the valley. The shores of Lake Valencia were the scenes of several successive Indian civilizations in pre-Spanish times. Moreover, they were Indians without any known connections with those of Perú, or many of the other Indian civilizations. Lacustrine dwellers, they lived in houses built on stilts over the edge of the lake. Doctor Requeña, who, as already mentioned, was long private secretary and physician to the general, divided his time between duties of state and archæological excavations on the shores of Valencia. He even turned part of his house, which stood next door to that of Gomez, into a museum.

The city of Valencia is still what it was before Gomez. The metropolis of the valley, the stolid old colonial city, and capital of the state of Carabobo, named for the battlefield a few miles away from the city where Bolívar won a decisive victory over the Spaniards, Valencia is as conservative today as it was fifty years ago. Its 75,000 people live much as they have for half a century. The old colonial houses, with their inevitable *patios*, grilled windows and doors, abut the narrow sidewalks of the correspondingly narrow streets. And their owners are a leisurely lot living on incomes from coffee, *cacao*, sugar cane and cotton farms scattered over the surrounding valley and hillsides. Its produce flows across the mountains and down the winding gorges to Puerto Cabello, by railroad and highway. Puerto Cabello, a seaport, is feverish with activity, where every day in the year ocean liners from Europe and the United States tie up, where cruise ships disgorge hundreds of tourists who drive up to Valencia and Maracay for the day.

If I were writing a guide book I should not hesitate to say that for any one wishing a taste of the Andes, of rural Spanish America, or a painless bit of South American exploration, here is the place to find it. Disembark at La Guaira, visit Caracas, motor over the mountains, down through the valley by Maracay and Valencia and rejoin the ship at Puerto Cabello. Furthermore, if I were in the business of boosting steamships and travel facilities, I should not find it difficult to grow enthusiastic about the delightful Santa ships of the Grace Line which recently began cruising the Caribbean and along Venezuelan and

Colombian shores. Not only because they open up to the traveller an entirely new region of tropical beauty and splendor, but because they have been built especially for the purpose, by means of governmental assistance, out of your and my tax money.

They are not old ships, built for the cold north Atlantic, with heavy hangings, velvets and plushes and all enclosed decks, doing intermittent Caribbean cruises just to coin a few extra American dollars in the off-European season. In my fifteen years of tropical travel I have suffered the discomforts of ships with galleys and dining-rooms three and four flights down, so that the smells of cabbage, onions, and steamy meat floated upward and saturated all the corridors and staterooms. The designers of such ships seem to have had a complex which made them feel that food was something you not only ought to live with every minute but that you had to "descend" to. No crowded tenement, with garlicky food smells filling every court, alley and hallway, was ever so unpleasant as the average smells of one of these old ships on a cruise in the tropics.

I waited for fifteen years for somebody to build a ship with the dining-room on an upper deck, where one can sit in the fresh air and breeze and enjoy his food. And it has remained for an American line to do it. The Santa ships are tropical innovations. There are plenty of wide wind-swept decks, outside swimming pools, tables and chairs for refreshments. They have put their dining-rooms on the promenade decks, with great French windows all around, and a roof which opens up to the stars at night, so that the breezes sweep through no matter from which direction they come. In the Caribbean the trade winds always blow westwardly, but on these ships this makes no difference. Best of all the galley is above the dining-room and aft, so that the odors are whisked away from the ship almost before they are created.

Anyway, the evolution of transportation and means of travel

Venezuela

to and in the valley of Valencia, is one of the newest developments in the conquest of the Andes—from Indian paths to buggy trails, from railroads to paved highways, and modern ocean liners bringing remote and almost unknown cities and towns within easy reach of all the world.

IV

Oil on the Waters

Venezuelan civilization, like that of ancient Gaul, is divided roughly into three parts. In the central region are a few coastal towns and the valleys of Caracas and Valencia, with their history, traditions and old culture, their bustling cities and sleepy, easy-going Spanish colonial towns, their old *haciendas* and busy *fincas* and the finest roads weaving in and out among them. To the east in the mountains bordering Brazil and British Guiana in the basin of the lower Orinoco River is "the fabulous Empire." In this region there are only a few scattered towns and some of the wildest and most inaccessible country in the hemisphere, where until now the only roads were the snakelike rivers and streams that weave their way across the high *llanos* and down through the jungles, and where, with but one or two exceptions, it is still impossible to travel except by airplane or on muleback. In the Maracaibo Bowl in the west, including a lake, or arm of the sea, seventy-five miles long and twenty miles wide, surrounded by high mountain walls, enough oil bubbles up out of the ground and the water, to make Venezuela one of the richest of all the Other Americas.

Maracaibo, its principal city, a little world all by itself, is almost completely isolated from the rest of the country. Here old Spanish atmosphere and customs must compete with the onrush of modern business and industry. The city and surroundings present striking contrasts. An old town of narrow streets and latticed windows, a new town where oil companies have their own sumptuous homes, hotels, club houses and theatres; an old town of colorful shops and fruit stands and a new town where night clubs, dance halls and saloons run full tilt, from sunset to early morning.

It is midnight in the old Trujillo Bar. A spavined orchestra blares and toots. Many races and nationalities are packed into the place. It is a sort of strangers' club for roving romeos and roustabouts—brown, black and white. In the old days they fought, stabbed and carved each other just for the fun of it. But the carving days are over. And now they make only mild whoopee. They dance, drink and spoon in automobiles parked in vacant lots.

Ten minutes by plane from Maracaibo and you are over the Goajira country, the land of still primitive tribes of red men who are among the hardiest and bravest in Venezuela. The fierce old Spanish conquerors were never able to defeat them or subdue them. They could never even force their way across the Goajira peninsula, that narrow tongue of land that juts out into the Caribbean west of Maracaibo Lake. Here the Goajiros still live, unmolested, and almost uninfluenced by the white man.

Magnificent specimens of manhood they are—big-muscled, clear-eyed, fearless. From an airplane you see them here and there, their greasy, brown bodies glistening in the sun. Their scorched villages of palm shelters stand out against the eternal green of the jungle. In the tiny clearings half-wild cattle and horses scamper to cover as the roaring demon of the heavens passes over.

Only a few of these children of the wilds have ever been out to see the white man's world and doings. But one old chief, El Torito, the little bull, is famous beyond the bush. He is their mouthpiece and ambassador to the palefaces. Also a good angel and protector to any souls who feel brave enough to go excursioning into their land. A powerful personage, too, with numerous families, one for every quarter of the compass. When El Torito chooses to travel it isn't necessary to cart a family along. He finds a different one wherever he goes, in every pueblo, so to speak.

Primitive though they are, according to our lights, the ways of the Goajiros are very strict. There is honor among them. They respect each other's property, and each other's rights, not to mention each other's families. Anna May McGrath, who, with her brother, Doctor Jim Tong, recently led an expedition among the Goajiros, says they are models of integrity and practical living. That is, if you are a Goajiro. They even have their own ideas of such things as health and sanitation.

For instance, they have never heard of members of that vast army of radio stars who lead the campaign for the care and culture of teeth. Yet like ourselves they brush their teeth regularly, not to say heroically. After eating a formidable half-cooked chunk of beef, the Goajiro sits down by the side of the stream, wets his forefinger, dips it in clear white sand, and massages his teeth and gums.

From this fantastic region, this jumble of wildmen, Broadway whoopee and old Spanish traditions, comes the wealth that has made a vast country with scarcely four million people—divided up between the progressive and cultured upper class, a couple of million *mestizos*, the countless tribes of Indians who inhabit the back areas, not to mention thousands of Sambos, an Indian and African mixture, in the coastal towns and villages—one of the richest and in some ways the most up-to-date of the Andean republics. Out of the income from oil, and up to now it was the oil of Maracaibo, they have built the highways, seaports, and kept the country out of debt for the last decade in spite of the fact that 90 per cent of the industry is in the hands of foreigners.

"The best governed oil country in the world," foreigners

Rural Highway in the Valencia Valley

Oil on the Maracaibo Waters

used to insist. "Oil laws that permit you to live and let live. Oil laws designed to benefit the producer, the government and the country." And why not? In the first place the oil men themselves helped to fashion the laws, which, after more than fifteen years have undergone few material changes. Back in 1921, soon after the first oil spouted up on the shore of Lake Maracaibo, an oil law was written by Doctor Pedro Manuel Arcaya, known as "the Venezuelan law-giver of the twenties." A superb rhetorician, and one of the finest legal minds in South America, as well as one of the most prolific of authors, if Doctor Arcaya was asked to write a law on taxes he turned it out in two days. If asked to draft a law on pearl-fishing he handed it in next morning. And his oil law was prepared with the same speed and finesse. It was a perfect piece of writing and a model legal document. But under it no foreign capital would come into the country, and so developments in the oil industry made practically no headway.

"Why," Doctor Arcaya asked a prominent American oil man, "does your company refuse to make any advances?"

Whereupon the Yankee who had long looked with covetous eyes upon the deposits of black gold which awaited only his command to be turned into fortunes, proceeded to explain his viewpoint of the question. "Doctor Arcaya," this gentleman told me recently, "was amazed at the conditions which his law would produce, the prohibitive cost of exploration and production. Finally he said, 'I never realized the mathematics of it.' "

Anyway, in early 1922 Doctor Rafael Requeña, then private secretary to Gomez, went to the oil men and said, "Benemerito General would like to have the oil men, those representing the leading companies—British, American and native—sit down with his officials and map out a set of laws. The General realizes if all hands plan the law it ought to be fair to all concerned, to themseves and to the country. You see," he went on, "you would naturally suggest a law fair to the country because you will have to live with us after it is made. It will be fair to all of you because each of you will see to it that no one gets more advantages than the other."

In June, 1922, this meeting took place. Within three weeks the law was perfected. It was immediately passed by the Congress and promulgated, and early in December the first big well was brought in—a 90,000-barrel well, which was the beginning of large-scale oil production in Venezuela.

In the very first year after the new law went into effect the Maracaibo region produced 2,398,000 barrels of crude oil, and in 1937 the total was 186,855,727, or 511,933 barrels a day. Continuing along the primrose path of the statistician, up to and including the year 1937, 1,495,472,000 barrels of the product had been pumped, shipped, refined and used up by automobiles, steamers, airplanes and clothes-pressing establishments throughout the world.

And lest some otherwise unoccupied oil man or interested party should venture to read this far, and be disappointed because the particulars of the Venezuelan oil laws are not given, I hereby submit the chief features of them for his or their edification.

First of all, exploration concessions, that is, areas of land upon which you may go exploring for evidences of oil, are each limited to 10,000 hectares, or 38.61 square miles. And the total of these concessions which any one company may acquire is limited to 300,000 hectares, or 1158.3 square miles. Such concessions run for forty years. After that, even though oil has been produced on them, they revert to the government. A period of three years is allowed for exploration work, with an additional time, up to four and a half years, by special permission. At the end of the period of exploration the entire acreage must be divided up into lots of 500 hectares, or 1235 acres, of which the company may select half, any half it desires, while the remaining half of the lots must revert to the government as national reserves. Incidentally, the government may in turn grant concessions on national reserves.

Originally the concessionaire had to pay to the government ten *centimes* of a *bolivar* for each hectare granted it, about a cent and a quarter an acre. This has been recently increased to an average of about a dollar and twenty cents an acre, subject to special agreements. In other words, this tax may be called an acquisition tax, or lease tax. Then comes the exploration tax. That is, when you begin to explore there is an initial tax which must be paid at once of two *bolivars* per hectare or twenty-five cents an acre, indicating, of course, that after you start exploration the concession is worth more. In addition to this there is a surplus tax of fifty-one cents per acre per year for the first three years, which is increased to nearly sixty-four cents per acre for the next twenty-seven years. For the remaining ten years the tax amounts to a little over a dollar per acre per annum.

The companies are beginning to complain about these particular taxes. They say that these charges, when added to the export taxes, which will be discussed in a moment, hastens the end of profitable production. Moreover, they say that, since the companies and the government are really partners, anything that shortens the productive period will be harmful to both.

So far we have discussed only the initial charges on leases or concessions, and the taxes levied during the period of exploration. When the production begins, export tariffs as well as other taxes and restrictions are imposed. .

To begin with, oil companies must pay fifteen per cent in cash of the commercial value of all oil extracted—five per cent more than was paid in the days of Gomez. Concessions covered by navigable waters get a reduction of twenty-five per cent on royalties. These laws have worked to the great advantage of the Venezuelan government. When oil was selling for ten cents a barrel in the United States, the Venezuelan government was getting fifty-nine cents a barrel in royalties. Under certain conditions, however, the government has the option of taking its royalties in kind.

Oil lands in Venezuela seem to be limitless. So far they have scarcely been tapped. There are numbers of scattered wells in the Maracaibo Basin but most of them have been drilled along the western edge of Lake Maracaibo, within a narrow strip of territory forty-three and a half miles long and nine miles wide, four of it on the shore and the other five out in the water. In this area there are six different fields bearing picturesque and delectable names—Ambrosio, La Rosa, Punta Benitez, Tia Juana, Lagunillas and Bachaquero. As this is written the daily average production of the three leading companies is 257,000 barrels for the Standard, 191,500 for Shell and 57,400 for the Gulf.

The wells of the Standard Oil Company are all in the lake, the derricks standing forty to fifty feet deep in water. As one official puts it, "We are entirely a marine operation, our oil upon the waters, so to speak."

Although the big companies have been transporting their crude product to the great refineries on the Dutch Islands of Curaçao and Aruba, just off the Venezuelan coast, the government is now demanding that a number of refineries be built within the country, thus bringing the industry and all its operations more and more within the jurisdiction of the Venezuelan government. All of which indicates that the lot of the foreign oil operator in Venezuela is not exactly a bed of roses. He makes money if prices are good, but if prices are bad, he at least makes less money.

The old charge about "exploitation of the workers" cannot be aimed too directly at the oil industry, or any other large foreign enterprise, in Venezuela. Venezuela's social and labor laws are already among the most advanced in the entire hemisphere. They provide for minimum wages, an eight-hour day, and collective bargaining. The duration of work for both laborers and salaried workers is forty-eight hours a week for both sexes. For office employees this period is only forty-four hours a week. The lowliest unskilled worker in the oil fields must receive not less than the equivalent of $2.50 in American money, for eight hours' work. The average actually is paid over $3 a day, while the pay for skilled white-collar and all other workers ranges still higher. Compare these wages with the average pay of government employees. For instance, a laborer on the highways receives an average of $1.60 per day. The daily wage of a bus driver is around $3.50, while a policeman gets only a little over $3 a day plus his uniform.

At least seventy-five per cent of all salaried employees and laborers must be Venezuelan citizens, while the positions of superintendents and all employees in immediate contact with the workers must be filled by natives. Besides, if a man has worked with the same concern for a year, he cannot be discharged without being given a month's notice in advance.

New provisions of the laws provide for compulsory profit-sharing by employers with employees "in the proportion," so the statute reads, "to be established by the Federal executive, or the President, after consultation with commissions which are to be created for this purpose."

It can be said for the oil companies that they not only live up to all the provisions of the laws now in force, but in addition provide the workman with many other advantages. They furnish him with free housing, free water, free electric lights, medical and dental care and all the health improvements with which the company can surround him. They also provide free schools and teachers for his children, as well as churches. In some cases they even pay the padres so that weddings, funerals and other church benefits cost him nothing. Last year one American company spent more than three million dollars in welfare work alone.

Unlike Mexico, Venezuela is comparatively free of powerful political or labor agitators. The government, although unusually democratic in inclination and operation, has been able to secure the passage of national safety laws, under which it is legally possible to restrict agitators. Nevertheless, like any other political organization, it is sensitive to the wishes and tendencies of labor. And, although I have pointed out that the oil companies pay the best wages in the country and have spent millions to provide their workmen with the best living conditions that exist in the republic, labor leaders are not to be satisfied. They will continue to ask for more and more concessions.

Some oil men in the country are already becoming jittery. In view of the expropriation or confiscation, as they call it, of the entire oil industry by the government of Mexico, every one is asking himself, "Is Venezuela next?" Indeed, an entirely new set of laws, all more drastic than those in effect, are in the offing.

There is no doubt in my mind that as the years roll by foreigners will meet with increasing restrictions. In fact, I am fully confident that eventually the present happy arrangement will be only a memory. Because, as everywhere else on the continent, nationalism is growing by leaps and bounds and any government, no matter how conservatively inclined, will be compelled to squeeze big business, especially if it is foreign big business, or take the lonely road to political limbo. If I owned a large mining or metallurgical industry in any country south of the Rio Grande, I would think of ways and means either to dispose of it profitably or to put at least part of it into the hands of natives within the next ten years.

However, many believe that there is no likelihood of the present government of General Eleazar Lopez Contreras following in the footsteps of Mexico. They feel that his long association with Gomez and his intimate familiarity with the oil industry, its beginnings and development, as well as his appreciation of the value to the country of businesslike operations, are all a guarantee that he will continue to favor private operation in preference to government operation.

And the President is a man of outstanding ability and experience. He began as an old-time revolutionist, having come down from the state of Tachira in the Andes near the Colombian border thirty years ago as an associate of Cipriano Castro and Juan Vicente Gomez. A hard worker, he took advantage of every opportunity to fit himself for public duty. And unlike most of the other Gomez lieutenants, he even went to school in his spare time. Having applied himself in the schools of Caracas, "the General" sent him to the Military Academy in Paris. History is one of his hobbies, and in the course of a busy life, he has found time to write several volumes dealing with Venezuelan events and personalities.

He shared military responsibility in the long rule of Gomez, having risen from private to general and minister of war. According to many influential Venezuelans he was actually the choice of the old dictator to carry on after the latter's death. Anyway, he was the only man able to control the situation once Gomez had breathed his last.

He looks every inch a quiet college professor. When I met him I could not believe that a man with his thin, sharp features, his dark eyes with the completely detached look in them, could be a soldier and strong man. He is tall and slim, so slim that he actually seems frail and anemic. But a man who has lived the strenuous life he has lived, and still lives, has to have iron nerves and an unbreakable constitution.

In spite of his long military career, he is the most democratic of men, simple and unassuming. Contrary to Spanish-American custom he doesn't surround himself with a phalanx of officers in gold braid and shiny swords. Four policemen guard the gates of his home in Paraiso, and a couple of aides sit on the front porch. Inside, he usually greets his callers himself, and invites them into a small library to talk.

He has not abolished all the Gomez ideas, but he has departed radically from the Gomez methods. The Congress is no puppet congress, and although he does not kowtow to it in the slightest, he does not encroach upon its prerogatives. The legislative and judicial branches of the government at the present time act with complete independence, but the executive department keeps a firm hand on all the agencies of law and order. Today there is probably more democracy in Venezuela than has existed for fifty years.

"We have accomplished something already," he told me recently. "What we have accomplished so far has been principally in the betterment of the morale of the people. As citizens we now understand better our relationships one with another, as well as our public duty. On the government's side officials today are administering their offices for the public and not for the private good."

Replying to a direct question about the status of foreign capital and the effects of Mexico's recent actions, he said, "I believe we have the right idea about nationalism. That is, we appreciate that proper guarantees ought to be accorded foreign capital and investments, as long as those who administer them think not only of their own welfare but the welfare of the country as well. There have been some small difficulties with the oil companies, mainly in the improper procedure and formalities respecting regulation. However, the government wants to have only a moderate equity for its rights. In other words, where properties in the past have been procured or administered improperly, if the companies and the government cannot arrive at a mutual understanding, then the government will insist that the matter be handled through the regular legal processes.

"Those extreme situations," he went on, "that have come about in other countries have been due quite often, I believe, to improper manipulations between the officers of the companies and the officers of the government. We are proceeding carefully and meticulously so that there will be no excuse for such situations arising in this country."

On the subject of alien influences—Fascism or Communism —President Contreras believes "There is little possibility of extreme radicalism or other foreign ideologies taking root here. We have lived a long time without any consideration of such doctrines, and consequently the people do not take any interest in them. The people here really believe in the Bolivarian idea of democracy, and we are going to promote this idea. From the richest to the poorest there are no foreign ideas about politics. When there have been demonstrations against government in this country they have merely been against local governors and were not due to foreign influences behind them.

"We have the best intentions," he concluded, "to promote sound ideas in the nation."

But Contreras is not content with properly administering the present laws of the land and keeping the social structure of the nation on an even keel. He insists upon moving forward. In fact, he has already embarked upon a great program of improvements, "a three-year plan." The program calls for an increase in production, especially foods and other necessities of life, so as to reduce the cost of living. To do this, agriculture and stock-raising are being encouraged, more funds made available through the labor and industrial banks to help people build homes, buy land and become farmers. Even bounties are to be paid on increased production of certain products. So far no plans have been made for the lowering of tariffs, which would contribute to cutting down prices. In the matter of imports the United States has a reciprocal trade agreement with Venezuela which has worked to our advantage.

Since the country is underpopulated, so that there is a shortage of labor, as well as a shortage of production, new immigration and colonization laws are being planned, but with safeguards against the influx of "undesirables, extremists and trouble-makers." Only people who are willing to go on the land will find a hearty welcome. Even the newcomer must be able to support himself for a time after his arrival in the country. Today no country in the hemisphere is more difficult to get into, whether you are an immigrant intending to make it your home, a business man trying to sell goods, or a mere tourist travelling alone.

Under the general heading of health, education and population are many specific projects. Syphilitics who are warned by the signs on the La Guaira-Caracas road, to "cure themselves" will not be left without facilities for the purpose. Health centers and dispensaries for the treatment of all diseases are being established throughout the nation. General and maternity hospitals are to be erected and maintained at strategic centers, especially in the larger cities. But more attention is being given those conditions and improvements which will prevent the spreading of disease and ill health, such as sewage disposal plants and modern water works in the cities, towns and villages.

Three hundred modern new public schools are already being constructed in populous centers, while in the future others are to be provided for the remoter communities. Meanwhile, school trailers are to visit the out-of-the-way places and provide limited instruction until more ample facilities can be provided. Hydro-electric expansion is provided for as well as an increase in the postal, telephone and air communications. Highway construction is to continue at full speed. Besides the completion of the port works at La Guaira and Puerto Cabello, the sandbar at the mouth of Lake Maracaibo is to be dredged and a port constructed so that regular ocean liners may call at South America's richest oil metropolis.

"In other words," say Venezuelan business men, "if the oil wells continue to flow and the money holds out, we will become in the near future the most modernized and up-to-date nation on the continent."

V

Record of the Rehabilitator

I HAVE made continual reference to General Gomez. And this is as it should be. The story of modern Venezuela up to the present moment is the story of the old Dictator, who, until July 17, 1937, was absolute ruler, not to say owner of the country. Whatever progress there was in the past quarter of a century was due solely to his will and efforts, because he was the Government and the Law. Nothing was done without his consent, and everything done was the result of his initiative.

Gomez was the most interesting personality I have ever met in South America. I saw him the last time in 1932. It was high noon, and as usual he was in the front yard at Las Delicias, a favorite little farmhouse just outside of Maracay, transacting government and private business in the most informal manner. Dressed in the khaki uniform of a general, high shiny boots and Panama hat, he was seated in a large wicker chair, with his old companion and secretary, Doctor Rafael Requeña, master of ceremonies.

Diplomatic protocol played very little part at these meetings, which were usually very brief. In rapid succession cabinet ministers, the representatives of foreign governments and other officials came up, spoke briefly and retired. The affairs of state concluded, private individuals, foreigners and natives, were received.

New Roads to Riches

On this occasion one of the Yankees having business with the General was H. T. Harden, connected with a New York firm with large interests in Venezuela. When Harden was presented he addressed the General in fluent Spanish, which not only won him immediate favor but inspired a characteristic gesture upon the part of the old Dictator. In response to a nod from Doctor Requeña, a soldier led up a somewhat non-descript mule. At the same time an officer advanced and began recounting the animal's qualities and virtues. In true Latin fashion he told of the origin and pedigree of the lazy, indifferent creature, which he had evidently been commissioned to purchase.

Gomez listened patiently and when the speaker had finished, turned to his guest and said, "What think you, Señor, of this mule?"

Somewhat surprised at the question, but quite sure of his ground, Harden replied, "Well, I should say the mule seems to be underweight. It is not suitable for heavy work, and certainly not to be ridden."

"Do you hear what the gentleman says?" the Dictator asked the officer, indicating that he was impressed by the visitor's remarks.

"But, sir," argued the officer, attempting to defend his position, "the gentleman is not acquainted with the mules of our country. He is comparing this one with the large, heavy mules of the United States!"

"I lived for many years in Spain and Argentina," countered Harden, "as an engineer and road builder. I used to buy and sell mules in Mexico. And I am thinking of the mules I have bought in those countries."

Recognizing the weight of expert opinion, the Dictator impatiently motioned the officer and soldier away with their charge. Such was the manner in which Gomez blended public and private business. He would have agreed with that classic

Venezuela

Coolidge phrase, "the business of government is business." Literally and figuratively he brought it right down to earth, too. In fact, the earth was a controlling factor in his life. Although a soldier and the powerful head of a nation, he kept himself and politics close to the soil. For he was first and foremost a rancher and farmer, in his time one of the richest ranchers and farmers in the world. It is quite probable he himself did not know the extent of his own private wealth and properties. Among his personal possessions were a dozen farms, plantations and ranches, and 600,000 head of cattle, 10,000 of them milk cows. He produced coffee, cotton, corn, wheat, sugar cane and many other products, all on a big scale. And on his various estates and properties 20,000 people were employed.

In Caracas, the doors of the old presidential palace of Mira-flores were seldom opened. In fact he spent very little time in Caracas. In order to be close to nature and the great outdoors, he lived in Maracay, in a two-hundred-year-old one-story Spanish colonial house with a leaky roof which still stands undisturbed on the plaza diagonally across the street from the old village church.

In addition to all his public responsibilities he personally directed all his own properties and activities. He actually worked and worked hard, at the business of farming. He even found poetry in the thought of cultivating the soil. For on a bulletin board at Las Delicias I read this favorite Gomez maxim: "The earth weeps when it is left idle, but rewards in gold the sweat of the brow."

At the age of seventy-six he put in more hours of work every day than most men of half that age. This I learned on my first visit to Maracay. Besides I learned it very early on the first morning. I was sleeping soundly in the Hotel Jardín, when a bugle split the quiet morning air. I leaped out of bed. Just then another blared in the distance, quickly followed by a third which seemed to be right in the building. Light began bursting out of windows in every direction. There was the sound of tramping feet on the pavement. The local brigade of the national army was hurrying to reveille. It was five o'clock and the day began in the valley of Valencia at five.

Gomez himself not only rose at five every morning, but, after a cup of steaming black coffee, he and Doctor Requeña went over important mail and state papers. At seven-thirty they went out for an automobile ride. After three quarters of an hour, their lungs full of fresh morning air, they returned to a simple, frugal breakfast and another two solid hours of work. By ten-thirty, they were off to the country again to spend another hour or so inspecting some farm or dairy before beginning the accustomed midday reception of officials and visitors under the trees at Las Delicias.

At two o'clock he was back in Maracay ready for the daily siesta from two to four. Then another two hours' work, a drive into the country, to one of his farms or ranches, or to the Maracay Club to sit for an hour or so with his family, officials and visitors, in the shade of a giant tree which stands in the front yard. Dinner was at seven, and the movies at eight. He attended the movies almost every night and insisted that all the official household and their families go along with him. But at ten o'clock all was quiet in the square around Casa Gomez. By that time the General was already deep in slumber.

Such was the routine day in and day out. And as lived the General, so lived the nation. Regularity, efficiency, thoroughness. He tolerated no idleness, no slovenly activity among those around him.

Gomez was never outside of Venezuela, yet his own business enterprises and the affairs of the nation were conducted according to the most modern methods. He sent scouts all over the world to study the latest developments in agriculture, engineering and industry, and bring him their reactions. Visitors like H. T. Harden who came to see him on business were usually plied with questions on all sorts of subjects. Those who came to interview him always found themselves being interviewed. He was as likely to ask a total stranger his opinion on Venezuelan road building or sheep-shearing, as he was his own experts in charge of these jobs.

Gomez was a *mestizo*, Indian and Spanish half-breed, born in the Andes. His beginnings were not only humble but hard. His family was poor, and at a very early age he was shouldered with the responsibility of taking care of brothers, sisters, aunts and uncles. Gomez himself never went to school and had already reached middle life before he learned to write his own name. These facts he never allowed himself to forget, and that others might know them he erected along that tree-shaded road on the way to Las Delicias, an exact replica of Quinta La Mulera, the old house in which he was born—thatched roof, home-made furniture and all. He passed by it every day in the week and often dropped in unannounced.

Early in life he joined the local militia, and became associated with the notorious old revolutionist, Cipriano Castro, who eventually gained power and proved to be one of the worst tyrants in Venezuelan history. He repudiated the foreign debts, causing other nations to make demands and threats of blockades. President Theodore Roosevelt once had to warn Germany that the United States would not permit any such tactics. Finally Gomez deported Castro, sent him out of the country and himself took the government in hand.

He turned the nation into a feudal estate. His government was entirely personal. No official or important businessman of the nation ever left the country on business or pleasure without reporting personally to him before leaving and upon his return. Every official of the government not only had to run the nation's business with meticulous efficiency but had to take care of his family, his wife, his children, or his woman and their offspring.

New Roads to Riches

There was the case of Victoria, mistress of one of Gomez's old friends, the Jefe Civil, in his old home town. The two had lived together for forty years. Victoria had slaved for him, borne a dozen children, grown fat and wrinkled. The Jefe Civil had become rich, the ruler of his community, and so he decided to marry an eighteen-year-old girl. Victoria went to see Gomez, told him the situation. Gomez advised her to leave the matter to him. She went away, and the General waited for his old friend to come and announce his plans. He finally came. "Benemerito," said the Jefe, "I have come to announce that I am going to get married."

"Fine," said the General, "I congratulate you. You should have done so before now. Victoria has been faithful to you and deserves this final recognition from you. I shall come to the wedding myself and be best man."

Gomez himself was never married, but he made the nation acknowledge his women and their children. Although there are many rumors to the contrary, he lived openly with only two women during his long rule of Venezuela. The first was a French woman who, when their children were grown up, became too domineering and bossy to suit the Dictator. So he gave her money and sent her back to France. He made one of their sons Vice-President but the offspring proved to be a public nuisance, and Gomez expelled him from the country.

The other woman bore him a large family and remained by his side until his death. That he had scores of children by other women has been rumored, and no doubt it was true. But he would not have thought this immoral. For he was personally unmoral, not immoral. Yet no man ever treated more gallantly and circumspectly the wives, daughters and womenfolk of his hundreds of officials and associates. Any one who ever met the wife and charming daughters of Doctor Requeña, who occupied the house joining that of Gomez in Maracay, would know that.

Venezuela

Gomez had hordes of enemies. Many of them tried to overthrow him, but they never got to first base in their efforts. In his early days he jailed such people or shot them. In his later years he deported them. Toward the last he was capable of clever, not to say humorous treatment of those who attempted to displace him.

Two hundred men, under the leadership of an old revolutionist by the name of Rafael Simón Urbina, set sail one dark night from Willemstad on the Caribbean Island of Curaçao for the Venezuelan coast. Most of the rank and file, as well as all the officers, were Mexicans of long experience in the great game of revolution. Several of them had fled from Mexico following the failure of a revolutionary plot against their own government. Months had been spent in planning the expedition. Immediately upon landing, thousands of Venezuelans were to rise in revolt against the Gomez dictatorship.

As the ship approached the village of La Vela on a sparsely inhabited section of the coast near Coro, on the eastern side of the Paraguana Peninsula, lights were sighted on shore indicating that the friendly forces were on hand to meet them. But no sooner had the bulk of the expedition reached land than they were surrounded by Gomez troops and taken into custody. Instead of negotiating with friends in Willemstad the leader of the expedition had unsuspectingly negotiated with Gomez spies.

The cautious Urbina, however, had not gone along with the vanguard of his forces, so that upon learning the sad news he easily escaped. The unfortunate Mexicans were immediately taken to jail to await trial and execution. While they languished in prison they contemplated with horror the punishment which would eventually be meted out to them. Finally, a day came when they were told to make ready for a long trip, which they felt sure would be a trip to some other horrible prison or before a Gomez firing squad. Early in the morning they were called, loaded into large buses and driven into the countryside. The polite officers informed them that before the final disposition of their case the government wished them to see something of the orderliness and beauty of Venezuelan rural life, the fine roads, the splendid farms and *haciendas*. All of which they realized was just another form of cruelty designed to make them suffer mentally as well as physically. At noontime they reached the city of Caracas, and were taken to the magnificent Moorish Pabellon (the famous Paraiso restaurant) where a band was playing and a sumptuous banquet had been arranged. They were told to seat themselves at the long tables and make ready for the feast. One more evidence, they realized, of the tantalizing terror of the Dictator.

Presently a group of official cars drove up bringing high government and military officials. In one of the cars was none other than Gomez himself; the official party proceeded to the head of the main table and sat down. Word was passed along that every one should proceed with his meal. But scarcely one of the unfortunate men had any appetite. As they gazed upon the man who was to pronounce their doom, their hearts sank within them. They were sure that the cynical smile on his face suggested a sadistic cruelty and enjoyment of the sufferings of others.

The meal over, an orator representing Gomez arose and began to speak, "Gentlemen," he said, "you have committed a grave offense. You have invaded a peaceful country with the intention of creating disturbance. We marvel, however, at your being so simple and trusting as to follow the leadership of a professional trouble maker. So what could you expect of us under the circumstances? Naturally you must have expected to be punished for such a grave offense.

"You are now about to begin a long journey," he told them. "But before you begin that journey we want you to see with your own eyes the actual conditions of the country whose

The "Gomez Club" and Gardens in Maracay

On the Road to Maracay

misery and unhappiness your leader no doubt so vividly described to you. Therefore, we have taken you on a tour of the countryside this morning. And here we have served you with a sumptuous meal which we hope you have enjoyed. This afternoon you are to be taken on a tour of our historic capital city. You will be shown our treasured monuments, our fine buildings, and public institutions, our schools. You will be taken on a visit to the Pantheon, the burial place of Venezuela's noble dead, and the tomb of the great Liberator—Simón Bolívar."

Their heartstrings strained to the breaking point, they contemplated with increasing horror the terrible fate which they must meet. They were almost unconscious with terror. And then the orator finished his speech. "At the close of the day," he said, in what seemed to the unfortunate victims a gloating manner, "you are to be taken down to the coast where your ship, the same ship on which you arrived, is waiting to take you back across the Caribbean and the Gulf of Mexico to your native land, where we hope you will be happy."

In the quarter of a century he was ruler of Venezuela, Gomez transformed the nation socially and industrially, if not politically. Through careful experiments and crossbreeding, he developed an entirely new type of cattle that thrives in the torrid climate of this tropical country. Many people think that the hot, damp tropics are not suitable for the raising of good milk cows and especially first-class beef cattle. I have heard such opinions expressed by people in our own southeastern states—Georgia, Alabama, and Mississippi. Although Venezuela lies in the very heart of the tropics, Gomez proved that climate is no obstacle to successful scientific cattle raising. Two decades of intensive experimenting on his estates produced a type of animal that not only stands the heat perfectly, but furnishes a quality of beef second to none and produces milk on a scale equal to the best milk cows in the United States.

First, he imported cattle from England, Holland, and the

United States—Herefords, Holsteins, Jerseys, and many others. After a time it was found that, although the Herefords were among the finest of beef cattle they did not stand the heat. The Holsteins were milk producers but they did not thrive in the terrible tropic sunshine. Then he conceived the idea of crossing the Holstein with the East Indian zebu, the sacred cow of the Hindus.

The Holsteins being good milk producers and the zebu not only a native of the Far Eastern tropics, and therefore accustomed to the hottest climate in the world, but a good meat producer as well, the combination produced splendid results.

But first the feeding problem had to be solved. Native grasses were found to be very poor for grazing purposes. And it was necessary to experiment with grasses and grains that would not only be suitable for the new breed of cattle, but that could be produced easily in the country. He imported dozens of varieties of plants from everywhere. Some grew well and others did not. Among the plants that did thrive were alfalfa and soya beans from the United States, Sudan grass from Central America, and Para grass from Brazil. Thus the feeding problem was solved.

Henry Ford once advanced the theory that agriculture and industry ought to be more closely allied, that farms ought to surround factories, thus carrying diversification to its ultimate conclusion. Gomez put this idea into practice in Venezuela nearly twenty years ago. He turned most of the raw materials produced on his own plantations into finished products on the ground in his own small factories and plants. He had his own slaughterhouses and dairies with facilities for distribution of meats, butter, and milk products in the cities. He had cotton mills that converted the native cotton that grows around Lake Valencia into everything from towels to fancy dress goods.

While Gomez carried on all these activities as strictly business propositions he was not unmindful of their importance as examples to the nation. Why shouldn't his own people know how to do all these things at home? Why shouldn't the labor-ing class become accustomed to modern methods of industry?

When he built his first cotton mill he had to import textile workers, for Venezuelans knew nothing whatever about ma-chinery. So, he went to Catalonia, the textile center of Spain, for his laborers, because they spoke Spanish and his own people could understand them. But beside every Catalonian he put a Venezuelan to learn how to handle the spindles and looms. Eventually Venezuelans ran the entire plant.

He did the same in agriculture. At first he brought in ex-perts from abroad—the United States, Germany, and other countries, not only to direct experiments and oversee plantations but to instruct the natives. Meantime he sent scores of young Venezuelans to school in the United States and Europe, and when they returned they took charge of the various prop-erties.

By instituting on his own farms a system of daily wages, and an eight-hour day, Gomez went a long way toward break-ing down the old *medianeiro* system of farm labor. The average daily wage paid by Gomez—equivalent in Venezuela to about a dollar a day—may not have been comparable to that paid for similar work in the United States, but it was certainly a far cry from the *medianeiro* plan, and, according to Venezuelan standards at the time, rather high.

Land ownership was another step in the constructive social development of Venezuela. Farm workers were encouraged to become property owners. And since agriculture is the basic industry of the nation, they were urged to invest in farm property, to remain on the land and become self-sustaining. It was he who fashioned the present tax laws of Venezuela. Imagine a farmer in New York or Mississippi or Iowa or Cali-fornia having to pay no land taxes! Yet the farmer, small or large, in Venezuela under Gomez was free of this burden. The royalties on oil provided most of the government revenue, as I have pointed out.

He was responsible for the simple and reasonable tax laws governing the property of the city dweller, also the Industrial Labor Bank which lately constructed the workingmen's houses at Bella Vista in Caracas. Besides he started a plan by which the government would lend the farmer money to maintain and improve his property. A mortgage bank was established for the special purpose of making loans to small farmers. A farmer might borrow up to fifty per cent of the value of his farm for a period of twenty years, at eight per cent interest. Actually he paid only three per cent interest, for five per cent was applied to the reduction of his loan. Furthermore, he was not asked to buy stock in the bank in order to get a loan, as has been the case with agricultural land banks in some other countries. The result was that at the time of Gomez's death there was a waiting list at the bank, and still is.

He provided several of the cities with excellent sanitation, water, and cheap electrical power. Even foreign power companies were rigidly regulated so that light and power might be within the reach of all. He was a devout believer in conservation of natural resources, not only of oil and mineral lands, but of everything else. If his plan of forest preservation lives there will never be a timber famine in Venezuela. Tree culture and care became a sort of religion with him. In fact, no tree could be cut anywhere in the country without the formal consent of his government. Paraphrasing Joyce Kilmer, of whom he probably never heard, he said, "Trees are the handiwork of God, and man cannot replace them."

That is the reason the highway from Caracas to Maracay is lined with trees. No tree was ever cut down to make way for a road. If one stood in the way, instead of allowing it to be cut down the road was built around it. For trees injured in a storm or dwarfed in their youth, a tree surgeon was provided. Those bent over on the ground were provided with supports, blocks of cement or posts, like crutches for crippled old people.

He frowned upon Venezuelans living abroad on the income from their properties in the homeland. He invested every cent of his own fortune at home and believed other people should do likewise. Some members of his family apparently did not adhere to the old man's practice. Although by no means unfriendly to foreign capital or industry, he didn't like to see farms and agricultural land fall into the hands of outsiders.

He once paid five million dollars for the great Trompillo coffee plantation near Valencia to keep foreigners from buying it. This plantation in the hills above Lake Valencia produced two million pounds of coffee beans a year, and originally belonged to a wealthy old Venezuelan who had grown old and decrepit and was unable to look after it himself. An English syndicate had already agreed to the price required. Gomez heard about it and immediately offered more.

The day after he came into possession of the place he erected a flagpole on a high hill some distance up the road from the main entrance, from which the flag of the republic always fluttered in the tropical breeze as a reminder to all and sundry that Trompillo was still in Venezuelan hands.

From a purely business standpoint, Gomez was the most remarkable and successful of South American dictators, at least in modern times. He ruled twenty-seven years absolutely and with an iron hand, and yet died peacefully in bed with officials and friends standing by. He took a backward, bankrupt, chaotic country and made it a marvel of financial integrity and order. He transformed a country of mountain trails into a nation with some of the finest highways in the entire hemisphere outside of the United States. He insisted that the government live within its income in good times and bad. All through the world depression it was prosperous and debtless. It owes nobody anything, about the only important country in all the world, except the United States, which has no bonds or loans abroad. In 1930 the one hundredth anniversary of independence from Spain was celebrated by discharging every penny of external obligation.

The lasting influence of these policies and practices is already evident. Recently the Contreras government planned to raise several million dollars by means of foreign loans to carry out its "three-year plan." But such opposition arose that the loan was finally postponed, if not abandoned altogether. According to one of the leading bankers of Caracas, "the prospects for a foreign loan have disappeared. Public opinion in Venezuela is completely hostile to the idea of borrowing money in the outside world. Here is a curious psychological phenomenon, based upon reasons of a sentimental nature, which always predominate in our Hispano-American countries. The blockade to which we were subjected in 1902 by England, Germany and Italy, and the subsequent humiliating arrangements for the payment of our international debts is still keenly alive in the imagination of all the thinking people of this country.

"It has been the style among us recently to revile Juan Vicente Gomez and his régime in all keys and apropos all problems. But when the question of a loan came up voices were raised all over the country and even in the halls of Congress in praise of what many call the rehabilitating work of the old Dictator in paying off the external debt. This unanimous trend of opinion compelled the government to postpone the proposition indefinitely."

To all Venezuelans Bolívar was the liberator from Old World domination. To his friends and an increasing number of people familiar with his record, Gomez was the rehabilitator. He liked to think of himself as having begun where Bolívar left off, as a sort of successor to the Liberator. He was born on the same day of the month as Bolívar. He believed he possessed the same powers, at least he pretended to possess them, until the pretense finally became an obsession. Even on his deathbed his faith in his own powers was tremendous. On the 15th of July, two days before his actual death, he went into a coma and even the doctors thought it was all over. They tied a cloth under his chin and around his head to hold his mouth closed. After a few minutes he reached up, took the cloth away and whispered, "No, today is not the day—not until the 17th." And he died on the 17th, the same day of the same month that saw the passing of the liberator.

Already he is a legend among many of the peasants and even the simpler-minded foreigners. An old peon near Maracay who had worked all his life on a Gomez farm found himself in difficult circumstances—no job, no food, and his family ill. He declares that Gomez appeared to him in a dream, told him to go to a certain party at a certain place and ask for help. He immediately went and received money and a job.

An Italian barber—an amateur sculptor—made the Gomez death mask. Today he insists that hair is growing on the mask. Probably some of the skin and hairs were pulled off with the plaster, and, of course, hair will continue to grow under such circumstances. But to the artist the death mask of the old General is taking on life.

Whatever hatred toward Gomez existed upon the part of many of the people living in Venezuela, both citizens and foreigners, was directed more toward his grafting relatives and overbearing officials than toward himself. As a prominent Venezuelan in no way connected with Gomez told me the other day, "If upon his death Gomez had been embalmed, mounted on a pedestal and set up in the government house, he would still be ruler of Venezuela."

For two months during his illness, part of which time he was unconscious, there was never one effort upon the part of his enemies to cause any disturbance. And they might have revolted then as easily as they did later. His funeral was a reverent occasion. Thousands and thousands of peasants and others passed by his casket while he lay in state. He was buried in the public cemetery at Maracay with all of the honors due a ruler, and his grave remains unviolated.

COLOMBIA

I

Gibraltar of the Spanish Main

COLUMBUS discovered a large portion of the earth's surface which turned out to be two tremendous continents surrounded by more than 2000 islands, large and small. For his pains he suffered disgrace and died in despair. Today these continents and their numerous brood are divided into twenty-one independent nations and several dominions, as well as dozens of colonies and possessions, most of which belong to Great Britain, France, and Holland. Yet when names were being passed around the old Italo-Spanish sailor was practically forgotten. In all of Spanish-speaking America few cities, towns or villages, except the Canal Zone community of Cristobal, and its Siamese twin, the Panamanian city of Colón, remembered him. Of the nations only one, the republic of Colombia, has honored itself with his name. Even that was an afterthought, because for two hundred and eighty years it was known as New Granada.

For that matter, the territory of New Granada itself was practically an afterthought. That is to say, for nearly three centuries after the first settlement the Spaniards were so occupied with looting Mexico and Perú that they gave little thought to the possibilities of the vast region which was destined to become one of the richest pieces of territory in the world.

[75]

Finally when they did give it any importance it was for military and not economic reasons.

I like to think of the incident which occurred one bright summer morning in 1735. The audience hall in the Royal Palace of his Castillian Majesty was jammed with nobles and high officials—dukes and admirals, counts and courtiers of the Spanish court, all resplendent in flashy uniforms and shiny accouterments. Above the chattering and the rattling of swords as the imposing company awaited the pleasure of King Ferdinand VI, one of the waiting gentlemen was heard to say, "I understand that his Majesty is to receive reports from the Viceroy of Perú this morning."

"No," said another, "I think it is a report from New Granada, another one of those Indies."

Just then the double doors at the end of the great hall swung open, and a page shouted, "His Majesty, the King!"

The royal party entered and the King took his seat and inquired in a low and indifferent voice, heard distinctly only by those nearest to the throne, what business there was to report.

"His Majesty," the Court Chamberlain announced, "may be pleased to learn that the forts and fortifications of Cartagena are now completed."

"You mean to say," the King spoke up with a show of surprise, "that the work on the north coast of New Granada, begun a hundred years ago, is at last completed?"

"That is the business we have to report to his Majesty today," the Chamberlain answered. "The work is completed and Captain Navarro arrived only yesterday bringing the final reports."

"Oh, then," said the King, "we will hear Captain Navarro himself. Let him tell us what has been done at Cartagena."

The Captain, in a brilliant new uniform, stepped forward and bowed, his face flushed with pride in this sudden honor which had come to him. He had not even expected to be presented

Colombia

to his Majesty, much less become the orator of the occasion.

"While Cartagena guards the jewels of a vast and fabulous region of his Majesty's empire," the Captain began, "it occupies the most strategic point on the coast of the Caribbean Sea. It is not only a door which permits us to enter and exploit the resources, the gold and precious stones of New Granada, but it is a sentinel guarding the path to Panamá, and therefore to Perú and the other vast outposts throughout the Indies. In the past two hundred years the city has suffered attack after attack from notorious English and French pirates, such as John Hawkins, Sir Francis Drake, and others. In all, his Majesty may recall, we have already been attacked seven different times and captured twice."

"Yes," the King interrupted, "we are still mindful of the ransoms exacted by Drake and the French, five hundred thousand dollars by Drake and even more by the French. Proceed, Captain."

"But his Majesty will be pleased to know," the Captain reassured him, "we shall never again suffer such losses and indignities. Today Cartagena is impregnable."

"Impregnable?" the King broke in, casting a skeptical eye over the assemblage.

"Yes, we can assure his Majesty," the Captain repeated with great finality, "Impregnable."

And laying an ornate map before the royal eyes, which by now showed less indifference than when the audience began, he went on. "Here, on this map, your Majesty may see for himself. The entire city is surrounded by a great wall, forty feet high and from fifty to sixty feet thick, which is lined with powerful guns. This wall can be entered only through six gates, each of which is guarded by its own fortress. Out here two miles from the city, are the two narrow entrances to the bay and harbor. One we have closed permanently, with underwater obstructions known only to us. An enemy attempting to negotiate it would surely come to grief. On either side of Boca Chica, the other and even narrower entrance, are fortresses in which we have installed the most powerful guns of the age. Farther inland along the shores of the bay is still another group of forts with guns of the same caliber."

"Here," the King again interrupted, as he leaned eagerly forward and pointed to the words "San Felipe" in the very center of the map. "What is that?"

"That," the Captain replied, "is the largest of all the forts, San Felipe, the crowning glory of Cartagena. San Felipe stands on the brow of a high hill overlooking the entire harbor and city. We have dug down five hundred feet into the hill and constructed great underground chambers, large enough to accommodate several companies of soldiers. What is more interesting still, these great underground chambers are scientifically ventilated and equipped with their own water supply."

By which time every one present had moved forward full of interest and curiosity. The orator, warming to his task, continued, "There is not a fort in all of Europe so equipped. Moreover, this and all the other widely separated forts and fortifications on either side of the bay and throughout the city are connected by secret underground passages. One great tunnel extends from Fort San Felipe all the way under the bay to the cathedral a quarter of a mile down in the city. This enables his Majesty's officers and soldiers on duty at the fort to attend secret mass every morning without even the people of the city observing them."

"But now tell us," the King suddenly broke in, "what is the cost of all this?"

Captain Navarro, sensing the royal concern for what he realized only too well was a fabulous outlay of money, was glad enough to yield the floor to some one else. "The cost sheets," said he, "have been delivered to his Excellency, the Royal Treasurer."

Colombia

The grim and grizzled old official stepped forward, mindful that, in contrast to all the other American transactions, this one was a problem of outlay rather than income.

"Read me the main items," commanded the King.

"First of all," he began a little haltingly, "the main fort of San Felipe—let's see—San Felipe costs eleven million dollars."

"What!" exclaimed the King. "One fort alone costs eleven —eleven million dollars?" He paused in deep reflection, as if contemplating every remaining coin in the royal coffers, while a stony silence fell over the assemblage. Finally he looked up and commanded the treasurer to proceed with the baffling figures.

"The cost of the remaining forts and fortifications—fifty-nine million dollars."

Again the King broke in, mumbling more to himself than to the others, "Fifty-nine million—plus eleven million—nearly seventy million dollars. One hundred years to build them and seventy million dollars!"

He arose, crossed the room and stood before the great terrace window facing westward. Again he was heard to murmur to himself, "Seventy million dollars—seventy million—there, in that direction, across the Atlantic." He turned and announced in a firm voice, "I don't see them."

For an entire minute no one spoke. Even the Court Chamberlain wondered what strange condition had taken hold of the royal mind.

"I can't see them!" the King repeated.

The Chamberlain, seeking to relieve what was rapidly becoming an embarrassing situation, made out to inquire. "What is it—what is it his Majesty cannot see?"

"The walls and forts at Cartagena," said the King. "One hundred years to build them, at a cost of seventy million dollars! I should be able to see them from here!"

Of course the King was amazed at the staggering cost of

the project. Three and a half centuries ago, seventy million dollars was more than a king's ransom.

But there it stands today, on the north coast of Colombia, just where the blue waters of the Caribbean swirl northward, one of the oldest and perhaps the most unique of all the cities of the Southern continent. The first stones of its foundations were laid three quarters of a century before the first settlement in this country. In 1933 Cartagena celebrated its four hundredth anniversary, celebrated not only its age as a city, but its history as the Gibraltar of the Spanish Main.

The grim old walls and forts of Cartagena are not only symbols of ancient power, as well as of ancient fear and suspicion, but silent reminders of present-day exclusiveness. The stranger or foreigner in Cartagena even today is not received with much cordiality, unless he travels in a tourist party and is carefully herded from ship to shore and back again. In the present year of our Lord when a ship drops anchor in that historic port, a bevy of white uniformed officials go on guard —captains, lieutenants, sergeants, and privates of the armies of immigration and customs. And when it ties up to the modern new docks they oversee every transaction, watch every piece of freight that is loaded or unloaded and scrutinize every passenger along with the goods.

Not only must every article imported into the country pay an almost unheard-of duty, but the law says that a ship's canteen or shop must not sell a citizen or resident of Colombia any article whatsoever, not even a tube of toothpaste or a package of Lifesavers. Which seems to make such shops an open sesame for the customs and immigration officials—they usually go ashore with their pockets bulging, while the lonely private citizen looks on with resignation and contempt.

"One of the political inequalities from which my noble country suffers," said my old friend Rafael when I arrived in Cartagena recently. Rafael himself had come on board that

The New and Old, Cartagena

Gasoline Refinery on the Magdalena

morning with hopes and designs to smuggle ashore on his person, or perhaps on the person of his "dear Yankee friend," a supply of silk hosiery to be divided between his Señora, that is to say his wife, and "perhaps some lady friends." About one of these lady friends I was to hear more and startling things in the days to come.

Even as we talked an official emerged from the corridor leading to the barber shop, the barber in this case being also the shopkeeper, stuffing silk stockings into his inside tunic pocket. Rafael touched my arm and said, "You have observ-ed?" (The last syllable of all words ending in "ed" receive special attention from Rafael. Otherwise he speaks flawless English.)

"That, Señor, is what I mean by political inequalities. Because of his position he may purchase expensive articles which the citizen may not. He then presents them to his family, or to his mistress. The mistress shows her gifts to her friends, which in turn makes it difficult for us. You understand, Señor?" Of course I did.

"You see, Señor," he went on, a little wistfully. "Silk stockings are particularly desir-ed by one's mistress in Cartagena. And one must be patient with the wishes of his mistress. Because of the terrible duty the government is pleas-ed to impose upon silk stockings the price in Cartagena is, how you say, prohibit-ed."

And I confess it was in this noble cause of political equality that I found myself going ashore in the ancient city of Cartagena with a pair of ladies' silk stockings in each pants and coat pocket.

Having baked in the blistering tropic sun these four centuries, the quaint old town resembles a page from a book of faded etchings. The battered buildings with their great open *patios*, time-worn churches and cathedrals, along with the crumbling forts and fortifications, make it one of the most colorful cities in South America. And the life of Cartagena is no less colorful than its historic buildings. In the late afternoon the little squares and plazas are full of chattering people, like characters in a historical pageant seemingly unmindful of the glamor of their past. Donkey carts, burros with bundles and packs piled high on their swaying backs, and automobiles with ear-piercing horns vie with one another for room to pass.

Riding at sunset with Rafael along one of these narrow streets where the humbler among the white people live, he reminded me that most of them were direct descendants of the soldiers and sailors of colonial days, poor but prouder of their family heritage than anything else in the world. We had to creep along to keep from taking toll of dozens of screaming, playing children. Though appalling poverty was the lot of many of them, the freedom of propagation has suffered no embarrassment. Big families are the rule, and the love of family an ancient right. Latticed and grilled windows, just like those we read about in the story books, open right out onto the streets. And there was hardly one without a barefooted lad on the outside and a dark-eyed señorita on the inside, each looking longingly at the other.

"Love," said Rafael, "is being made just as it was centuries ago in old Castile."

At least life offered them some reward, some compensation. But romance among their betters is subject to broad application. Rafael styles himself a *licenciado*, which, subjected to plain English, means merely a member of a profession. A muchly schooled and travelled gentleman, Rafael has studied in the Universities of Cartagena and Bogota, and also in the old University of Salamanca. He has travelled frequently to New York and Philadelphia. Yet, in spite of his apparent cosmopolitanism, he still treasures the ancient customs, especially in regard to his social habits and relations.

"You see, Señor," he frankly confided, and Spanish Americans are nothing if not frank in such matters, "your ways are not for us. We not only inherit the traditions of the Latin and the Spaniard, but also of the Moor. Besides, the climate, the tropics, how you say, dictate the more frequent resort to the physical pleasures. I myself am devoted to my family, my señora and my seven children. But I am also devoted to my mistresses, Madeleine and Olga. Señor, Olga! She is Russian. She is stately, blonde—ah, it is the unrecorded law of man."

But I soon found that the system was not wholly ideal, and certainly not without occasional unpleasant consequence. For, the very next day, after assuring me of his devotion to both of them, it seemed that Olga, not having been previously aware of Madeleine, and having just learned of such competition, had raised violent objection to such divided attentions. And even before he unbosomed himself, figuratively and literally, it was evident that there had been physical violence. A long scar traversed one entire side of his countenance.

"Señor," he told me, with extraordinary emphasis and appropriate gesticulations, "it is unbelievable that my actions should be question-ed. I am a man, and I but exercise a man's rights. No woman, and more especially a mistress, has the right to inquire into a man's romantic activities. Yet, Señor, last evening, when I call-ed at her *casita* she greeted me with abusive language. When I objected, she thrust one fist into my stomach and the other into my face. And when I attempted to choke her into submission, she disfigur-ed my face, as you can plainly see."

Then, unbuttoning his shirt and pointing to a ten-inch gash across his chest, he shouted, "This, Señor! This she did to me. How ungrateful. I give her my devotion. I provide her with a luxurious *casita*. I present her with presents, and now I am humiliat-ed! I am outrag-ed! I am scratch-ed!"

And then, after a moment's reflection, he added, "But, Señor, what is one to expect when the national government permits the influx of aliens into our beloved country?"

New Roads to Riches

In spite of such unfortunate alien penetration Cartagena is still the apotheosis of Spanish tradition. Its population is almost wholly of Spanish or African descent, except for the not inconsiderable number who share both Spanish and African antecedents. They maintain inviolate the long *siesta* period in the middle of the day, as well as their inalienable right not to interfere with the refuse and smells that have accumulated through the years in some of the back alleys and side streets.

The national government has engaged North American engineers to build some of the finest docks and warehouses, and the most modern of derricks and marine equipment to go with them, all of which it meticulously maintains. But by the time you travel one block away you realize that much is to be desired insofar as sanitation is concerned.

The venerable University, whose chief prerogative is conferring degrees of engineering and doctorates of this and that upon gentlemen who complete the equivalent of a junior course in law, medicine or the mechanical arts, consists of a two-story building, surrounding a large *patio* or quadrangle whose state of repair, the last time I visited it, remained much as it was when the last Spanish Governor departed for the homeland.

Old families still figure prominently in the native business of the city. The Velez family is perhaps the leading as well as the richest. Their most conspicuous enterprise is typically Spanish. They raise bulls for the ring, having been given special permission by the government to import breeding cows from the old country for this purpose. Yet, in spite of their efforts, bull fighting in Cartagena is a rather tame affair compared with bull fighting in Venezuela under Gomez. According to my friend Rafael, the original Señores Velez attained their financial standing in the community in a rather ingenious manner.

"Years ago," he told me, "the government decided to tear down the old city wall and build a new one. One of the Velez brothers was awarded the contract for tearing down the wall, while another secured the contract to build the new one. The first brother transferred to the second all the material from the old wall, out of which he erected the new one. Thus, Señor," Rafael concluded, "as you Yankees would wish to say it, the family profited from both ends of the wall, no?"

The capital of the coastal state of Bolívar, Cartagena's contacts with the national government and civilization of the interior, before the coming of airplanes, was by rail across country to the Magdalena River, and then by river boat to Bogotá. In fact it was long the chief seaport on the Caribbean. Until comparatively recent times there were no port facilities at Barranquilla to take care of ocean-going steamers, so that the coffee of Medellín and Antioquia was transferred from river boats at the port of Calamar, brought to Cartagena by rail, and shipped out to the world from there.

Today new riches flow through its gates. A pipe line brings oil from the fields which Canadians and Americans have developed along the jungle-lined Magdalena, four hundred miles in the interior, and pours it into tanks and ships to be sent out over the world. This oil in turn brings millions of dollars, pounds, guilders, lira, and marks to Cartagena and Colombia.

The principal signs of renovation and improvement in Cartagena today, with the notable exception of the government-owned and operated docks, are the new water works and sewerage system, both of which are presenting tremendous problems since most of the city is below sea level. There are few new buildings except the more or less imposing edifice which the oil company has erected in the heart of the commercial section, a section distinguished by stuffy narrow streets and the stifling aroma of roasting coffee beans.

In spite of the excessive heat, coffee-stands vie with soda fountains at Cartagena. Coffee is drunk by every one every few minutes during the day. Incidentally, the foreigner soon learns that a cup of coffee in the hot tropics is more refreshing than iced drinks. The narrow sidewalks are occupied by Syrian and Jewish merchants, who display their wares so profusely that the pedestrian must take his chances out in the middle of the streets along with the donkey carts and automobiles, and the army of hawkers who carry on their heads trays the size of small canoes, laden with everything from ice-cream and cookies to miniature furniture stores.

In the streets and tiny plazas surrounding the cathedral, a building distinguished by its nightmarish, half-sculptured, half-painted frescoes, the great old Moorish houses are not to be passed up. Occasionally, through the grilled doorways, your gaze may be rewarded with a fleeting glimpse of a buxom señorita.

The father of my old friend Rafael occupies one of the most antique of these houses. Here at five o'clock, when coffee is served for the dozenth time during the day, I observed the devotion of Cartagena's family life which Rafael so often and so eloquently proclaimed. For the rambling old structure houses not only the unmarried daughters but practically all the sons, their wives and their children, as well as the grandmother and all the "Afro-Colombian" servants and their numerous progeny.

Incidentally, the contrast between the gracious and democratic deference the grown-ups, both servants and served, show to one another, and the barbaric behavior of the gosling male children was something to be remembered. The hilarity and abandon of the latter could be compared only to that of a gang of New York street urchins engaged in laying siege to a peanut-stand—except that eventually a cop would subdue, or at least scatter, the Gotham vandals. This probably accounts for, or at least explains, Rafael's philosophy of the "inalienable right of the male," and the horror which floods his soul when the world, or his woman, leaves him "bruis-ed" and "scratch-ed."

But then when I permit myself such unfair reflection, I am reminded of the unselfish, unrelenting labors of some of Cartagena's early citizens. There was the immortal old priest, Pedro Claver, who built the first of its churches close by the main gates of the old city walls. His long life of unrelenting labors in behalf of the poor African slaves, more than half a million of whom were imported for the purpose of building the historic battlements of the city, remains one of the most engaging characters in the early annals of Cartagena. Only a Livingston at large among the teeming tribes of darkest Africa craved and claimed the souls of more black men than Pedro Claver.

He is credited by some historians with having baptized more than three hundred thousand of those immigrants from Africa. In fact, a special niche in the great wall leads from the landing wharf through a side door to the baptismal font in his church so that their souls were always saved from Purgatory in the Hereafter before they were forced to sacrifice their bodies in piling bricks and stones on the walls and forts of the city. Whether by accident or design, if one single African was allowed to escape this routine, Pedro Claver never permitted himself a moment's rest until such an accident had been repaired. He would arise in the dead of night and march the creature mercilessly through the heavy rain back to salvation lest in sin he should fall a victim of yellow fever or be crushed by a caving wall the next morning.

One old darky managed to escape the ministrations of Claver for twenty-five years. In fact, in the household of a spiritually careless officer he had served faithfully and devotedly all this time. He had learned to read and write to the extent that he had become quite a scholar and philosopher, with deep moral convictions of his own. Finally he fell fatally ill and already waited patiently the grim messenger of time, when news of his impending demise reached the ears of Claver.

Although himself aged and failing, the old Padre rose from his bed, trudged several miles through a driving rain to rescue the spirit of the departing slave. All night long he wrestled with the stubborn old man, who even in his weakened and half-delirious condition parried every one of the Padre's arguments, almost up to the very last. Finally, just before dawn, the priest himself limp and exhausted, the determined old sinner was convinced, or had become too weak to hold out longer. History is not altogether clear on this point. Anyway, he murmured submission and received the last ministrations, thus assuring the priest a perfect score.

In any case, the mortal remains of Pedro Claver now sleep in a glass coffin close by the altar of the church of his name, just inside the main gate of historic Cartagena.

II
Life on the Colombian Nile

I SAILED from Cartagena for Santa Marta on a hot, almost stifling August night. The moon spread a silver sheen over the bay as the little old British freighter pulled away from the dock. But once beyond Boca Chica we turned eastward into the teeth of the trade winds that churn the Caribbean most of the year. I stood on the forward deck watching the waves as they broke into gossamer sheets of spray against the nose of the ship. Two garrulous old sailors took their stand near by. After relieving their minds about the heat and the treatment they had received at the hands of "mercen'ry sinoritis" during their four days in the ancient city, they became entangled in the meshes of history.

But then it is impossible to resist history in these parts. In fact, it was for this reason that I shipped for Santa Marta instead of Barranquilla. Cartagena and Santa Marta are Colombia's most venerable cities. Besides, in the early days of independence, when Simón Bolívar gave up the fight against the politicians and came down from Bogotá only to have the puny patriots of Cartagena desert him coldly, he went aboard a small boat and sailed away to Santa Marta.

"It's a shime, I sez," grumbled one of the Britons, "that Sir Francis Draike took a ransom instead of blowing up the blahsted plaice. Some of the smells in that 'arbor 'ave been there ever since 'e left."

"Ay," said the other, "but ye've more nose than eyes. W'y cahn't ye see a bit o' the 'ist'ry—them cahstles and anchient walls. We've not much in England to beat 'em, rially, ye know."

"Can I 'elp it, if me nose rebels at w'at me eyes see?"

He was unconscious of the smells of the old tub on which we were travelling, proving that nature has been kind in the matter of certain of the senses, making it easier to smell the other fellow's odors than our own. Anyway, the argument continued.

"I laike the plaice," insisted the more optimistic one. "I don't forget that part of its 'ist'ry was made by the British, not only by Draike, but there was Admiral Vernon. Mind ye, the Yankees shouldn't overlook the fact that the Admiral was the uncle of George Washington. Washington thought a lot of the old adm'ral too, enough to name 'is estaite on the Petomic after 'im."

Marvellous how an Englishman never forgets the glories of his race. But then the entire Caribbean might have had a different history had it not been for the daring and deviltry of the Drakes, the Vernons and the Morgans. Anyway, as I lay in my bunk that night I took sides with the Englishman who could think of the history and glamor of Cartagena in spite of the ancient odors that still surround it.

Next day, when we oozed over the horizon and sailed into the mountain-circled bay at Santa Marta, I at first refused to be impressed by the trim white fruit steamers flying the Stars and Stripes, and the fact that the banana fields of Santa Marta are among the largest and busiest in Latin America. Instead, I immediately engaged a dilapidated old taxi and hurried away to San Pedro Alejandrino, that tiny white Spanish colonial house where Bolívar spent those last tragic days, the house which all Colombians and Venezuelans approach uncovered, as they would a holy place. I am not very sentimental, yet I confess that when I go to San Pedro, as when I go to Mount Vernon, I am filled with a certain quiet emotion. The towering peaks of the Sierra Nevada, like hatless white-haired giants looking silently down upon the place, the tropical breezes that whisper reverently through the trees, suggest that something called unearthly peace.

Although founded in 1525, eight years before Cartagena, and for more than two centuries overshadowed by the martial pomp and colonial importance of the latter, today Santa Marta is not only the mecca of Latin-American patriots, but it probably touches the pocketbooks of more Colombians than its classic sister. By day it is as quiet as a deserted village. There is no activity. The steamers hug the wharves from mid-morning throughout the day, with scarcely a soul above deck. The wooden shutters of the old one-story houses are drawn—for it is a law of the tropics, if not the prophets, that no person in his right mind, except perhaps the Yankee tourist, would be at large in the middle of the day.

But when the long hot day is over and the evening breezes begin to blow, the waterfront twinkles with thousands of lights, laborers swarm over the docks and the ships. Trains in from the banana fields puff up and down and soon long lines of workers are moving in rhythmic cadence from train to ship where great mechanical conveyors gently lower millions of bunches of the pale green fruit down into the holds.

Curiously enough, the first banana plantation at Santa Marta was established by a Paris syndicate in that fabulous period when Frenchmen had completed the Suez Canal and had already embarked on a plan to sever the North and South American continents at Panamá. The company furnished plenty of money to a group of engineering dilettantes, not to say idling ne'er-do-wells who built a palatial château, planted trees and trusted to fate to tend and make them bear fruit. Meanwhile, succumbing to the enervating climate, they spent more and more time in the shade drinking wines imported from the home-land until the stockholders in Paris stopped sending cash.

Today only the crumbling walls of the château remain as a monument to French inability to discriminate between the virtues of labor and the love of life. For many miles inland well-tended plantations spread out over the soggy coastal lands. Although developed by Americans, most of these plantations today are owned by Colombians who learned the business from the Yankees and then went into producing for themselves, the Yankees buying the fruit in the field. Last year only twenty per cent of the 7,295,488 stems of bananas exported from Santa Marta were grown by the foreign companies. The balance of eighty per cent came from the farms of natives.

"You have here," one of the native plantation owners told me, "a splendid example of how Yankee industry can best function in South America. Only a few years ago the North American company controlled production in this entire area. And, although it paid good wages, provided workers with houses, hospitals, medical care and all manner of conveniences they never enjoyed before, yet it experienced endless labor troubles, even strikes and riots. Periodically the government saddled it with new taxes and regulations. It was a constant target for politicians until anti-American sentiment was rampant, and business was bad for both the company and the country.

"Look at the contrast today," he said. "The company not only buys its bananas from us, but assists us in every way to produce the very best of fruit. It furnishes experts in agriculture and agricultural engineering who analyze our soil, tell us how to treat it, drain it properly, keep down plant diseases and so on. The result? We make money. We take pride in the industry, because it is really ours. There is little labor trouble. We understand how to deal with our own people. There are fewer government restrictions. It is to their and the country's advantage for the politicians to treat us right.

Colombia

"This is an advantage to the American company, too," he went on. "It gets its fruit regularly, and with little or no interference. It is put to less expense here, so that it has more money to spend at home, to advertise, to promote a larger market, which means the employment of more of your own people. It doesn't have to fight our laborers, the politicians or the government, so that there is more good will on both sides, to the mutual benefit of all concerned. And, what may be more interesting to you, it makes a better market here for American goods. We have more money to buy things from you. Your ships have cargo both ways. They bring down your machinery, cloth and luxury goods, and take back fruit."

Carrying water for large Yankee enterprises in the Other America is not among my specialties. But some of the professional anti-imperialists who insist that every phase and activity of every Yankee business in the countries beyond the Rio Grande is a menace, administered purely for the purpose of enslaving the lowly Latin, could display a great deal more logic. There have been outright crooks and selfish and designing characters who have fleeced and bullied the more trusting and dumber among the people of the Caribbean countries, but more often they have had the able assistance of designing characters among native officials.

A few hours on the wharves among the workers and local officials, and in the fields along the Santa Marta railroad, served to shed an interesting light upon the imperialism of one of our large companies in Colombia. For instance, Colombian labor has little room for complaint against the banana industry. The wages received by Colombian banana laborers are higher than those paid in any other Latin-American republic. For here labor is rigidly organized, and its interests are scrupulously protected by the national government.

The average man engaged in loading bananas at the dock in Santa Marta makes from $5 to $6 a ship. Even in the de-

[93]

pression there were three and four ships every week. Translated into local living costs he is three to four times better off than those who unload the same fruit at New York or New Orleans.

Also those Colombian politicians who during the presidency of Alfonso Lopez, from 1934 to 1938, hounded big business, especially foreign big business, with even more fervor than the most rabid New Dealer during the same period hounded the great corporations in this country, may be reminded that their government levies an export tax of one and three-quarters cents on every bunch of bananas that leaves Colombian ports. This export tax the North American consumer must pay. They might also be reminded that the companies made the American people banana conscious by spending countless millions of dollars in advertising and promotion, and that they maintain, at tremendous expense, gigantic organizations for the sale and distribution of the golden yellow fruit. In other words, Colombians can produce and sell their fruit only because Yankee ingenuity and money have created a market and demand for it.

Even if the Yankees themselves produce only a fifth of the bananas in Colombia, they have to buy, lease, or rent the lands from Colombians for which they pay whatever is demanded. They give employment with good wages and salaries to thousands of Colombian citizens. They pay taxes of all classes within the country.

Ever since that day in 1866 when Carl August Franc, at the time employed as a steward on one of the vessels of the Pacific Mail Steamship Company, brought some wild bananas to New York and peddled them along the Battery, hundreds of millions of dollars have been spent in scientific research. Specialists in all the ramifications of science have been and are still busy searching for new ways of cultivating and ripening the fruit so that it may have increasing appeal to the public's palate.

In the Santa Marta lowlands there are soil experts, students of climate and rainfall and drainage engineers whose studies determine the effect of the marshy soil of one field, or the sandy soil of another, and the amount of moisture and sunshine, the sugar and chemical content, which in turn determines the time required for ripening, and thus the flavor and grade when it reaches the fruit stand at Detroit or St. Louis. The experts have to know the amount of chlorophyl, that is the green, in the fruit in one field as compared to that from another field. It always varies, and it is vital because the amount of this determines the length of time required for it to turn yellow, or ripen.

But before I become so hopelessly involved in the science and culture of bananas that I cannot find my way out, I am going to rush on to Barranquilla, the most important of Colombia's three Caribbean cities. Located at the mouth of the Magdalena and about midway between Santa Marta and Cartagena, Barranquilla is the Cairo of the Colombian Nile. It is the principal seaport—the gateway to the interior. Yet until 1939 ocean-going steamers had never been able to reach it. The river which for four hundred years has served as the chief highway for Colombian commerce and travellers was still cut off from the sea insofar as ships from the outside world were concerned. Through the ages the internals of the continent, mud and sand, had flowed down from the mountains and accumulated at the river's mouth, making it impossible for a ship or a sailboat to enter. The volume flowing down at all times had been so great that any attempt at dredging was about as effective as trying to dip up water with a horseshoe.

The British, who are not only the world's most prodigious accumulators of concessions, but for a hundred years were the principal port and dock builders of South America, finally and at great profit to themselves provided something of a remedy for the situation. They signed the Colombians to a long-term agreement, built a mile-long pier right out into the sea seventeen miles west of the city. For the concessionaires this was, of course, a convenient distance from the community they expected to serve. For then they were able to build a narrow-gauge railway from the port to the city and charge such exorbitant tariffs on freight and passengers that if the stockholders didn't receive unusually satisfactory returns on their investments they should be considered pikers. If they didn't do so there will be no opportunity in the future, for the concession has reverted to the Colombian government.

Meantime, through the initiative of man, coupled with the intervention of Providence, the mouth of the Magdalena has at last been cleared of its age-old accumulations, and ships are sailing directly into the Magdalena and tieing up at the new and imposing docks which have been built on the mosquito-ridden marshes several miles inland.

Two years ago Yankee contractors and engineers surveyed the watery scene at the river's mouth and, for a not inconsiderable sum, took on the task of building jetties and dredging a narrow channel across the bar. By the time they had completed the jetties, nature took a hand, and with a vengeance. It seems that the obstruction had piled itself up right on the brink of a bottomless undersea chasm. Suddenly one night the entire area washed overboard, taking one of the jetties with it, but leaving a hundred feet of water, and making Barranquilla one of the most desirable seaports on the north coast of South America.

Barranquilla was already a modern metropolis, full of foreigners, *gringo* factories, shops and modern homes. Its red and green traffic signals somehow prevent the careless occupants of donkey carts and high-powered automobiles from ending up in masses of wreckage. More than any of the other cities of Colombia, it has experienced the inroads of foreign business. There are cotton mills like those in the Carolinas that turn semiwild Colombian tree cotton into ready-to-wear, snow-white suits for three dollars and fifty cents. Because of the increase in the production of this cotton, the French have just erected a rayon plant and announcement has been made that

Bridge Across "The Colombian Nile"

San Andres Gold Mine, Antioquia

four or five more are being moved from England. There are German beer-brewing establishments that might have been transplanted from the Rhine. A German colony, an Italian colony, an English and American colony, each maintains its own clubhouse, tennis court or golf links.

Still to be seen among the foreign establishments of the city is a memorial to Ivar Kreuger. The tentacles of the late match manufacturer even reached down into Colombia. Citizens of the lower Magdalena will tell you that significantly enough the mill closed and Kreuger's representative in Barranquilla sailed secretly away to France only two weeks before the financial Fu Manchu blew out his light in Paris.

No stranger is permitted to leave Barranquilla without visiting the *Acueducto,* the modern water works which might have been transplanted from Kokomo or Kalamazoo. It was built and is operated for the municipality by a burly and blustery Westerner by the name of Hollipeter, whose name has become synonymous with his product. Even barkeepers in Barranquilla will inquire whether you wish *agua mineral,* or *agua* Hollipeter with your Scotch. The *Acueducto* was made possible by the persistency of a Chicago banker back in the Coolidge era. It has been from the first a most profitable enterprise, which until recently had meant little to the American bondholders. Every month the city government set aside the money to pay the bonds, but exchange restrictions made it impossible to send it out of the country. So Hollipeter reinvested it. He built a magnificent athletic stadium in the new part of the city, which is evidently yielding splendid returns, since football is a most popular sport. Now the growth of the city has made necessary an expansion of the *Acueducto* itself.

A characteristic story is told about the building of the original plant. In spite of the great campaign for its establishment, one of the most prominent, if not the most patriotic, of the city's medicos almost defeated the project. He warned the unsuspecting citizens of the metropolis that the drinking of this water would result in dire and devilish disaster. "Señores," he warned in effect, "the devastating chemicals used in the so-called purification processes will but render the procreative organs impotent. Therefore, it will bring to our beloved community a diminution of population, marital unhappiness and an unholy social state."

The three Obregón brothers, Rafael, Pedro and Evaristo, are the most prominent and influential among the old Spanish families. Unlike most Colombians, the members of this family have never broken their ties with Spain. They have maintained estates at Barcelona and Seville, each taking his turn in the administration of their Barranquilla enterprises. However, the Spanish War has caused them to alter the practice somewhat, and they are all taking a more active part both in their possessions and in Colombian public affairs. The stalwart Martinez brothers, headed by Carlos Martinez Aparicio, manage to put out one of the two best daily papers in all of Colombia, a paper printed in both Spanish and English. I should say the English edition is even better than the Spanish. But then the North American and British colony constitute a potent if small element in the life of the town. Carl Parrish, a North American, fathered the first modern real-estate development in the country. On the outskirts of old Barranquilla he built California bungalows, golf clubs and the Del Prado, architecturally the most imposing Spanish-American hotel on the continent. But Elios Muvdi, a Syrian Jew, is today the real-estate wizard of the city. He has surrounded the Parrish section with a half dozen new subdivisions and has accumulated such a fortune that he has become the most lavish contributor to social and patriotic causes in the country.

P. P. Von Bauer, a tall gray-eyed Austrian gentleman, is responsible for starting another modern movement with headquarters in Barranquilla. He came to Colombia as a very young man long before the Big Parade began sweeping across Europe in 1914. Trained as an engineer and scientist, he learned to speak a half dozen languages, including Spanish. Then, fulfilling a strange ambition, he came to Colombia and went exploring in the hinterlands of the republic. For a long spell he lived among the untamed red men of the Amazonian regions, hundreds of miles from civilization. He studied them, learned their dialects, meantime observed the riches of nature—trees, plants and soils. Then he took up residence in first one city and then another, in order to learn the customs and the culture of New Granada.

Meantime he had forgotten to take out citizenship papers before going on a visit to his family in Vienna. While there the Archduke fell a victim of an assassin's bullet in Sarajevo. Austria descended upon Serbia. The Kaiser's legions went goosestepping into Belgium and, having been an officer in the army of Franz Joseph, Von Bauer suddenly found himself in a uniform and marching at the head of a column of soldiers. For four years he dodged the bullets of the Allies until the lull in 1918, when he hurriedly set sail once again for the New World.

Back in Colombia he got hold of a second-hand airplane, and in a desultory manner started flying between towns. Thus was born the idea for the first and oldest commercial air transportation system in all South America, in fact, in all the hemisphere, a project that wiped out the barriers of distance, inconvenience and time, and brought the most remote inland cities of Colombia into intimate touch with the rest of the world.

Before Von Bauer arrived upon the scene, Colombia's largest cities, even the capital of the republic, were so far off the beaten track of travel, that the outside world had known nothing about them. Even today there is not a single railroad or highway extending from the sea to Bogotá. To reach the capital city from the Pacific port of Buenaventura, it is necessary to travel in three stages.

New Roads to Riches

Leaving Buenaventura in the morning, the first stage is by train over the coastal mountains to the important city of Cali on the western side of the Cauca River, then across and down the valley to the railhead at Armenia, some four thousand feet up the Quindio Mountains. Here you spend the night. Next morning by automobile you climb over the 10,000-foot spine of the mountains and down to Ibagué and another railhead. At Ibagué you take a train on a road that twists, turns and switches back and forth the rest of the day, across the Magdalena Valley, reaching Bogotá late in the evening. That is, if there have been no landslides or washouts, and there usually are. Sometimes during the rainy season traffic over this route is held up for weeks.

The distance from the Caribbean to Bogotá is 700 miles. Flat-bottomed old river boats struggle up the lazy snakelike river in fifteen to twenty days. Small, more modern ones occasionally make it in seven if the rain god has been at all generous. Even this must be made in three stages. Deep-draft boats ply from Barranquilla to the rapids at La Dorada, where you must take a train for forty some miles where boats of shallow draft make the trip on to Girardot.

Towns and communities not located directly on the river are reached by every known method from canoe and muleback to cable way. From the port of Gamarra one of these ingenious contraptions, with basket cars, each with a capacity of 500 pounds strung a hundred feet apart, swings passengers and freight from the river up to the town of Ocaña on the top of the mountains. Farther up another cable way connects the city of Manizales, way over in the Cauca Valley, with the railroad which extends on down to the ports of Honda and La Dorada. This one actually swings cars in successive stages up and over an intervening mountain range a distance of seventy kilometers, or a little over forty-three miles.

The local planes of the Von Bauer lines take you from

Colombia

Barranquilla to the foot of the Andean shelf in four hours and on over the 9000-foot parapet in thirty minutes. Express planes now make the trip non-stop in two hours. By air Bogotá is now less than two days and nights from Broadway. You may take the night plane to Miami, then next morning fly in a forty-passenger clipper ship straight across the Spanish Main to Barranquilla and have lunch the following noon in Bogotá.

The Sociedad Colombo-Alemana de Transportes Aéreos, to unfurl it completely, is no longer an infant. And though it now affiliates with the giant Pan-American system it still clings to the treasured ways of the builders, whose reputation for carefulness has become a tradition in the republic of Colombia.

The other day I took the air from Barranquilla within a split second of 6:30 A.M. Ten minutes later we were deep in the heart of the Continent. The brown muddy river oozed through the ageless jungle beneath us. Pale puffballs of clouds played hide and seek over and under the ship, now and then spraying us with a shower of rain. On either side only a few miles away, billowy green mountains lifted their heads high above us.

Now and then we swept down upon some quiet town of mud huts to exchange mail and give the natives a chance to gather on the river bank and enjoy the chief excitement of their lives. Barranca Bermeja was one port of call. It is from here that the Tropical Oil Company's pipe line begins its 400-mile journey down to Cartagena. For three and a half hours the process continued, until we reached Girardot at the foot of the Andean wall. Then the plane lifted its nose and prepared to go over the top. From the valley of the Magdalena we rose for 13,000 feet above the soupy mist that even shrouded the tops of the Cordilleras. Within a few minutes we dropped down blindly through the clouds and presently came out on the windy *Sabana* of Bogotá.

As I sat comfortably in the plane that day watching the

strange mysteries of this jungle world sweep along beneath me, I remembered the story of the epic journey of Gonzalo Jiménez de Quesada and his 150 Conquistadores who negotiated the first trip from north to south through these regions. Four hundred years ago doing the impossible had already become an old Spanish custom. But this trip of Quesada's remains until this day one of the most amazing of all Spanish accomplishments.

Rumors had come down the river of a rich civilization in the interior—of gold and precious stones and the fabled story of Eldorado, rumors that had some foundation. Anyway, down in Santa Marta the ambitious old Spaniard rounded up a party of hardy adventurers like himself. He told them the story of the mysterious civilization in the interior, of its fabulous riches. His eloquence must have known no limits, for he thrilled them with the prospects. Without delay they drank to the King of Castile and began the journey. From Santa Marta they sailed in five small ships, with horses, stores and equipment, entered the Magdalena and made their way as far as the rapids. From there they took to land, or what in the sodden jungle would pass for land. Plunging into this endless stretch of green hell, they followed as best they could the watery tentacles of the river, its countless branches, tributaries, slues and lagoons. Every step of their way was a superhuman battle. Disease and pestilence travelled with them mocking their every movement. There was the heat, killing heat, myriads of varieties of death-dealing insects, hungry crocodiles, all the slimy creatures in the category of reptiles, and horrible fever and disease germs in every drop of water, not to mention unfriendly and primitive Indians at every clearing. Day after day dragged by. Every day their numbers diminished. Every day they left Pedro or Carlos or Luis behind, a hostage to the pestilential wilds.

Finally, one late afternoon in 1538, thirteen years after the founding of Santa Marta, 166 ragged, fever-racked members of the once glorious party, together with fifty-nine of their horses, straggled up over the Andean ridge and out onto the *Sabana* of Bogotá. But imagine their astonishment when they found that a group of Germans, from a colony which had settled near Lake Maracaibo, had made their way southward, while fellow countrymen of theirs had gone by way of the Pacific and arrived just ahead of them.

III

The Capital of Liberalism

It was the "Dia de la Raza," the 12th of October, "The Day of the Race." As one Colombian puts it, "Didn't the immortal Admiral discover the New World on October 12, thus founding the American race?" Anyway, like all the other Spanish-speaking nations of the New World, Colombia celebrates Columbus Day with reverence and gaiety, with Te Deums in the churches and *fiestas* in the streets. But if the Bogotaños, on the occasion in question, celebrated with poetic gaiety, the city itself greeted me in a very prosaic manner. Immediately upon my arrival at the Hotel Granada, I was advised to report with as little delay as possible to the Police Department.

The travelling stranger in Colombia is seldom free from the dizzying process of trying to conform to the laws and regulations of the republic. But, although the laws seem almost as silly as some of our own, the officials themselves meet courtesy with courtesy, no matter how slow and thorough they may be.

"Si, El Señor is expected," said a young officer at the door of the department, and took me immediately in tow. I followed him across a *patio*, up a winding stairway, through numerous hallways filled with nondescript characters, around the *patio* balcony, through back halls, and rooms half filled with palaver-

ing officials and attachés. Finally, somewhere in the remote
recesses of the yawning old building, a pleasant gentleman
asked for my passport, and sat down to inform himself of all
of its details. Although it was not my first visit to Colombia,
and I was only a transient and my credentials revealed that I
had complied explicitly with every regulation before and upon
entering the country, it became necessary for me then and there
to be fully investigated and once again put on record with the
national forces of law and order.

"But, first of all," he said, "you must supply us with a set
of six photographs of yourself, three profiles and three front
views."

Much to his surprise I was able to produce the required
number. Whereupon, to the enthusiastic interest of those standing around, I was weighed, measured and fingerprinted not
once, but in duplicate. My health was attested to, the color of
my skin, hair and eyes and my physical idiosyncrasies were
minutely described in the bold and ornate script of a clerk
who contemplated his handiwork letter by letter. At this stage
of the ceremonies I was permitted to sit while the same deliberate servant of the state recorded in an individual six-page
booklet the complete details of a lengthy inquiry into my whole
life's history, my mental and social traits and habits, as well as
my future plans and aspirations.

In return for all this I was presented with a tiny brochure,
or *cédula*, to be carried on my person at all times. Any one
would think that a document resulting from such endless investigation and effort would admit its bearer to any place, institution or official at any time, day or night. But I soon found it
would only allow me to present myself for approval to the
police in any and every city and town I might visit. It would
qualify me, when about to take leave of Colombian territory,
to call upon the Minister of Finance or his agents for the purpose of undergoing an investigation into my income while in

the country, as well as an examination of the amount and character of whatever funds I might be taking out with me. And finally it would only permit me to request of the police headquarters at the port of departure a written, signed, stamped and sealed permission to depart.

Such rigid supervision over travellers is necessary, so I was told, in these troubled and perilous times. "There are so many destructive doctrines and ideologies abroad in the world," it was explained, "that the government must take all precautions to protect its institutions."

Considering the difficulties of reaching Bogotá, even if you have money to pay for a river passage from the North, or overland transportation from the Pacific Coast, not to mention the more pretentious air service, I should think enemies of the republic would be slow to attempt an invasion of the capital when so many other fields are easy of access. However, Bogotaños may be excused their suspicions, since the old Conquistadores themselves appeared to have been such a suspicious lot.

For the most part the metropolitan centers and capitals of other South American countries are either on the seacoasts or in the heart of their most populous districts. Bogotá, on the other hand, is really the outpost of Colombian civilization in the interior. Beyond it to the south and east lies the vast, wild, most of it unexplored, hinterland of Amazonia, two thirds of the land area of the republic. Like a lighthouse on a promontory it stands on a balcony of the Andes, looking south, west and north, with practically all of its developed resources on the hillsides and in the valleys of its two great rivers—the Magdalena and the Cauca. The plateau of Bogotá is really a high shelf, 2000 square miles in area and a mile and a half high, while the shelf itself is surrounded by a steep ledge, or higher wall of mountains some 1500 to 2000 feet in altitude. Bogotaños refer to this plateau as "the *Sabana* country," and to the lowlands, as "the hot country."

Colombia

Climate in Colombia is not a matter of north and south, but a matter of up and down. Since all the republic lies within the tropics, winter and summer are designated by the rainy and dry season respectively. Generally speaking, rain falls from March to May and from September to November. In December, January and February, in June, July and August, grassy lawns and shrubbery turn brown from the lack of moisture and the long hours of scorching heat and sunshine. On the *Sabana* the thermometer ranges around fifty degrees throughout the year. Much of the time the sky is gray. At night and in the morning it is cold and damp and as a friend of mine put it, "The skin of the foreigner is always covered with goose pimples."

You cannot know Colombia, "the hot country," or the *Sabana*, until you have met the man who recreates them on canvas—their scenery, their people, their life, their moods. He is Don Ricardo Gomez Campuzano. An afternoon in his old house is a pictorial tour of all the republic. Seek out a certain number in a drab, narrow street. Dangle the knocker of an ancient battered door, and wait. Presently the door creaks and swings slowly open. A sheepish little maid, speaking the lisping Spanish of the Old World, invites you to enter. You follow her down a narrow corridor and out into a broad open *patio*, filled with the hardy plants and shrubbery of the highlands. Then you climb a winding stairway to the second floor and walk into a great drawing room.

At first it is a room, then suddenly it becomes a countryside inhabited by all manner of people and creatures. There is a typical Spanish colonial house with a vast rolling field stretching away behind it. The field is crowded with cattle, sheep, donkeys and what not. The house and its old pink-tiled roof are bathed in tropical sunshine. Sunbeams fairly dance on the bougainvillea blossoms that hang in cascades along the dilapidated adobe wall or fence. Over there crowds are leaving a village church. And here is a marketplace with hundreds of people milling about. These are the pictures of the "hot country."

In an adjoining room the mood is different. The pictures are less cheerful. Most of them make you want to turn up your coat collar. They depict the highland country around Bogotá. There are few bright flowers. Trees are hard-bitten with leathery foliage and little of that except for the Eucalyptus trees, which, of course, have been imported. Here and there on the *Sabana,* rows of these have been planted, and, as in the valleys of Utah, Colorado and other mountainous regions they seem to thrive in spite of cold winds.

Gomez Campuzano is one of Colombia's institutions. He paints for the joy of painting. He even likes his own pictures and frequently buys back canvases he has already sold. A friend bought a life-sized painting of a lone cow. She was out on the cold dreary *Sabana.* Storm clouds rolled toward her. The scrubby trees were bent low in the wind. She had evidently lost her calf and was frantic. She called appealingly to it, but it never came.

Some years afterward Don Ricardo saw the painting in the house of his friend who now spent a part of each year abroad, so that the great house was closed and the shutters drawn for months at a time. He got to thinking of the unhappy cow, shut up in a dark, deserted house, so he bought her back and hung her in one of his large cheery rooms so she would not be alone.

Next to the Colombian scene, his wife and daughter are his favorite subjects. He is always beginning new paintings of them, for Don Ricardo is both an artist and a Latin, desperately, hopelessly in love.

The most remote of Colombian cities, Bogotá has a population of more than three quarters of a million people. When you look at its imposing buildings, at the cathedrals and churches, the great colonial capital, fronted by the sunken gardens and fountains of the central plaza, the sprawling stone structures on Fifteenth Street, the banks and other modern buildings, you marvel how all the materials that went into their construction and equipment, as well as the fixtures and facilities for maintaining them, were ever brought to a spot so far from the world's highways. And again you are compelled to admire the daring and resourcefulness of the Spanish race, meantime overlooking the cruelty of its past and deploring the tragedy so recently heaped upon it in its original home.

So little has been the cultural, or perhaps better the social, influence of the outside world that next to the people of Medellín, in the valley of Antioquia, the inhabitants of Bogotá, aristocrats and peasants, probably speak the purest Castillian in the world. Many of them speak it with the same accent and inflection, the same lisping lilt, so characteristic of the old aristocracy of the motherland. Of course, Bogotaños of the servant classes are not Spanish. In their veins is the blood of the Chibchas, who are descendants of the ancient Incas.

One of the Incas, or emperors of Perú, sent missionaries to convert the wild tribes of red men in the far north. One of these missionaries finally reached the *Sabana* of Bogotá and established himself in the vicinity of the present capital. He made friends with the primitive people, taught them agriculture and other industries, even art and music. As the centuries passed his descendants grew into a numerous tribe. Anyway, when the Spaniards arrived these people dominated the surrounding country. Like the aborigines of every other section of the New World invaded by Europeans, whether by Anglo-Saxons or Latins, the Chibchas soon found themselves in the tyrannical clutches of the newcomers. Something may be said for Quesada personally. He seems to have been an exception among the old conquerors in that he was about the least cruel of all of his cohorts. He even named the city he founded after "Bacata," one of the chiefs of the region.

New Roads to Riches

I have no doubt that poetic as well as practical reasons prompted Quesada and his compatriots to settle in such an inhospitable climate. There was already the nucleus of a civilization. Then, too, if the heathen had settled there undoubtedly rich treasures existed thereabouts. Besides, it was the authentic bailiwick of one of the cleverest Indian chiefs who ever lived, and whose exploits whetted and excited the imaginations of more men—rulers, soldiers, traders, explorers, adventurers— than any other character in New World history. No American since his time has displayed more publicity genius. The title, or appellation which he chose for himself inspired and thrilled the men of all Europe to go out and hunt for and conquer new worlds. If Mussolini and Hitler had pondered the story of this denizen of the Andes, they might have been wiser in the selection of their titles, their various conquests might have proven more popular. The terms "Il Duce" and "Der Fuehrer" excite awe and fear instead of admiration and envy.

To attract attention to himself, to sell himself to his people the Chibcha chief of Guatabita did not resort to military demonstrations or the warlike displays of a bully. He did not surround himself with fierce braves fitted out with the largest bows and the longest, sharpest arrows "ever made." He sent out no armies on forays against the weak to prove his prowess. Nothing so cheap as that. He made sacrifices instead of conquests, sacrifices to his gods, but not human sacrifices. He didn't even follow the practice of many of his contemporaries and throw beautiful girls into deep wells. History, according to Doctor Philip Ainsworth Means, has it that he demonstrated his sacrificial nature by throwing material riches—gold, silver and precious stones—into a lake. An act which no doubt would have sickened the heart of any civilized paleface, but which to my way of thinking proved him a lily-white sacrificer, as well as demonstrating a strength of will that has not been equalled since.

Colombia

At night, as a final act to his performance, he rubbed a sticky substance over his skin, then had himself sprinkled with powdered gold, and all-glowing and glittering in the dim flickering lights of the camp-fire, he did a rousing and, I have no doubt, sexy dance. After having disported himself sufficiently, he climaxed the occasion by himself leaping into the lake and allowing the gold, but not his fame, to be washed away. For the story of the Chibcha chief, *El Dorado*, "the man of gold," has endured through the centuries, yet, sad to say, his descendants still do the drudgery for Quesada's progeny.

In spite of the preponderance of Chibcha blood among the Bogotá peasants few traces of the ancient customs of their forebears remain. As in each of the South American countries, the customs and folk habits of Colombia are entirely her own. Remoteness and climate as well as racial antecedents give the people of the Colombian highlands characteristics not found in any of the other South American nations. In every Spanish country on the continent men of the peasant or peon class wear some form of *poncho*, a great piece of heavy cloth with a slit in the middle through which the head is extended. This piece of cloth is known by a different name in practically every country. The Colombian peon calls it a *ruana*, and the damp, chilling winds of the *Sabana* make it his closest earthly companion. He may be without shoes, his pants, which reach only a little below the knees, may be in shreds, but his *ruana* is always in good condition. And what the *ruana* is to the man the great black shawl, or *manta*, is to the woman.

However, there are very distinct class lines among these peasants, lines that are seldom crossed. Day laborers, such as janitors in public buildings, look down upon laborers, say in the building trades, and vice-versa, while the second cook in a legation, or home of an official, high-hats the first cook in the home of a prominent merchant or banker. Maids and butlers in diplomatic households have even begun to discard the *ruana* and the *manta* and do not associate with the other servants of the same household, such as gardeners, scrubwomen and dishwashers.

If class distinctions exist among the peasants, or the servant and working classes, it is natural to expect unusually rigid social distinctions among their self-styled betters. More than any other capital of the Andean country, more even than the Peruvian city of Lima, historic capital of the Viceroys, Bogotá is socially the city of the colonial Spaniard. Although the foreigner who takes up residence in Bogotá must do a period of probation, eventually he will be invited to formal affairs and finally, upon occasion, be admitted to the family circle of intimate acquaintances, but he will still be a foreigner. To certain exclusive clubs he will seldom be admitted, except on sufferance. Until the world depression few foreigners, except those in the diplomatic service, might become members of the Bogotá Country Club. Economic disaster, however, sometimes serves as an outward social leveller, and so to help pay expenses and maintain the establishment, the financially better-to-do among *Los Gringos* were accepted. Today a Yankee or a European may lunch, or chase the little white ball from green to green in a friendly atmosphere.

In spite of the purity of language and the preponderance of white people in Bogotá, Colombia has its marked racial distinctions, even in the populated centers of the interior. Conservative Colombian estimates place the population of the country at 7,000,000, thirty-five per cent of whom are white, and five per cent Negro, the latter located principally in the hot coastal regions. The Indian population, about two per cent of the whole, is concentrated largely in the Amazonian hinterland, and the regions east of the Magdalena, all the way from Bogotá to the tip end of the Goajira Peninsula, between Santa Marta and Lake Maracaibo in Venezuela. The remaining fifty-eight per cent are of various mixtures, white, Negro and Indian.

Colombia

Among the whites there is, even among the oldest families, a very large element of Jewish blood. Some of the earliest Spanish colonial settlements were made by Spanish Jews fleeing the Inquisition and other oppressive conditions in the Old World. In addition to these descendants of the Sephardic Jews, who came over from Spain in early colonial times, many Syrian and Near Eastern Jews have settled in Colombia more recently. Previously I have mentioned Elios Muvdi, the merchant and real-estate philanthropist of Barranquilla. Then there is the eminent Doctor Gabriel Turbay, outstanding political leader, and perhaps the Liberal Party's candidate for president in the next elections, who is of Syrian-Jewish descent.

As nowhere else in the world perhaps, the Jews of Colombia, that is the old settlers, have become thoroughly assimilated and merged with the people of Spanish blood. Invariably the only remaining suggestions of their ancestry are their Semitic features. Interestingly enough, most of them, although Jews by race, are Catholics by religion.

Incidentally hundreds of Jewish immigrants from Germany and Austria have entered Colombia within the past two years. Unfortunately so many have settled in the one city of Cali and the surrounding rich Cauca Valley that local protests are going up, not because the newcomers are Jews, but because there are so many of them they have glutted the labor market, surfeited the community with small shops and overcrowded certain of the professions.

The not inconsiderable contingent of German and Austrian, as well as Italian, settlers should not be overlooked. In spite of the Bogotaños' aloofness toward the foreigners of today, these Europeans are rapidly becoming assimilated. Representatives of banks and trading companies in Hitler's realm, as well as the agents for German steamship lines plying the Colombian coasts, may outwardly assume a Nazi mien, click their heels and beer mugs and heil Hitler in their clubs, but many of them are

[113]

quietly putting their money into Colombian land and property, signifying their intention to remain in the New World. Many of the older settlers have already taken out Colombian citizenship and broken ties with the Old World forever. As one old-time German settler put it, "the climate as well as the easy freedom of democracy in Colombia tends to undermine the sense of strict discipline and regimentation instilled into us in the old country. It is not easy to be strict and strenuous in the tropics and especially in a country so rich as well as politically democratic."

So far as Colombians themselves are concerned, Fascist doctrines, whether of the Italian or German stripe, are not popular. There is a tiny so-called Fascist group in the country, but it bears no relation whatsoever to European Fascism. It is exclusively native. Its leaders and followers are the extreme conservatives, some leaders in the Catholic Church who cannot abide the works of the Liberal Party which replaced the old Catholic conservative government eight years ago. They insist that the party's liberalism is so extreme it approaches Communism.

"As a matter of fact," a former conservative cabinet member told me, "so far as I am concerned, the four-year administration of President Alfonso Lopez was almost as radical in its action toward foreign enterprise and business in general as the Cardenas government in Mexico."

I thought that the conservative Republicans and Democrats in this country entertained strong opinions regarding the politics of Franklin D. Roosevelt. But a few minutes in the company of groups of old-time business men in Colombia gave me a better idea of the exact meaning of "strong opinions." They expressed themselves in the most eloquent words, punctuated with all the picturesque profanity peculiar to the Spanish language, concerning "our former Communist president."

In spite of their anger and protests, the Liberal Party overwhelmed the conservatives in the last elections and another Liberal president was inaugurated on August 6, 1938.

The attitude of Colombians in the Spanish civil war must have proved a disappointment to any pro-Fascists or pro-Nazis with ambitions in Colombia. In practically all the other South American nations the majority of the people who were at all opinionated on the subject were pro-Franco. In Colombia, except for the more conservative elements and the Church leaders the great majority of people were pro-Loyalists. When the new Franco ambassador dared to criticize a Bogotá newspaper for its uncomplimentary remarks about his chief there was a mass condemnation and demand for the recall of his Fascist Excellency.

Government in Colombia is democratic in practice. The country has enjoyed orderly political procedure and change of administrations by ballot, instead of by revolution, for some forty years. Today there is a universal opinion against all authoritarianism or government by dictatorship. Some observers even call Colombia the only genuine democracy on the continent and one has dubbed Bogotá "The Capital of Liberalism."

What one old conservative calls "the present orgy in Colombian liberalism" began August 7, 1932, when, due to a split in the old Conservative Party, the liberals elected Doctor Enrique Olaya Herrera, to the presidency. Before he became president Doctor Olaya was for years Colombian Minister in Washington, where he was popular and highly regarded. He was a scholar and a statesman of the first order, worthy to rank with any, living or dead. To him politics was a science. He captured the imaginations not only of liberals but of conservatives as well. It was his personality as well as his cultured statesmanship and sound common sense that made him outstanding. The hold which the Liberal Party has on the country today is due to the lasting imprint which he left on the people of the nation. He was one of the notable examples of the mixture of Spanish and Chibcha blood. El Dorado, if a little poetic license be permitted, was among Olaya's ancestors. He looked the part. He was tall, with the torso of a Dempsey or a Tunney. His enormous head rested squarely upon powerful shoulders. He had high cheek-bones, a firm chin and a mouth filled with glistening white teeth. In conversation he spoke deliberately in several languages, including English, and he looked squarely at you through sparkling black eyes.

Olaya was a remarkable orator, but not of the typical Latin type. He spoke with profound dignity and his voice was like the rich low tones of a great organ. It rose and fell in rhythmic cadences.

I knew him as Minister in Washington and I visited him several times in Bogotá while he was President. The last time I saw him we sat in his private study in the old presidential palace at Bogotá, and he chatted freely about his long residence in the United States. Although passionately Colombian he liked the people of North America, made no bones about patterning many of his works after theirs. He invited American capital to the country and, as long as he was in office, accorded it liberal treatment. Although ready to check the head of any foreign business enterprise who overstepped the limits of Colombian laws and customs, he was generous in his efforts to see that the enterprise was protected. He floated bonds in this country to finance public works and scrupulously paid the interest on them. He began the work of building modern ports at Buenaventura and at Cartagena, as well as roads to the interior, but without becoming lavish in his plans or his spending. He encouraged the development of the oil industry and many other business enterprises.

The constitution of Colombia does not permit a president to succeed himself, although he may again run for the office after an intervening four years. And Olaya was no man to alter the constitution for his own convenience. So when his four-year term was up he passed on the administration to the ultra-liberal-radical Alfonso Lopez, and, if death had not claimed him in the meantime, overwhelming public demand would have led him back to power once again after the unpopular four years of his successor, who liked to refer to himself as the Colombian "New Dealer," and whose son once reminded me, "Don't you realize that my father's is an Anti-Conservative Left Wing Government?"

It may be said that if the Alfonso Lopez government was Left Wing and Anti-Conservative, it was also superrestrictive and antiforeign, insofar as business was concerned. The features of the New Deal which seemed to appeal to him mostly were its regulations of big business. He wanted to apply all the Rooseveltian ideas to business in a country where practically none of the circumstances surrounding business in the United States prevailed.

A liberal-minded old Colombian professor expressed it this way: "Lopez seemed to think that what Mr. Roosevelt did to utilities, the oil industry, and to manufacturers in a country where all these things have long been developed could be applied with equal vigor in Colombia, where such things are only now getting under way. He wanted to stifle all of them with taxes, regulations, and prohibitions before they even got into production.

"But," he went on, "that has been a failing of most of our so-called liberals. Back of their political liberalism is economic and cultural reactionaryism, for it is reactionaryism not to let business progress by itself. Our liberals have usually wanted to pass laws protecting us from competition before we develop anything ourselves, or before we are even prepared to develop them ourselves. They have usually restricted foreign business so that it couldn't demonstrate to us how to develop our industries. They have protected us from foreign professionals, before we developed a professional class of our own. It is nearly as easy to throw an elephant over the Andes as for a foreign doctor to pass a medical examination and get a license to practice in this country. Yet if a person with enough money to get out of the country has to have an operation, he rushes to the hospitals in Panamá, to the Mayos in Minnesota, or to Europe.

"Lopez," he concluded, "practiced this philosophy. With one hand he tried to drench the people with the broth of radical liberalism. The other he applied to snuffing out forward-looking enterprise by surrounding it with imposing legal handicaps."

However, Eduardo Santos, the democratic, high-minded, scholarly, clever newspaper editor who succeeded Lopez, has returned the government to something of the Olaya equilibrium —liberal administration without fireworks, a human approach to the problems confronting him, without violent upset to the institutions of the country. He believes the nation should progress, but without sudden revolutionary changes. He thinks government should give aid to the common man and the people who work, that business should be regulated but not persecuted. He is a businessman himself and sees no incompatibility between liberal politics and wisely operated business. Although not a rich man, he built up, owns, and runs *El Tiempo*, the leading newspaper of the country, runs it so successfully that its net profits average a quarter of a million *pesos* a year—about a hundred and forty-five thousand dollars. He not only preaches liberal democracy, but practices it. For a hundred years presidents have lived in the old government palace, which significantly enough is next door to an army barracks. Santos lives in his own private residence on the outskirts of the city with a single policeman at the gate. He goes to and from his office and strolls in the streets unaccompanied. He returns his salary to the State and pays all of his own expenses and those of the presidential office. But in his newspaper he preaches a doctrine that most observers will agree is good for Colombia, a country in which politics is the most advanced of the sciences. His words and actions make it unmistakably apparent that he agrees with the old Colombian professor who said Lopez was politically liberal but economically reactionary. Even before he became President Santos pointed out in an editorial in his paper, "That Colombia was a nation of great politicians and poor administrators.

"There is no doubt," said the editorial, "that our capacity as politicians surpasses that of many countries that are already old in the concert of nations. Colombia has plenty of poets and orators but a dearth of people who can run business and industry. We suggest the formula of less politics and better administration. We have the necessary talent for maximum planning. The one thing that we lack is the will to make plans effective. We have not exercised intelligence in financial matters, but only in the noble use of words."

While politics is the most advanced of the sciences, "the noble use of words" is the most highly developed of the arts. Music, dancing, and even painting find few devotees. Gomez Campuzano is the only outstanding painter living, but no country in the world has produced more poets to the dozen of its population, especially among the upper classes. A popular poet who can read his poetry in public can still fill the largest hall in Bogotá at so much per. In the old conservative days the ability to reel off verse was a splendid recommendation for a presidential candidate. Even such a statesman as Olaya was known to indulge in such pursuits now and then.

"It used to be impossible," one old traveller has pointed out, "to stroll through a plaza in Bogotá without encountering clusters of poets trying out their verse on one another."

Times have changed little. Stroll through one of the plazas around the university, upon those none-too-frequent occasions when the sun shows its face, and you will find plenty of evidence of the poetic urge today.

Surprisingly enough women poets are and have been quite as numerous as men. But then, curiously enough, there are more women in Colombia than men, which suggests a skeleton in the closet. In spite of its peaceful practices of today, and its devotion to democracy, Colombia was, until comparatively recently, one of the most war-ridden of the South American nations, having experienced some thirty-five or forty real revolutions, anyway enough revolutions to decimate the male portion of the population.

As recently as ten years ago there were three women to every man in some towns of the country. With little prospect of ever acquiring a man whom she could call her very own, the woman either resigned herself to fate, or took to poetry in self-defense. Doña Silvera Espiñosa de Rendon sang of the cross and the Virgin Mary, and the beauties of friendship, all of which is highly suggestive of a melancholy longing for male companionship.

Yet, curiously enough, not to say flattering to the male, the outstanding ones among Colombia's feminine versifiers were usually married women. Perhaps the good fortune of getting a man filled them with such ecstasy that it was impossible to restrain lyrical outpourings. Doña Mercedes Alvarez de Florez showered her poetic fancy on her husband, and the joys of kissing. When he fell ill, and was expected to die, she urged him to fight death "by drawing strength from my kisses." Even Hollywood might have learned something from her.

IV
The New El Dorado

IF YOU have to take an early plane out of Bogotá on Sunday morning, it is not necessary to leave a call. Bogotá is a city of churches, churches whose priests have acquired something in the nature of ecclesiastical perpetual motion, for they seem to ply their calling without ceasing day and night. Mass is early on the first day of the week. And no late rising is permissible or even possible in this devout metropolis.

I left Bogotá the last time on Sunday morning. Long before five o'clock I came to consciousness with the peal of a bell, a peal as staccato and piercing as the report of a machine gun. One in the distance answered it back, then a third, a half dozen, twenty-five—a million, until the morning air was rent with bells. I arose and looked down into the plaza below my window. In the dim morning light it was thronged with hurrying peons in *ruanas* and *mantas*, as well as somberly clad aristocrats. Gradually the bells died away, and presently there were only a few stragglers. Twenty minutes later when the streets were empty and silent, another bell, miles away it seemed, began ringing frantically—some good padre had slept late and rushed to the church lest some of his flock forget and fail to put in an appearance.

An Englishman, E. H. Riley, was also flying that morning. Although bearing a name of Irish origin, there was no doubt that Riley was a devoted subject of King George, the way he reeled off remarks about "His Majesty's Government," "His Royal Highness, the Duke of Connaught," and other British royalty. Anyway, he was going for his biennial vacation in dear old London. We rode together to the flying field, which is miles from the city, in one of the most open of all open spaces on the *Sabana,* where the damp chilling winds have perfect access to your ankles. But then I could not tell whether the sudden siege of shivers was due to the climate or to the prospect of flying the mountains in bad weather. The sky was overcast on the high Andean wall, while bilious-looking clouds were getting ready to roll down the outside and deluge the tropical lowlands.

Herr Klotz, our smiling, blond German pilot, looked his tin bird over with the eye of an eagle contemplating a hypnotized sparrow. Sure of his machine, he next scanned the heavens in the direction of where the horizon should have been, but wasn't. Then shouted, "Vee go."

Riley and I looked at each other, but said nothing. Somehow you never question or hesitate when a pilot tells you to get into a plane. Another fellow, with face as white as a sheet, and hands trembling, appeared from somewhere and climbed in beside us. He proved to be a tenderfoot making his first flight. What a day he had selected for his initiation!

Herr Klotz "gave her the gun," and she rolled across the wind-swept *Sabana* and ascended into the soup. Up, up, up, and then nothing. The world below was only a memory. Riley and I glanced knowingly at each other. That is to say, we knew we were in a flying machine that had parted company with terra firma. Our companion sat like an ancient mummy, his countenance frozen with fear.

The motor roared and purred—roared as it climbed, and purred as it kept on an even keel. For twenty minutes—hours it seemed—we floated in the milky firmament. Finally there was a glimpse of Mother Earth and life became less tense. We zoomed down, only to discover we had returned to our starting place.

Thirty minutes later came the crisp command, "Vee go." As meekly as lambs we responded, climbed into the machine to repeat the process, and twenty minutes later sat down again on the same windy field.

For an hour and a half this time we watched the surging of the clouds. Finally a few more gallons of gasoline were added, and we were off once more. But minus our companion. He had taken thought, or taken flight, or both.

This time there was no search for an aperture in the clouds. It was up and up—14,000 feet above sea level and out into the early morning sunshine. Below us was an ocean of clouds. In the distance a single snowy peak of the Andes stood like a lone sentinel in a fantastic universe.

We flew straight westward for fifteen minutes, to clear the mountains, then plunged into the boiling foam, with the hope of finding something in the lowlands of the Magdalena River. Fortunately we found it—a narrow, crooked valley with a canopy of clouds suspended between the two high ridges. And if we had thought of the peaks we had missed getting down, we would not have had time to think of the perils now before us. It was necessary to follow, like a fly in a water-pipe, down this valley to Girardot on the banks of the river, flying so low that the fronds of the palm trees flapped frantically in the wake of the plane.

To say that it was a relief to be seated in the airport café with a couple of bottles of good German beer under my belt is to tax the word conservative. Nor is my admiration for the skill of Herr Klotz and his associates any the less, if I say that on my next trip to Bogotá I shall leave the plane at Girardot and make my way leisurely by train or automobile the remaining 112 miles from "the hot country" to the *Sabana*. In fact,

New Roads to Riches

I shall make the trip by automobile over the new modern high-way which is one important link in the projected Bogotá-Medellín road northward across the republic to the Gulf of Darien.

A Colombian friend in Barranquilla once explained that when visiting Colombia "the only reason for travelling to Bogotá is to see our monastic or secluded government which, geographically at least, is not of the country but quite apart from it. The President, the Congress, and the high courts, as well as the foreign diplomats, sit in their official box high on the mountains and look down upon us. Surrounded by a considerable portion, though by no means all of our social and cultural aristocracy, they wait for us of the lowlands to do the work of the nation, run its business and industry, develop its resources, and furnish the money to maintain them."

Anyway, having observed the government, the high officials and the political world apart, I had, thanks to Herr Klotz, come down rather breathtakingly to "the hot country" to appraise, if not to see personally, all of Colombia's principal industries and riches, industries and riches enough to transform the land of the golden man into a new El Dorado.

Colombia is the fourth largest of the ten South American countries, ranking after Brazil, Argentina, and Bolivia. It stretches nearly two thousand miles north and south at its greatest length, and at one place it is thirteen hundred miles wide. You could put our two prize states of Texas and California into it and have more than enough space left over for New Hampshire, New Jersey, and Delaware. For political purposes, it is divided up into fourteen states, *intendencias* and seven *commissariats*. The latter need suggest no Russian significance, since *commissariats*, or territorial divisions, existed in Colombia long before there were soviets in Russia.

Its lowland civilization lies principally between the three mountain ranges that traverse it and in the valleys of its two

great rivers, the Magdalena and the Cauca, both of which rise
in the far south, at the base of the 14,550-foot Mt. Sotará,
near the old town of Popayán. The Cauca finally joins the
Magdalena in the far north just before the latter reaches the
sea at Barranquilla. The most highly developed region of
Colombia lies principally in the Cauca Valley. Here are located the majority of its cities, Popayán and Cali in the far
south, Manizales and Medellín in the central region. It is the
home of the greater portion of the stock-raising, agricultural
and mining developments, and others. The bulk of Colombian
coffee comes from the states of Manizales and Medellín.

On the other hand, except for the regions along the Caribbean coast, the Magdalena Valley is virgin territory, not to
say virgin jungle. At the same time it is the scene of what may
be called Colombia's virgin industry. The middle stretches of
the valley, like the lower basin of the Orinoco, are bubbling
with oil. Just below Girardot around Honda, and La Dorada,
the Shell Oil Company has been feverishly active in exploration work, with every indication that oil may be found in paying quantities.

However, the proven fields are farther north, the oldest
around Barranca Bermeja, four hundred miles from the Caribbean coast, where the Tropical Oil Company, the first company
actually to produce oil in the republic, has already invested
over sixty million dollars in wells, refineries, and pipe lines. It
has opened up an industry in and for the country which did not
exist before. This it did with United States capital and brains,
and against odds which existed practically nowhere else in the
world. Engineers, scientists and mechanics of this company
went out into the heart of the sodden, steamy no-man's land,
drilled wells, and built towns where no Colombian had ventured his money or his effort. They built a pipe line from these
wells three hundred and thirty-five miles through the marshy
jungle to the city of Cartagena on the coast.

New Roads to Riches

Once again an appreciation of the difficulties of getting Colombia's vast riches to the world's markets due to the lack of transportation and the absence of railroads or highways may be gained from the experience of this company in laying an eight-inch pipe line between Cartagena and its fields. Supplies, tools, living quarters and, most important of all, field hospitals had to be carried up the river on rafts the entire distance. When the cost was counted it figured more than $25,000,000. Even today, in spite of this tremendous investment, no other way exists by which officials or workmen may reach the Barranca Bermeja fields and refineries except by airplane or slow river steamer.

Colombia insists that its people patronize native industry, and here again lack of transportation imposes excessive hardships. At present the only oil refinery in the country which, incidentally, makes Essolube and Ethylene, is the one at Barranca Bermeja, about halfway between Bogotá and Barranquilla. In order for automobile owners in Cali, in southern Colombia, to get these products, they must be transported by barge four hundred miles to Barranquilla or Cartagena, shipped by way of the Panama Canal to the Pacific port of Buenaventura and by rail to Cali. By this time the cost is so great that it is like burning liquid gold in a machine which, also because of poor transportation into the interior, not to mention high tariffs, becomes a luxury so expensive that few but the wealthy can afford one.

So far, considering the restrictions which the government has placed upon other foreign enterprise, the oil companies have been allowed to operate with comparative freedom, although neither the government nor the nation in general suffers from the bargain. Ten per cent of every drop of oil that comes out of the ground is handed over to the government. This she receives without spending a *peso* or turning a hand. At the present rate of production this amounts to around 5000 barrels a day. In addition to this she is given the use of the pipe line, free of charge, for so many hours a day, to pump her own oil to market. Besides this the company and all its employees pay the government an income tax of eight per cent. At the same time it provides employment at high wages for about 4500 Colombians.

Nor does the Colombian Government permit any exploitation of labor either by the oil or any other foreign companies. Some of the features of Colombian labor laws are even more unusual than those prevailing in Venezuela. In 1934–35, Congress passed what is called "the Private Employees Contract." A private employee is described as any employee not in official service and not a manual worker, but who performs work for some one else for a fixed remuneration, a participation in the profits, or any other form of compensation. The law requires that there must be a written contract between every such employee and his employer, that "the contract must be written on plain, unstamped paper in duplicate, and that both the employee and the employer must have copies." The contract must specify the exact kind of work the employee agrees to perform, the amount of remuneration he is to receive, and the manner in which it is to be paid and the time. It must set forth the exact duration of the contract and the causes under which it can be terminated. The contract must be accompanied by a health certificate signed by a doctor whom the employer selects and pays. In case any dispute arises between the contracting parties the contract itself becomes "complete evidence" of the various obligations.

In cases where no contract has been written and signed, as provided by the law, the court "presumes that one has been executed in accordance with the law." The law goes on to point out that any foreign company operating within the country cannot and must not attempt to grant greater guarantees or advantages to foreign employees than it grants to Colombian employees under similar circumstances.

However, apparently there is no fear upon the part of the

big companies that Colombia will be directly influenced by Mexico in its treatment of the oil industry. Additional millions are being poured into the development of new fields, refineries and pipe lines. Two new fields are already in production at Petrolea and Rio de Oro, over in that eastern strip of territory along the Venezuelan frontier. Geographically, of course, these new fields do not lie in the valley of the Magdalena. But, since patriotism and practical politics must be served, Colombian oil cannot be permitted to flow out to the world through alien territory, although it would be comparatively simple to lay a pipe line or even build a railroad and highway eastward down the mountains to Lake Maracaibo. Therefore, the product must be syphoned westward across the high Andean cordillera down into the Magdalena lowlands and to the sea.

Before going into all that, these new developments revive once again the stormy saga of one of the most famous of all oil concessions in Latin America. Way back in 1900, after Colombia's last revolution, General Virgilio Barco, victor and hero in the conflict, returned to his native town of Cúcuta, capital of the eastern state of Santander, now the frontier city on the new Bolívar highway—between Bogotá and Caracas, Venezuela. Interested in cattle raising, which until then had been the principal industry in this eastern region, the General set about to develop new markets. The northern cities of Barranquilla and Cartagena of course constituted one of the largest meat markets in the country. But at the same time there had been no way of transporting or even driving cattle to them from Cúcuta. With help from the government and the cooperation of the local cattlemen he began hacking a cattle trail through the jungle-covered mountains to the Magdalena River, down which they could be shipped by steamer.

Work progressed and the General's enthusiasm grew. New markets and new wealth loomed before him, when suddenly the picture changed. He ran on to mysterious seepings along the headwaters of a river that flows northeastward toward the basin of Lake Maracaibo. Ah, oil and gas for the lamps of Colombia, not to mention the pockets of the General. He rushed to Bogotá, where his prestige as saviour of the country was still strong enough to win for him a vast concession covering the area of his discovery. Next he began a long pilgrimage to North America and that citadel of light and lubrication among the minarets of steel and concrete on Lower Manhattan Island. To be specific, he was bound for the holy of holies, on an upper floor at 26 Broadway, where he would be greeted by none other than John D. Rockefeller himself.

Alas, nobody at 26 Broadway knew him or had ever heard of the Ulysses S. Grant of Colombia, South America. Besides, as one attaché of the citadel has since said, "He was the funniest-looking old codger I ever saw. He wore a strange comic opera outfit, and, though he acted as if Mr. Rockefeller himself should have met him on the sidewalk below, he couldn't even talk English so we could understand him. Naturally we had to throw him out."

This act later caused misgivings upon the part of many a Standard Oil mogul, for General Barco soon found a welcome among other groups. No one with oil on his fingers, no matter how funny his dress or attitude, could long escape the clutches of the smart gentlemen of Wall Street. They wined him, dined him and dickered with him, no doubt until his brain was addled and his constitution undermined from the excitement. Anyway, at last he sold three quarters of his concession for what was to them a song, but fortunately to him a sufficiency, and made his way back to his homeland to live and die in peace.

Then began the usual orgy of speculation, a succession of sales and transfers that would confuse the mind of a card shark. The boys who frisked the old man so successfully formed an operating company, that is, a company to operate in Wall Street, which it did with considerable success. They sold three quarters of their three quarters of the General's concession to the Cities Service Company. The Cities Service Company in turn formed the Colombian Petroleum Company, which sold the contract to Andrew Mellon's South American Gulf Oil Company. In 1926, to the consternation of all, from the General to Andrew Mellon, the Colombian Government cancelled the whole concession. This act was followed by a long period of wrangling, name-calling, and negotiations, until the reticent magnate of Pittsburgh, already a mighty force in Washington, and, according to conservative Republicans, "the greatest Secretary of the Treasury since Hamilton," brought his ingenuity, not to say pressure, to bear on Colombian diplomats. Finally a new agreement under a new name was effected, and ratified by the Colombian Congress.

If the transactions that preceded the cancellation of the concession constituted a trading orgy, what followed the ratification of the new contract was a trafficking nightmare. Mr. Mellon's Gulf Oil Corporation immediately sold its interest in the South American Gulf Oil Company, which held seventy-nine per cent interest in the Colombian Petroleum Company, to the Texas Corporation and Socony-Vacuum for the tidy sum of $12,500,000. "The profit from this," says one observer of the proceedings, "in a way compensated Mr. Mellon for his personal handling of the matter and left to him a little pin money with which to salve his conscience by building art galleries and memorials in his declining years."

After taking over the Mellon interest, the Socony-Vacuum and Texas Corporation then went foraging for the holdings of General Barco's original benefactors which they found in the portfolios of the Colombian Petroleum Company, and succeeded in acquiring for $2,500,000. All of which about cancels the horrible blunders of the attachés of 26 Broadway who in a manner of speaking "threw the funny old codger from the jungles of South America out on his ear."

Colombia

The concession is to run for fifty years from the date it was ratified by the Colombian Congress. After that it reverts to the nation. Royalties and other conditions of the contract are similar to those governing the operations of the Tropical Company.

If by now any one is still interested, the trading having gone on long enough for a large army of bankers, high-powered economists, lawyers, counsellors and fixers to grease their pockets, not to mention explorers, experts and engineers who furnished the facts and probably received a pittance, the famed Barco concession at last is a liquid reality, and a booming bonanza.

By May of 1939 thirty-odd wells with an eventual capacity of 70,000 barrels a day were already in operation in the Petrolea field. At Rio de Oro, thirty-five miles away, there were half a dozen producing 10,000 barrels a day. A $12,000,000 twelve-inch pipe line, two hundred and sixty miles long, was practically completed. It is estimated that $40,000,000 were spent before a single barrel of oil found its way into a market.

The physical problems and difficulties encountered in developing these new fields approach the historic feat of old Quesada himself. The oil fields themselves are not only located in one of the most inaccessible spots of the South American jungle, to which the drilling machinery, equipment, and supplies had to be transported by airplane, but it is a region infested by the fierce Motilones, the wildest and most unfriendly Indians left on the Continent.

Since the earliest Spaniards invaded New Granada the Motilones have taken toll of every party of palefaces that has attempted to contact them or invade their secluded homeland. In fact, few white men have ever actually contacted them or even seen them except from airplanes. The first evidence of their presence is usually made known by a shower of arrows with poison darts propelled by powerful bows, or shot from six- to ten-foot blow-guns, or long hollow reeds. About all that any one knows, who has looked down upon them from the air, is that they live in great palm-thatched communal houses that stand in small clearings here and there. The aerial observers estimate that some of these houses will accommodate as many as one hundred men, women, and children.

To fly into the middle of nowhere, establish a camp and surround it with protection is one thing, but to venture afield on exploration trips with safety is another. No less than a dozen explorers, prospectors, and engineers have been known to lose their lives since white men became interested in the oil deposits of this region.

I have mentioned the difficulties that confronted the Tropical Oil Company in the laying of its pipe line from Barranca Bermeja to Cartagena. That was a simple matter compared with laying this new pipe line from Petrolea to the sea. The Tropical line follows more or less north and south along the Magdalena River. The new one has been laid entirely overland from east to west across the Sierra de Perijá, the northern backbone of the Andes. The lowest pass in this range reaches an altitude of more than 5000 feet. To force the oil from the field and over the top, three powerful pumping stations are required in a distance of seventy miles. From there it plunges the remaining one hundred and ninety miles right down the mountains across the valleys of the Magdalena and the Cauca to Puerto Coveñas, on the Gulf of Morrosquillo. The terminus is near the Port of Tolu, from which comes the famed balsam of Tolu. To eclipse the feat of laying the pipe line, the companies, to comply with another provision of the concession, must next begin constructing a parallel highway from Petrolea to the Magdalena Valley.

Thus in spite of engineering difficulties and expense, in spite of wild men and arrows with poison darts that have baffled white men for four hundred years, the relentless machinery and genius of twentieth-century industrialism is pushing back the jungle, scaling the mountains, and bringing the riches of Colombia to the markets of the world. The bankers, economists, and oil experts predict that within five years oil production will become the chief industry of Colombia, and make it the third oil-producing nation of the entire hemisphere.

Oil is the only major industry in Colombia which has been developed entirely under foreign leadership and direction as well as by foreign capital. Going to the opposite extreme, emerald mining in Colombia constitutes a government monopoly entirely under government operation. Significantly enough, in the opinion of many natives this industry presents a shining example of the lack of native administrative ability. It justifies the suggestions made in President Santos's paper, *El Tiempo*, that what Colombia most needs "is fewer politicians and more people trained to operate business and industry." In fact, two years ago it was pointed out in an editorial in *El Tiempo* that "In ten years the Muzo and Coscuez emerald mines cost the government 1,640,000 *persos* while they produced only 283,000 *pesos*' worth of emeralds."

Although foreigners have not been excluded from them, private Colombian capital and Colombian citizens have usually dominated the live stock, agricultural, platinum and gold-mining activities. However, these activities belong principally to another valley and therefore to another chapter.

V

The Gold Trees of Antioquia

Bogotá is the seat of national government planted high and remote on the Andes above the Magdalena. Medellín is the capital of the State of Antioquia, the secluded metropolis of business and industry nestling peacefully in a green valley a little way from the Cauca. Bogotá is a land of perpetual autumn where fever germs and the winged pests of the tropics find life overly strenuous, a land full of health and buoyant airs where you sleep under blankets. In Medellín spring is eternal. There may be cool nights but there are always warm and sometimes hot days. A man can sweat, and get thirsty. In Bogotá there are politicians and poets, both actors, who like the parts they play, but who take life and themselves very seriously. Medellaños work, not too hard, but they work, drive a bargain upon occasion, laugh at the world and even themselves. I vote Medellín.

Although Medellín is the second city in size, by land it is even more remote from the world than Bogotá. To reach it comfortably, it is necessary to fly there from Bogotá, from Barranquilla, or directly from Panamá. That is, you may fly from east, west or north—until you are directly above it. Then you must spiral down to it, since it is completely surrounded by mountains. If you insist upon the hard way, you can go by boat from up or down the Magdalena to Puerto Berrio. There you take a train that worms its way by hairpin curves, tunnels, and switchbacks one hundred and fourteen miles over the mountain range that separates the Magdalena and the Cauca valleys. In the dry season you can be fairly certain of getting there within a day. In the wet season you only hope. Some portion of a mountain may go sliding down into the depths below just ahead of you.

Anyway, after following the oil story up and down the Magdalena, I found it just as convenient to go by steamer from Barranquilla to Cristobal and the Canal Zone, then fly directly in two hours by the Pan-American short line. It was just as convenient, but I confess that one of the chief reasons for taking this route was the certainty of finding Don Gonzalo Mejia at the airport.

Don Gonzalo is a promoter of business enterprises, of communications, friendships, and good will not merely for himself, but for his friends, his city, and his country. He is the Grover Whalen of Antioquia. And the airline from Panama and Cristobal to the Antioquian capital is one of his promotions. He journeyed all the way to New York to convince Pan-American officials that even if they did have lines operating clear around the continent and along the Colombian coast, they couldn't afford to neglect the most unique city in South America. They could not have resisted his arguments even if they had wanted to. So in record time the "Umca," his fellow townsmen dubbed it, was shuttling back and forth. Week in and week out, whether the skies are clear or pouring down torrential sheets of rain, Don Gonzalo will be on hand to greet passengers and crew.

Nor can you miss him even if you never have seen him before. Officials and friends in Cristobal will have told you about him, described him in detail, his six feet three inches and 220 pounds of soldierly erectness, his command of Yankee English and slang, his fabulous sense of humor, the smile that rivals a sunrise over a dewy meadow in its effects on the people and atmosphere around him, as well as his unbridled hospitality.

Clerks in the Washington Hotel at Cristobal will have related with chuckles the story of Gonzalo's first visit to Mexico —of how he fell in love with the very first Chihuahua he met, and the tender solicitude of the Colombian giant for the tiniest of all species of the canine world. After being flown in one day from its 10,000-foot Mexico City habitat down to sea level, the poor creature was prostrated from the Panamanian heat and humidity. Fortunately the prostration was not fatal, or the course of Don Gonzalo's life might have been altered. It is still a favored and privileged member of the Mejia household in Medellín.

From the plane we went directly to the Union Club, an ancient two-story structure on a narrow street with a high iron fence in front, a courtyard paved with priceless old Spanish tiles, and a succession of dining rooms and banquet halls stretching backward from the entrance. "We are lunching here today," he told me, "so that you may taste without delay Filet Antioqueño and what all Yankees insist is the poorest coffee in the world." And the filet was something to record in history—tender, juicy, with a flavor that has lingered. Even now I can smell its aroma and my palate is tingling. But the coffee: after that first cup it was never difficult to choose between the beverages suggested by the respective electric signs on the two cafés across the street from my hotel. "Bueno Hasta La Ultima Gota," good to the last drop, flashed one. "Cervaza Pilsen," winked the other. I choose Pilsen.

"You see, our filets," Don Gonzalo suggested as we left the table, "are like the best of wines, of ancient vintage. In this valley the cattle are of the very first stock, the Orijinerros. They were brought over by the earliest settlers over two hundred and fifty years ago, and have been kept absolutely pure. Since then not a single cow of another breed has been brought

Colombia

into the valley. Besides, the succulent grasses are highly flavored
by the unusually salty volcanic soil, peculiar to this region, not
to mention the pure rain waters that trickle down from the
high mountain tops. But the coffee growers, you see, after the
fashion of the orange growers of Florida and California, send
their best coffee beans abroad."

And then, according to ancient custom we went our separate
ways, he to his house and I to my hotel for the daily *siesta*.
I had hardly dozed when a clamor in the streets below caused
me to rush to the window to see what I felt sure must be the
latest revolution, but which turned out to be thousands of
students demonstrating against new decrees from the Federal
Department of Education, adding an extra year to the courses
of the local schools. Without the completion of this extra year,
said the decree, no one could enter the National Universities.
To the proud boys and girls of Medellín this was not only a
cruel imposition, but one more affront, not to say indignity,
from "those common *hombres* on the other side of the river,"
meaning the people as well as the officials of Bogotá. The
rivalry between the Medellaños and Bogotaños, or I should
say the contempt of the former for the latter, begins to develop
in the cradle.

After youth had marched on I returned to bed and to sleep,
only to be brought suddenly to consciousness once again by
loud voices from the bar at the end of the hall. A tall, black-
haired Texan lad, on vacation from the Shell Oil Company
prospecting gang down at Honda, on the Magdalena, "aged
twenty-three and no woman hater," he said, was arguing with
the barkeeper about the "foolish customs of the country,"
aided and abetted by a bottle of Scotch which was gradually
gaining the upper hand.

"Why I should have signed up for three years and come
down here to this country I don't know," he exclaimed. "I
wouldn't mind it so much if I could go out with the girls here

just like any other human being, and they are gorgeous, mind you. But, think of it, if you take one to the movies you have got to have the whole family along. What a hell of a custom!"

But customs in these matters are strict. They are old Spanish. Medellín is old Spanish America, the only genuine Spanish America on the Continent. From the aristocrat to the lowliest peons of the countryside all are white. No Indians or Negroes have penetrated this valley. The people, like the cattle, are the original stock, mostly from the ancient Basque country. Even those not of the Spanish race are Spanish in character, custom and religion. All are devout Catholics, especially the Spanish Jews. Medellín, it is said, is not only a Spanish but a Jewish city. Yet only an anthropologist would be convinced. With rare exceptions, even the names offer no clue.

San Pedro at Medellín is the finest, most aristocratic and exclusive Catholic cemetery in the republic. It is a great campanile, with snow-white columns where natives and aristocrats sleep tier upon tier around the circle. In the center a few families maintain their own mausoleums or tombs. The most imposing is that of the Catadavids, an aristocratic Jewish family, long prominent and influential in both Bogotá and Medellín.

But the most striking gravestone marks the last resting place of one of the Colombian immortals, Jorge Isaacs. Although born and raised on a *hacienda* near the city of Cali, in the upper Cauca Valley, his last request was that he be buried at Medellín. Of all the poets and authors of Latin America the name Jorge Isaacs is the most famous. At least, he wrote the greatest Colombian novel, *Maria*, the best-selling book ever published in all the region between the Rio Grande and Cape Horn. *Maria* is a superb picture of devout Catholic-Jewish home life in Colombia. As a best seller, *Gone With the Wind* was in the small-time class. More than eight million copies of the Colombian novel have been sold in Spanish America alone, while it has been translated into dozens of foreign languages. Yet the artist who chiselled Jorge's likeness on the headstone of his tomb relieved him of every Semitic feature. In stone he has taken on the facial features and mustache of that classic and noble old Scotsman, the late Arthur Balfour.

Custom and the Catholic faith make big families and industriousness popular even among the intellectuals of Medellín. Seventy-year-old Don Juan de La Posada, patriarch and elderly statesman of the valley, is a graduate of the University of California. He and his charming wife find supreme happiness in their seventeen living children, all of whom are married, prosperous and prominent in the business and professional life of the city.

Having founded and built up several of the large industries of Antioquia, including the enormous factory of the Colombian Tobacco Company, makers of Pilrojas, the Chesterfields of Colombia, and other Colombian cigarettes, Doctor Posada has long since retired from strenuous activity. Today he merely spends three days a week in the saddle at his cattle ranch along the Cauca, and two more days lecturing at the University, where serious young men, loafers and dandies alike crowd his classes and hang on his words. Another day he spends looking after his business affairs, preparing his lectures and writing on philosophical, financial, social, political and other subjects. Sunday he spends going to church and visiting with his children. Simple, unassuming, sincere, convincing, he is overflowing with good humor, seasoned wisdom and a gracious philosophy. He typifies the substantial citizen of this remote Colombian city.

If you forget the surroundings, the houses, the furniture, the pictures on the walls, the bric-à-brac on the tables and shelves, the churches and the family customs, Medellín might be Boston, Baltimore or San Francisco. In business, conversation, and intellectual interest the people are thoroughly cosmopolitan. But the atmosphere and the environment in which they live is that of old Spain. As an example, there is Andalucia, the home of Don Gonzalo's sister, Señora Amalia Mejia de Botero, in an old country village down the valley from Medellín. Stop your car before great wooden doors in a high white-washed adobe wall on the main street, push the bell and wait. Eventually the doors swing slowly open, and you gaze down a long avenue of giant trees, an avenue that leads through several acres of orchards, carpeted with brilliant flowers in every color of the rainbow. At the end of the avenue is a low Moorish arch with a cross above it, like the entrance to an old Spanish mission. Pass under this and you are in the outer courtyard of a dream house, a house that remains just as it was when built over two hundred years ago. Modern conveniences of every description have been installed but they have been carefully camouflaged.

To the right of the entrance is the drawing-room; chairs, chests and tables of exquisitely carved hardwoods, candelabra of hand-beaten silver and priceless paintings by old Spanish masters. On the left and quite separate from the remainder of the house, is a large room with a giant canopied four-poster bed, boggy, thick carpets and every masculine fixture and trinket, the bedroom of the master of the house. His women-folk, in the manner of ancient Spanish households, occupy smaller rooms across the *patio*.

In this house it seems strange to find every one talking English, the ladies smoking cigarettes, and the men drinking regular Scotch highballs from enormous old silver goblets, and discussing Myrna Loy, Clark Gable, the recent offerings from Hollywood and the New York and London stock quotations. One señorita insisted upon giving me her reactions to many of our latest, as well as some of our raciest novels. She liked the historical ones best.

Medellaños travel—to Europe and North America. Whether they study abroad or at home they learn other languages, and especially English. "English," volunteered Don Gonzalo, "is our second language. Anyway, it is the commercial language.

Colombia

Twenty years from now most people in Latin America will speak English and I should think many of your people would speak Spanish."

Wherever I have gone I found them, young and old, able to converse in my own tongue, much better than I could converse in theirs.

Leading business and professional men commute by air between Medellín and Manhattan. Meeting them for lunch at the Country Club is like meeting the leading business and professional men of Omaha, Tulsa or Denver at the Country Club. They talk about cattle raising, coffee growing, oil production and mining. I have listened to Luciano Restrepo and Mejia discuss the relative importance of oil and coffee to Colombian economy, while Daniel Pelaes, proprietor of the famous San Andres Gold Mine, was outlining to Ingeniero Alberto Jaramillo Sanchez the latest developments in the gold-mining industry. And, if I had closed my eyes, it would have been hard to believe I was in Colombia instead of the United States.

Along with oil and coffee, one of the three major native industries in Colombia is gold mining. Antioquia is the largest gold-mining center in South America. If gold figures are in order, between 1932 and 1937 Antioquia's 500 mines produced exactly 1,138,746 fine ounces of the yellow metal, more than fifty-five per cent of the total Colombian production. It may be added that fifty-seven per cent of this output was financed by foreign capital. Other leading production centers are in the departments, or states of Caldes and Cauca, both in the Cauca Valley south of Antioquia, and the territory of Choco which lies along the Pacific.

When I expressed to Don Gonzalo a desire to see some of this gold, he said:

"We will just go over to the mint."

We crossed a shady plaza, turned down a side street and entered the arched doorway of an old Spanish colonial building.

[141]

"No, we don't need any guards," he explained, when I expressed surprise that the great door stood wide open to the public. "Gold is a very common object here, and besides, it would be difficult for any one to get over the mountains and out of the country with any considerable amount."

In a large room opening on a grassy *patio* two men sat at desks. When our wishes were made known one of them motioned us toward an inner room, where gold bars were stacked about the floor. One stack contained $1,500,000 worth of the newly mined metal.

"But all Antioquia's gold does not come out of the ground," Don Gonzalo reminded me. "It grows on trees as well—our golden coffee beans."

"And coffee growing," I assured him, "is what I actually came to see."

So at daybreak one bright morning we set out for La Amalia, one of the largest and finest coffee *haciendas* in the Cauca Valley. We travelled via the "Graveyard of Antioquia," the burial ground of millions of United States dollars, as well as Colombian workmen—the Ferrocarril de Amaga. This eighty-mile section of the Antioquia railroads, which operates by main strength and awkwardness—between Medellín and the coffee and cattle districts along the river—was built by means of money raised from bonds sold in the United States and long since defaulted. "They spent all the money they could get," says an old Yankee resident of Colombia, "as much as $100,000 a mile, and then damned the Yankees for lending it to them."

But it is a friendly railroad. Signs in the locally built passenger cars, cars with springs and shock absorbers that neither spring nor absorb, read: "Señor Conductor, your duty is to serve the passengers. Keep it in mind and see that you do it." Whether, as I suspect, it was the presence of Mejia, a personality in the community, or whether it was the printed injunction, our conductor was the soul of courtesy. He always smiled reassuringly when I braced myself and clutched the seat to avoid being pitched against the opposite side of the car, or maybe through the glass window, as the train suddenly careened around a curve at what usually seemed like an angle of forty-five degrees, or after speeding down the face of a mountain, stopped short with a sudden jerk in the middle of a spindly legged trestle over a bottomless cavern.

At every stop people crowded the station, milled in and out of the train, greeting friends and relatives. In these mountain-locked valleys, every one, especially every peasant, seems to be related to every one else. And somewhat contrary to the attitude of the Anglo-Saxon, the Latin peasant treasures his friends and relatives instead of avoiding them. Even though barefooted and their pants a crazy quilt of patches, they all smiled, laughed and joked, opened their *carrieles* and shared their cigarettes and knickknacks. The *carriele* is an institution in this region. A little accordion-like satchel, with many compartments, swung by a long strap over the shoulder, it serves as a carrier for everything imaginable, tobacco, food, money, trinkets and valuables. No peon is ever without one.

We left the train near Venecia, fifty miles from Medellin, and drove back into the hills, to our destination, arriving just in time for lunch. Doña Amalia Madriñan de Marquez, the aged matriarch of the plantation, greeted us personally. Quiet, gentle, shy, Doña Amalia looks the part of the typical Spanish grandmother, the sweet old lady who sits in the corner knitting while others do the talking. But in her case nothing could be more deceptive. Her career proves that one should never believe that Spanish-American women are helpless, unable to take care of themselves, their families and their properties, if it becomes necessary.

Doña Amalia, a member of one of the old and aristocratic families of Medellín, and her young husband came to this virgin valley in 1888, cleared the land and established the plantation. Hardly had it begun bearing when he died, leaving her a widow with several small children. Instead of returning to the home of her family, as is usually the custom, she took charge of affairs herself. She put on pants, literally as well as figuratively, buckled a revolver around her waist, got astride a mule, and rode up on the hillsides and directed the workmen herself, making a tremendous success of what her husband had so well begun.

Doña Amalia was very sad the day we arrived. She was grief-stricken over the loss of her only son, an eccentric old bachelor who left behind him a plantation house of such complicated architecture that it could have been designed only after a severe nightmare. It consists of Roman arches, Moorish windows, Greek columns and Turkish fountains. His bedroom was built on stilts, or tall columns, and his bathroom was an overhanging balcony with full-length double French windows on three sides. The walls were done in deep orange, the tub was of robin blue mounted on a raised dais, while the stool had a pink lid. On the offside, of course, but to Doña Amalia he was the son of a Latin mother, and that means that sane or crazy he was next to the gods.

"It is so lonely without him," she said as we sat down to the table. And if Don Gonzalo, realizing that we might become hopelessly involved in a family tragedy, hadn't maneuvered the conversation so cleverly, I should never have found out the ingredients of some of the dishes served us, particularly the *Masamorra* and the *Arepas*. Human tragedy may be the same, whether in Colombia or Hoboken, but *Masamorra* and *Arepas* are found only in Antioquia. Yet they would be equally at home in Georgia or Iowa. Therefore, why not *Masamorra* and *Arepas?* The base of both these tropical delicacies is corn. The *Arepas* are nothing more than a glorified species of old Southern corn dodgers. Sprinkle a portion of salt into extra fine powdery ground corn meal, add just enough water to make it stick, knead

The Peon of Antioquia is White

Sheltered "Gold Trees of Antioquia"

it as you would to make flour biscuits, except more so, say until the arm is limp, roll it into tiny round balls, bake them until the crust is brown and crisp, serve red hot, with butter, and the world immediately takes on new interest. For variation, you may mix Parmesan cheese with the meal and you have cheese balls, or *bunuelos*. If you boil the whole grains of fresh corn, not on the cob, until thoroughly tender, then serve with a piece of *panela*, the native hard, candylike sugar, which in Venezuela we called *papelón*, you would either like *Masamorra*, or you would not. I did!

Anyway, my muleback tour of the plantation was much easier after I had taken on several portions of *Masamorra* and several *Arepas*. In fact, it requires a heavy diet to stay in the saddle as you climb up and down the steep, almost perpendicular hillsides. That is, if you are outfitted according to native requirements, and again custom is law. The saddle must be fastened on with *grupas*, a special harness anchored fore and aft to prevent sliding forward or backward according to the tilt at which you are climbing or descending. You must wear *zamorros*, full-length leather or heavy padded canvas chaps drawn on over your pants. Then hook on a pair of *estribos*, or stirrups made of stiff leather or metal in size more suitable for riding an elephant than a mule. If you are barefoot, as all the workmen usually are, they prove a bit bunglesome. But booted, or barefoot, one doesn't ride forth without *estribos*.

On the subject of going barefoot, the barefoot workmen at La Amalia interested me. For that matter, barefoot workmen all over Colombia and Latin America, whether Indians, Negroes, *Mestizos* or *Sambos*, interest me. But the barefoot Antioqueño, with his pure white blood, his rosy fair skin, his brown or gray, and sometimes blue eyes, fills me with sadness. His rightful heritage entitles him to something better. But how can he afford it? Throughout the coffee country of Antioquia he receives an average of fifty-five or sixty *centavos* and a piece of *panela* for a day's labor. He is usually provided with a one-room house for himself and family, and occasional access to a doctor of sorts. He is welcome to the plantains and bananas on the place and he may have a garden and a few chickens. When coffee-gathering time comes he is paid on a different scale, about eight *centavos* for every three-and-a-half-pound basketful of coffee beans he picks. And yet he smiles. He even takes pride in La Amalia, pride in its fame, the fact that its product is at a premium in far-off Estados Unidos.

La Amalia occupies an ideal terrain, almost a round bowl with hills sloping gradually upward on all sides. The bottom lands are planted in sugar cane for the making of *panela*, while the hillsides are a mass of coffee bushes with their protecting shrubbery and trees.

Coffee bushes are kept trimmed and dwarfed so that they average four to five feet high. They must not be exposed too openly to the hot tropical sun. In fact, the sunlight must be diffused so that the cherries or berries, each containing two coffee beans, may mature and ripen uniformly. For this reason other shrubbery and trees with spreading foliage must grow along with them. A variety of plants are used for this purpose, according to the location and the viewpoint of the farmer himself. The *piñon* tree with its umbrella top, something like the *saman* tree of Venezuela, and long a favorite, is now thought to be too tall. It allows too much sun to spill through. *Cambulo* trees are used extensively in some sections of the country, but not in this particular section. The *guamo*, lower and more shady than the *piñon*, along with the *durazno*, which grows more quickly than any of the others, are predominant at La Amalia, while banana trees are always thrown in for good measure.

Proper shading, and, therefore, regulation of sunlight is but one of the conditions contributing to the flavor and quality of coffee. Too much humidity or too little is bad. Colombia's alternating dry and rainy seasons, each of about the same dura-

Colombia

tion, is a special boon. Proper elevation or altitude is also
important. Finally, Antioquia's soil, "the salty volcanic ash,"
which we are told lends flavor to the filets, also gives the
proper tang to the coffee beans.

When coffee cherries have ripened, shrivelled and been
picked, they are placed in large concrete vats to soak in water
until the pulp is soft and easily removed. Then the beans are
spread out in the sunshine on broad concrete floors until thoroughly dry. After that they are polished and graded by machinery, and then regraded by hand, according to size and
color, and the best grades shipped to the United States.

"And there you have it," Gonzalo Mejia reminded me, "the
reason you get better coffee in New York, Boston or Chicago
than we do in Medellín."

Whether in reality this is the reason I wouldn't pretend to
say. I do know that Doña Amalia's coffee tasted no better than
that served at the Union Club in Medellín. I also know that
the most delicious coffee I ever drank in the United States
was made of Colombian beans.

It was in the dead of winter. I had gone from Boston to a
small town upstate to spend the week end. Snow was three feet
deep on the ground and icicles hung from every tree. I got
the wrong train, missed a connection, but finally, chilled to the
bone, arrived in a horse-drawn carriage. I went to bed to thaw.
They sent up a pot of coffee. As I drank it my tongue tingled
with pure delight. "Still anything would taste like nectar under
the circumstances," I said to myself. But next day it tasted
just the same, and the next day. And I spoke to my hostess
about it. "Ah," she said, "this coffee is bought in the green
beans just as it comes from Colombia. I put it in small cloth
sacks (about a pound in each) and hang it up in the pantry to
dry for a year. At the end of a year I begin to use it. I roast
the beans slowly, in small quantities, until they are a deep
brown. Then I pulverize them instead of grinding them.

New Roads to Riches

(Hark back to Venezuelan *Café Aguarapado*.) I put the pulverized coffee in a canton flannel bag, which is fastened to a metal ring that will fit over the top of a pot. I pour freshly boiled water through it and serve at once."

The coffee industry in Colombia has grown into the highly scientific business it is today because United States coffee roasters began years ago to use Colombian coffee for blending purposes. Seventy-five per cent of all our coffee comes from Brazil. But a certain amount of mild coffee from the Colombian highlands is usually mixed with larger amounts of stronger Brazilian coffee, with the result that today there is hardly a coffee distributing company which does not utilize both Brazilian and Colombian coffee in the same blends. Because of this Colombia finds a ready and regular market in this country for some 400,000,000 pounds of coffee every twelve months.

Anyway, coffee growing and the making of good coffee constitute serious business, just as serious as the growing, shipping and ripening of bananas. Because of the location, content of the soil, moisture and amount of sunlight at one plantation the flavor of the beans may be entirely different from those grown on another plantation three miles away.

We buy one half of all Colombia's coffee output and, as in the case of the bananas we import from the fields of Santa Marta, the government charges an export tax, yet it pays no entrance fee, no import tax, when it gets to New York, New Orleans or San Francisco. Besides coming in free, it sells for cash. Much has been said about our high tariffs, about the prohibitive duties we impose upon the products of other countries. On this score Colombia has no room for complaint. But the few things which we are able to sell Colombia, and which are becoming fewer all the while, must pay about the highest tariffs that you can find this side of a tariff-maker's paradise. Some one has said that Colombia's present tariff laws make Messrs. Hawley and Smoot look more like free traders than the arch-protectionists they were.

Colombia

"But you won't find many Antioqueños defending tariffs," according to Gonzalo Mejia. "It is the Bogotá government and those people on the other side of the river."

On the way down from La Amalia we met Doctor Posada and a friend returning from a visit to the Cauca Valley, and for hours I listened to a thrilling discussion of the tariff and other related subjects.

"I come from Cartagena," Doctor Posada's friend remarked. "On the coast we have no problems in transportation. But because of high tariffs Chesterfield cigarettes sell for thirty and thirty-five cents a pack. A tiny cake of Palmolive soap costs twenty-five cents; Carnation milk for babies thirty cents, and imported butter $1.40 a pound, while a small can of peaches costs forty cents to fifty cents."

"Ah," Doctor Posada chimed in, "in Medellín they would cost much more. Anyway, these are luxuries affecting only you and me. It is the peons that suffer most because of high tariffs. We don't produce enough rice in this country to supply our needs, yet imported and native rice is sold for ten cents a pound when it should not be more than five cents. Beans sell for eight cents a pound; they should be four cents. Corn is equally expensive. Lack of proper diet is depleting the vitality of our people. Medellaños go barefoot because there are no cheap shoes, and there are no cheap shoes because the tariff on shoes is prohibitive. Therefore, hookworm and thus human deterioration. High tariffs are ruining the country. Thus in the end we are in danger of becoming a degenerated race."

"But here," says Gonzalo Mejia, "you meet the greatest problem in this country, the lack of transportation, the need for roads."

No matter what subject or problem is under discussion, Don Gonzalo will show you how it could be solved by more roads, better transportation and communication. He is Colombia's highway apostle.

"We can't get our products out of the country without performing miracles," he went on. "Every bag of coffee leaving Antioquia must travel one way. From La Amalia it travels by truck or mule to the railroad, which takes it to Medellín. From the station it goes to the agency. Then it is trucked to another station on the opposite side of town. By train it is taken over the mountains and down to the Magdalena at Puerto Berrio to wait for the steamer which will eventually land it at Barranquilla or Calamar, where it must be transferred to a railroad or smaller steamer for Cartagena. Then it finally connects up with ships for New York."

"Yes, if we could transport products in and out easily," Doctor Posada agreed, "we wouldn't have to charge high tariffs. Or we could levy high tariffs and still buy things reasonably if the physical inconveniences and cost of distribution were not akin to those provided in the dark ages."

"Here we are with a plethora of oil," Don Gonzalo continued, "and yet we have no roads to drive automobiles over. What is more, an automobile is too expensive for any but the rich to buy. The tariff on an automobile is eighty per cent of the value at Barranquilla, at the seacoast. The freight and charges from Barranquilla to Medellín is another $150. Besides, it may be damaged to an extent of one hundred or one hundred and fifty more dollars when you get it.

"This damage," he explained, "may be caused by delay and exposure. In the dry season it may take as long as four weeks by boat from Barranquilla to Puerto Berrio, where it must wait its turn for the train trip over the mountains. Because of lack of cars and locomotives, freight is often tied up at the river from four to five months. That is why we must finish the road from Medellín to the sea."

That is why Don Gonzalo is determined to build the road from Medellín to the Caribbean. Don Gonzalo is the reason portions of it are already completed. When this road is completed the feat of old Quesada will no longer be the chief epic in Colombian transportation. At the moment the indomitable Mejia is really interested in the road from Medellín to Turbo on the Gulf of Darien, that neck of the Caribbean where Panamá joins onto Colombia. As he says "so we can get our coffee out, so a farmer can take his own crop down to the sea by truck." But in Bogotá he spreads out elaborate charts and maps made at his own expense and shows them how it would revolutionize the entire country by laying a ribbon of concrete or asphalt, or even grading a highway, from the capital 560 miles to the sea.

"What is more," he now tells them, "it is already two-thirds completed. Here," he points out on the map, "you have already blasted and graded a road from the *Sabana* of Bogotá to Girardot and down the Magdalena to La Dorada, 161 miles. Then there is a gap of 100 miles to Sonsón where the mountain is only 8000 feet instead of 10,000 as it is between Armenia and Ibagué on the Cali-Bogotá route. And this part is already surveyed, mind you. At Sonsón you would connect with the road to Medellín, which is already completed. Think of it! The two greatest cities and the richest state of the country connected up for the first time in history."

Then he smiles with satisfaction and continues, "Already we have completed 125 of the 225 miles of the remaining distance. We have scaled the two ranges of mountains and spanned the Cauca Valley and are now beginnning the last lap—100 miles— to Turbo and the sea. It is already a certainty. It is inevitable. We must not fail."

And without catching his breath, or allowing any one else to catch his breath, he moves on to the climax. "This, Señores, would mean that the most difficult portion of the Pan-American highway would be completed, and Colombia would have made its supreme contribution to Pan-American unity."

Five years ago nobody would have listened to Don Gonzalo. They would have pitied him. The very idea of climbing those mountains, mountains that become moving masses of mud once you cut the vegetation or break the crust. And after the mountains a long stretch of soggy, fever-ridden impenetrable jungle, the South American jungle at its worst!

My friend, A. F. Tschiffely, famed author and engineer, who in nine hundred days succeeded in transporting himself and two hardy Argentine mustangs from Buenos Aires to Washington, found it absolutely impossible to ride, walk or crawl from the Colombian highlands over this section of the continent to Panamá. He had to go from Medellín to Puerto Berrio, take a river boat to Calamar, then ride to Cartagena and take a steamer to Cristobal. When I asked him the possibility of laying a paved highway across this no-man's land he merely smiled.

And yet it now seems on the way to becoming a reality. When I took the plane from Medellín over the same route to Turbo and the Canal Zone the last time, Don Gonzalo's last words to the pilot were, "Show my friend the road to the sea. Point out to him how it wriggles its way over the mountains, the bridge across the Cauca, and then show him the course it will take through the jungle."

"You see," the pilot chuckled later, "Don Gonzalo established the Umca as a means of advertising this road."

And why not? From the plane when the weather is clear it is an inspiring sight, a child's crayon mark scrawled in curves and curlicues across a blue-green slate which will eventually tie Medellín and the riches of Antioquia to the markets of the world!

PANAMÁ

I

Isthmus of Vanity Fair

At four o'clock in the afternoon the clans begin to gather about the long tall counter in the back room of the Stranger's Club in Cristobal. At four o'clock civilian and military activities in the Canal Zone have begun to lag. The army has done its daily chores. The heavens are no longer rent with deafening zooms and booms. The sky riders have come to earth and put their machines away. Offices and banks have closed the front doors, though not always the back doors.

"This one's on me," some one says.

"No, it's on me," counters another.

"Not on your life," shouts a third.

There is only one way to settle it. The bones begin to rattle in the cup. They clatter across the counter—once, twice, three times. There are laughter and banter. Others gather around eager to witness the trimming, no matter who loses. Life is neither complicated nor strenuous in the Panamanian tropics. Small matters are important. Anyway, it is important who pays for the drinks today.

Again the bones rattle and clatter across the counter—one, two and a third time. It is over. Sam or Bill or John pays. And so it goes, until every one in turn has paid. Every one except the stranger. This is the Stranger's Club. On his first visit he is not allowed to pay; that is, if he has been invited to join the circle. He is the guest and must drink with every one else until he has gone the rounds—if the crowd is not too large, and it often is.

They are a friendly lot, these Yankees who carry on the affairs of "the Zone." Some one has called them the friendliest in the world. They like each other and they like the stranger, especially if he is a Yankee. They want to entertain him, ask him questions.

"How is New York, or how is Chicago, or St. Louis? What is business like in the States, who will be the next Governor of Missouri, or of New Jersey, or of California?"

Every one of them, whether civilian or soldier, is still rooted in the home soil, still loyal to the old home town, still clings to the hope of retiring to the land of his birth. He is merely doing time on the Isthmus. He will "go back" some day. If he is an army officer he will do his turn, go on somewhere else and then return to continental United States. Even if he is an agent for a steamship line, an insurance company, or an automobile concern, whatever he is doing, he expects eventually to go back to the home office.

Old Gerald Bliss settled down at Miami when his thirty years in Uncle Sam's postal service were up. As postmaster, first at Pedro Miguel and finally at Cristobal, Gerald was on the firing line so long he had become one of the monuments along the Canal. His office was, and is, one of the busiest and most important in all the world. Letters from Tokyo and New York, Melbourne and Stockholm, Istanbul and Honolulu, pause in Cristobal on their way across the world. It is the transfer point for the air mail that flies back and forth between the two ends of the hemisphere.

Upon the slightest provocation Gerald would show you a priceless collection of "first flight" stamps. He dispatched air mail on thirty or more first flights to Latin-American countries, including several of the Lindbergh flights. He might even allow you a brief look at his joke book, a priceless volume containing more than five hundred tall tales and anecdotes which he had collected and written down, tales of the sea and ships, told him by grizzly old captains from the Mediterranean and the Indian Ocean, from the China coast and the Baltic Sea. The editor of one well-known magazine offered him a thousand dollars for the privilege of printing a dozen selections, but the thousand never changed hands.

One of the most picturesque yarn spinners in captivity, Gerald could tell every one of these five hundred stories, and tell them better than a professional. He could tell them hour after hour, a yarn to fit every occasion. And most of them he told again and again in the back room of the Stranger's Club, in late years to the great annoyance of some of the local boys, but to the genuine delight of the passing stranger.

Another colorful character, in a community full of colorful characters, is Bob Wilcox. Rich in this world's goods, Bob is a highly respected and genial gentleman, around whom many legends continue to revolve. Some of his friends enjoy telling you he got his start by engaging in commerce with the San Blas Indians, a tribe of semicivilized red men who inhabit a string of islands along the eastern coast of the Isthmus, some ninety miles south of the Canal.

An old-time drummer was stranded in Cristobal, so one story has it. He was forced to sell his samples, which consisted of a trunk full of English "bowlers" or derby hats. Bob bought them for a song, but without any very clear plans for their disposal. However, one day he disappeared. It was later learned that he went down the San Blas country and indulged in a little barter. He swapped them for cocoanuts and bananas, which he brought back and peddled to Canal laborers. This deal netted an unbelievable profit, for there was a tremendous market for fruits in those times. Besides, every son of the San Blas was so anxious to own a derby that he was only too happy to pick bushels of cocoanuts and dozens of stems of bananas to give in exchange. Hurry-up orders had to be sent to New York for additional supplies, until the entire male portion of the tribe had been completely covered. For years afterward, it is said, the bowler hat was the prevailing headgear in the San Blas country.

But the bowlers did not wear out easily and Bob spent months in deep thought. He must find a product that required replacement or renovation, or spare parts, or something. Continued sales, replacements, continued service. Twenty-five years ago this was already the spirit of modern business. Eventually fate sent another salesman to Cristobal with no money and ten dozen alarm clocks on his hands. Fortune put him in the path of Wilcox, and it was not long until he had parted with his entire collection in exchange for enough cash to buy steerage passage on a freighter to New Orleans.

Bob immediately took the noisy, shiny objects to the land of the bowler hats for demonstration. They were a hit from the very first. Every Indian had to have an alarm clock, not in order to keep up with the time, which means less than nothing in the life of a San Blas Indian, but because of its beauty and the fact that it did such amusing and unexpected things as making music in the middle of the night.

The new product proved a much better business than the bowler hat trade. In fact it made business practically perpetual. Naturally the clocks would run down and the ingenious merchant had kept the only key with which they could be wound. This service, of course, necessitated an additional charge each time. So every few days the Cristobal merchant made a voyage to the San Blas country, wound the clocks, filled his boat with cocoanuts and bananas and returned triumphantly to his growing fruit market. And so, they tell you, Bob's fortune grew until today he owns a goodly portion of the city of Colón and lolls in a private yacht on the blue waters of the Spanish Main.

Panamá

After the Stranger's Club in Cristobal, it is proper to call at the Tropical Bar in Colón. Cristobal and Colón are two towns not easy to separate. Cristobal in the Canal Zone is governed exclusively by Uncle Sam. Colón, in the republic of Panamá, of course is under the jurisdiction of the Panamanian government. Each melts or dovetails into one another at no place in particular, so that one is totally unconscious of passing from one to the other.

Nobody takes any notice of where this happens until he comes to vote or pay taxes. In Colón a citizen enjoys both these privileges. At least he enjoys the franchise and endures the taxes. In Cristobal you do neither. For Colón, in fact all Panamá, is genuinely, dizzily democratic in its social complexion as well as politically. Every clan, tribe and nation of the human family is represented in its population. By comparison Vanity Fair was a homogeneous gathering and the Tower of Babel a temple of linguistic silences.

Bilgray's Tropical Bar, day or night, year in and year out, is the lodestone for the oddest assortment of people this side of Shanghai; sailors, soldiers, Chinese, Japanese, Turks, British, Swedes, and Yankees from Maine, Florida and Oregon, each with a colorful history. Bilgray himself, once proprietor of a pre-prohibition bar in one of New York's old Times Square hotels, is not to be overlooked. Always dressed in immaculate white, he is one of the most genial and generous of hosts. He knows everybody from Turkey to Timbuctoo, and befriends every one. His museum of bad checks is a monument to his hospitality.

Look the old timers over. There are countless specimens of the sons of adventure. Some bear the stamp of cruel adversity, others are eloquent examples of light and careless living. But they are all interesting. I cannot forget Colonel Slater, who recently passed on. At eighty he was still a daily visitor, but to sip a glass of milk, not to indulge in alcoholic beverages.

New Roads to Riches

The Colonel had known all the thrills of life—romance and misfortune, fame and prison, and then all of these over again. His title came from having once been a colonel in the Chilean Cavalry, the first colonel among the mounties of that republic, so he said. Then he was boss of a gang of pneumatic drillers who helped to build the great steel gates and locks of the Canal. Later he meandered up through Central America cutting a wide swath as he proceeded. He was Chief of Police in Guatemala City, until a revolution literally flung him out into the middle of the public square. Fortunately not without a portion of his monetary accumulations. With $18,000 in cash on his person, some of it in solid gold, he trudged across the mountains to the little seaport of Puerto Barrios on the east coast, slipped aboard a tramp steamer and sailed lazily away.

Next he was in the Black Republic of Haiti, when one day a thief in Port-au-Prince stole his wallet, and he wielded a hammer with such force and precision as to relieve the unfortunate creature of all earthly responsibility. This necessitated another quick move, another hairbreadth escape. So he went over the mountains to the city of Santo Domingo, or as it is known today, Trujillo City. In the Dominican Republic all went well until news of his Haitian escapade reached the ears of the local police. By this time his feet had lost their cunning. He was too slow, so to jail he went, although not for long. Lady Luck came to him once again, that is, if the lady had anything to do with the nice handout to the guards. Anyway he escaped, went to New York, then back to Panamá to acquire and operate a string of saloons and cabarets.

But one day the wheel of fortune turned again, this time in reverse, and left him penniless. After this, fate was ungenerous for many a year. He lived from hand to mouth. Bilgray gave instructions to his employees to look the other way when the old man would take on generous portions of free lunch. But just when he had completely resigned himself to an ignoble fate, and every one had come to look upon him as a hopeless, pathetic figure, a well-to-do niece in New York passed on and left him a handsome sum in cold cash.

And there is Antonio Tagaropulus, a gentleman from the Athenian hills, whose father evidently met an Italian signorita on his way to America. Antonio started out peddling fruit and knickknacks from a pushcart. Today he is the fruit and grocery king of the Isthmus. His chief competitor is Lee Chong, an industrious Chinese who operates a string of *cantinas*, one on every corner in Colón. And, of course, there are the other famed Asiatic merchants who sell everything from teakwood figures to silk suits from the Island of Ceylon.

Front Street in Colón, facing the Panamá Railroad tracks, is more spectacular than any set in an Oriental movie. Hindu shops, Turkish bazaars, Chinese and Japanese stores are filled with the most fantastic of wares, a tourist's paradise, where bargaining becomes the most exquisite of arts. When the cruise ships are in, the "trippers" descend upon Front Street until it becomes a nightmare of chattering, shouting Orientals. Barkers stand in front of every establishment minutely describing the wonders that are within, begging, pleading, for the sake of your immortal soul, to come in and view the magic wonders. If you only come in, there is no worry about what follows. Any but the most iron-willed eventually yield to the cunning and skill of psychologists with thousands of years of training behind them, and come away with arms full of laces and linens, perfumes and shawls, jewelry and rugs, which could be bought in any store back home for ten per cent of the Colón price.

The Fawk River Market is worth an hour any morning. Coal-black Jamaican expatriates who helped dig the Canal and then remained behind to eke out an existence and raise large hordes of children, gather along the banks of a lazy stream on the edge of the town to swap the wild gifts of Mother Nature —bananas, green cocoanuts, yucas and yams, plantains and papayas. Papaya: fruit of the tropical gods, which in Havana, Cuba, you must always refer to as *paw paw, fruta buena* or something else, unless you are interested in commercialized romance. From the outside, the papaya resembles an overgrown canteloupe. Inside it looks like a cross between a peach and an old-time muskmelon, with a few dashes of yellow persimmon added. Saturated with lime juice and served at breakfast time it would tame the most profound dyspeptic.

The Central Market in the heart of the city not only offers papayas in quantity but it is a good place to make an inventory of all of the fruits and vegetables of the Panamanian tropics. It is a spotless place where a fly is considered a visitor from another world, and whose presence is made extremely uncomfortable, thanks to the vigilant eyes of Uncle Sam's Sanitary Corps on the Isthmus.

Be sure to stop at one of the market bars and sample *estofado de patito*—cows' heels stewed with bits of potatoes and onions and seasoned with such mysterious delicacies as *achote* seeds, and *oregano* herbs. A pot of *estofado* is always stewing in every native saloon and restaurant. It is strictly a Panamanian dish, the Panamá of the interior, the villages and small towns. Which suggests that it is impossible to know this Isthmus of Vanity Fair unless you see the interior of the republic as well as the Canal Zone and surrounding communities.

Maps are sometimes deceiving. Panamá itself is not a negligible piece of territory. In area about the size of the State of West Virginia, it is divided up into nine different provinces. It is even more mountainous than West Virginia and the geographers tell us it has 180 rivers flowing into the Atlantic and 300 into the Pacific.

Late in a recent October I flew north from Cristobal to see something of the outer world of Panamá. One night I stopped in the mildewed old town of David or, as the natives call it, Daaveed, near the Costa Rican frontier. In what was called a

Panamá

hotel I succeeded in arranging for accommodation, that is to say, shelter, if the word is used in its most literal sense. The hotel, which occupied the upstairs or loft portion of the old frame building, was divided into stalls, with partitions extending only a little way above the head, so that every one might get plenty of air and at the same time share freely in every one else's slumber.

I was greeted by the fattest and most ingratiating proprietor who ever wore a long tapering mustache and spoke English without any suggestion of an accent. In the course of the long night I learned that he had been born and reared in the environs of San Gabriel, and that he had spent years travelling from town to town purveying to the ruralites of southern California a certain tropical tonic guaranteed to restore youth to the fading spirits of those in whom life had not begun at forty. He had wandered southward following some slight disagreement with those responsible for the enforcement of the Yankee Pure Food and Drug Laws.

The señor greeted me in the manner of an old-time Spanish Lord Chamberlain welcoming a foreign diplomat to the court of his Castillian Majesty. "You, Señor, do my humble house and myself great honor by pausing, as it were, for the night. You shall be my guest at the *Fiesta de La Cumbia*, which transpires in my ballroom here between the hours of eight and twelve."

The ballroom occupied the entire lower floor of the edifice, which in addition served as bar, dance hall and community meeting place in general. Anyway, it was here that the *Fiesta* of *La Cumbia* "transpired." In spite of one of the hardest, wettest tropical downpours I have ever experienced, by eight o'clock the entire population of northern Panamá, it seemed, descended upon the place. First the señores with glazed hair and an unusual collection of mustaches, each of whom the Señor presented to his "honored guest." Later came the señoritas, not the señoritas alone, of course, but señoritas with their mamas and papas and brothers. Although their pink and blue, red and yellow organdy dresses, with cascades of ruffles and flowing sashes, were spattered or soaked, they seemed not to mind. What with sable hair, brownish red skin and sparkling eyes—like black diamonds set in dull copper—many of them were not difficult to look upon.

"David," my host explained, with engaging frankness, "is Panamá, primitive and colonial Panamá, Panamá of the days when the red men first met their conquerors and where the ways of those former years are still in vogue. These people, Señor, as you will observe, still suggest the time when the noble Christians of Castile blended freely with the first Americans. This is rural Panamá where people still hurry to mass in the morning, and as often as occasion comes to pass, to dance *La Cumbia* in the evening. And, Señor, if you gather the import of my words, they dance it with transcendent delicacy, as well as abandon."

That night they danced *La Cumbia*, if not "with transcendent delicacy," certainly "with abandon." Twice too many people were gathered in the hotel ballroom. It was filled to suffocation with smoke from cigarettes of potent and fearful contents. There were the odors of rain-soaked shoes and boots, the fabulous fragrance of colognes, old-time Hoyts and others that never should have been invented, all perfectly blended and brought to a slow boil in the heat of the tropical night. But this did not deter the gathering in its hilarious pursuit of happiness.

The orchestra was stationed in the center of the hall, a little man with a cornet who had evidently blown himself down to a skeleton, a couple of portly fellows with drums, another with an old-time concertina, and still another with the inevitable *maracas* or pebble-filled gourds. After considerable palaver as to what they should play they finally began warming to the job as they proceeded. And they warmed quickly. Such tooting of a cornet, such merciless squeezing of an accordion, such beating of drums and shaking of *maracas* I never heard before or since.

Soon every one was afoot, except those too young or too old to stand alone. Taking their places by couples in a circle around the orchestra, they stood for a moment, then some one began to clap his hands and pat his feet to the music. All the men joined in. Then they began to swing and sway, the men and women dancing around each other and all moving to the right around the musicians. There were laughter and shouting. Every step and stamp and hand clap and shout in perfect time with the drums.

Finally, there was an intermission, since the orchestra was all but exhausted and perspiration flowed in rivulets down the faces of the dancers. But it was only for a moment or two. They took their dancing seriously, or if not seriously, certainly in a businesslike manner. The music resumed, this time with even more vigor, and the dancers rushed to their places. Lights were lowered or dimmed. Each man lit a candle and held it aloft as if to see the face of his partner. Again they began to swing and sway. Each danced around the other, the great circle revolving on its musical axis and the candles raised and lowered in perfect rhythm with the music. The music swelled. The laughter and shouts grew louder, feet moved faster and faster until the assemblage was a nightmare of frenzy and joy.

That is *La Cumbia*, the native dance of rural Panamá. At least, that is *La Cumbia* as it was danced in the jungle metropolis of David on a rain-drenched October night. But then it was no less lively or interesting because of the rain. Rain never dampens the spirits of the Panamanians, because rain is an ancient and honorable institution, at least from April to December. Every day and often several times a day during this period of the year the heavens open and let go. At David it rains as much as a hundred and forty inches a year. Yet life moves on definitely, if leisurely.

This northern region is a rich and prosperous agricultural and stock-raising country—in fact the most prosperous section of the republic. Chiriqui Province in the north has long been a prosperous cattle-raising center. Coffee is grown on an increasing scale. Along both coasts are some of the largest and newest banana plantations in the tropics. The banana business has become so prosperous that native land-owners have been curtailing their cattle business and planting more and more bananas, a practice deplored by the government because it means a diminishing meat supply in the country. Serious effort is being made to open up new grazing territory and to improve the breed of cattle so that meat will bring better prices, therefore a new impetus to the industry. With the assistance of one of the large United States tire manufacturing companies, rubber growing is being introduced in Panamá. A large acreage has already been planted in trees. Some of them are nearly two years old now, and there is every reason to believe that they will turn out well. If they do, intensive cultivation will follow. Timber lands are also extensive in the far north.

David, remote as it may seem on the map, and primitive as it may appear from the standpoint of hotel accommodations, is by no means out of the modern world. It is the third largest town in the republic, a busy and growing community and a regular port of call for the Pan-American planes that fly between Brownsville, Texas, Mexico City, the Canal and South America. A modern highway, the greater portion of which was paved more than seven years ago, connects it with Panamá City 250 miles away. This road, incidentally, is a portion of the Pan-American Highway which may eventually connect with Gonzalo Mejia's Colombia Highway at Turbo on the Gulf of Darien.

At the moment Panamanians complain about the free use

made of this road by the United States military forces. "We are trying to improve the road," one high official told me recently. "But that is difficult. In the first place the road was not built to withstand heavy truck traffic, yet every year the army uses it for maneuvering purposes, tearing it to pieces. But they refuse to pay us anything for its upkeep."

I could have reminded him that it was built out of money borrowed from the United States, that is, from private United States citizens who bought Panamanian bonds which, like the bonds of many other countries, are now in default. Therefore the United States army might as well get some use out of it.

This David-Panamá City road furnishes ample evidences of the difficulties that road builders will always encounter in the rainy portions of the tropics. (Later we shall find that some portions of the tropics are desert lands.) During the wettest period of the year hardly a day passes that disastrous washouts do not occur, or that some important bridge is not carried away by floods. In fact, because a bridge had disappeared the night before I was to drive south, I found it necessary to take a plane to the capital and that Duke's Mixture of communities surrounding the Pacific end of the Canal.

While the urban section on the Atlantic side consists of twin cities, the Pacific side is divided, or to speak more accurately, combined into interlocking triplet cities. If the Colón and Cristobal frontier is imperceptible to the newcomer, it is next to impossible to distinguish the dividing line between Balboa, the Pacific terminus and headquarters, Ancon, the residential section for employees of the Canal, and sprawling, cosmopolitan Panamá City.

Strange as it may seen, when I arrived in the capital I was hardly settled in my hotel before a messenger brought a special invitation to a fashionable dance at the Union Club that same night. It seemed that dancing was to become an important item in my tour of Panamá.

[167]

New Roads to Riches

The Union Club, like the Stranger's Club on the edge of the bay in Cristobal, rests on piers over the waters of the Pacific so that at high tides the waves dash up furiously against the floor. On this particular occasion Isthmian society was holding forth in honor of the President of the Republic. A thousand people attended, Panamanians and Yankees, civilians and soldiers, Panamanian gentlemen in tail-coats and white ties, and Yankees in black pants and those white monkey jackets so typical of the tropics. That night they danced everything known to the night clubs of Broadway and ended with the *Tamborito*. What *La Cumbia* is to rural Panamá, *El Tamborito* is to the capital. Without becoming terribly technical it is a combination of *La Cumbia*, the *Rhumba* and the *Tango*.

As the music began the dancers stood in a great circle around the hall, but not necessarily in couples. There was a clapping of hands. A man stepped into the center of the circle, selected his lady and bowed to her. She accepted his invitation and stepped out to meet him. He danced to her and around her. Others joined them until everybody was in motion.

The dance is important to the Isthmus, whether it is the urban *El Tamborito*, or the *Fiesta de La Cumbia* of the remote countryside. Whether you are a native of the interior or a *gringo* in the cities, it is leaven for the languid tropical nights. Dancing you will usually find, either at the Union Club, in the various cabarets and night clubs, at the imposing and now fashionable beer gardens on the edge of town, or even at the modest and democratic Yankee-frequented Century Club, the place to meet the *gringo* personalities of the Pacific shore. It was at the Century Club that I first met the Duke of Balboa.

Among the nobility of the Isthmus the Duke is the only member who boasts a title, a title which he did not inherit, nor buy, nor even assume. It was thrust upon him. He started out in life with a name somewhat mixed in origin. He was born Theodore McGinnis in the United States, and Theodore Mc-

Ginnis he remained for many a year until a group of inspired convivials generously elevated him to the Panamanian peerage.

There are many versions of the story. One version has it that on one of those dark and stormy nights so characteristic of the Isthmus, a group of gentlemen had paused in a life-giving station to wait for the weather to subside. As fate would have it, behind the bar was an attendant by the name of Jerry who proved to be in league with the elements. While the heavens deluged the streets and roads with water, Jerry plied his guests with frothy, foamy beer. The rain continued and the beer held out until the night was ripe and the party was uproarious. Suddenly the most eloquent member of the group held aloft his glass and began to speak.

"Melor's and gen'l'men! In graceful, that is to shay gratchful acknowle'gment for the liquid benefac'ions which our fellow citizen, Ted McGinnish, has bestowed upon us, it is meet, not to shay drink, that we should offer him shome fishing token of our humble eshteem."

Which outburst brought forth resounding response, response sufficient to move the orator to even more forensic efforts.

"Melor's and gen'l'men!" he went on. "Le's drink, le's drink to Ted, to Theodore, yea, le's drink to the Duke of Balboa, peerless beer baron of the Isthmus of Panamá!"

From that night on, Theodore McGinnis, long president and proprietor of the Balboa Brewing Company, has been known far and wide, from Panamá City to Pittsburgh and San Francisco, as the Duke of Balboa. And, if I may observe in passing, for many long years the Duke brewed practically all the beer drunk on the Isthmus, millions of gallons, enough to quench the tropical thirst of all the natives and soothe the parched lips of legions of travellers from the scorched Sahara of North America during the age of Prohibition.

All during those days the Duke never permitted the great vats of the Balboa Brewery to be empty, day or night, month in and month out. Moreover, during those long months of the tragic depression, when not only the engraved masterpieces of great industry, but even the gilded promises of many foreign governments lay faded and useless in the bureau drawers, Balboa Brewery stock paid handsome dividends. Many a Yankee expatriate, whose business or profession kept him in the regions of the "Zone," was able to buy a new car, replace the old icebox with an electric refrigerator, or spend a vacation back home because of his beer-soaked income.

I predict history will not overlook the Duke, and that his memory will remain as moist as the tropical rains that fall so freely upon the grassy hills of Balboa, not to say the sprawling beer gardens that now flourish on the fringe of Panamá City. Meantime the Duke takes his ease in New York, Los Angeles and points beyond and lends his placid personality to gatherings of the Adventurers Club, the Circumnavigators Club and other organizations and societies of wandering and widely travelled convivials.

You may dine, drink and visit with the Yankees at the Century Club. But as the evening grows you will feel the need of fresh air. The thing to do is literally to go out and hire a hack, and do the narrow winding Avenida Norte for an hour or so. In Panamá there are still horse-drawn carriages, open Victorias, *carromatos*, the natives call them. In the cool of the evening long lines of them, filled with foreigners, jog up and down the avenue that twists and turns along the waterfront. The natives, at least the more affluent among them, have their country cottages with gardens and picturesque swimming pools where they spend their evenings and do their entertaining.

Natalio Ehrman is a leading businessman and well provided with the things that bring leisure and luxury. He entertains informally, but sumptuously. His country home is mostly garden, a cottage built on high piers with wide porches around it. Underneath is a tile floor with swings and great wicker chairs. In the back is a veritable forest of trees and flowers. Scattered through it are fountains and bird baths, and in the middle of it a great pool done in mosaic with sculptured water nymphs, and often live ones, to watch you as you dive or flounder about.

Natalio's hospitality is unstinted. He invites Panamanians and Americans to come and bring their friends. Tables are placed around the cool basement floor and piled high with roasts, salads, fruits and drinks. You may don your bathing suit or not, and swim and eat intermittently. Or you may sit on a garden bench, and tell some glorious creature what you think of her, as mother strolls occasionally by.

On such evenings you find out that the Chinese and the Hindus and the Greeks and the Italians and the Yankees, who run the shops, and markets and saloons, the Canal and the Army and the Navy are not the predominant element in Panamá City. The Ariases, the Jiminezes, the Pachecos, the Navarros, the Arosemenas, the Alfaros, and the Boyds are the all-powerful element. They don't sell you laces and shawls and fruits and fish. They and their kind are the lawyers, the doctors and the bankers the *hacendados* and the politicians of the Isthmus. They are the native Smiths and Joneses of the country, names you will find in high places and public affairs.

An Arosemena is president now. A Jiminez is the Minister of Foreign Affairs. Some of these old families are survivors of Spanish colonial days. Compared to them our proud old Southern and New England families are newcomers. Their forebears were in Panamá stacking gold into ships bound for Spain and the Old World long before the Cavaliers came to the James River or the Pilgrims to Plymouth Rock.

II

The Dream of Alvara de Saavedra

CIVILIZATION along the Canal looks new and modern, as if it had been set down in wild and virgin country, yet it is impossible to be long on the Isthmus without becoming hopelessly entangled in history. You are continually reminded that some of the giants of the story-books have tramped its trackless jungles, sailed up and down its palm-fringed shores, scaled its mountain peaks and spattered its valleys with heroic blood. Whether on the Atlantic or Pacific side, there is romance and glamor aplenty.

Even the dauntless Christopher himself who, with the exception of the Maid of Orleans, saw visions in more places and rivalled George Washington in the number of nights spent away from home, did considerable discovering in Panamá. Cristobal Colón, as he is referred to in all Spanish-speaking countries, hunted for India all along the Panamanian coast from Costa Rica to Colombia. He sailed his little ship into the wild recesses of Limon Bay, and dropped anchor just back of the Stranger's Club where in our time giant steamers from the ends of the earth tie up to imposing docks. And what's more, Christopher died in the belief that he had reached the fabulous lands of the Indian princes.

Then there was that other frenzied discoverer, Señor Vasco Nuñez de Balboa (shall we say forerunner of the present

[172]

Panamá

Duke?) who fought his way westward across the jungle and conquered the Pacific. At least he must have conquered it, judging from his peculiar behavior. For we are told that he drew his sword, stuck out his chest, waded right in and claimed it for his Royal Lord and Master. You cannot overlook the courage of a man who takes an entire ocean singlehanded.

And of course there could not be Spanish discoverers without English discoverers, not even in Panamá. No matter where the rowdys of Barcelona went in those days, they were followed by the envious roustabouts from the Thames, and vice versa. In the footsteps of Columbus and Balboa came that old devil dog, Sir Francis Drake. Sir Francis found the Isthmus all cluttered up with Spaniards, and could not at the time even get across it, so he could not very well say he had discovered the Pacific. But he insisted that he was the first Englishman to lay eyes on it. According to the chronicles he went to a mountain top in Darien, climbed a tall tapering tree and viewed the mighty waters from a distance. If you can picture a man who was soon to become a brave knight of old England removing his shoes and "shinnying" up a tree to claim the Pacific Ocean for her Britannic Majesty, Elizabeth being the sovereign at the time, that, too, goes into the poetic epic of Panamá. Or perhaps this was proof of her way with men. Once under her spell there was no difficulty too great to overcome or, in this case, no heights to which they would not climb.

Like all the English buccaneers, like all or any buccaneers, Sir Francis was looking for gold and silver which he knew only too well the Spaniards were bringing up from Perú by the schoonerful, transferring it across the Isthmus and shipping it to Spain. He made several desperate efforts to surprise convoys or caravans and capture some of it, and did succeed eventually in taking Nombre de Dios, then a port on the Atlantic, or Caribbean side, and by arson, torture and murder take from the frightened inhabitants and officials a considerable sum. But this

[173]

incident was not nearly so exciting nor fruitful as many of the old pirate's other adventures and acts at Cartagena and on the islands of the Caribbean.

A hundred years after Drake another subject of Britain not only made several visits to the region, but captured numbers of communities and finally crossed the Isthmus where he performed one of history's outstanding feats of perfidy and crime. He was Henry Morgan, Esquire, afterward honored as Sir Henry, if I may at the beginning speak formally. Later on it will be difficult to refer to him formally or even tolerantly. Mr. Morgan was not only extremely envious of, but downright disgusted over the good fortune of the Spaniards. So upon reaching the Isthmus the first time he subjected the town of Puerto Bello to a microscopic examination, and, because he could find nothing that resembled gold, became so angry he demolished the place almost stone by stone.

Determined to catch the Panamanians unaware, he returned in 1671, bringing along some 1800 of his fellow British and friendly French pirates, so as to be prepared for any eventualities. After weeks of preparations and exploration in the environs of Puerto Bello, and skirmishing with outposts all the way across, he finally arrived on the outskirts of Panamá City at daybreak one morning. He looked greedily down upon the town from a hillside, a splendid sight. The tall spires of the cathedral towered benignly over the great stone houses and the massive flower-covered walls surrounding them. A few minutes later the sun splashed the red-tile roofs with its golden rays. Bells began to ring, bells presented by Queen Isabella herself to "the finest church on the Spanish Main." But the bells which had so often called the faithful to prayers were now sounding the alarm of impending disaster.

Bravely the Panamanian, or Spanish, soldiers went out to meet the enemy but were driven back, their lines shattered. People began to flee for their lives, to the sea, to the hills, anywhere. Very few got beyond their own doorways before they heard shouts and to their utter amazement saw the armed demons making right into the heart of the town. It was gold that Henry wanted, and silver. Plenty of it at that—and right away, too. But alas there wasn't any. The Morgan jaws clamped together and the big gray eyes squinted. What, no gold? Did they dare to greet him empty-handed? Then they could take the consequences, the contemptible swine!

Guns barked, sabers rattled and glittered in the morning sunlight. The battle went on. Men died in their tracks defending their homes and families. Women and children screaming with terror were shot down in cold blood. Houses were set on fire and gutted by the flames. Walls were battered in. All day the battle raged, until sunset, and when the curtains of night were lowered all that remained of a city of 10,000 was a handful of terrified captives, a few stone walls, heaps of ashes and the lifeless bodies of hundreds of Spanish settlers and soldiers.

Henry had always considered himself quite adept at uncovering hidden or buried treasure but when he had finished his memorable day's work he was grievously disappointed. For very little precious metal had been found. With the first rumors of Henry's arrival at Puerto Bello and the memory of his former mission of arson and murder at Nombre de Dios still green in their minds, the people had rushed out and hidden, or buried, their valuables, especially every gadget and trinket that had any gold about it.

Even the famous cross of gold in the cathedral had eluded him. High and low he had searched for it but it had completely disappeared. Little did he realize that he had been close enough to it to touch it with his own hand, that he had even looked squarely at it several times during the day. And how exasperated he would have been had he learned that the clever padres had outwitted him. They had not buried the priceless piece, nor even hidden it. They had merely covered it with a coat of whitewash and left it in its place. But, gifted with a one-color vision, Sir Henry could only distinguish yellow. So he had passed it up.

And in this coat of whitewash the cross of gold remained for many a long year, until 1904 in fact, when Panamá became a republic. Throughout all these years the padres took no chances. Too many people, even after the Conquest, were coming to this crossroads of the world, fortune hunters, gentlemen with itchy palms in search of gold and precious metals. But today the republic is free from danger or threats from buccaneers and armed fortune hunters; the golden cross of colonial times, a revered and priceless relic, belongs to the modest little church of San José.

Drive seven miles from Cathedral Square in the present capital of the republic along a paved highway of the modern day, past the old bridge of gold on the Camino Real, its graceful arches still intact, and you may view the ghosts of the Morgan crime. Only the vine-covered tower of the old cathedral and a few piles of stone remain as grim reminders of the gentle disposition of the old Anglo-Saxon.

And so it has been with Panamá from its very beginning. No country has had a more checkered career. Discoverers and conquerors came and went. Cities sprang up and then were destroyed. Ships brought gold and silver from the south and the north, from Perú and Mexico. It was hauled over to the other side and shipped to Spain and the Motherland. Or it was captured by others and shipped elsewhere.

For a century and a half after Morgan, the murderer, merchants and traders, people from Chile, Perú and all along the Pacific travelled back and forth across the Isthmus, over the old highway. In 1848 and 1855 Yankees built a railroad, and thereafter the Vanderbilts and the Astors trafficked with California and the far West by way of Panamá. Today, the old highway having long since slipped back into the jungle, the railroad and the Canal are the only overland methods of transit.

Main Street on the "Isthmus of Vanity Fair"

A Ship Enters the Canal Locks

Panamá

The present Canal, which is barely twenty-five years old, was by no means a recent inspiration. For centuries the possibility of digging an artificial waterway across Panamá engaged the fancy of every adventurer and soldier of fortune who knew a shovel from a sailing ship. In 1529 Lieutenant Alvara de Saavedra, one of the young Spaniards who stood by that afternoon when Balboa waded out and conquered the Father of Waters, was probably the first to put such a plan on paper. He got so far as to prepare a set of charts for the project.

Later on Englishmen discussed the possibilities of doing something of the sort. But, perish the thought, it had not been written in the book that they should do it. Finally the French attempted it, at first with great promise of success. The same Ferdinand de Lesseps who built the Suez Canal tackled the job. But fighting mosquitoes, fevers and other terrible diseases in a tropical rain-soaked swamp was not like digging a ditch across a fairly level stretch of dry land. So it was left for the Yankees to unloose their purse strings, count out some five hundred twenty-six million dollars, tighten their belts and unite the two great oceans in everlasting matrimony, making Panamá forever the crossroads of the New World, and the key to all the Americas.

Many of the world's industries and business houses have branch offices on the Isthmus, headquarters for their trade activities throughout Spanish America. Dozens of steamship companies, including several owned by United States capital, register their ships under the Panamanian flag because the government of Panamá makes it very attractive for them to do so. They are shouldered with fewer restrictions and regulations, such as a ship registered under the United States flag would be subjected to. Technically Panamá has one of the most imposing merchant marines in the world. At the present time there are 261 ocean-going ships under Panamanian registry.

Every day in the year Panamá plays host to important

officials, diplomats, business men, writers, observers, from many climes. Traders from Tokyo, Shanghai, Bombay, Barcelona, Hamburg and Amsterdam visit in Panamá on their way to the Central and South American countries. Sooner or later every influential business man in Nicaragua, in Mexico, in Colombia, in Chile finds his way to the Isthmus. High officials of the various republics pass through it en route to or returning from important diplomatic missions. It furnishes refuge to unpopular politicians from far and near. If a Nicaraguan, or Honduranian, or Peruvian president finds it necessary to take sudden leave of his post, he goes to Panamá to await developments or to make plans to recoup his fortunes. Even dignitaries who still enjoy public favor come to the great hospitals and clinics of the Isthmus in search of health and relief from their ailments.

Panamá is to the Other Americas the great example of how Uncle Sam treats his weak and smaller neighbors. As one Peruvian official puts it, "Your treatment of Panamá is taken by the other Spanish-American peoples as the measure of your attitude and intentions toward all of them. It is the show window of your Latin-American policy."

With no other country in the world are our relations so intimate and delicate. Thousands of our citizens are on the Isthmus engaged in operating the Canal and other purely American interests. Thousands of our soldiers and sailors have the run of the country, mixing and mingling freely with the Panamanian people. Under such circumstances the maintenance of respect and good will between Panamá and the United States is a tremendous as well as a vital problem.

Right through the middle of the republic from sea to sea runs a strip of land ten miles wide and forty-seven miles long over which we rule supreme. In this piece of territory there are upwards of 10,000 civilian Americans, 12,000 Yankee soldiers and sailors, 20,000 dark and dusky West Indians, mostly Jamaicans, whose government is the War Department of the

United States, and whose governor is a West Pointer. It is also well to bear in mind that the Canal Zone, strange as it may seem, is not United States territory. We govern it but we do not own the land. Which is to say we merely lease it in perpetuity to accommodate the Canal. We paid Panamá $10,000,000 down in the beginning of things and still contribute $250,000 a year in gold, or the equivalent, as an annuity. It may be well to clear up one point just here, for it seems to be taken for granted, both by Panamanians and Americans, that this $250,000 is paid as a rental for the Canal. Such is not the case. Before the Panamanian republic came into existence the Yankee owners paid the government of Colombia $250,000 annually for permission to operate the railroad across Colombian territory. After Panamanian independence, the United States took over the railroad and the building of the Canal, so it was thought only right that the new government which would be in need of a steady income should receive the $250,000 annually.

Before his term of office expired, Doctor Harmodio Arias, the President preceding the present one, succeeded in wringing from the United States material concessions in the Canal Zone and, in 1936, an entirely new treaty between the republic and the government at Washington respecting the Canal.

Agitation in Panamá for concessions under the treaty of 1903 had been increasing during recent years. So, early in the Roosevelt administration, at the request of the Panamanian government and in line with its good neighbor policy, the President made certain restrictions upon the commercial activities of the Canal commissaries. To prevent competition with stores, cafés and theatres in Panamá, the patronage of citizens and residents of the republic is no longer accepted by the Canal Zone commissaries, restaurants and movie houses. Likewise the commissaries are forbidden to sell direct to the thousands of tourists and passengers on ships passing through the Canal.

New Roads to Riches

At the same time the regulations under which Canal Zone restaurants and shops were at one time required to buy their supplies exclusively from government commissaries have been abrogated.

Notwithstanding these concessions, various groups and individuals on the Isthmus were loud in their demands for more than commercial favors. Political critics and leaders of propagandist organizations advocated everything from the sale of the Canal to an international corporation, to the complete scrapping of the treaty of 1903 under which the Canal was constructed and by which it was maintained.

"The United States should demilitarize the Canal Zone," one communistically inclined member of the Panamanian Congress told me in 1934. "The big guns should be pulled down and the army withdrawn from the vicinity. This great waterway should not be dedicated to war but to the pursuits of peace."

"The Canal should be in theory, as well as in reality, an international highway," suggested another talkative politico. "The United States," he explained, "should sell it to an international corporation in which are represented all the leading nations of the world. This corporation would in turn operate it for the benefit of the whole world and not just for the United States alone."

And then there was Señor Rivera Reyes, founder and head of the Panamanian Society for International Action, an organization which would free Panamá from "United States domination" through international coercion. Señor Reyes insisted that the 1903 treaty "born of fraud, perfidy, dishonor," and so on, be abolished before any other negotiations were attempted. Indeed, in a memorandum addressed to President Roosevelt on the occasion of one of the latter's early visits to the Isthmus, the Society declared—"Panamá denounces as absolutely null and void the treaty entered into between this country and the United States of America on November 18, 1903."

Panamá

At the same time the opinion was shared both by responsible Panamanians and a great number of the Americans living on the Isthmus, that the republic of Panamá had certain grievances against the practices of the Canal Zone government toward the republic which seemed eminently worthy of consideration by Washington officials.

For instance, the Panamá Railroad, which is owned and operated by the United States government, though separate from the Canal, is the only railway in the entire country serving the general public. Panamanians and Americans have long advocated the construction of a highway across the Isthmus between Panamá City and Colón. In this age of motor transportation a highway across the Isthmus would be an important addition to the defense of the Canal, as well as a boon to commercial intercourse between the republic's two principal cities. Yet it is pretty generally conceded that the Panamá Railroad Company had consistently opposed the building of such a highway.

Strangely enough, there are American grievances against the Panamá Railroad Company, grievances from American interests not located on the Isthmus. The company also owns one of the most successful steamship lines operating between New York and Cristobal in competition with privately operated lines. In fact, among the finest and most modern of our newly constructed merchant ships are the three new 10,000-ton vessels of this line, the *Panamá*, the *Ancon* and the *Cristobal*, commissioned in 1939. The particular objections raised by the private companies is the fact that the line allows all Canal Zone employees specially reduced rates which the private lines cannot meet.

The Panamá Railroad also owns a great portion of the best commercial property in the Panamanian city of Colón, property over which from the beginning it has exercised complete control and regulation. Panamanians believe, and so do some Americans, that these properties should be subject to the same rules, regulations and taxes as any other properties owned by foreigners in the territory of Panamá.

Then too, in spite of the restrictions already mentioned, the Canal Zone commissaries, which compare favorably with any small city department store in the United States, since they carry everything from Persian rugs to French perfumes, still had a monopoly on the sale of provisions to the ships which pass through the Canal. The commissaries pay no rent or taxes, and everything they sell, no matter from what source it comes, either from the continental United States or from other countries, enters the Canal Zone duty free. Consequently, Panamanian merchants who must pay tariffs, taxes and high transportation costs cannot compete with them.

Another particular grievance of the Panamanians was the fact that, due to the tremendous expansion of the Canal, the army, the navy and Panamá Railroad activities in recent years, and the continual appropriation of additional territory, the Panamanian city of Colón had become completely isolated from the rest of the republic; in other words, completely surrounded by the Canal, navy and army properties. Because of this situation, overcrowding in the old section of Colón is becoming a serious problem to the Panamanian government, not to mention a possible menace to the Canal Zone itself. In a space eight blocks wide by sixteen blocks long live over thirty thousand people, making the problem of sanitation one of the most difficult to be found anywhere in the tropics.

On the other hand, a considerable portion of the land now occupied by the Americans, particularly a section or strip extending southward along the Caribbean, and known as New Cristobal, has been filled in as a result of great dredging projects carried on by and at the expense of the United States government. On this land one of the great hospitals for the Canal, an imposing high-school building with playgrounds, and houses for hundreds of Canal Zone employees have been constructed. But since most of this land was filled in along the waterfront of the old city of Colón, as well as adjoining the original Canal Zone proper, Panamá insists that it is Panamanian territory, and should remain under the complete jurisdiction of the republic. For that matter, old Colón itself was built in 1850 as a result of American enterprise, and on a mudflat, as the starting point for the Panamá Railroad.

This is one of the most ticklish of all the questions that have arisen between the two governments. The land for New Cristobal was already filled in, the buildings constructed at a cost of millions of dollars, before any question was raised by the Panamanians. It is an accomplished fact. What it amounts to is that a part of the Canal Zone, its activities and its employees are and will continue to be subject to the laws, regulations and rule of Panamá.

Already there are constant clashes between the Americans in New Cristobal and the Panamanian authorities, particularly the police force, most of whose members are colored. In fact, the bulk of the population of Colón is either black or a mixture of African and other dark races. While the national government of Panamá rabidly insists upon maintaining its complete sovereignty over the community, and no doubt wishes to furnish complete protection to the property and residents, local authorities often make a poor showing when it comes to carrying out their responsibilities. In fact the overbearing and often unfair attitude of many of them is perfect evidence of an inferiority complex and, although understandable, is inexcusable upon the part of the national government.

Dozens of annoying incidents pile up every week. I witnessed, or from unimpeachable Panamanian sources learned of many such incidents during a recent visit. A colored taxi driver deliberately ran into a white employee of the Canal Zone who was driving his own car. The policeman on the beat let the taxi man go but gave the American a ticket which resulted in his having to pay a fine.

An American doctor connected with the New Cristobal Hospital returned home one evening after a walk with his wife to find a colored man sitting on the front steps making love to the Panamanian cook. When the doctor told the visitor to move on, the latter, although not in uniform, showed his police badge, shoved a gun into the doctor's ribs and began to spout abusive language. The doctor's wife rushed to the telephone and called the police department, only to be told, "You will have to come down to the department and personally swear out a warrant before we can do anything about it."

Two neighbor friends, both Americans, drove out of their garages one evening and accidentally backed into one another. They apologized and each agreed to take care of the damages to the other's car, but a policeman intervened and said, "Oh no, you must both go to court."

A colored taxi man ran over an old colored woman, drove on and left her lying in the street. A young white man came along, found her, picked her up, put her in his car, took her to the American Hospital, then went down to police headquarters and reported. They immediately put him in jail without any investigation.

Two Americans went to the police department and complained about their houses being continually robbed without the police making any effort to apprehend the robbers. "It already costs us $25,000 a year to police New Cristobal where you Americans live," was the reply they got, "and we can't do any more than we are doing now."

This inferiority complex about national sovereignty, and the attitude toward the United States is easily understood. The population of Colón and Panamá City is quite different from what it was ten and fifteen years ago. The bulk of the poor and simpler classes have moved in from the interior. They know nothing of what the communities were like before the Americans built magnificent buildings, parks, paved streets and roads, made them spotless and freed the whole Isthmus of every kind of insect and disease. When these people first arrive they look at Balboa, Ancon, New Cristobal, the beautifully kept hotels and homes of the Americans. So it is easy for them to believe the Yankees took all these things away from Panamá, particularly when petty politicians and cheap news sheets find it so profitable to keep them in ignorance.

But then the Yankees also have shortcomings. Some of them, especially the newcomers, naturally resent having to be subjected to Panamanian rule. Altogether old-timers who have been through the mill, and have helped to keep relations between the two peoples on an even keel for so long, and live in New Cristobal by choice, are not unreasonable in their demands. Besides, Americans employed on the Canal are engineers, artisans of all kinds, and substantial people with families.

One prominent Panamanian said to me, "I am afraid that the attitude of some of our people toward the Americans is not due altogether to those who live in Panamá, but to the multitude of visitors, the cruise ship passengers, the tourists on a holiday, who swarm into the community every day in the week and while here engage in what you Yankees are pleased to call 'doing the town.' It is natural for many of our people, who, until recent years, have had few of the advantages of education, travel or substantial jobs with which to afford reasonably good living conditions, to be offended at these things.

"For instance," he explained, "this is a very warm climate. You and I realize that persons arriving from New York, the eastern and middle-western United States in January find the heat oppressive. Yet it is unfortunate that so many of them start shedding their coats, or, as the Panamanians say, 'undressing,' as soon as they get into port. They take off their ties, open their shirts, so that their hairy chests are bared to the world. Then they remove their shoes, put on tennis slippers or sneakers to walk about the town. In the shops they talk loudly, ridicule and browbeat the clerks, make slighting remarks about Panamá before the proprietors and the customers.

"My dear sir," he concluded, his anger rising perceptibly, "this is one source of contempt that many of these people develop for United States citizens. You see, the poor Panamanian, never having been to the States, and having seen so many of this type of obnoxious person, although of course you and I know they do not represent the real Americans, thinks he has seen representative citizens of the great and powerful United States."

The new treaty, as far as the fundamental problems concerning relations between the two countries are concerned, covers practically all of them. New Cristobal will continue under the sovereignty of Panamá, the commercial and trade restrictions imposed upon the Canal Zone commissaries become permanent. It specifies that the payment of the $250,000 annuity in gold shall be paid in balboas, the Panamanian unit of currency, to the amount of 430,000 annually. Moreover, this payment shall be retroactive to 1934 when Panamá refused the first payment in depreciated dollars. The United States renounces its guarantee of Panamanian independence, also its responsibility as well as its right to intervene for purposes of restoring order in Colón and Panamá City.

The two articles of the treaty which are of the most immediate importance are first: "In case of an international conflagration or the existence of any threat of aggression which would endanger the security of the Republic of Panamá or the neutrality or security of the Panama Canal, the governments of the United States and the Republic of Panamá will take such measures for prevention and defense as they may consider necessary for the protection of their common interests. Any measures, in safeguarding such interests, which it shall appear

Panamá

essential to one government to take, and which may affect the territory under the jurisdiction of the other government, will be the subject of consultation between the two governments."

And second, "The provisions of the treaty shall not affect the rights and obligations of either of the two high contracting parties under the treaties now in force between the two countries, nor be considered as a limitation, definition, restriction or restrictive interpretation of such rights and obligations, but without prejudice to the full force and effect of any provisions of this treaty which constitute addition to, modification or abrogation of, or substitution for the provisions of previous treaties."

But the State Department in an exchange of correspondence with the Panamanian government has established clearly or to the satisfaction of the Senate Foreign Relations Committee that nothing would be allowed to restrict the free action of the United States in case of war with a foreign power or any sudden major emergency. At any rate, the treaty has already been ratified by the Panamanian Congress and the United States Senate.

And yet the extreme Nationalists are not satisfied. They will never be satisfied, and if the government at Washington makes a practice of listening to all the agitators and makes concessions every time they are requested, a very unhappy situation will eventually result on the Isthmus. Of course, it is not only right, but even good business, for the United States to be as generous as possible in its treatment of the little republic. Nevertheless, practically everybody, whether American or Panamanian, whose head is fastened squarely on his shoulders, and who knows the facts first-hand, feels that whatever may have been the circumstances surrounding the negotiations of the treaty of 1903, and regardless of the intemperate and extravagant contentions of the propagandists today, the Panama Canal is now a reality and nothing whatsoever should be permitted to interfere with its efficient maintenance, operation and protection.

III
The Listening Post

I NOW know why fire engines are so alluring to small boys, and to not a few larger ones as well. At least I know why every boy in Panamá City wants to be a *bombero*, as the citizens of this southern metropolis are pleased to call their fire-fighters.

Firemen in the capital of Panamá are the gayest-looking sheiks I ever saw, except the bullfighters of Caracas, Venezuela, or perhaps the chorus men of a Broadway musical comedy. Most of them are in their late teens. They are slim, dark and dapper, with shiny hair that tapers into a very pointed V at the temples. A few even sport those wispy mustaches of the hot-house variety. And how they dress! They wear blood-red shirts, snow-white pants, glistening black boots and patent-leather helmets. When there is a fire in Panamá nobody misses it. But then who would? What señorita would not enjoy being rescued by the boys of such a brigade? It is a wonder that the city does not break out with fires every day.

It is an honor to be a *bombero*. In fact, it is strictly an honorary position. Nobody is hired to fight fires. Membership in the department is entirely voluntary, but strict. You don't put on the red shirt to strut in public. You put it on to serve your country as well as your city, to learn obedience and practice discipline. The rules are severe, and to break them wilfully is national disgrace.

[188]

Panamá

There is one man behind all this, an old man too, a patriarch. He is Comandante Juan Antonio Guizado. Daddy Guizado, as he is affectionately known, the idol of the small boys of the city, has long been the spirit and the law of the department. He founded it, surrounded it with an air of romance, even a bit of the glamor of a King Arthur's court. Anyway, the lads of the Red Shirt Brigade pay Daddy Guizado just as much homage as the Knights of the Round Table paid to Arthur himself.

The home fires may be kept burning in many a town but they do not burn long in this city on the Isthmus. What is more, whether it is a fire or a famine, a riot or a revolution, Daddy Guizado and his boys are always standing by ready for action.

A few years ago, in 1931, the population of Panamá became very angry about the wily ways of the political bosses. They became so angry they boiled over. In the early hours of a January morning they quietly laid hands upon the Chief of Police, then swooped down upon the Presidential Palace and sent His Excellency on a long vacation. Having already met with such startling success, they next proceeded to subdue one by one His Excellency's satellites and henchmen, and otherwise rid the community of all those gentlemen who had practiced the old art of political plunder. By that time their enthusiasm was all but sufficient to wreck the town. Every one was anxious to join in the chase of politicos. Not since the days of the Texas bad men has there been on display in one community such an assortment of ancient pistolry and hand artillery.

Whereupon Daddy Guizado gathered up his gay *bomberos*— those in reserve, as well as those on active duty—and went forth to save the town from itself. In no time at all he had pacified the frenzied patriots, calmed the multitude and stood by while a wiry little brown-eyed lawyer brought passable government out of hopeless chaos.

And that brings us to Doctor Harmodio Arias, no relation

incidentally to the Ariases of the aristocracy mentioned in the previous chapter. On the night in question Doctor Arias became the saviour of his nation, as well as the moulder of Panamanian history. He is one of the biggest little men who ever started from taw in the tropical jungle, strolled down the classic cloisters of Cambridge University in England and sat on the high bench of the International Court of Justice. And if that sounds perfectly Horatio Algerish, it cannot be helped. It is the gospel truth.

When the enraged populace first began to apply the public boot to political pants, Harmodio Arias probably had no expectation that he would have to pilot the Ship of State through such troubled water. He wasn't the leader of the revolutionary group. He wasn't even the moving spirit. He is much too quiet and retiring for that. But when the revolutionists had gotten rid of the old crowd, Harmodio was the one man in the country whose ability and disinterestedness they trusted. They simply demanded that he act, and so he acted.

As fast as the wheels would turn he ground out a temporary régime, then planned an election to re-establish a constitutional government. All this done, he was ready to slip back into his accustomed niche as a private citizen and the most respected lawyer in Central America. But soon the old crowd began to lick their chops and creep back one by one to look for places at the public trough. The people again sniffed anger. And so did Harmodio. His Latin temperament and his Indian blood completely aroused, he became a candidate for the presidency and again took the field in a fight to the finish. Election Day came. The ballots were counted and the fighting attorney was again the man of the hour.

Inaugural ceremonies were held on an August afternoon, and it was such a day as the republic had not seen since it came into being. It was a day of rejoicing, like a gala Saturday at an old-time county fair. From every town and village in the

Panamá

republic, from Chiriqui Province and the San Blas country, pilgrims came to the capital—black men, red men, brown men, and those of Spanish descent—women, children and babies—all to see the diminutive doctor inducted into office. For by now he was the little father of all the faithful.

The National Opera House was the scene of this spectacle because the opera house serves as the official residence of the National Congress. Not that the Congressmen sing or play on musical instruments. They merely act—that is, for the people. The people may even sit in the galleries and watch them perform. And who shall say that a theatre is an unsuitable place for a Congress to meet, since so many Congressmen seem to be given to histrionics and Thespian behavior?

A ticket to the opera house was as easy to find as the Lamp of Aladdin. But I was fortunate. I went as the guest of the American Minister, then the clever Missourian Roy T. Davis. He even sent Edward Latham, a member of his staff, to see that I got safely by the doorkeeper. But getting by the doorkeeper was not the problem. It was getting to the door. For when we arrived the place was being mobbed—peacefully mobbed, of course. Nowhere, except possibly at a demonstration of the Italian Fascisti, or the German Nazis, could you find such a crowd. The streets and squares for blocks around were a solid mass of seething Panamanians.

Just as we got within eyeshot of the front doorsteps they began flowing and ebbing like waves on the seashore, a phenomenon that dampened the dignity of the diplomats, in fact bruised the dignity of more than one. A flock of these gentlemen got caught in the surge and were thrown bodily toward the door. Several missed the opening and landed up against the façade of the building. Some were caught by the tails of their coats and held back in the scramble. A few lost their canes and gloves while silk hats went bouncing above the surface of the human sea. Latham and I got on the crest of one of those waves and rode it to the door. And but for the bayonet of a soldier, whose unintentional thrust we managed to parry by a hair's breadth, we would have flowed right on through to our seats without stopping—but luck was with us. As we stood in this perilous predicament an attaché of the Ministry of Foreign Affairs saw us, and rushed to our rescue.

Already the walls of the theatre were bulging from the pressure of the perspiring crowd within. The aisles were jammed. The balconies were overflowing. People hung over the edges and clung to columns. Diplomatic boxes were invaded in a frenzied scene. Visiting admirals and generals in glittering regalia, office clerks and scrubwomen, diplomats in standing collars and tail coats, truck drivers in greasy shirts and overalls, like too many sardines in a can, stood wedged against each other throughout the proceedings.

It was democracy with abandon, hilarious democracy, people mad with joy, anxious to pay tribute to their idol. But in all the confusion nobody got angry, nobody except a few of the prominent and exalted foreigners who got their spats soiled or their silk hats mashed. I have never witnessed anything like it— the eagerness to see, the reverence of every one who could see, the high and the low. Those who got in hung on every one of the simple but profound words of the little man's speech. They might have been hypnotized, so serious were the expressions on their faces.

Afterwards officers and officials were full of apologies for any mishap. They had simply been swamped. To tell the truth they had expected a perfunctory affair, as in the good old days. One man said, "We hadn't even dreamed of such a thing. You see, we never had a president before that people paid much attention to." Personally I think few of the southern republics have ever had such a president.

Doctor Harmodio Arias has lived enough experiences to fill volumes. Fifty-odd years ago he looked out upon the world

Panamá

from a tiny village in the wild interior of the Isthmus. When Harmodio was old enough to take notice of such matters, his father, a backwoodsman of the first order, possessed a few runty cattle, a seedy old mare, a wife and a half dozen children. But somehow that mysterious power which flings obscure men into the solar plexus of world activity took this lowly lad of Spanish and Indian parentage out of the Panamanian waste lands and stood him in the fashionable courts of the world.

He went to Panamá City in his teens and, Abraham Lincoln-like, got a job as a clerk in a little store. Between customers he read odds and ends—papers, almanacs and whatnot. He passed up the strange sights and wonders of the city. School was his consuming ambition and he finally got into one. Then a war broke out. Panamá revolted from Colombia, seceded, or whatever one's personal opinion on that controversial subject may be. Anyway, it became a republic. After which young Arias went back to school, then to a straggling college where he lapped up what they had to offer and asked for more.

The new republic had wisely provided for several scholarships, with the idea of sending bright youngsters abroad so as to provide the country with a group of citizens trained in world affairs. Harmodio asked to be examined for one of these scholarships, won it, and immediately set off for England, and the University School at Southport, to prepare himself for Cambridge.

A few years later he strolled out of Cambridge with honors, but his desire for learning was not yet satisfied. So straight down to London he went, and to the University of London where he prepared and published a thesis on the exciting subject of International Law. For this, the staid old professors gave him the degree of Bachelor of Laws and sent him back home to hang out his shingle, or whatever a lawyer in Panamá hangs out, and later to build up the most distinguished practice on the Isthmus.

New Roads to Riches

As the years passed, other honors began raining down upon him. He was sent as Special Minister here and there. He was Panamá's first representative in the League of Nations, from which place the trail led to the Hague and the International Court of Justice to sit as one of the distinguished jurists of the times. Then he went back to Panamá and, as you have already seen, to the presidency, to lead his people out of a tragic crisis and through the mazes of a world depression.

As his regular term as the nation's chief executive drew to a close, he entertained no thought of succeeding himself although he could have been re-elected almost by acclamation. Instead he supported Juan Demostenes Arosemena, his Minister of Foreign Affairs, for the presidency. Arosemena was a former mayor of Colón and afterwards governor of the province of Colón, a rather gruff and outspoken, but extremely able, man.

The depression dealt Panamá a severe blow. The republic enjoys prosperity only when the world is prosperous, when world trade flourishes and the sea is full of ships. The livelihood of Panamá's citizens, the majority of whom live in Colón and Panamá City, is dependent upon the Canal Zone. For several years, traffic through the Canal fell off, tolls shrank, so that forces had to be cut down. Thousands of laborers were laid off, army and naval activities were curtailed. Consequently Panamanian stores and shops suffered severe losses, and there was little work for thousands of Panamanian laborers.

Throughout this difficult period Arias not only succeeded in feeding the unemployed and carrying on a program of public works, but kept up payments on the country's foreign debt. A foreign debt of more than $18,000,000 originally and a large additional internal debt is no small obligation for a country of scarcely half a million people, few of whom are even well to do. Besides, much of the debt had been contracted during previous régimes. But Arias was a stickler for promptness and fairness to the private individual who had put his money into the country's bonds, no matter what the circumstances surrounding the floating of these bonds. During his last year in office, there were many Panamanians who thought he ought to suspend the payments, "because," as they expressed it, "hardly any one else is paying its debts, not even such powerful countries as England and France. Why should little Panamá pay?"

I shall never forget his reply when I asked him his personal views on the subject: "I would consider such a step most unfortunate both for the government and the country," he said. "I know many people think credit isn't worth anything anywhere, therefore why should Panamá think about credit? But even if this were true, which it isn't, I would still be in favor of keeping it up. When I have given my word to do a thing, I can think of no excuse why I should not live up to it. Only one condition would cause me to suspend payment on the debt while I am president, and that would be to prevent my people from starving to death."

His sense of propriety as a private citizen, even if he is still the most respected figure among his own people, would never permit him to voice open criticism of his successor who suspended the debt payments. But I have reason to know that he has not altered his opinion on the subject.

Although it was Arias who won so many concessions from the United States government, and who negotiated the new Panamanian-United States treaty, whose ratification has been completed, he is no enemy of the United States. Because he himself is a gentleman who feels that doing the fair, honorable and just thing by every one should be a privilege and not an obligation, he cannot bring himself to see why little Panamá should not be allowed the privilege of being friendly and generous to her powerful neighbor instead of being told in a treaty that she has to do it. This is to say he insists that the United States should trust Panamá to realize that her best in-

terest lies in close co-operation with her neighbor. He would
uphold the dignity of his nation, its right to discuss with the
Washington government, as an equal, questions involving its
relationship with the Canal Zone, and as they arise, instead
of giving to the United States what some one has called "a
blank treaty right to do as it pleases at any time, as was permitted by the original treaty of 1903."

To those who have feared that by giving up its right to interfere in the political affairs of Panamá the government might
at some time make agreements with other governments, or
allow other countries, say Germany, Italy or Japan, privileges
on the Isthmus that might endanger the safety of the Canal,
it may be said that Arias and his successor have carefully
guarded against this, even in cases where such things were not
even forbidden by the old treaty. In 1930, during the administration of the government which Arias succeeded, Panamá had
entered into a trade and immigration treaty with Japan. Under
the treaty each country made concessions to the other in the
matter of commerce and Panamá was to permit Japanese citizens to settle in various parts of the republic.

This was a very serious question. It meant that Panamá was
giving privileges to a country which was later to be lined up
with the European totalitarian states and the enemies of the
very democracy which Arias was to insist should govern her
relations with the United States. The agreement had already
been ratified both by the Japanese government and the Panamanian Congress. But fortunately the formalities of the exchange of ratification had not taken place. Therefore it was not
in effect before the revolution of 1931 when the government
which had made the agreement was overthrown.

Arias was under no illusion about the possible dangers of
the situation, especially since the agreement had already been
ratified by both governments. Nevertheless, when he came to
office he carefully neglected to exchange the articles of ratifica-

tion. He put the matter off time after time, figuring the Japanese would take a hint. But the Mikado's officials are nothing if not persistent, or naïve, even if intentionally so. The Japanese minister made overtures to the Foreign Minister, Doctor Arosemena, now president of the republic. The Foreign Minister came to Arias about it. The President gave him instructions to tell the Japanese envoy, not in writing, but orally, that "Panamá unfortunately is experiencing a crisis and thousands of our own people are unemployed, and, under the circumstances, we do not feel that we can afford to permit any further immigration at the moment."

The Japanese minister then lodged a protest, suggesting that Panamá was not keeping faith. Arias replied that his government did not make the agreement in the first place and that it was made by a government which, because of unfortunate practices, had been overthrown. The Japanese then made it a question of an affront to the Emperor of Japan. The Arias government humbly but cleverly suggested that such a small country as Panamá could hardly be important enough to affront the great Japanese Empire.

Later on an admiral came through and, of course, asked to present his compliments to the President. He was received by Doctor Arias. Naïvely he remarked on the good relations between Panamá and Japan. "I believe," said he, as if such matters were entirely outside his field, or knowledge, "we even have a treaty for the promotion of trade and immigration?" Arias graciously replied, "Oh, unfortunately, I am afraid not. The formalities of ratification were never exchanged." The admiral appeared "so surprised," knowing very well that he and his country's minister had hatched up that method of reminding Arias of the treaty once again.

Even after this the Japanese minister came forward with suggestions for a compromise. Japan would be willing to forego the immigration features of the treaty if Panamá would only exchange ratification. However, Arias found other and continual excuses until his term of office expired. But the moment he retired, and Doctor Arosemena came into office, the request for ratification was renewed by the Japanese. Naturally the Oriental mind figured that, while Doctor Arosemena was Minister of Foreign Affairs his Latin cordiality and extreme courtesy meant that he was merely carrying out the orders of his chief, but, now that he himself was the head of the government, he might be induced to complete the transaction. That is to say, as Foreign Minister Doctor Arosemena was compelled to make excuses for some one else, and he had made so many excuses that now as president he would have to give in. But so far he has not.

There are some who still feel that Arosemena is personally unfriendly to the United States. They recall certain of his criticisms of the Yankees during his earlier years as mayor and governor of Colón. Yet it is hardly possible that he would have had the support of Arias for the presidency, or, to be more explicit, that he would have been the Arias candidate, if he had not proven himself a man of the highest integrity and extreme sound judgment, who knows that Panamá has nothing to gain by any act that is detrimental to the efficient operation of the Panama Canal.

It is true that he suspended payments on the public debt, which Arias so rigidly kept up while he was in office. But his reasons for this were not without logic. In a recent conversation he said, "The situation for us is this. The United States government isn't paying its debts to us, so how can we pay our debts to citizens of the United States. The stipulations of the treaty of 1903 say that the United States shall pay us $250,000 a year in gold, not depreciated currency. But it has refused to pay us in gold—and a quarter million gold dollars a year cut from our income is more than a serious loss."

When I suggested that that point had been taken care of

in the new treaty, he was quick to reply. "Yes, we promptly ratified the treaty but the United States has not, even though the treaty was drawn up and signed more than three years ago. Considering the fact that the United States went off gold in 1933 and would not pay us in gold, it means that you still owe us more than a million dollars, that is, gold dollars. In fifty-nine-cent dollars, it is actually nearly two million.

"Of course," he said, "we might have accepted the checks which were offered us each year, checks for $250,000 in present-day currency. But that might have jeopardized our claims for the gold or its equivalent."

Whatever President Arosemena's attitude toward the United States may be, or whether he would be likely to give aid and comfort to any country or government that might have designs against its best interests in the Canal Zone, informed and influential Panamanians are outspoken against the forces that are leading the fight against democracy.

In *The Panamá American,* one of the two leading newspapers in the country, of which he is publisher, Doctor Arias himself has recently spoken in no uncertain terms against having any truck with the Fascist states. He even advocated that all democracies break off relations with Germany, "as a demonstration of the intense aversion, profound disgust and a reaffirmation of the democratic sentiments that respect the rights and liberty of peoples." He expressed the hope that the American nations will adopt this attitude and demonstrate the continental solidarity revealed at the recent Lima conference.

Close on the heels of this statement, T. Gabriel Duque, also a former president of Panamá, and publisher of *The Star and Herald,* the other leading newspaper, goes farther and calls upon all Latin-American countries to take steps against the Nazis, or any others not satisfied with conditions in this part of the world. "We could imitate a well-known Nazi institution, the plebiscite, conducted, however, on democratic lines of freedom of vote, by which German residents would have to declare whether or not they were in sympathy with the Nazi ideology and program."

Duque asserted that the cry of Yankee imperialism comes from Old World interests for their own benefit. "With the United States as its frankly recognized leader—a leadership based on the democratic principle of equality—Latin America can act to offset any aggressive attempt by Nazi Germany or Fascist Italy," declared the editorial.

Even before these two leaders spoke out, plain citizens themselves were making their own views known. An Italian cruiser paid a good-will visit to Panamá. When the officers, dressed up in their gold braid and shiny swords, were on their way to present their respects to the government, they suddenly found themselves targets for all manner of dejected and rejected fruit and vegetables.

"Fascism, Nazism or Nipponism," as one high official sees it, "will get no farther here than it does in Georgia or Missouri or North Carolina." The same personage, under whose jurisdiction such matters would be taken care of, spoke out on the subject of Japanese spies, living in Panamá but operating against the Canal. "Of course there are Jap spies here," he said, "and have been for twenty years. But they are so naïve they don't fool anybody. Their every movement is known and their every movement has always been known."

In this matter there is the closest co-operation between the Panamanian authorities, the officials of the Canal and the army and navy forces. Let no citizen entertain any doubt about the vigilance and the all-seeing eye of Uncle Sam in these matters. There is little about the Canal that cannot be known by anybody who lives near it or who passes through it. The important thing is to know who the foreign agents are and what they plan to do, or could do. With more than 25,000 Yankee soldiers, sailors and employees on the Isthmus, not only to guard and patrol the Canal itself, but to dress up in civilian clothes and keep circulating in every nook and corner of the cities, towns and area, not much could be or is going to be planned without its becoming known.

Some of the smart uncoverers for certain of the Hot Stuff periodicals have recently put out very scary stories about the dangers of our treasured waterway, and the impotence of our Secret Service forces around it. One or two have gone down in person, looked the situation over and learned—in two or three weeks, one of them in six days—things that none of the fellows who have been constantly on the job for years had known. But why dignify such pitiful presumption with discussion? It is enough to say that if army and navy officers, and a host of highy trained civilians, men Uncle Sam has trained from boyhood, and who have spent years studying, observing, and figuring ways and means of apprehending, circumventing and unearthing the plans of spies and foreign enemies, don't know everything that is going on in Panamá, it is hardly possible for an itinerant journalist to learn much more than they know in a few days.

Meantime, entirely aside from the fact that we operate the Canal and therefore have intimate and sometimes delicate relations with the Panamanian government and people, Panamá is diplomatically one of the most important countries in the hemisphere to us. It is our Latin-American Listening Post. In the new drive for closer trade ties with the countries to the south, the Embassy (the legation has only recently been raised to an Embassy) in Panamá is one of the most important links. Its occupant should be a highly trained and able man, one intimately acquainted with the people of all the Other Americas, their customs and characteristics, their weaknesses and their virtues. Such a man can help to guide successfully the course of Uncle Sam's relations with all the near-by countries.

We are fortunate that we have had in Panamá a number

of men who thoroughly appreciated this fact. In recent years we owe a great deal to such men as Roy T. Davis and George T. Summerlin, both well trained in the school of common sense, as well as the intricacies of diplomacy. Roy T. Davis, United States Minister in Panamá from 1929 until 1933, was called upon to handle the difficulties which grew out of the only revolution the country has experienced since it became a republic, and since the Canal has been in operation. He handled it in such a way that not a single Panamanian of any importance could criticize him or us, and at the same time he preserved to the letter the dignity and integrity of the United States government.

And George T. Summerlin, who before his service on the Isthmus had been able to keep up friendship with Venezuela's Juan Vicente Gomez and at the same time make the picturesque old dictator show the proper respect for American citizens and business in that country, will long be remembered among both Panamanians and American citizens on the Isthmus.

Both these men during their incumbencies entertained an army of dignitaries who came through, made friends with them, listened sympathetically to their complaints and their gossip. Each of them could put on a diplomatic reception in a hayloft and send the guests home feeling as if they had been to Buckingham Palace. And indeed that is just what they did. When you see the old legation, now the embassy building in Panamá, you smile, and, if you have any appreciation of the importance of our country's foreign affairs, you come home determined to write a letter to your congressman. It is one of the rattiest looking and most ancient structures in the city. It might well be one of the few relics that survived the Morgan raid.

According to a Panamanian friend, "It was built one hundred years ago and lost in a poker game twenty years later. Then the French took it over and housed their Canal superintendent in it. Later you acquired it when you bought out the French.

But when the engineers took it over they decided it leaked too much to use it as a warehouse, and it was too far away from the job to keep the mules in it. So they turned it over to the American minister as a residence."

ECUADOR

I
Tropical Adventure

Among the men who started from less than scratch and planned, surveyed, and built their own roads to fame and fortune, Francisco Pizarro is a superlative example, provided one is not too exacting as to the quality of his fame or the methods by which he acquired his fortune.

He was conceived in bastardy—but not, as one well-known writer has said, "born no one ever learned where to a mother no one ever knew." The good people of the old city of Trujillo in Estramadura were by no means ignorant of this juicy morsel of community waywardness. The man in the case was a well-known "gentleman," Captain Gonzalo Pizarro. The historians have discreetly failed to give the name of the girl. But they knew her well enough to assure us she was "an old Christian," which meant she was not of Jewish or Moorish blood. What is more, the Captain did at least half-way right by her. He would not himself take her as his wife but he saw to it that she got married off to Señor Fulhano de Alcantara, a steady, if not overly particular, farmer. In later years the Captain even recognized his son.

Meantime, in infancy the potential conquistador had been deposited, for better or worse, at the door of an old church. The padres took him in but it seems they were put to it to keep him alive. Apparently nothing but sow's milk agreed with him, and his behavior in after years was proof that it was more than wholesome. Moreover, it must have taken effect almost immediately, for he early proved too much of a problem for the patient and faithful fathers so that even they got rid of him. That he ran at large for several years there is little doubt, because it is generally agreed that he grew up unable to read and write. Eventually he wandered down to Seville and afterward made his way to the New World.

His first stop was at the oldest European city in the New World, the one built by the discoverer himself, Santo Domingo. Then he gravitated to Havana, and finally to Panamá. He, too, along with the young engineer Saavedra, was present that day when Balboa took over the Pacific, a performance calculated to inspire any ambitious young man. At least it must have touched off a spark in Pizarro. He began at once to volunteer for odd and difficult jobs, to make himself useful to officials. Having proved himself a good fighter, he was sent by the governor on several dangerous expeditions about the Isthmus, to trade with and, if necessary, chastise the Indians.

On one of these voyages southward along the west coast he heard rumors of the great cities and the fabulous wealth of Perú. Back in Panamá he teamed up with another adventurous gentleman by the name of Pedro de Almagro. After a high-pressure campaign they got together the necessary funds, rounded up a few roustabouts and set forth on a long voyage. They set forth, but they did not reach much of anywhere. Along the coast of Colombia storms buffeted them about, tropical fever befell them, and almost any other calamity the mind may imagine. They made several more voyages over a period of years, each time getting a little nearer their goal but each time encountering more hardships. But it was not in Pizarro to give up. Not even when his men refused to follow. Once on the shores of Ecuador, in the vicinity of the present town of Esmeraldas, the entire company balked. Their clothes in shreds, hungry, almost too weary to resist the rigors of the equatorial sun, or to fight the tropical pests, they demanded to be shown why they should go one step farther.

Once again Pizarro demonstrated his superb leadership and his ability to make men carry on though the heavens fall, which they did for hours every day during most of the year. Having experienced a few of the rains that fall in these regions I am willing to classify the downpours in northern Panamá as heavy dews. At Esmeraldas the old boy stepped forward, and with his sword drew a line in the sand and delivered one of the most dramatic he-man speeches ever made. It deserves to rank among the great orations. Translated by the late Cunninghame Graham, himself a Spanish Grandee, as well as a Scottish Earl, his mother having been a member of the Spanish nobility, it reads as follows:

"Gentlemen," said Pizarro, "this line means toil, thirst, hunger, weariness, wounds, illnesses and all the other dangers and the difficulties that in this conquest we shall have to pass, until life finishes. Those who are brave enough to risk and conquer them, let them pass across the line, in sign and proof of the stoutness of their souls and in testimony that they will be my faithful followers, and those who feel themselves not worthy of so great a hazard, let them return to Panamá, for I force nobody; but with those who remain, no matter if they are but few, I trust in God for His greater honor and His glory, and the perpetual renown of those who follow me, His eternal Majesty may so assist me that I shall never miss those who elect to go."

Thirteen ragged, sick and emaciated members of the party crossed the line and stood at his side. With these thirteen he waited, while Almagro returned to Panamá for more recruits and supplies. Eventually they got far enough south to make contact with Incan outposts and to see with their own eyes evidence of the rich treasures to which they eventually were to help themselves. But it was not until after the illegitimate, the outcast who was living only because he had been suckled by a sow, had made a trip all the way to Spain, gained the ear of the King, secured his support and been admitted to the company of the nobility, that success was in his grasp.

Even so, when he got back to Panamá it was necessary to patch up differences with his old friend Almagro. This done, he sailed away southward again, this time on the most daring of all his journeys, down the coast to northern Perú, then inland, through the desert lands and up into the Andes. He passed on horseback through native communities and cities, getting acquainted, making friends and gathering information. Finally he rode down into the valley of Cajamarca, just then headquarters of the Inca, or Peruvian emperor, and almost the entire royal army. With a few horses and guns, a handful of men, each equipped with intestines enough to supply an army of thousands, he conquered an empire, strangled its ruler, who was also its living god, pillaged its riches, made himself supreme over a great people and died at the hand of an assassin in his own palace.

I never set sail or take the air from Panamá and along the Pacific coast of South America that I do not marvel anew at Francisco Pizarro and his escapades. To me he is not only the most picturesque of the conquistadores who set foot on the South American continent, but one of the most colorful figures in all the early history of the Other Americas.

Of all my travels along Pizarro's old trail, a trip I made with John D. MacGregor, a ruddy-faced, progressively rotund and perpetually youthful Scotsman, remains the most interesting. Pioneering general manager of the Pan-American Grace Airways from its infancy until his heathery wisdom suggested that he ought to be thrifty with his years, John D., as he has been and ever will be known to me, invited me along on a leisurely inspection and good-will flight in a tiny Sikorsky amphibian

Ecuador

to the various coastal towns and villages of Colombia and Ecuador.

From Panamá City we followed one of the first and longest of the regularly scheduled over-water routes, 350 miles to Buenaventura, Pacific port for travellers and freight bound to and from the Colombian southland and Bogotá. A river town with one of the most modern of seaports, Buenaventura is surrounded by a community so backward that it beggars description. After the place was partially destroyed by fire a few years ago the national government erected modern docks and wharves, an imposing Customs House office building, a new modernistic railroad terminal and a hotel. Along the river banks, formerly lined with huts and shacks, it has constructed a concrete *malecon*, or promenade, and studded it with bright lights. All of which serves to intensify the contrast between the modern and the primitive, as well as to hasten the departure of any one with the price of a ticket, or even a canoe.

Seventy-five miles out of Buenaventura we circled the historic island of Gorgona, where Pizarro once marooned himself for nearly three years while his partner in crime, Almagro, returned to Panamá to gather more men and supplies for his expedition.

"Every time I look down at this lonely bit of jungle-covered earth sticking out of the Pacific," John D. observed, "my feelings toward Pizarro soften a bit. I no longer roundly condemn him for being covetous of Peruvian riches. If I should be marooned on Gorgona for even one day, I should feel like leading a ruthless conquest upon the first bit of civilization I ran across afterwards."

Another eighty-five miles and we called for gas and oil at Tumaco, the last of the Colombian ports, a few minutes from which we rounded Cape Manglares and entered Ecuador. Next we visited Esmeraldas, the first of the Ecuadorean cities, scene of the Pizarro mutiny—or shall we say, the first of all Ecuadorean revolutions. Considering the number since then, this is a historical distinction worthy of note.

After Esmeraldas, the low flat beach having given way to a high bluff, we were forced out to sea. After looking down for hours at the lazy whitecaps of the Pacific, I finally fell asleep, only to be suddenly awakened by the imminence of disaster. The plane dropped, then lunged forward, turned half around and was plunging downward. I clawed at the seat in front and, in an effort to brace or save myself from being mangled as the plane nose-dived onto the sandy beach, almost lacerated the neck of the radio operator. As she settled back on an even keel, I was still holding on with the tenacity of a leech. Just then the pilot looked back, smiled and handed me a neatly engraved document, signifying that I had just crossed the Equator and had become a full-fledged member of the flying order of the Condor, all to the immense enjoyment of John D.

At Manta we found two steamers anchored offshore taking on several of the unique products for which Ecuador is famous. First of all, fish, fresh out of the water and still kicking, red snapper and corbina, for the crew and passengers. Then cargoes of ivory, not ivory that grows on elephants, but ivory that grows on trees, one of the important products of the republic. In South America the ivory nut is known as the *tagua* nut, used for the manufacture of cuff buttons, collar buttons, and buttons for countless other more intimate purposes, as well as umbrella handles and poker chips.

The *tagua* tree is a species of palm, about fifteen feet high with large drooping fronds resembling giant green ostrich feathers. It grows wild in Panamá and Colombia, but principally in Ecuador. Its fruit is a burr about the size of a large cocoa-nut growing at the base of the leaves, eight and ten to the tree. Each burr weighs from fifteen to twenty pounds and contains from six to nine nuggets, or seeds, of the hard white ivorylike substance. Ecuador exports from 25,000 to 40,000 tons of *tagua* nuts a year, quite enough to button up—well, a considerable number of persons, both young and old.

I have learned many things in my travels. But I have also found it a splendid way to unlearn things. This visit to Manta served to impress upon me for all time the fact that Panama hats are not Panama hats at all, and that if you are looking for an argument, or wish to see a human being transformed into a living, seething volcano, just tell a one hundred per cent Ecuadorean that Panama hats come from the Isthmus. Just let him suspect that you think they do not originate in his equatorial homeland and he will let loose a torrent of words. For he wishes all to know that what we call a Panama hat is a *Sombrero de Jipijapa* or a *Sombrero de Montecristi* according to the particular community in which it is made.

I overheard this conversation between a native vendor and a tourist, evidently one of the most verdant of all greenhorns, from one of the ships in the harbor, who was looking at a stack of unblocked and folded hats.

"What are those?"

"Those are the *Sombreros de Jipijapa*, Señor."

"Mm. They look like Panama hats."

"No, no, Señor, what you call the Panama hat, it is the Ecuador hat, the *Sombrero de Jipijapa*, or *Sombrero de Montecristi*. These are the *Sombreros de Jipijapa*."

"But, Señor, the Panama hat is much worn in my country."

"No, Señor, it is too bad that—how you call it—the Yankees, they should think that the marvellous product of our glorious republic—it should originate in the exterior—that is, on the outside of our borders."

"But can it not be that there are hats in Panamá as well as in Ecuador? Isn't there a—well—a *Sombrero de Panamá*?"

"*Sombrero de Panamá*? No, no, Señor! It is *Sombrero de Jipijapa!*"

"But what is this *Sombrero de—de—de———*"

[213]

"*De Jipijapa*—it is made from the plant which grows most prominent in the soil of my country."

"Then Panama hats really come from Ecuador?"

"Si, Señor."

"Why, then, are they called Panama hats?"

"Because, Señor, foreigners bought them first in the markets of Panamá."

"So the real name is *Sombrero de*——"

"Si, Señor—these being the *Sombreros de Jipijapa*. The *Sombrero*, that word it is much in the common with you—but *Jipijapa*—it is not so universal maybe. In the way of our pronunciation we call it He-pee-hop-ah."

The finest of these hats are now produced in the regions around Manta. The plant from which the raw material comes resembles a saw palmetto about eight or ten feet high with fan-shaped leaves. According to one authority on the scientific and technical aspects of the industry, "in selecting the materials it is important to watch the color, length, thickness and number of threads to the strand or skein of the freshly gathered straw or palmetto. The fan-shaped leaves must be cut from the trunk of the plant before they open, or just as they ripen. Stripped of their outer filaments, they are then dipped for a few seconds in a vat of boiling water, withdrawn for a moment to be again immersed for an instant, taken out and shaken vigorously, hung up to dry in the shade and a day or two later put out in the sun to be bleached. If lemon juice is added to the hot-water bath, the result is a much whiter straw.

"In a day or two," he goes on, "the sprouts shrivel into a light, compact cylindrical form, like cord or string, when the straw is ready for weaving. It was formerly stated that the hats were actually woven under water, which is not strictly true, although the straw must be kept thoroughly moistened while in the hands of the weaver."

Anyway, the good citizens of Ecuador have recently been

Ecuador

much agitated about the serious injustice to their profitable and almost exclusive industry. Only recently an Ecuadorean gentleman telephoned me in New York, imploring me to write and speak over the radio about the matter. There was a choke in his voice, and, although I could not see him, I do not doubt great watery globules were flowing down his cheeks and dripping from his chin. In fact, you can move an Ecuadorean to poetry and pathos any day in the week if you attempt to deprive him of his *Sombreros de Jipijapa*, his *Sombreros de Montecristi* or any of the others.

"And," as John D. puts it, "if we are to save ourselves from some awful end we must never entertain the thought that our aristocratic summer headgear came from Panamá, and whether we can pronounce it or not, we must remember that it is spelled *Jipijapa*, and is made in Ecuador."

After all, it is no easy matter to make one of them. It requires three or four weeks for a poor Indian to weave a genuine *Jipijapa* which sells for twenty-five dollars in Manhattan, Minneapolis or Memphis, a job for which he receives the munificent reward of perhaps one dollar and seventy-five cents.

Mention is also made, although there is no visible grief or shedding of tears about the misuse of the word *cacao*. Ecuador is the home of much of the cocoa we use in the realm of Uncle Sam. In Manta I soon found that cocoa and chocolate are merely the trade names of products that we make from *cacao* beans.

"Cocoa?" said one Ecuadorean. "Why, cocoa undoubtedly comes from the cocoanut." And it does seem logical. The *cacao* tree averages about twenty-five feet high, and, curiously enough, the fruit or pod which is about the size of and resembles a clenched fist, grows on the trunk of the tree and not on the branches. Each pod contains a number of seeds which look much like almond seeds.

The curing process is a very scientific matter which deter-

mines the flavor and the quality of the finished chocolate. The
pod is cut with a large knife, carefully, so that the blade does
not pass through the outer shell and injure the seeds. It is then
broken open by hand. The seeds are separated from the fibrous
tissues that surround it, and put into a tight warm room, or
sweating house, until fermentation takes place. No one seems
to know exactly what happens to the bean during fermentation.
Anyway, after it has fermented, or the moisture has been taken
out of it, it is dried in the sun, after the manner of drying coffee
beans, or with the aid of hot-air furnaces. The dried bean turns
to a bright red color outside while the inside is brownish
chocolate which crumbles easily in the fingers.

Of course there are great *cacao* plantations of highly cultivated trees. But many of these giant beans grow in the depths
of the jungle and are brought down rivers and streams to
market, by the sun-baked children of the wild in those narrow
little boats, which they dig out of the trunk of the *balsa* tree.
Sometimes they paddle for days in order to reach the coast
and exchange their meager holdings for a handful of pennies—
a fabulous sum to them, since it buys enough rum or other
frivolities to separate them for a week or so from life's dreary
realities.

Balsa is another important product of Ecuador. It is exported in large quantities to the United States and in smaller
quantities to Europe. *Balsa* is a very light wood but it has the
strength of many of our heavier woods. It is much in demand
among builders of display models and of airplanes. The *balsa*
grows wild and is not a cultivated product.

All this and more I had learned on the way along the Ecuadorean coast. And then late one evening we sat down, or the
plane sat down, on the quiet waters of the crescent bay at Salinas,
otherwise known as the Atlantic City of the republic. Just as
we climbed out on the beach and looked westward the sun
fell like a ball of fire into the Pacific and its scarlet rays shot

Cacao Bean Sorters Enjoy a Photographic Interlude

A Highlander Ready for a Cockfight

Ecuador

across the heavens like a giant open fan. Some one shouted the Yankee football scores of the day, another one mentioned President Roosevelt's speech to the Budget Committee, while some one else mentioned the elections in Maine. Although a long way from the mad rush of Manhattan, Detroit or Cincinnati, Salinas is only an instant from all or any of them. It is a meeting place for the secrets of two continents.

Known to some people as Santa Elena, which is the name of one of the fingers of land that helps to make the Half Moon Bay, Salinas has long been the relay station for the All America Cables that bind together all the cities and important towns of all the Americas. Here the messages between the continents, as well as the news that flashes from one to the other, pause for more power before they are shot on to their destination. Also it is next door to the Anglo-Ecuadorean oil fields that skirt the low-lying country along the coast and the Guayas River.

The moment we stepped down into the sand of the snowy beach, Spanish flowed in torrents. All talked at once—old and young, grandfathers and children. All because John D. had greeted them in his racy Castillian.

That reminds me that the only adverse comment I ever heard about his linguistic accomplishments was from a red-nosed Irishman in Chile, who said, "the only trouble with Mac-Gregor is that he speaks Spanish so much better than the rest of us the natives think we're particularly dull. Why, if he had been in Pizarro's shoes he would never have strangled the Inca in order to get hold of his kingdom. He would have charmed him into submission with the music of his Scottish tongue."

As I was saying, when John D. burst forth in Spanish it so thrilled the inhabitants of Salinas that they all but smothered us with welcome and hospitality, because so few *gringos* know more than a few halting words of the principal language of the Other Americas. As we started down the beach to the inn, which staggered and groaned under the name of "Salazar's International Hotel by the Sea," the entire community insisted upon sharing in the transport of our luggage and belongings. I was actually afraid they were going to open up the bags and distribute everything from collars to undies in order that every one might have something to carry.

Señor Salazar himself came out to welcome his distinguished friend, "Señor Juan," and to escort us to the specially reserved presidential suite, which turned out to be the second floor front room facing the sea, in which there were two iron beds and a tin washstand.

Presently dinner was served on the breeze-swept second-story porch, served between courses of beer. The food was somewhat incidental for reasons which I shall not mention. But with good beer, a tropical breeze, swishing surf and a low moon, food was not so vital. And then there were John D.'s stories, Scottish stories, stories of tropical adventures and, on this night, stories of Spanish gold.

"There, on the Punta Santa Elena," he said, "is where the rainbow ends for a lot of these people. The bag of gold was spilled right there on those rocks. It is a sort of Treasure Island, or it would be if it were an island instead of just a spit of land extending out into the sea. There are people around here who have grown gray in their search for fortunes on Santa Elena. And out there you may still find gold and silver if you search long enough. You may find them any time of the year. But March and October are the best times to look for them.

"You see," Mac went on, "for two hundred years and more Spanish galleons bucked the winds up and down this coast, taking Inca riches to Panamá and bringing back supplies from the motherland. It was the heyday of the Spanish reign in South America, the Arabian Nights period in New World adventure. Sometimes a consignment of money, doubloons, pieces of eight, came back to circulate among the colonial conquerors. One of those old galleons carrying such a cargo came to grief out there. A storm swept in from the west. The ship was washed against the Punta and broken into splinters. A fortune in coins was scattered over the rocks like the spray of the sea. They settled down into the cracks and crevices. Time and tide have covered them with the slime of the briny deep, so that it is difficult to see them.

"But twice a year, in March and October, when the equatorial tides come in and the Pacific rises over the rocks, they are lifted out of their old hiding places and washed to new positions. Then when the tides go out, the gold rush is on. Every living soul in Salinas, native and *gringo*, begins hunting for fortunes—'Pieces of Eight' as old as history in the Americas."

And as Mac spun out the tale the moon spread a silvery path across the lazy waters of the bay and out toward rocky Santa Elena. And just beyond the point I could see, silhouetted against the sky, a tiny Spanish galleon—floating along—even if it did turn out to be a fishing smack coming home from the catch.

Finally our bedtime stories were rudely interrupted by Señor Belalcazar, a descendant, he stoutly claims, of the founder of the Ecuadorean capital of Quito, and the city of Guyaquil, an itinerant merchant, purveyor of almost any product imaginable, whether made in Ecuador or East Orange, N. J., and himself no mean raconteur. Knowing that our plane would be leaving at daybreak in the morning, he waited upon us the night before. He had Spanish shawls and the inevitable Panamas—that is, *Sombreros de Jipijapa*—Indian rugs and wraps, chocolate bars and tropical fruits, and the dried skins of jaguars and boa constrictors. All these he spread out on the floor before us, and then proceeded to regale us with the quality and history of each.

He told us about the buxom *chola* woman who knitted the rug, but I was particularly interested in the señorita who made the shawl. In fact, when he got through describing her—her eyes, like glistening diamonds in limpid pools, her glossy hair, her

golden velvety complexion, her voice, her juicy lips of scarlet—
I bought the shawl, half believing I would find her hidden away
in its folds. And then the jaguar skin, the cloak of the beast
who slew the grandmother of a friend of the Señor. And, oh yes,
the boa constrictor's skin was the eloquent remains of the same
wriggling monster that swallowed the first born of the chief
of the headhunters.

If you are a tenderfoot in Salinas and South America, when
you encounter Señor Belalcazar the first time you buy many
things. You buy them for the figure he asks. If you have visited
the city once before you pay only twenty per cent of the quoted
price. But if it is your third call at Salinas you buy nothing.

However, the night passed. Next morning just as daylight
flickered up from behind the eastern Andes we crawled out of
our dreams, dreams of jaguars wrapped in Spanish shawls and
señoritas wrapped in boa constrictors—and rushed to the plane.
I used to tell John D. that in South America the laws of aero-
nautics must have been invented just before daybreak and that
they wouldn't start working after sun-up, because his pilots
never let the sun catch them on the ground.

On our trip from Salinas to Guayaquil, thirty-five miles up
the muddy swirling Guayas River from the sea, we flew across
the edge of the green billowy jungle and came out twenty
miles below the city. Then we followed the left bank in order
to see the alligators plunge off the shore into the water as the
plane roared over. Fat, ancient-looking reptiles who could
make a mess of succulent *gringo* meat any day in the week.
We weren't lucky enough to see any such sight this time, but
John D. told me that in the flood season, the season of its
heaviest rains, great hunks of the jungle flow down to the
Pacific, and that sometimes various members of the animal kingdom take a ride to the sea on them. He once knew of an unfortunate old jaguar who floated down on a log and passed
right out to salt-water eternity.

Ecuador

"Swim?" he said. "Of course he could swim. But a million years of instinct told him that it was all his life was worth to start for land. He didn't relish the thought of becoming a choice tidbit for some school of sharks."

II
Shanghai in Miniature

H<small>E HAD</small> many things planned for the trip down to Guayaquil. He was even going to invite a friend along. His own railroad passage, of course, was provided for. But the friend could
ride down in the box-car with the automobile. He could arrange
that easily. As chauffeur for the President of the Republic, he
would have to be very busy during the day, what with all the official calls, receptions and parades. But his activities would begin
when his Excellency retired for the night, and the nights are
long in the tropics. Besides, even if he did not sleep during the
trip, what of it? There would be plenty of time to sleep when
he got back to Quito.

The day came. The presidential automobile and the friend
securely stowed away, he hurried forward to the day coach,
and the train began its laborious journey from the top of the
world down to the sea. At Durán, which has recently been
renamed Eloy Alfaro and is the terminus of the railroad across
the river from Guayaquil, the friend was to jump out just as
the train was coming into the station so as not to be detected.
Imagine the chauffeur's surprise when he hurried to unload the
automobile to find the door of the car securely fastened and
sealed. And imagine his amazement when the door was opened
to find his friend lying dead on the floor.

In their effort to keep Guayaquil free of bubonic plague,

which at various times has ravaged the population, the Public Health Service, under the direction of the Pan-American Sanitary Bureau not only inspects every ship and person approaching it by sea, but all trains and travellers coming down from the interior as well. At Bucay on the Yaguachi River, at the foot of the Andes, all passenger cars are cleared, cleansed and disinfected and all box-cars fumigated and sealed airtight. Of course, every precaution is taken so that no one may be harmed. An officer opens the door of each car and shouts two or three times, "Any one here?" Then he deposits specially prepared hydrocyanic acid, slams the door, fastens and seals it.

The particular preparation of hydrocyanic acid suited to this type of fumigation is a German product called Zyklon put up in special cans, each can containing about an ounce of the poison mixed with Fuller's Earth. If the contents are shaken out on the floor of a freight car and the car sealed, within two hours it will have done its work and not a rodent, beetle, bug or insect will have survived. This was the procedure on the occasion when the president's chauffeur arranged for his unfortunate friend to travel contraband down to the coast. Naturally the two ignorant Indians from far-away Quito would hardly have known anything of such strange and scientific matters.

During his lifetime, and with remarkable success, the late General Gorgas, along with the famed Doctor Connor, the immortal Noguchi and others, gave of their wisdom and energies in the fight against the various tropical scourges that held sway in Ecuador's chief seaport. Through numbers of campaigns carried on over a period of years, yellow fever and smallpox were finally brought under control. So far as these two diseases were concerned, however, their problem was more or less a local one. When mosquito havens and other germ-nurturing hideaways were destroyed, ponds of stagnant water drained off and back alleys cleaned up, much of the fight was won. Through generous loans from foreign countries, as well as assistance from private foreign enterprises, a modern water system was put in, streets paved, hospitals built and a measure of hygienic precautions instituted in schools and business houses. These and other civic improvements contributed very materially to the success of the doctors' campaigns.

But bubonic plague was another matter. The plague may be brought in from distant ports of the world in many ways. Infected fleas may arrive on the backs of mice and rats, or they may arrive in cargo from far-off India, such as fiber bags, one of India's chief exports, transfer themselves to and bite the men who unload or handle it, thus starting an epidemic. However, by 1930 the plague too had apparently been banished from Guayaquil.

Unfortunately, in 1935 it reappeared. No clue to its arrival by steamer could be found, nor any evidence that it had lurked in any dark corner without the knowledge of the sanitary experts. Doctor John S. Long, that tireless apostle of public health in the Other Americas—a member of the United States Public Health Service and now in charge of all field work of the Pan-American Sanitary Bureau—and his associates began reconnoitering beyond the environs of Guayaquil. Eventually they found that the scourge which formerly arrived by sea was now stealthily descending from the mountains of the interior.

Curiously enough, during its heyday in Guayaquil it had travelled along the Guayaquil and Quito railroad all the way up to certain small towns around Riobamba. Once more they put the languid old town through the sanitary wringer, isolated and stamped out whatever germs there were. In the interior it still leads a desultory but threatening existence, and but for the relentless precautions taken at Bucay might any day descend upon the city once again.

Unfortunately the tenure of government at Quito has been so frequently interrupted in the past four years that no administration has been able to give its attention to anything but staying in power. During these periods of political chaos, resulting in disruption of the Health Service, there have been outbursts of smallpox, fever and plague. Under the circumstances, it is remarkable that the fatalities have been so few.

Known for a hundred years as the death hole of Pacific South America, home of the most venerable and virile germs in the realms of tropical scourges, ready to make merry on the helpless carcass of any native or stranger who ventured near, Guayaquil enjoys periods as a decent self-respecting community, when life is not imperilled and the citizen may go the even tenor of his way, but only when the health officers and experts are unhampered by ignorant politicians, given a free hand and supported by local and national government.

Nature herself battles against the city. The thermometer sizzles around ninety throughout the year. As the weather man puts it, "in the wet season a mean temperature of eighty-one, with the accent on mean." From January to March it rains and rains and rains, and the moisture is like vapor from a vat of boiling tar—sticky and clinging. Your clothes stick to you, your shoes mildew overnight, and in twenty-four hours turn blue with mould. Although the natives are immune to them, the outsider is all but asphyxiated by the simmering smells from the open markets, and even the best kept offices and houses give off dank odors.

The years as well as the climate have lain heavily upon Guayaquil. Every one of the four hundred and four years since old Sebastian de Belalcazar, one of Pizarro's immortal band of plunderers, planted the city on the muddy banks of the Guayas has left its mark and taken its greedy toll of life. The population of the spotless city of the dead on the side of the only hill in the vicinity, with its gleaming snow-white tombs and burial terraces like mail boxes in a post office, rivals the population of the city of the living. Although most of the old houses, even the ancient cathedral, are wooden structures, all fast decaying and giving way to concrete structures, they are giving way very slowly.

Señor Isaac Abaob has been five years constructing his new six-story Hotel Metropolitano. Its lower portions are already splotchy with age while the languid workmen tinker away on the tile swimming pool which is to grace the roof. Ordinary two-story structures, already under way a year and a half ago, are still unfinished. Time does not march on in Guayaquil. It crawls except when a fire breaks out or tropical blood pressure rises, both of which exhibitions occurred the last Sunday afternoon I was there.

First, I went to see the cock fights in a side-street enclosure. It was three o'clock. The sun beat mercilessly down as I left my easy chair in the cool arcade of the Grand Hotel. Scarcely a half dozen natives were in evidence, and they hugged the shady side of the street. But a party of Yankee tourists from Boston, typical of their kind in being persistent in their belief that sunshine at the Equator is no different from sunshine in Back Bay, hurried gaily down the middle of the main boulevard lest they be late for the bloody carnival of the Guayaquil Sabbath.

At a wicket in a board fence I put down a *sucre* and picked up my piece of brown paper which answered for a ticket, passed through the gate and into the yelling, smelly mob. I found a seat on the second tier of benches above the cock pit, by the side of a local steamship agent. Two stringy raw-boned old birds were pecking away at each other, already too tired to fight, but urged on by their handlers. Finally, the umpire ordered them taken away. The next pair, one a satiny black and the other a dull red, in the arms of handlers as alike as two coffee beans, would apparently present a different performance. The moment they were placed on the ground they had blood in their eyes and, as they were held by the tails awaiting the moment to be released, they clawed the ground and stretched their necks into feathery strings in an attempt to reach one another. The handlers glared at each other no less angrily, and when the word was given they leaped from the pit and watched with hawklike concern as the encounter proceeded.

It was a fifty-fifty fight for minutes. The black leaped over the red and the red over the black. Then the black lunged forward, slitting the comb of his adversary with his rapierlike gaff. But before he was on his feet the red plunged after him and tore a sheaf of feathers from his breast to the frantic joy of the spectators, and the venomous anxiety of his handler. Again the black leaped forward and missed, because the red swerved aside. After this the red carried the battle to the black. He made several sudden lunges and the black lay trembling on his side, blood streaming over his shiny sable feathers.

As the crowd yelled there was another encounter. The two handlers leaped into the ring and before friends could separate them one was on his knees, blood spurting from his face and arms, the result of a half dozen gashes from a knife which no one saw. The crowd which but a moment before had been shouting itself hoarse stood silent and amazed.

"It was a strange enmity," said the man at my side. "They were twin brothers. The owner of the vanquished black married the sweetheart of the owner of the victorious red. And now they are both avenged. The owner of the black has now wounded the owner of the red."

Whether the wounds proved fatal I do not know. No one had waited to see. For at that very moment sirens began blaring and bells began ringing and the spectators who had paid to enjoy a cock fight, but witnessed the sudden and gory climax of a feud between brothers, now rushed out to see a free-for-all fire. In fact, they rushed with such speed and abandon that they took with them some of the boards from the surrounding fence. Streets, which had been deserted a half hour before, were now alive with people of all ages and conditions of dress, for the *siesta* hour was still in progress when the alarm was given.

As in Panamá, a fire is equal to a dramatic operetta, only more so. The volunteer fire department of Guayaquil is the finest and best trained organization in town, maintained by 3000 volunteers. Interestingly enough, it was organized by Daddy Guizado of Panamá, and the *bomberos* wear the same blood-red shirts, white pants and patent leather boots. But in Guayaquil, when a building is in flames, to add to the spectacle the city band turns out and plays martial music to inspire the boys as they fight the flames.

How hundreds of these fellows had donned uniforms and rushed from all parts of the city to the scene of the conflagration so quickly is still a mystery. Before they brought the fire under control it had gutted a small jewelry store and a drug shop that occupied an ancient one-story structure. But when the flames died away and their battle was won, the multitude cheered to the echo, and to the strains of the national anthem.

Old Spanish customs persist in spite of a population in which there are not more than a dozen families of pure Spanish descent. The average native of Guayaquil, like the average native of nearly all the other cities from Panamá to northern Chile, is of varied and generous mixture, Indian and Spanish, Indian and African, with the Indian always predominant. The majority of the descendants of the old Conquistadores live in Quito, exclusively in the highlands.

Until the world depression (the one ranging from 1930 to more or less recent date) few of the leading families of the country, Spanish or otherwise, forsook the boulevards of Paris and other Latin cities of Europe "more than occasionally," as one Ecuadorean journalist put it, "except to collect and count the profits from their *haciendas*. But the universal problem of exchange which dealt Ecuador an overly hard blow, brought most of the expatriates back to the land of their bread and butter."

Victor Emilio Estrado, however, kept an eye and a finger on his prosperous and influential Banco La Previsora throughout the dark period; probably because he had, and still has, to compete with the growing Banco Italiano, which at the moment is financing much of the real-estate construction which in turn is being done by an Italian construction company. Likewise the lawyers who profit by and attempt to render legal protection to large foreign enterprises seldom wander far from Guayaquil and the capital. Among these is Doctor Alejandro Ponce Elizalde, who nurtured the banana industry in the Guayaquil regions, which, by the way, is among the very newest developments of the United Fruit Company. Then there is the polished and charming Doctor Eduardo Salazar, lawyer, adviser and friend to the American and Foreign Power Company, which supplies light and the noisiest street cars in the world, to the city of the late Belalcazar.

Perhaps the foremost figure of this group, however, is Doctor Carlos Arroyo del Rio. Two of his lucrative clients are the Vanderbilt South American Development Company, which owns gold and silver mines up in the interior near the towering volcano of Cotopaxi, and the Anglo-Ecuadorean Oil Company, whose wells are down near the Punta Santa Elena, and a half dozen other such companies—"guardian of the Guayaquil *gringos*," one politician has called him. But then why shouldn't a man with his picturesque name find prosperity? It is so expressive of the locale—"Arroyo del Rio"—little stream of the big river. Without the rivers and the industries and prosperity which they bring to Guayaquil, the dominant legal mind of the city would be completely lost. There would be no prosperity. In fact there would probably be no city. For the rivers are the *raison d'être* of Guayaquil.

The Pacific tides force their way in right up to the city's

door, even hard by its main street. But they must battle the muddy torrents that flow down into the Guayas on all sides, the surging melted snows from the central *cordillera*, the rushing torrents from the *colonche*, or coastal range, and the sprawling lazy rivers and creeks from the valleys in between.

If you take a launch and travel up one of these bilgy waterways, in the rainy season, it is not only easier to appreciate the poetry of William H. Hudson's *Green Mansions* but easier to understand how little Noah Webster knew about a jungle. Now and then there is a strip of grassy shore with clumps of low bushes so thick they look like balls of deep green wool, scattered over a lighter green carpet. Back of this, masses of vine-covered trees push their gangling heads upward in an attempt to escape the dark shadows below, shadows so forbidding that only the boldest adventurer bent on doing the impossible, so as to qualify as an exploring hero, or the author of a jungle thriller, would try to penetrate them. Occasionally shafts of sunshine break through the hovering clouds and fall like aerial searchlights on this verdant unknown, bringing out the myriad different shades of green. Here and there are palm-thatched huts which the lacustrine Indians, like the ancient dwellers on the shores of Venezuela's Lake Valencia, have built —huts that never seem to be inhabited. But there are good reasons why they are usually vacant. The builders are always in transit, either back in the wilds to gather the products of the jungle, or on their way down to Guayaquil. They travel by various methods, but all fluvial. If on a quick trip they travel by stream-lined *balsas*, those long, slim trough-like dug-outs, hollowed out of the trunk of a tall tapering *balsa* tree. If it is a leisurely trip they build a raft of *balsa* logs, shelter it with palm fronds and take the entire family along, cook, eat and live aboard for weeks at a time, after the fashion of the Chinese who live and die on their junks along the Yangtze.

The less primitive inhabitants of the towns along the rivers equip their *balsas* with a single sail, or build miniature sailboats and travel lazily with the indifferent breezes. Seaworthy sailboats are constructed at Guayaquil to ply between the cities and the towns and villages up and down the coasts. Nearly all the great *haciendas* of the coastal regions are on the tributaries of the Guayas, and their only means of transportation is by water. Day in and day out the river bank at Guayaquil is a solid mass of these quaint types of craft, making the old city a Shanghai in miniature.

Even the *Eloy Alfaro* will be anchored offshore. Formerly an old Vanderbilt yacht, reconditioned and mounted with guns, the *Eloy Alfaro* constitutes the Ecuadorean Navy. Two years ago the *Eloy Alfaro* went on a practice voyage down the west coast to Chile, a voyage which resulted in many experiences for the crew. Engine trouble developed en route. It grew so serious that the ship barely succeeded in reaching its destination. At the Chilean navy yards in Talcahuano, an attempt was made to overhaul it, but the attempt failed. Entirely new machinery had to be built and installed. Meantime the officers and crew entered the naval academy of Chile and spent a year in profitable study before the ship was able to sail back homeward.

But besides the sailboats, *balsas* and picturesque rafts, freighters and ocean liners from Japan, Germany, Italy, England and all Europe and North America are to be found in the river at Guayaquil. Warehouses and market places are crowded with traders from Texas to Turkey who come to buy *tagua* nuts, *cacao* beans and bananas, as well as *sombreros de Jipijapa* and *sombreros de Montecristi.*

Private individuals, merchants, doctors, lawyers, just plain laborers and all public officials reap their livelihood from the river, its industries and its shipping, and none so exclusively as the officials. When a passenger and cargo steamer arrives the parade of launches from the shore begins. First the boat doctor and his staff, then the boat captain and his aides. After these two departments have slowly, but courteously, discharged their missions, they hurry to the dining-room for a good breakfast, lunch or dinner, according to the time of the ship's arrival. Free meals must be furnished, that is if the company expects to enter the port thereafter without encountering innumerable little annoyances.

The next boarding parties are the immigration officials and the army from the department of Resguardo or customs service. Whether the ship is large or small, there will be the administrator of customs, two comandantes of customs, three captains of customs and four to twelve customs guards to see that the ship's shops do not sell so much as a pocket handkerchief while in port. There will also be five marine police and six immigration officials. "A nice way," an Ecuadorean business man suggested, "to solve the unemployment problem. It beats the New Deal."

Incidentally, all of these officials, assistants, helpers and hangers on, are expected to come out in their own launches, but, since the launches are usually out of order, due to broken or lost parts, or to having been run without oil and the like, the ship's agents must transport them. While I am attempting no economic treatise, a few examples of Ecuadorean public and private salaries and wages may be interesting. The government pays the various officials I have mentioned for eight hours' work, or for eight hours of more or less inactive service, but the steamship companies must pay for all overtime, which is never so little as "time and a half," either. No ship ever gets away without overtime. The stevedores and lighterage workers see to that, because they too get overtime pay.

The lighterage service in Guayaquil is a government monopoly. And while lighterage laborers receive from the government only four *sucres* a day for eight hours, a little more than twenty-five cents a day, the steamship companies must pay three *sucres* an hour for all overtime. Stevedoring at Guayaquil is

Ecuador

José Obando's private monopoly. It has been in his family for three generations, his father and his grandfather before him having controlled it. A stevedore laborer gets sixteen cents an hour for eight hours, and twenty-four cents per hour for overtime. A stevedore laborer is the highest paid laborer on the river. They are, of course, paid in *sucres*, the monetary unit of Ecuador. The *sucre*, at this writing, is worth about six and seven-eighths cents in United States currency.

Common laborers in Guayaquil, of the pick and shovel variety, average thirty-four cents a day, while a policeman receives, or is supposed to receive, according to whether the government is in office long enough for him to get his pay, six dollars and eighty-seven cents a month, barracks, board and two uniforms a year.

Since Ecuador lives primarily by exports and trades with all the world, competition is an all-important topic in Guayaquil. And, when any mention is made of commercial competition in South America, people in this country wish to know if the Fascists and Nazis aren't taking all the trade away from the United States.

For a time the Germans met with considerable success in their commerce with Ecuador. In fact Ecuador is one of the few countries of the continent where they have made any trade gain at the expense of the United States. But the Italians have made no headway whatever, although they have made several ingenious plays for trade.

Until a year ago members of the somewhat new and small Ecuadorean flying corps were under the instruction of private United States aviators. However, the government insisted the salaries were more than it could afford, so the Americans received six months' pay in advance, their contracts were cancelled and an Italian military and aviation mission at small, if any, salaries quickly moved in. The commercial angle is the fact that the Ecuadorean flyers were not only supposed to learn their profession from Italian instructors, but would fly in Italian and German planes.

Arrangements were immediately made to bring in several Italian planes, while the purchase of German planes had been made during the time the late Fritz Hammer, representative of the giant German aviation combine, Lufthansa, was negotiating for a flying concession. Late in 1937, just before he made a last fatal flight into a cloud-covered Andean mountain peak, Herr Hammer had succeeded in inducing President Alberto Enriquez, one of Ecuador's transitory dictators, to sign a contract giving the German company an exclusive right to transport all mail and passengers within the republic. But Herr Hammer's tragic death, and the subsequent fall of the dictator then in power, made it impossible for the Germans to carry on. In the meantime the Pan-American Grace Airways got a concession to fly its planes into the interior of the country.

For two years or more Hitler's propagandists waved the swastika. They tried, with some success, to keep their own countrymen faithful to the present regime in the fatherland. Some of the local Nazis were even outspoken about the number of German-Jewish refugees, most of them doctors and professional people, who had entered the republic. Their protests seem to have gotten nowhere, however, for the refugees are still going about the business of building up patronage and organizing their lives according to the conditions of their new country.

In 1937 and the first half of 1938 the Germans increased their trade considerably. They bought large portions of Ecuador's chief export, *cacao*. Most of the *cacao* beans which previously came to the United States went to Hamburg and Bremen in German ships to be distributed by German firms throughout Europe. Of the 250,000 bags of *cacao* beans shipped out in 1937, more than 150,000 of them were bought by German exporters.

Ecuador

As everywhere else, this trade was a matter of barter. The Ecuadoreans exchanged their raw materials for German manufactures or blocked marks. German commercial representatives worked hand in hand with the agents and operators of German ships. Nazi buyers refused to purchase any product unless it was shipped by a German steamer, and there were and still are plenty of German steamers. The port of Guayaquil averages óne German ship every day in the month. German vessels carried away from Ecuador in 1937 forty-three per cent of all of its exports. However, the American-owned Grace Line steamers alone, with an average of only two and three calls a week, took care of thirty-two per cent, while the British, Dutch, Italian and others divided the remaining twenty-five per cent among them.

Today there are anti-Nazi and anti-Fascist rumblings. The aviators are not only displeased with their Italian instructors, but particularly so with the Italian and German planes. They not only suspect but have reason to know that the Italian planes they bought were second-hand, that they were merely revamped, after having been used to bomb the natives of Ethiopia in the conquest of the little African nation, and then sent out to Ecuador. The *cacao* producers also are dissatisfied with the Nazi method of doing business. "We are anxious," one of them told me, "to sell our crops for exchange, dollars or pounds sterling, instead of bartering them away or having to take blocked German marks.

"You see," he went on, "for a time I could afford to take tractors, trucks, wire fencing, washing machines, and so on, in return for my crops. I really needed most of them. Likewise I could take a portion of the pay in aski-marks or German blocked exchange, because I could swap these marks to local German merchants and trading companies for other things I needed. But now I am overstocked with goods and materials and I can't use any more German marks.

"Yes," he concluded, "you can take goods for your crops and products until you are overstocked with goods. Then when you want to buy a Yankee automobile or radio, or take a trip to New York or London, you are up against it. The Yankee distributors and American and British steamship agents won't take depreciated German money for their automobiles or steamer tickets. So you see the Nazis finally run into difficulties and their trade cannot expand further."

III

Politics among the Volcanoes

E CUADOR?" asked a gorgeous creature at a high-toned New England college. "That is the land of the headhunters, isn't it? We had a famous British explorer here who told us all about the Ecuadoreans."

Well, there are some hardy headhunters in the wild regions of Ecuador, or hunters of hard heads, as the case may be. At least their fame has travelled to every corner of the United States. We read about them in story books. Not only "famous British explorers," but numbers of Yankee explorers, tell us about them. We see their handiwork in the museums, in the windows of curio shops and among the mementos of private collectors. By means of movie close-ups we may see for ourselves the very whites of their eyes. We are even permitted to watch them ply their deadly trade. As to the commercial aspects of the craft there can be little doubt if one half the specimens on display round and about are authentic.

In a New York movie house recently I sat glued to my seat for forty minutes, cold shivers playing leap-frog up and down my spine, as I watched a solemn old medicine man of the Jivaro tribe, oblivious to the grinding of the camera, which was all of three feet away from him, remove the bone, heat and otherwise take the swelling out of the head of some poor unfortunate.

[237]

New Roads to Riches

I am already on record to the effect that I know little if anything about the South American wilds, except for the broad expanses of it which I have seen from airplanes, or the close-ups from the decks of river steamers. My line is whatever of civilization, or semicivilization there may be, with an occasional foray into the not too remote sections. I know there are many wild, even undiscovered, regions in the vast hinterland of several of these countries, in which dwell countless primitive peoples. But it does seem that the Jivaro headhunters of Ecuador have been a bit overworked, especially by certain professional gentlemen.

When I read or listen to some of the stories about the ferocity of these peoples, and see them in the pictures, I am always left wondering: if these aborigines have such a yen for collecting the heads of palefaces, how do all the adventurers, camera men and story makers get back with their own heads? Of course it may be that the medicine men are choosy in their selection of specimens.

But now that dude ranches have made their advent in Ecuador, and three-weeks-all-expense-tourist-adventure-expeditions are being featured, with satisfaction and possibly a miniature head guaranteed, it may be that the old-fashioned game of headhunting will eventually give way to head counting. Wild men have little chance of preserving their ancient crafts or even of surviving against the onslaughts of professional travellers and tourists.

Ecuador and headhunting are by no means synonymous. Yet like Venezuela, Colombia and Panamá, the greater portion of it is primitive and wild. Its two and a half million people are concentrated along the coastal region in the valley of the Guayas and the narrow strip of high plateau country lying between the two ranges of the Andes. Even if all its claims to territory are granted, it is still the smallest of the six countries dealt with in this volume except Panamá. According to native claims the land area of the republic is 275,936 square miles,

Ecuador

excluding the Galapagos Islands some 600 miles off the coast, which are about 2400 square miles in area.

Ecuador proper is more than five times larger than New York State. It occupies a triangular slice of the continent, just where it bulges out into the Pacific, and right astride the Equator, from which it derives its name. One side extends some 500 miles along the ocean, while the other two follow eastward across the Andes in the direction of Putumayo River in the north and along the Marañon in the south, way over into the valley of the Amazon. If the none too modest claims of Perú be taken into consideration, Ecuador consists of a mere rectangular insert, bounded on the west by the Pacific, on the east by the eastern cordillera and on the north and south by Colombia and Perú respectively. Peruvian maps claim all territory from the eastern watershed of the Andes right up to the border of Colombia on the Putumayo.

While these century-old claims, except for occasional flare-ups, had been more or less dormant for years, the relationships between the two countries for the past two years have been punctuated by fiery periods of oratory, charges, counter charges, threats and several encounters between border guards and raiding parties. Throughout the years many attempts have been made to settle the difficulties by arbitration, all of which have bogged down in the quicksands of questionable old Spanish grants and other mildewed documents representing the double-dealing and horse-trading of early Spaniards all the way from the crown itself to the lowliest of the Conquistadores.

Finally in 1937 the dispute was submitted to a conference between commissions from the two countries, whose members were to arbitrate the question at Washington, under the benevolent eyes of Franklin D. Roosevelt. If they themselves could not find a solution, they were to agree to lay the matter on the lap of the squire of Hyde Park.

"The commissioners," says one caustic Washington observer,

"spent two years collecting their salaries and expense funds, sending their children to school and enjoying the easy society of Washington. They engaged in occasional desultory discussions and at frequent intervals issued statements. Finally, having attained less than no results, and without even agreeing to let Mr. Roosevelt do it, they gathered up their progenies and possessions and sailed for home."

Thus it can be seen that the last and, next to the recently composed Chaco dispute between Bolivia and Paraguay, the most difficult in a long list of territorial and border problems in South America, not only remains unsolved, but is no nearer a solution than it was fifty years ago. Besides, it may well continue to serve the purposes of politicians in both countries. That is, there is no better way of cooling the political hot waters at home than to find that the enemy is marching across the sacred frontier of the fatherland. And when the frontier in question consists of an imaginary line in the middle of an uninhabited desert, or unexplored jungle, convincing military incidents can always be arranged.

Anyway, I shall leave these undeveloped and still disputed regions where the diplomatic conferees have left them—divided between the uncharted portions of the map and in the hands of the two governments—and return to the regions where there is some contact with the outside world.

In this regard, insofar as its main cities and centers of civilization are concerned, Ecuador, although much less developed materially, socially and politically, is at the same time much more fortunate than Colombia. The capital city of Quito, like Bogotá, is located far in the interior, behind high mountainous walls, but 10,000 feet above the sea, 2000 feet higher than the Colombian capital. Yet, unlike the latter, it is on the main line of the Pan-American Grace Airways from Panamá to Lima, Santiago and Buenos Aires, exactly two days from Miami or Brownsville, Texas. It is even possible in the dry season to travel northeastward from Quito by bus to Bogotá and even on to Caracas, Venezuela, over the Bolívar Highway, the longest continuous stretch of passable, if crude, international highway on the continent.

But more important still, the Ecuadorean capital is directly connected by rail and convenient and comfortable trains with its chief seaport of Guayaquil. Among the five or six west to east, or ocean to Andes, railways in western South America the Guayaquil and Quito line is one of the most efficiently operated. Built under the direction of United States engineers and financed by North American stockholders, who have never received any too much return on their investment, it was, like all these railroads, a super-ingenious feat of engineering.

Ecuadoreans themselves, that is the government, actually began the project. From Durán, rails were laid across the lowlands fifty-seven miles to Bucay. But when they ran up against the solid walls of the Andes, help had to be called in. In 1897 General Eloy Alfaro put the project into the hands of Archer Harman of Virginia who succeeded in raising enough cash to make another start. Turning the actual work over to his brother John, he continued beating the bushes around Wall Street and other moneyed thoroughfares. The two kept at it against all the physical odds, handicaps and disasters in the category of tropical railway construction, until the track was so near to Quito that the work on the last lap was not interrupted by their death.

The eleven years that elapsed between the arrival of the Harmans and the completion of the road might easily be chalked up as an epic in railway history. In the rainy season tracks would go sliding down the mountain sides and be buried under thousands of tons of soupy mud, while trestles floated down the rivers and streams like so many match boxes. In spite of the doctors and sanitary precautions, fevers and smallpox raged continually. Workmen died by the scores every month. No railroad builders ever encountered such problems in the

Rocky Mountains of our own country. In places tracks had to be supported by retaining walls on the sides of perpendicular cliffs. There are four and a half per cent grades, and curves of almost thirty degrees. Barely eighty miles from Durán, and when they were little more than halfway up the heights, they had to deal with the Devil's Nose, "La Nariz del Diablo," a mountain of solid rock, like a colossal proboscis, pointing forbiddingly at any engineer who might attempt to scale it.

In other words, the Harmans found their path completely blocked. There was no valley either to the right or the left by which they could surround the impediment, so they made a daring frontal attack. They hacked and blasted away until they had zigzagged right up to the top. Today as the train climbs hundreds of feet in a few minutes, it oscillates back and forth until you feel a little as if you were attached to the pendulum of a clock. In a distance of forty-nine miles, in which the climb up this particular mountain is included, the rise is from something less than 1000 feet at Bucay to over 10,000 feet at Palmira, the top of the first range of the Andes.

At Riobamba, one of the four largest towns in the country, you may stand in the main plaza at 9000 feet and gaze upon famed and majestic Chimborazo which rears its shaggy white head 20,702 feet into the firmament. In fact at Riobamba you may feast your eyes on snow-capped peaks and volcanoes. There is Altar, 17,728 feet, Carihuairazo, 16,747 feet, and Tungurahua, 16,685 feet.

Farther on from Riobamba volcanoes spout and low subterranean rumblings are heard, rumblings which the superstitious if poetic natives call "the voices of the volcanoes, the gentle breathing of mother earth." At Urbina the railroad crosses the second Andean range at 11,841 feet and, after passing through the picturesque and delightful town of Ambato, you may stop at Latacunga for a session with another quartet of mountain peaks and volcanoes. Most notable is Cotopaxi, the twin sister of Chimborazo, 19,493 feet, the highest active volcano in the world, and one of the most magnificent. It has been called the Fujiyama of South America, or the Huziyama, as the Japanese now prefer to call their terrestrial protrusion. Every now and then her ever-boiling cauldron spills over, sprays fumes and lava, terrifying the poor Indians in the surrounding valley. Near by are Iliniza, 17,400 feet, Quilindaña, 16,134 feet and Quilotoa, 13,057 feet.

At Quito you are still in the presence of terrestrial exaltation. The city itself clings to the base of 15,925-foot Pichincha. In fact, scattered up and down this strip of the Andes are more than a dozen of these mighty peaks. Looking down from an airplane upon this region of Ecuador, "these white peaks," as one visitor describes them, "appear like giant chimney pots upon the roof of the world."

While the products of the tropical lowlands are today Ecuador's chief sources of wealth and income, this volcanic plateau of the interior possesses many potentialities. To some extent the gold resources are already being explored, some silver has been mined, while the government itself operates large sulphur mines. But there are deposits of copper, iron, lead and gold, discovered years ago, that have hardly been touched. Once upon the heights, all along the railroad agriculture becomes the chief activity of the natives. In one place corn, wheat and, of course, the ancient potato which originated, not in Ireland, but in the Andes, are cultivated. In another they specialize in fruit growing. For flavor, the apples, pears, plums, apricots and grapes of the Ambato community are not to be passed up lightly, while the milk, butter and cheese from the Latacunga district are of superior quality.

This central region, and especially Quito, constitutes an entirely different world from that around Guayaquil. It is hard to believe that the two cities are in the same country. Climatically, going from Guayaquil to Quito is like going from the mouth of the Congo to Geneva, Switzerland. When you go to Guayaquil, take a fan with you. When you go to Quito, do not forget your overcoat, no matter what month of the year it may be. In dry weather you won't need it in the daytime, when the direct rays of the equatorial sun fall upon the city, but the moment Old Sol hides his face behind the mountain peaks you will begin to shiver. Although only fifteen miles from the Equator, the thermometer at Quito hovers between fifty and seventy the year round. It is called "The land of perpetual spring," but personally I have never found a night in Quito that seemed exactly springlike.

From the standpoint of tradition and history, going from Guayaquil to Quito is more like going from Shanghai to Lhasa, Tibet, from an old river town with a stuffy climate and population of colorful nondescripts, foreign merchants, traders and shrewd business men, to a remote and ancient city of history and religious tradition.

Quito is said to be the oldest capital in all the Americas, north or south. At least it is the site of more capitals than any other place in all the hemisphere. Ages ago, probably ever since the red men or their progenitors first set foot on South America, there has been a town or capital city where it now stands. It got its name from the Quitus, one of the dozens of races that inhabited the spot. The Quitus were conquered by the Caras about 980 A.D., who in turn were conquered by the Incas, already the masters of a great empire farther south in which are now Perú and Bolivia. In turn it became the northern and later an independent capital of the Inca empire. Then came the Spaniards, after Pizarro had taken over the Incas and established himself in Perú. Belalcazar, already mentioned as the founder of Guayaquil, went first to the interior where he took over, plundered and set up a government in Quito in 1534.

Architecturally, Quito is still the most baroque of all the Spanish colonial cities, particularly as regards its churches and,

Ecuador

even more from Bogotá, it is still a center of religion and de-
voutness, a city of early morning bells and priests, as well
as politicians. Some of its churches rival in picturesqueness any
in Spain itself. The entire front of the church of the Company
of Jesus is extravagantly carved and decorated. The Church
of San Francisco is famed the world over for its rare panels
and paintings, its fabulously sculptured and decorated chancel,
the work of artists whose names are immortal in church history.
Then there are altars and sacristies covered with solid gold and
silver and studded with priceless precious stones.

Clustered around the public square or Plaza Major is the
enormous old cathedral filling one entire side, wherein repose
the remains of General Antonio José Sucre, another of Simón
Bolívar's companions in the fight to drive the Spaniards from
South America. Sucre not only gave the country its independence, but also the name of its money. Fronting the cathedral
is the imposing Bishop's Palace. On its right flank is the many-
columned government building and on its left the City Hall.
Elsewhere to be found are stately old buildings, such as the
old University and the National Theatre. To a Yankee familiar
with Washington the exterior of the National Theatre looks like
our Treasury Building.

There are narrow cobbled streets with the inevitable overhanging balconies leading up and down the steep hillsides.
At certain hours the streets are filled with the descendants of
the Quitus, Caras, the Incas and the others. All bear eloquent
evidences of a generous mixture of Spanish. When you look
into the faces of the lowly Quitaños, you realize that although
the Spaniard in the Andes could not and did not try very hard
to keep his own race pure, he left his unmistakable imprint
upon those he conquered. Spanish colonial architecture, brown-
skinned Indians and half-breeds seem to blend perfectly.

In Quito you meet for the first time the tiny camels of the
Andes, the llamas, the ancient beasts of burden of the Incas.

[245]

New Roads to Riches

Although not as numerous this far north, they serve the rural Indian well, bringing his fruits, vegetables and trinkets from distant villages to the markets of the capital. The Quito markets, like those of any other Andean city, are not only marvels for the variety of their products, but riots of color. Indians come not only from all the near-by villages, but from the eastern foothills of the Andes, on the edge of the Amazonian jungle, from north and south, and from toward the Pacific. Sometimes they travel for days, spending the night wherever it overtakes them, and making use of whatever shelter or housing facilities there are, no matter to whom they belong.

If you go to live in rural interior Ecuador, and you find a family of Indians corralling their llamas in your front yard and bedding themselves down on your front porch for the night without bothering to ask your permission, think nothing of it. They will harm nothing. At daybreak they will have vanished, leaving everything as they found it. It is just an ancient Ecuadorean custom, probably a tradition which has come down from the days of Inca rule, when shelters and inns were provided for travellers and their beasts at the end of every day's journey. It is another indication of the manner in which the Indian mingles traditions with the customs and civilization of the Spaniard.

Whether in his own village or abroad in the land, the Ecuadorean Indian has even combined the folk music of the conquerors with his own ancient rhythms, thus adding vigor and originality to both. When produced by a combination of his own primitive instruments, including the unique *rondador*, and one or two of the white man's, it will haunt you ever afterward. The *rondador* is a sort of harp made of reeds the shape of a lyre and played like a flute by blowing into the ends of the reeds. The sounds are not unlike the shrill tootings from a calliope.

Not long ago I went with an old friend, Pedro Cortez, on

Ecuador

horseback to a village in the valley below the city to witness an Indian *fiesta*. We arrived after nightfall. The sky was so clear and the moon so bright we could see for miles. In the distance the snow-crowned peaks and steaming volcanoes were silhouetted against the sky. As we drew near we could hear the chatter and laughter of the people and from a lonely hut across a trickling stream, the shrill flutelike music.

"Some aged minstrel," said Pedro, "serenading the moon, perhaps, his ancient goddess. Of course the Incas worshipped the sun, but don't forget that the sun god's wife was the daughter of the moon. Anyway, I often think some of these older people still worship their ancient gods."

When we reached the village the little square was packed with people who had already taken on enough rum to fill them with a hilarious happiness. Soon the musicians began playing a quaint, languid dance number.

"The *Yaravi*," Pedro explained, "an old serenade, probably one of the oldest of the folk tunes. That is also what the minstrel was playing up in the valley as we came along."

Finally they changed the tune and began playing a much faster rhythm, something reminiscent of the Venezuelan *Joropo*, yet very different. And then a few of the people began to dance.

"This," my friend explained, "is the *San Juan*, one of the gayest dance tunes. The *San Juan* is a very old rhythm too, probably hundreds of years old, but it is newer than the *Yaravi*. Like all this music, it is a combination of Indian rhythm and Spanish *fandango*."

Soon every one was dancing, old and young. In fact they danced for hours, growing more excited all the while. What the Yankee rhythm kings and their jitterburg satellites could do with some of this old folk music of the remote Andes!

Some years ago a brilliant young Italian, Hugo Gigante, went to Quito to teach in the National Conservatory. Fascinated by these old folk melodies and rhythms, he travelled by

New Roads to Riches

muleback from village to village throughout the surrounding country and copied down hundreds of them. Since then he has returned to Italy and has composed some splendid works based on this ancient music.

Except for his pilgrimage to the market place and his village *fiestas,* the lot of the Ecuadorean peasant Indian is prosaic and unpromising. His government does little or nothing for him. In fact, in four hundred years it has rendered him so little, and his only experiences with it have been so disappointing, not to say disastrous, that his dearest wish is merely to be left alone. It is not this peasant Indian who engages in revolution and political upsets in Ecuador. All such antics he leaves entirely to the half-breeds in the cities and larger towns. He is not interested in anybody's isms or ideologies, and, left to himself, he is a kindly, quiet and dignified human being, inheritor of great traditions.

Some sporadic efforts have been made to legislate for the benefit of those employed by industries and government, but even this legislation works successfully only in connection with large enterprises, particularly those controlled by foreigners.

But then, government in Ecuador has been and is so uncertain. With few exceptions, presidents, legislators and even dictators have not had the chance to do a great deal of constructive planning. In fact, the instability of government has been Ecuador's most serious handicap. In Quito, politics dominates everything. As a prominent Quito newspaperman says, "Politics in Ecuador is as volatile as its volcanoes."

General Eloy Alfaro, father of the present able and popular Ecuadorean Minister to Washington, although a dictator, attempted many improvements for his country. He backed and co-operated with the Harmans in building the railroad from Guayaquil, an accomplishment which alone distinguishes his memory. Yet he was overthrown and deported by another General, Leonidas Plaza Gutierrez. Later on, when General Alfaro

Rural Life Near Quito

Weaving the Sombrero de Jipijapa

returned to the country, Gutierrez had him jailed. While languishing in prison there was a supposedly popular and very suspicious uprising among the hoi polloi, during which the old man was taken out and burned alive.

Afterward came an Indian medical man, Doctor Isidro Ayora, one of the most honest and able, and probably the most succesful of recent presidents, in many ways a great man. Ayora gave first attention to the public health and social welfare. Under him education received a shot in the arm, about the only boost it has had lately. He was at least successful enough to stay in office until the pestiferous politicians and army officers, who in Quito are usually one and the same, became so annoying and unbearable that he voluntarily retired to private life.

Doctor Ayora was President and played host to President Hoover when the sage of Palo Alto, then President-elect, went swishing around the continent on a tour of good will in 1928. Today he goes about the business of running his private clinic, of administering to the sick and afflicted, loved and respected by all, while the professional politicians kick the government about like a badly deflated football.

Ecuador's political history is one of dictators and despotism, of fiery politics and revolutions. Yet no country has ever produced more ardent and brilliant opponents of such persons and conditions. Some of her poets and intellectuals have been giants in the fight for liberty, order and human rights. One of them towers above all the others. He was Juan Montalvo, one of the greatest, perhaps the greatest, writers South America has ever produced. From Quito he showered the southern continent with his wisdom and wit—wrote a life of George Washington and said that the man of Mount Vernon was greater than Napoleon, because his work lived after him while Napoleon's died with him.

He put up a ceaseless fight against dictatorship and oppression. No ruler was ever powerful enough to scare him or even awe him. He was an eternal enemy of all who mistreated, double-crossed or tried to short change their fellow men. As a matter of fact, one critic has called him the John Milton of Ecuador. Not that he wrote like Milton, but "because his writings, like *Paradise Lost,* are praised by all, but read by few." Another has called him the Cervantes of South America. Among his prose writings there is a character who even imitated the talkative and irresistible old Don Quixote. In a most excellent work on *The Literary History of Spanish America,* Doctor Alfred Coster has translated a conversation between the Montalvo character and a naïve old village padre.

It seemed that the South American version of Quixote was looking at the various treasures of a village church—its furniture, its communion pieces and especially its pictures. They were pictures depicting some of the miracles performed by the patron saint of the community. Quixote was much interested in the one which represented a terrible shipwreck.

The good padre quickly explained, "This happened in the Bay of Biscay, my son. All the passengers were saved except those who were drowned."

"All saved except those—ah ha, I see. Then they were all saved, weren't they, Father?"

"Oh, no, my son, not a third of them were saved."

"Well, then, tell me where are those who perished?"

"Wherever the Lord may have put them, my son. You see, the artist painted only those for whom the miracle worked."

Montalvo was not only a great writer, but he possessed brains and backbone in equal proportions, a man who lived fearlessly and died fearlessly. He was very ill. It was necessary for him to undergo a severe operation. The doctor arrived and made ready for the ordeal. Montalvo insisted upon observing every step in the operation. He said, "I have always been conscious of every one of my acts and experiences and I propose to be conscious of this one."

Ecuador

He never recovered from the shock. The Grim Reaper soon came to gather him to his fathers, but the old boy must have saluted and stood in reverent admiration for a spell; because in his last hours, Montalvo made his friends dress him up in his Sunday best and prop him up in an armchair. He had them bring flowers and place them around the room, and as he sat and waited for death to come, he said to those about him, "Whenever we are going to perform a solemn act, or when we expect to meet a person of consequence, we dress in our best. Well—no act is so important as quitting this life. So when death comes, we ought to receive her as we would receive a beautiful lady—gallantly and with great dignity."

If here wasn't a man, then John Paul Jones was a water nymph. To have produced such a man is alone enough to have distinguished the whole history of Ecuador. And when I am inclined to become overly critical of South American public men—generals, dictators and politicians—I generally pull myself together and contemplate the Montalvos.

Such men you can find not only in history, but even in the flesh, all over these Other Americas. Call them temperamental, sentimental Latins, or what you will, but courage is their middle name. Danger or disaster doesn't make their knees tremble. They are not equipped with chicken livers or cotton spines. That is why I have faith in the future of all of these countries, even in Ecuador, in spite of its politicians.

PERÚ

I
Ghosts in the Canefields

Perú is the California of South America, geographically at least, only it is 1400 miles long and 700 miles wide, nearly three and a third times the area of our great western state. Easterners may more readily appreciate its extent when they find that it is almost nine times the size of Georgia, the largest state east of the Mississippi. Looking at the maps of South America and the United States, with Lower California added, Perú is similar in shape to California, a long, curving, mountainous country occupying the bulge of the continent.

Its position in western South America is much the same as that of California in this country. The two northwestern countries of Ecuador and Colombia lying above Perú correspond to the states of Oregon and Washington, while the long, slim shoestring republic of Chile to the south resembles the narrow, tapering Mexican peninsula that joins onto southern California. The great difference is the fact that California's eastern border gets all tangled up in the Rockies, while Perú sprawls clear across the Andes and far out into the lowlands of Amazonia. While California's Sacramento and other rivers flow westward into the Pacific, Perú's three mighty rivers—the Marañon, the Huallaga and the Ucayali—flow north and eastward into the Amazon, which also rises in Perú.

Historically Perú is the Egypt of the southern continent,

a land where empires had risen and fallen a thousand years before Columbus started east by sailing west, where the old Spanish conquerors themselves found cities of fabulous wealth, temples whose walls were splashed with gold and studded with precious stones, palaces where pomp and splendor had reigned for centuries when the Alhambra still smelled of plaster and varnish. The remains of its ancient temples stand calmly in the presence of such brazen modernism as sugar mills, cotton factories, copper mines and smelters, and oil wells. There is a new building for every ancient ruin, a modern industry for every old one, and even nature offers a surprise on every hand.

Just a few hours from Ecuador's chief seaport, down the muddy Guayas, and along a palm-fringed coast with a lazy surf lapping the shore, you come to the end of the jungle and the beginning of the desert. On the Pacific slopes of South America vegetation and tropics are not synonymous. As far as the northern hump of Perú the billowy green jungles stretch westward until they roll up like giant green breakers against the mighty mountains. Then suddenly the scene changes.

Near the frontier, if you go by air, the pilot tilts the stick and the plane rises suddenly from the water's edge and soars inland. Eastward are the gleaming white peaks of the Andean cordillera. Beneath are seared crumbling hills and gullies and ahead the misty brown of the desert coastal region which extends not only the length of Perú, but for more than two thousand five hundred miles clear down to the central valleys of Chile.

The change is so sudden and definite it looks as if a green living map of Ecuador had been neatly pasted on to a dead brownish map of Perú. This sudden change in topography is due to the blighting ocean current that sweeps up from Little America, and named for its discoverer, that roving old German scientist who gave South America so much geography and cli-

matology to think about, Baron von Humboldt. The cold of
the current works havoc with the clouds, driving them back
against the mountains where their moisture turns to snow, so
that there is practically no rainfall along the coast.

The scientists explain this peculiar phenomenon of nature
in this way: the warm Japanese current flows down the coast of
North America, Mexico, Central America and along the shores
of Colombia and Ecuador and then swings out into the Pacific.
Consequently the coastal regions of Colombia and Ecuador are
cursed instead of blessed with rainfall. As the Humboldt current travels northward it is constantly advancing into a warmer
climate so that "there are no cooling air currents off shore to
condense the vapor and no electrical disturbances to shake it to
earth in the form of rainfall."

Once in every five or six years nature slips a cog and it
rains and deluges thousands of square miles, during which many
people in the Peruvian northland watch their little adobe
houses melt and flow down the valleys and gullies to the sea.
Afterward plants of every conceivable kind pop up over the
face of the earth, only to wilt and die under the pounding rays
of the tropical sun when the clouds have passed away.

When the Japanese and the Humboldt currents do go to
war, and the former pushes farther south instead of turning
westward according to habit, and the latter advances north, a
marine catastrophe results. All the fish and most of the other
living creatures of the deep become the victims. Those accustomed to warm waters freeze to death when pushed into the
cold current and those native to the cold suffocate when forced
into warm waters. Persons who have observed this disastrous
phenomenon have seen the waters covered with the carcasses
of all manner of sea life.

The dusty northern point of Perú where the city of Talara
now stands has been a sort of entrance to the country ever
since Pizarro landed near by and began his famous march south-

ward into the empire of the Incas. More recently it has been a landing place for many notables. On one of his spectacular tours abroad a few years ago, his then Royal Highness, the Prince of Wales, Duke of Cornwall, Baron of Renfrew, and now the plain Duke of Windsor, left his ship at Talara and continued his journey southward by air. While Pizarro was looking for gold, the Prince was looking for oil. Talara is an oil town, the headquarters of fields and refineries, part of which are owned or controlled by various of Britain's scattered but faithful nationals.

One of the Talara fields is so old that even before the Spaniards the Incas dug holes and dipped the oil up in buckets and jugs. What they did with it is not known, since automobiles had not yet come to toot their horns in the dead of night, and nobody had invented a gasoline engine with which to turn the wheels of industry. The early Spaniards knew all but did nothing about these riches. They were too busy looking for the wealth which others had already gathered.

In the records of his travels published in 1580, one old Padre, José Acosta, tells of sailing along this stretch of the Pacific coast and hearing the pilot of the ship say that "Sometimes far out to sea, out of sight of land, I know by the odor of the bitumen where I am with as much certainty as if I could see land, so strong is the odor given off." In any case, oil now flows up out of some of these same old pits. In sinking several of the wells drillers and engineers have found the remains of old walls, numerous trinkets and even cannon used by the Castilian conquerors.

Perú possesses more soil resources than any of the Andean countries except Colombia and Venezuela. At least they have been more extensively developed. They lie in a strip of coastal territory stretching from the Ecuadorean border 280 miles south and some 18 to 55 miles inland, an area producing annually some 17,500,000 barrels of crude oil. The largest concession is that of the International Petroleum Company, Ltd., a Canadian corporation, made up of many and varied interests, with three separate fields and over 1700 wells in the Talara district. The Lobitos field, to the north of this concession, founded by an enterprising Scotch flour-mill owner, Alexander Milne, has a thousand wells in production. Still farther north the smaller Zorritos field, with some forty-five wells in operation, was founded by Faustino G. Piaggio, an old Italian settler in Perú, and is still operated by his sons and grandsons.

Today the government itself is exploring in all of these regions, and it is rumored that no more concessions will be granted to foreigners or even private individuals. Meantime, besides being on the outlook for oil of its own, the government does well for itself out of the income of the private companies. It collects various income and local taxes and an export tax of seven shillings sterling, about a dollar and seventy-five cents, on every metric ton shipped out of the country. The International Petroleum Company alone supplied nine and one-quarter per cent of the entire national income in 1937, and was the principal source of all the export taxes collected by the nation.

Needless to say the foreign companies not only pay comparatively high wages, about the highest wages in the country, but provide workmen with all the modern and up-to-date living conditions. For the 23,000 men, women and children under its jurisdiction, the International Petroleum Company, following the practice of the oil companies in Venezuela and Colombia, has provided good housing, schools, churches, recreation facilities and hospitals. One of the best equipped hospitals in all Perú, and perhaps the finest and most powerful X-ray installation in western South America, is to be found on the International Petroleum properties at Talara. I know a man who went all the way from New York for a spinal operation in this hospital; not only because the facilities and doctors were equal to any he could find in this country, but the dry, even climate, like that of Tucson, Arizona, would be a great aid to rapid recovery.

A little south of Talara and its oil field is the port of Paita in the valley of the Chira, and also the first of the oldest Spanish towns, Piura, founded on the spot where Pizarro camped on his way south. Then another hop, skip and landing, and you cross the Desierto de Sechura, the Sahara of northern Perú, and stop for a visit in the valley of Chancay in the department of Lambayeque, whose capital city of Chiclayo is the northern headquarters for the Peruvian flying corps. Since the flare-up over the Peruvian-Ecuadorean border question, Chiclayo has been an unusually busy place, with army planes in the air morning and afternoon.

About halfway between Chiclayo and Trujillo, but back up on the Andean plateau from the coast town of Pacasmayo, is the old city which was the scene of the most famed of all Pizarro's exploits, Cajamarca, where he captured the Inca Atahualpa and where the Spanish power in Peru began. This historic town is of little importance today and, except by air, is very much off the beaten track. Surrounded by a peaceful countryside of small farms, its principal distinctions are its old churches, one with a fabulously carved façade, and the house on the public square containing the room in which the Inca was imprisoned and which he promised to fill with gold in return for his freedom.

Travel north and south in the coastal region of Perú is a matter of jumping from valley to valley. Life and civilization exist only where the icy rivers flow down from the mountains to the sea, making possible irrigation in the fanlike flatlands at their mouths. From the air the country resembles a crumpled piece of brown paper with widely separated emerald streaks and splotches along the edge. Each valley is a little world by itself, devoted to its own individual industries. In the Chira valley around Piura it is cotton and in the Chancay and the Chicama, the two largest regions under cultivation in the north, it is sugar cane. More than half of the 350,000 tons of sugar produced in the republic every year comes from the Chicama valley alone.

Strung along the coast in this section are some of the largest of those tiny islands on which are located the world's oldest fertilizer factories for which Perú was so famed in the middle eighteen hundreds. It is on these islands that the millions of Guano birds, the principal species of which are the alcatraz, or Peruvian pelican, the piquero, and the cormorant, come to rest while their digestive organs convert all the fish they have devoured into the most potent of guanos. Incidentally, no other living thing seems to possess such an appetite. One scientist familiar with these smelly creatures estimates that a colony of 6,000,000 birds consumes approximately 1000 tons of fish a day. Anyway, for half a century their droppings constituted one of the country's most valuable exports, and it is still a source of considerable revenue.

The most extensive of the northern valleys is the Chicama. The near-by city of Trujillo, another town established and named by the old conqueror himself in honor of his own home town of Trujillo in Estremadura and now the capital of the province or department of La Libertad, is the metropolis of the north. Trujillo was not only one of the first cities of Spanish Perú, but the first town to rise against the King and all of his works, or shall I say all his plunderers, in the struggle for independence nearly three hundred years later. It is a city of halfbreeds and a few old Spanish aristocrats. Among the latter, blue-blood family traditions and the tenure of residence and occupation are still important matters.

You will see striking contrasts between the old and new in the main plaza. There is an old church with its inevitable golden altar, numerous old houses with some of the finest of all

New Roads to Riches

Moorish balconies, and in the center an outlandish statue, a modernistic monstrosity, a giant woolly-headed figure of brownish stone in keeping with the prevailing landscape, holding aloft a torch. I should say it is a cross between the Statue of Liberty and Paul Manship's famed fountain figure in New York's Rockefeller Plaza.

The long Calle Francisco Pizarro, which stretches eastward from the plaza until it loses itself in the dusty countryside, is lined with stores, shops, clubs, hotels and the uninhabited-looking old university. On this street are also many of the old Spanish colonial residences, the intimate life of whose *patios* are plainly visible to all passersby. But just as you begin to feel that Trujillo is a typically Peruvian-Indian-Spanish town, you run onto a statue in front of the city hall erected in memory of Captain O'Donovan, who commanded the town's own regiment in the war with Chile in 1880. After that the signs bearing the names of lawyers and doctors, such as Fernando Jacobs, Ricardo O'Sullivan and Togo Yamatoya and others, become quite significant. There are English and German trading companies, Chinese grocery stores, Japanese garages and auto accessory stores, one of the largest of which carries Yankee-made tires and tubes exclusively.

The Japanese and the Chinese are also in the barbering business. Why members of these two races go in so strongly for shaving and hair-trimming in Latin America I have not been able to learn. Perhaps the trade serves as a training school in which they may learn how to trim one another the more successfully. But the Oriental barber shops cannot compete with the time-honored tonsorial parlor of Señor Velasquez, who has been supplying haircuts and odoriferous tonics to the gentlemen of the old families for half a century. Last year the city fathers, on behalf of the male members of the upper classes, presented the Señor with a gold medal "in appreciation of his fifty years' service to the community."

Perú

In spite of its conservatism, its traditions and attachment to the past, its respect for old families, old tradesmen and old barbers, Trujillo is a hotbed of *Aprismo*, the radical movement led by the native Lenin—Victor Haya de la Torre—a movement which Peruvian conservatives term communism. In 1932 during a political upheaval in Lima there was an outbreak in this old town that rivalled in intensity at least the famous slaughter in Moscow's Red Square in 1917. Apristas, or radicals, and perhaps not a few men with age-old grievances, walked the streets shooting and killing wholesale. Hundreds of leading citizens lost their lives before a military dictatorship got itself established throughout the country. When it did, and in keeping with the best traditions of dictatorships, order was quickly restored after the murderous rioters had been corralled. In the end the army evened up matters very neatly by marching the culprits out to the old city of Chan Chan and leaving their bullet-riddled remains among its dusty ruins.

Incidentally, Chan Chan is the only reason any one should tarry long in Trujillo itself. Compared to those of Chan Chan, Trujillo's claims to fame are insignificant and inconsequential. This ancient capital of the Chimus, a race that flourished centuries before white men arrived in the New World, may not be much to look at, but it is something worth lingering over. Chan Chan's ascendancy is said to have lasted from about 900 to 1300 A.D. Its principal remains lie near the Pacific and only a few miles north from Trujillo's central plaza. It was one of the great cities of New World antiquity, a city of great artistry and industrial advancement, as well as a city of tremendous proportions and magnificence.

Fly above it and it looks as if it had been knocked down only yesterday. There are the long narrow streets, the outline of the parks and plazas, the remains of its palaces and the great walls which surrounded them. Its size and age are attested by the cemeteries which begin on the outskirts and reach right down to the ocean shores a mile away. The huge pile of debris which was the central temple still rose fifty yards above the surroundings before 1925, when one of the infrequent and historic deluges flattened it out. From the cemetery gorgeous pottery and other ceramic ware, carved stone and golden jewelry of amazing pattern and beauty, have been dug up only recently.

Chan Chan had already reached its decline and been conquered by the Incas long before the arrival of Pizarro. Religion, it seems, was one of the causes for rivalry between the Incas and the Chimus. The Incas worshipped the sun, while the Chimus worshipped the moon. This is as it should have been, of course. The home of the Incas was high in the Andes, where the frosty night winds chilled them to the bone. Why shouldn't they have loved the sunshine? Every morning it came to thaw them out, warm their blood and make them feel good. But the Chimus lived along the lowlands on the coast where the hot tropical sun beat mercilessly down upon them by day. They hated the days and loved the nights. They had no use for the sun. Therefore they worshipped the moon, goddess of the night time.

The Incas were of an uplifting turn of mind. You will recall they sent missionaries as far north as the Sabana of Bogota to convert the Chibchas. Like nearly every race in history whose civilization ever progressed very far beyond the cave, they could not let other people live in their own way. However, they failed at first to convince the Chimus of the error of their faith. So they sent them an ultimatum demanding that ·they come up and worship the sun. The Chimus naturally objected, and their reply was cloaked in matchless logic. "No," they said, according to one commentator, "we prefer the moon to the sun. The moon does not make us perspire in the day time. Besides it comes out at night when light is really needed."

There were many cities in the Chimu Empire, which extended all the way from the Tumbes valley next to the Ecuadorean frontier almost to Lima in the south, most of which yielded

tremendous riches to the white conquerors. Fortunately they
did not find all of them. They left a few for modern archæologists to discover and study. In December, 1937, in the Illimo
district of the Lambayeque department, one of the greatest
finds since the Spanish conquest took place. There was a 17-inch,
18-carat gold statue of a chief or god, exquisitely carved and
decorated with turquoise and mounted on a symbolic half-moon
knife. Along with the elaborate statue there was a solid gold
mask, numerous carved hair ornaments and enormous gold
drinking goblets encrusted with turquoise. These priceless pieces
are now locked in the vaults of the treasury at Lima.

But one of the most interesting of such discoveries came
from the cemeteries of Chan Chan and is now on display in the
private museum of Don Rafael Larco Herrera at his great
sugar estate, Hacienda Chiclin, in the Chicama valley, twenty-
five miles above Trujillo. One moonlight night two years ago
a *cholo huaquero*, or half-breed grave robber, who was grabbling
among the burial places of the ancients in the Chan Chan cemetery, came upon a piece of metal. Carefully he removed the
hard dry earth around it and lifted it out. It was a king's crown
two feet high made of solid beaten gold. Searching further he
found a golden staff, carved epaulets, or shoulder pieces, and
a large carved breastplate. By grapevine the news reached Señor
Larco, who immediately made contact with the discoverer just
as he was about to melt them down so that they might be sold
without arousing suspicion. Peruvian law forbids any grave digging, even by archæologists, without special permission. Fortunately Señor Larco was able to purchase the entire outfit and
save it for posterity.

During my last trip to Trujillo I visited Chiclin for the express purpose of seeing this magnificent treasure from the
ruins of the Chimu metropolis. Foreigners who explore and
write about Perú's ancient civilizations always gravitate to the
Cuzco district, to Machu Picchu and the other Inca ruins of the

southern Andes. Our own museums are full of their remains and wares and many books have been written about them. To me, however, these ancient regions of the north, scenes of the cities of great peoples older than the Incas, are just as important. Chan Chan, its ruins, its *huacos* and the crown of gold are equally fascinating and far more mysterious.

Since the Incas were still in their ascendency when the Spaniards arrived, there are few secrets about their life and works. Their cities and their palaces were still standing. Yet little if anything is actually known about the Chimus except what is surmised from their marvellous ceramic ware and statuary. The Larcos themselves, students and enthusiasts on the subject, will admit as much. With a museum stocked from floor to ceiling with the pottery and trinkets of the Chimus and the Mochicas who preceded them, they revel in research and speculation, with little certainty that they are on the right track.

Not even Borglum's sculptured heads of North American notables are so eloquent of character and personality as the *huacos* portraying heads of men, women, kings, soldiers, as well as of all manner of animal life, which have been dug up from the burial grounds of these ancient races. They worked in metals of all kinds from gold to copper, but none of it is so artistic as their ceramics, or sculptured photographs.

These *huacos* doubtless tell in symbols the story of the entire civilization, if, of course, they could only be read accurately. So far no Rosetta stone has been found, no key to the symbols. Each piece seems to express the individualism of the person whose likeness it is, his joys and sorrows, his longings and ambitions, while the symbols are supposed to describe the habits, customs, industry, the food he ate, how it was prepared, his trials, tribulations, his misfortunes, the plague or disease against which he struggled. In the back room of the Larco museum are thousands of *huacos* picturing the sad ex-

Perú

periences of people suffering from social diseases, including lifelike representations of all the sexual perversions and their consequences.

It seems that the finest of all the art work, the statuary, the *huacos*, were not for the use or pleasure of the living, but for the dead. The master artist modelled and painted only for those who had passed on. In life, except for the nobility and priests, only crude things were used. Sacrifices were made in this life so that in the life to come there would be ease and plenty. Conquering Christians should have tried to teach these people, or their descendants, about the Hereafter!

A visit to ·Chiclin makes a trip to northern Perú a memorable experience. If I were a Peruvian and I were looking for the ideal in romantic interest as well as material·and social activity, it is here that I would find it. Besides the museum full of priceless historic treasures, the surrounding countryside is hoary with traditions reaching all the way back into the dim mysterious past. Yet there are endless square miles of fertile fields full of perpetually maturing sugar cane, vast orchards and flower gardens. If the problems of crops, cane mills and modern financial responsibilities became too pressing, I could steal into the museum and roll back the centuries. If, at night, sleep became impossible I could stroll out through the canefields and commune with the ghosts of ancient artists, kings and empire builders.

The plantation is an institution. Besides its sugar industry and other crops, hog raising is carried on on a large scale and in a most scientific manner near by. Its hundreds of seemingly contented and happy workmen, who share all the privileges and responsibilities of the place, are housed in picturesque, but modernly equipped colonial structures. There is a hospital, movie theatre, school and church. Organized on its present scale by Don Rafael Larco Herrera, who has now retired to his library and his newspaper, *La Cronica*, in Lima, the Señores

Larco Hoyle, his three sons, all graduates of our own Cornell University, now operate the place.

If the sons seem to bear a slightly different name from that of their father, it is merely an old Spanish custom. In Anglo-Saxon countries, which boast of equal rights to the female sex, when a woman marries her own name sinks into oblivion. Her sons are known only by the father's name. In Spanish countries the son proudly embraces the mother's name as well. Since Don Rafael Larco's mother was a Herrera, the founder of Chiclin became known as Larco Herrera. His wife having been a member of the good Scotch family of Hoyle, his three sons in turn took the name of Larco Hoyle.

And what a diversified yet co-operative combination they are. Young Rafael, the oldest and general manager of the plantation, is the archæologist of the trio, following in the footsteps of his father. Quite logically Constante, whose avocation is painting and natural history, is the manager of all field activities, while Javiar, the youngest, a champion athlete, specializing in pugilism and fencing, directs all the welfare activities of the place. In true Yankee fashion he leads the employees in organized sport.

The Chiclin football team plays the teams of other plantations in the valley. An Indian employee who grew up from childhood on the plantation recently became a national star. Chiclin's champion boxers, pole vaulters and javelin throwers often go down to Lima to participate in national tournaments. They are even encouraged to preserve their ancient aboriginal dances and to revere them. When sightseers come to Chiclin the experts turn out in fancy costume and perform on the lawn. In addition to the aboriginal music and dances, they perform the *Yaravi*, and *Marinera* of post-Spanish days.

The comradeship of these three brothers is the apotheosis of old Spanish family tradition. Among them are no rivalries or pulling in opposite directions. If the father is present all three defer to him with the humility of lowly subjects to a king. In the absence of the father, Rafael becomes the head of the family insofar as the other two are concerned. To him they pay complete homage, defer to his every suggestion and his judgment is always final and unquestioned. They anticipate his every wish or desire. If seated in the living-room with visitors in the evening, you often hear one of them say, "Rafael, may I get you a cigarette?" Or if he offers a guest a glass of brandy, one of them immediately speaks up, "I will get it, Rafael." Ask either one of them anything about archæology, or the policy of the plantation, even if it is only a trivial matter, and he will give you "my brother's opinion," not his own. Meantime each is meticulous in his respect for the other and, although none of them is married, individual family responsibilities would not alter their devotion and deference to one another in the slightest.

Maybe this is why great estates in these countries so often pass unimpaired from generation to generation. Not only has Chiclin followed the general pattern and policy of the elder Larco, but it is even improving and expanding under the management of the sons. The father was such a liberal in his attitude toward employees and in his progressive management, he was called a radical by conservative friends and acquaintances in Lima. And the sons do not allow the paternal flag to droop in the slightest. The result has been that during the radical uprising of 1932, when there were riots on the other plantations in the Chicama valley, every employee from the foreman down to stable boy defied any agitator even to approach the premises, much less attempt to enter. In a region of great estates and plantations, Chiclin was the only community where no workman showed any sympathy whatsoever with the extremist cause.

It is no easy matter to maintain and administer a great plantation anywhere in the Peruvian northland. The chief problem is neither labor nor production, nor even the advantageous sale of crops, although all these call for more than ordinary skill and ingenuity in these times. Ordinary or common labor is cheap enough. The average on most plantations is from eighty centavos to one and one-half soles (or thirty-five to seventy-one cents in United States equivalent), a pound of rice and a pound of meat for a day's work. In addition the laborer gets living quarters and medical attention. At Chiclin, of course, he is especially favored.

On a sugar estate as well as any other, the chief problem, the great desideratum is water. One-third of the 1,120,000 acres of land in cultivation in Perú lies in these narrow coastal valleys. Every drop of water comes from the melting snows and ices of the Andean cordillera. There is a dam for every river and trickling stream and the quantity of water is never the same any two months or even any two days in the year. Without water land is valueless, and its value is determined entirely by the water rights. These rights in every valley go with the land in proportion to the acreage already cultivated and the percentage of the water varies every day. A farmer's wealth consists not only of his land, houses, and other visible properties, but also of whatever water he may receive. The roads to his riches are the irrigation ditches, streams and rivers that reach up into the snow fields.

Irrigation is a government monopoly administered by a commission in every valley. No farmer or plantation owner knows in advance how much water he will receive. In fact, the supply varies so from day to day that the commission gauges the water in the river four times in every twenty-four hours and apportions the water according to that particular day's supply. Every farmer has a main canal connecting his plantation with the river. His portion of water is turned into his canal, then he distributes it over his plantation as he sees fit.

As one plantation owner puts it, "Since water is the will of God, coming down from the mountains only in proportion as the sunshine melts the snows and ices, farming in Perú becomes a miracle."

This means that expansion of cultivation under present conditions is practically impossible. It is said there is less land in cultivation in northern Perú today than there was before the coming of the Spaniards; probably because the Indians grew mostly corn and beans, which required much less water than the present prevailing crops of cotton and sugar cane. Then, too, the method of irrigation, being the very same bequeathed from pre-Spanish times, has not been improved upon.

The farmer pays for his water by the month in cash to the government. Nor is there any standard rate for water either. Since the supply varies in the different valleys, the rates also vary. Water is portioned out on the Chicama *haciendas* in *riegos,* which is the standard measure and which denotes the fall of so much water per second in the gauge. The ordinary proportion is one *riego* of water for fifty *fanegadas,* a *fanegada* being about seven acres of land. To the owners of plantations of the valleys producing principally sugar cane, special concessions are now being made by the government on account of the low prices of sugar.

All these rules, regulations and prices apply only to large *haciendas.* Peasant farmers, or those of the *comunidades,* who still live under the old Inca community or, as some say, communistic system, receive water under entirely different rules and regulations, and far less advantageously, it may be said. A certain amount of water is apportioned to each community, and then the individuals must take it by turns. One farmer irrigates today, another tomorrow, and so on.

The Chicama valley is perhaps the richest and most progressive agricultural region in the north, with most of its watered acreage confined to a half-dozen large estates. Besides Chiclin, there is Casa Grande and its three adjoining plantations, about which there has been so much talk recently. One story has it that the Casa Grande estate and their half-million acres, stretching right along the shores of the Pacific, is owned by a German company which maintains its own flying field, its own private seaport and harbor facilities, both of which are carefully guarded by armed Germans in uniform.

"All this," says one traveller returning from Perú, "is within striking distance and apparently without the knowledge of officials and guardians of the Panama Canal."

In the present circumstances, with Hitler and Mussolini demanding more and more territory, a greater share of the world's raw materials, this story has not only gained considerable credence, but taken on more serious proportions with each telling. The latest rumors have it that German submarines and other naval craft, as well as regular German steamers, have been seen going in and out of this harbor. Such a state of affairs, if true, would constitute one of the boldest challenges in all history to the Monroe Doctrine and to the sovereignty of the United States itself. It would call for quick and decisive action from the government at Washington.

However, there is no such threat or danger to the Canal or to the United States. Casa Grande is owned by a company with a German name, but the German owners, the Gildemeister brothers, have lived in Perú longer than New York's famed Senator Wagner has lived in the United States. They are Peruvian citizens born in Perú. The so-called air base is an open space in the perfectly flat canefields used by local Peruvian air lines and listed on the charts of the Pan-American Grace Airways as an emergency landing field. Since a great deal of its sugar, molasses and alcohol is shipped to Europe, small German as well as other European freighters call at the little port of Chicama, a tiny bay or inlet at the edge of one of the plantations.

Only a little way from Casa Grande is Cartavio, a similar

plantation where sugar, alcohol and rum are produced in enormous quantities and which is owned by W. R. Grace & Company of New York. This plantation, as well as Casa Grande and Chiclin, is heavily guarded to protect crops, refineries, distilleries and other properties from marauding peasants and Indians, just as any similar property in this country is guarded and protected. Cartavio, like Casa Grande, maintains its own flying field. But the regular Grace steamers operating on the west coast carry passengers to and from this region, and particularly parties of tourists who visit the ancient ruins of Chan Chan. Consequently they use the port of Salaverry, twenty-five miles away and twelve miles south of Trujillo by railroad or paved highway.

Incidentally, Salaverry is the shipping point or port for Trujillo and the entire region, that is, if it could be called a port. In fact, along the entire coast line of Perú there is at this moment but one single port where ocean-going steamers may tie up to a dock, or even anchor in calm waters. That is Callao, the port of Lima. At Salaverry, as at all the others, the ship anchors a mile or so out at sea, and reels and rocks on the Pacific swells, making the loading or discharging of freight about as difficult a job as you can find anywhere.

Passengers take their chances down a heaving ladder and count themselves lucky if they make the bobbing launch without getting drenched. And if they do, after the launch, not unlike a ship in a Walt Disney cartoon, has successfully ridden breakers as high as a house and reached the long pier that extends out into the restless deep—they must be windlassed up by a block and tackle in a species of iron bucket, wondering the while what would happen if the uncertain hand of the indifferent *cholo* should slip or miss the lever of the electric motor which operates it.

Of all my adventures in South America by sea or air, the

last trip I made from shore to ship at Salaverry holds a choice place among the most hair-raising. It was a dark night and the sadistic, half-drunken proprietor of the launch held me halfway between the pier and the ship, with a rough sea growing rougher, and threatened to keep me there unless I paid him double what he had agreed at the pier to transport me for, "in order," he made it known, "to teach the *gringo* he is not superior to a Peruvian."

Shippers and importers, as well as passengers, find launchmen and stevedores a mercenary lot. Contrary to the practice at other ports, marine labor at Salaverry works on a piece basis. That means that every person who handles a bag or box of freight gets paid a fixed sum. To get a case of condensed milk ashore, it is necessary to pay the stevedores seven centavos and the launchmen ten centavos of a sole—the Peruvian unit of money worth a little more than forty-seven cents; that is, during regular hours from 7 to 11 A.M. and from 1 to 5 P.M.; from 5 to 7 o'clock in the evening the charge is fifty per cent more, from 7 to 9 seventy-five per cent more, and from 9 to 12 P.M. 100 per cent in addition. On Sundays or holidays the off-hour rates range from 50 per cent to 175½ per cent more per hour.

To the lowly citizens of Trujillo and the surrounding country these conditions put a can of condensed milk in the same class with a fifty-year-old bottle of brandy from ancient Brittany or somewhere. Likewise it gives an idea of the additional problems a Peruvian farmer, cotton or sugar producer must face in getting his products to the world market, even if he has won in the superhuman struggle against government and nature to grow and gather it.

My own experience also makes it certain that from now on I shall take the plane and not a steamer southward to Lima from Trujillo and the valley of Chicama. While it would be possible to make the trip now by automobile, I shall not go by land until the new highway has been completed all the way. Besides there is not a great deal along the way that compares in interest or importance to the far northern regions. In fact the far north with Trujillo as the base, Lima and the central sections, and the far south, with Arequipa as the hub, constitute the principal centers of Peruvian civilization.

II

City of the Kings

Just at nightfall we ran into a fog. At rhythmic intervals all through the night the ship's whistle blew until my eardrums seemed on the verge of collapse. Sleep was impossible. What a relief it would be to get into Callao, hurry up to the hotel at Lima and go to bed! Finally seven o'clock came and the breakfast gong, but the whistle still blew. Hurrying out on deck, I found that daylight consisted of a semi-opaque glow. The fog was like a heavy steam from a boiling kettle. "Callao is somewhere out there in it," the deck steward said. "This is June, and wintertime you know, and Callao and Lima seldom see the sun this time of year."

Callao remained "somewhere out there" until nearly noon when the heavy gray curtain lifted slightly, but only slightly. It still floated just overhead. Throughout my four weeks' stay it floated just overhead day in and day out, descending to earth at night, as if in repose. Atmospherically, such is Callao and Lima four and five months in the year, and sometimes longer. But only Callao and Lima and the lower Rimac valley. Ten miles inland at night the stars twinkle the year round and the sun shines nearly every day.

But on this occasion, even before the fog lifted, the ship was attacked by *fleteros*, or launchmen, who shouted and screamed at the top of their lungs. By scores they rushed the ladders, all trying to ascend at the same time. They rioted, cursed, pushed and bashed one another. Once up the ladder they swarmed over the decks like wolves, invaded the social hall, the dining-room, jammed the corridors, knocked and screamed at cabin doors and practically tore the clothing from the backs of such passengers as ventured out. Four and five would surround the passenger, hold on to his arms, and shout Spanish into his ears, all in an effort to arrange contracts for the trip from ship to shore.

I finally made an agreement with the largest and fiercest looking of them all to transport myself, my three bags, typewriter and brief case. No sooner had we started down the corridor than rivals began grappling with him, trying forcibly to divest him of the bags. While he engaged two of them in a free-for-all, one seized my typewriter and another my brief case, and, but for the intervention of two ship's officers, would have made away with them. By pushing, shoving, and threatening, we succeeded in getting down the ladder to the giant's frail-looking launch and on our way to the shore.

For fifty years, until October 24, 1934, such was the procedure at Callao. It was an exciting experience for a tenderfoot or stranger to disembark and get to Lima. Pizarro himself landed in the north, crossed the Andes and made his way into the very presence of the Inca with little more inconvenience and difficulty. In fact, he met with far more courtesy and co-operation.

As far back as 1869 the Peruvian government had built a small iron pier at Callao, and in 1877 the French constructed a so-called port and dock, but no sizable ship could ever get within half a mile of it. Today Callao has the finest, most modern port and docking facilities in western South America, designed, planned and built by the Frederick Snare Corporation. At a cost of about sixteen and a half million dollars, they erected a breakwater over two miles long, dredged channels and a basin thirty-seven feet deep, filled in acres of ground, built a dock over a third of a mile long from which half a dozen piers extend 590 feet out into the water, and surrounded the place with large office buildings, custom offices, spacious flower-filled parks and plazas. Not even at French Havre or Calais, English Southampton or New York, are passengers handled with more efficiency, dispatch or courtesy. No more wild *fleteros* fighting and rioting over your bags. Already the increase in business is taxing even these facilities. At this moment the government is spending over two and a half million dollars on a drydock, naval warehouses and additional piers.

Callao for hundreds of years was a sleepy, bedraggled old town with a few little plazas, a statue or two of native heroes and an old fort with oversized pop-guns built way back in the time of a famed, as well as romantic viceroy, Don Manuel Amat. In fact, it existed only to handle Lima's freight and travellers. But recently Callao has had the languor and sleepiness shaken out of it. Together with adjoining suburbs, it is now a city of nearly 150,000, with office buildings, brand new factories, and all the accoutrements of a hustling coastal metropolis.

Four great boulevards, a railway and interurban electric lines connect it with Lima and the various outlying districts of the capital, while connecting roads extend to smaller towns and villages in the surrounding communities. From the new port, broad Avenida Argentina is the most direct, or the new Avenida Colonial. The Avenida del Progresso leads through Bellavista. Another follows the coast southward by La Perla, the summer home of the president, through San Miguel to Magdalena Nueva and Magdalena Vieja and turns inland through the new and wealthy San Isidro and country club districts where a new Lima is springing up at the rate of one hundred houses a month, enough to make Hollywood, Beverly Hills and Miami green with envy.

Perú

My favorite route is the shore road by La Perla and the Magdalenas to Miraflores, the older of the better residential suburbs, with its enormous houses of old families, its legations and embassies, including the American, where brilliant geraniums climb riotously over walls, fences and houses. From Miraflores I take the double-laned, tree-lined Avenida Arequipa right into the heart of the city.

The glory of modern Perú is Lima. There are, in fact, two Limas, the historic and historical Lima and the new modernistic Lima. The old Lima is a Spanish colonial city unspoiled by the garish architecture of this hurried age. It is a city which, in spite of its extensive civic improvements and its modern business structures, is still filled with old houses with deep patios, narrow streets with overhanging balconies, a city where old Spanish courtesy and hospitality are still genuine, if hesitantly proffered to strangers.

For romance and glamor the historic Lima is the first city in all the Other America. Its record of wars, rebellions, loves, hates, duels, murders and spectacular fights is unsurpassed by any other in the entire hemisphere. As one of the very first cities that Europeans planted on the southern continent, Lima was christened exactly seventy-two years before Captain John Smith began his operations on the James River.

Countless spectacular characters have strolled its streets and plazas. To know Lima, to understand it, to get the feel of it, one must not forget them. Pizarro himself was of course the chief among them. When he got through strangling Atahualpa at Cajamarca and looting the ancient cities of the age-old empire, he came down out to the coast to organize a government. It took him about a year to get Atahualpa off his hands, from November 15, 1532, to August 15, 1533, so that he got down to the valley of the Rimac River about a year later, and on January 18, 1535, began levelling off and laying a cornerstone for what was to become "The City of the Kings."

New Roads to Riches

By this time, due probably to the accumulation of Inca riches, he had acquired many enemies within his own ranks. Nothing produces enemies so quickly as riches that have been taken away from some one else. Anyway, his old partner, Almagro, went away to Chile to do a little conquering on his own. However, he met with little success it seems. Chile was another world with few cities worth ransacking and much fiercer Indians, especially in the far south. He proceeded back northward to replenish his fortune by taking over the ancient Inca city of Cuzco. Pizarro could have none of this, of course, so he sent his none-too-trusted brother, Hernando, on a hurried trip to teach Almagro a few things. But Almagro wasn't so easily dealt with. They quarrelled bitterly; in fact, Almagro took Hernando prisoner, but, being of a rather generous disposition, he allowed the gentleman freedom upon his word of honor that he would behave himself. A grave error in judgment!

Hernando proceeded straightway to plot. He double-crossed Almagro and took him prisoner. Then he proceeded to do to Almagro what his brother Francisco had done to the Inca; only, instead of allowing his aids to do it, he himself arraigned Almagro, made the charges, convicted and passed sentence on him all in one fell swoop. One record has it that immediately after the record trial and conviction he himself administered the last sacraments to the condemned man and then led him to the scaffold. Following which he explained it all to the Spanish government in several hundred thousand words. Had he written a briefer explanation, or none, he might not have had to spend twenty years in prison for the crime. The Spanish government did not countenance the hothead's treatment of an old man who was over seventy, gouty and used up by the hardships he had already undergone in the service of King and the Empire.

Here Almagro's son took up the fight. He got together his

friends and went to Lima. One night while Pizarro was at dinner in the palace he rushed in and ran the old boy through with a sword. This seesaw of murder and assassination went on while first one and then another of the conquistadores ruled in turn; until one day there arrived from Spain a nondescript priest by the name of de la Gasca, nondescript in appearance but not in speech. He had one of the glibbest tongues of any man who ever essayed politics. At first he went about quietly in his threadbare cassock talking to the soldiers and citizens until the majority were enthusiastic about the humble priest. Having made friends, learned the inside of social and business, as well as political, affairs, he ordered the despot then in power to get out—the despot being the same Hernando who a little while before handled the Almagro case with such dispatch.

Hernando was enraged and ordered his forces to drive the padre and his friends into the Ancon, or somewhere. It seems the forces, or following, of the two gentlemen were drawn up in the Plaza de Armas in front of the Cathedral. Father de la Gasca began to talk. As he talked Hernando's men began to realize the situation. They started deserting and going over to the enemy. One record has it that in twos and fours and tens, and then by companies they went over until Hernando was left almost alone. Even then Father de la Gasca continued to speak, to exhort them to get on the side of King and Country, to forsake the murderer.

And any one, I think, will agree that it took eloquence to do that.

But here is the point of the story. The humble priest having rid Perú of the last of the inner circle of the conquerors and brought peace to the city of Lima, packed up his satchel, got on a boat and went back to Spain; thus proving himself the first and perhaps the most completely unselfish individual who ever ruled in the old land of the Incas.

New Roads to Riches

In a city that witnessed such an act upon the part of a simple priest you would naturally expect to find churches. I thought I had seen churches and cathedrals in the old cities of Europe. When I went to Lima the first time I changed my mind. In most of the old cities of Europe there is only one church to the square. In Lima there are some squares that average four, not garish and gaudy churches, but churches that look for all the world like faded old etchings come to life.

There is Santo Domingo, the church of Santa Rosa, the patron saint who was canonized in 1671. "Pope Clemente the 10th," runs the colorful English of an old historian, "declared her the principal and universal saint, not only of Perú, but of all and any kingdoms, isles and land regions of all Latin America, the Philippines and the Indies." Which seems quite inclusive. Santa Rosa is buried in this old church where a jewel-studded altar has been erected to her memory. The jewelled altar of Santa Rosa is only a little more gorgeous than the solid silver one near by—which is a memorial to Our Lady of the Roses. Connected with the church is the Convent of Santo Domingo which possesses priceless paintings and art treasures that few strangers without proper Catholic standing or sponsorship are ever permitted to see. Its main chapel with delicately-carved mahogany panels and its crystal chandeliers are things of exquisite beauty.

But the Church of San Francisco, known as the church of the miracles, is even more imposing. It has quite as many works of art, jewels and whatnot, as are found in Santo Domingo. However, its most important possession is the image of the Lady of Miracles. Along about 1630, a guide will tell you, when an earthquake made the old city do a perfect St. Vitus, the statue of the Lady of Miracles actually stretched forth her arms and made the earth stand still.

There is the dingy old cathedral itself, said to be the largest in South America, which, along with five naves, ten chapels, marvellously carved choir stalls with sculptured figures of the twelve apostles, some notable paintings by Murillo, and others, contains the last mortal remains of Pizarro, who himself laid the cornerstone of the cathedral. His shrivelled dried carcass now sleeps in the first chapel on the right-hand side of the main door. "His sepulchral monument," say the Peruvian guide-books, "is worthy of that sturdy soldier who swept away an empire and founded in America an essentially Spanish nation." It consists of a marble coffin with glass sides, on top of which sleeps a rather languid-looking lion, all of which is mounted on a marble pedestal. At either end of the pedestal are figures of peculiar significance. At one end justice and grief, at the other end faith and mercy. Since in life Pizarro possessed none of these virtues, they are at least with him in death. Having viewed the tomb and the skeleton of the old conqueror, and if your constitution is hardy enough, you may, after proper procedure, see jars in which has been pickled in alcohol the remains of those portions of his anatomy which made him the bold and daring figure he was.

Next door is the new archbishop's palace erected in the flush of his busy reign by the late dictator, Augusto B. Leguia. Designed in the true ornate Moorish style, with the inevitable dark wood portals, it is a handsome structure. If the old man's munificence was remembered in the days of his tragedy, it seemed to have had no effect on his enemies, for he died the horrible death of a common prisoner at the hands of the *cholo* government which overthrew him.

The churches are equalled in magnificence by the splendor of the old palaces of the viceroys and the early nobility. There is the home of the famed actress, Micaela Villegas, the Sarah Bernhardt of Perú, who in the middle 1700's was the rage of Lima, at least of all the sleek-haired young men, and not a few of the old ones. It was a dull day when some dashing don failed to challenge another to a duel, or to throw

himself into the sea, about her. In many cases the whole course
of family history was changed and entire dynasties wrecked, all
because of this remarkable lady.

But proving that age can sometimes put it over youth in the
matter of romantic adventure, none of the desperate dons succeeded in winning her hand. She finally succumbed to the
wooing of a lusty old boy of sixty-odd years, Don Manuel de
Amat y Junient, the same who in more practical, not to say
martial moments, erected the old fort at Callao—and practically rebuilt the city of Lima itself. When Don Manuel arrived
in Lima as viceroy he had already heard of the charms of the
great actress so he arranged without delay to witness one of her
performances. Immediately he went down under her spell.
Dressed in his fluffiest laces and gold braid, his curls trimmed
and perfumed, he presented himself at her feet with a proposal
of, shall we say, marriage. She refused him, but apparently did
not close the door too tightly. Anyway he persisted. He told
her if she would accept him he would build her the finest
palace in all the Spanish empire. He even described it. Its
gardens would rival the gardens of Versailles. He would turn
back the waters of the lazy Rimac River and make them flow
through these gardens, so that fountains might play in front
of her windows. Its walls should be covered with silver and
gold. By this time she was on the verge of giving in, but, when
the fountain of eloquence stopped flowing for a moment, she
had a practical, if feminine, second thought. If he would build
the palace first and she liked it, all might be well.

Don Manuel, having already made plans for a building
campaign, rushed away and assembled architects, artisans and
artists, and ordered them to draw up specifications and order
materials from the ends of the empire. The result was that in
record time the dream palace was complete, with gardens,
near-by parks and the Paseo de Aguas, on which the aristocracy
of Lima for hundreds of years afterward were wont to prome-

nade, and Don Manuel became the proud husband—in fact, if not in theory—of the dream girl of Lima. Anyway, his behavior created one of the juiciest social scandals ever to occur in Peruvian high circles—and yet today there are those who try to whitewash the old boy by insisting he was the victim of a designing woman!

Curiously enough it was long after this that she was dubbed with the expressive nickname by which she is known today—La Perricholi. She was a *chola*, which in Perú as in Ecuador and Bolivia means halfbreed, that is, having Indian or dark blood, a fact which may have accounted, at least in part, for her bewitching beauty and attractiveness. As time passed and his arteries began to harden, the old man grew jealous and suspicious and often showered her with abusive appellations, his favorite being a combination of chola and La Perra, the word denoting the female of the canine species. But apparently Don Manuel, although an exalted representative of the Spanish king, like the Pizarros sprang from rather humble beginnings. In any case he did not pronounce his Spanish very well, so that instead of referring to his love as La Perra Chola, he barked La Perricholi.

However, in the flush of early love revelry reigned in the new palace. Musicians came from Paris and Madrid to amuse the happy couple and their guests. The finest wines and champagnes were imported to quench the thirst of the aristocracy. Not even Cleopatra entertained more lavishly, if we are to believe the records and the tourist booklets. "The fountains played in the gardens and the fragrance of the flowers flowed through the house," runs one poetic description.

"Until one day," wrote the late Harry N. Foster, "La Perricholi was driving in her carriage through the streets of Lima. She came upon a religious procession and was suddenly stricken with contrition, with the futility of fame, riches and revelry. Then and there she got out of the carriage, directed the driver to return home, joined the procession and went humbly into the church." And incidentally out of Don Manuel's life forever.

There are other and varying versions of this last chapter in the romance of the celebrated actress and the old viceroy, but most of them spoil the story. So why dwell upon them? In any case, its splendor dimmed, its walls dingy and crummy, its tile floors worn, its gardens neglected, the palace of La Perricholi, which respected historians insist was the private residence of the viceroy to which the lady came by invitation but in which she did not reside, stands majestically in one neglected district of Lima—the temporary headquarters for a company of infantrymen. The Paseo de Aguas has just been restored to its former position by extensive improvements.

The University of San Marcos, founded in 1551 by Fray Tomas de San Martin is not only the oldest university in South America, but the oldest in all the Americas. Mexicans like to insist that the old university of Mexico City came first, but there seems little doubt that San Marcos has maintained a much more continuous activity these three hundred and eighty-eight years. In any case, it was turning out graduates in laws and the arts and other cultural subjects long before the College of William and Mary in Virginia was conceived or John Harvard had been born.

Its charter was granted by Charles the fifth and the university was to have begun its classes in 1550, but, due to some delay, perhaps a little *mañana*, its doors did not swing open until the following year. Its beginnings were in the old Monastery of Santo Domingo. During the next two hundred years it occupied other buildings, moving from place to place as its student body grew. And, although today its faculties of medicine, engineering and other practical subjects are scattered throughout the city, many of them splendidly and modernly housed, the departments of arts and law, its museum and historic-chapel, the burial place of Perú's immortal dead, occupy the simple two-story Spanish colonial buildings on the Plaza Universitario. Its dignified exterior, its numerous *patios* filled with palms and shrubbery, its great library and various lecture halls, make it one of the most inspiring structures in the city.

From its stately Hall of Sessions, the meeting place of the Board of Regents, with its giant mahogany table and high-back chairs, each containing a gold embossed coat-of-arms of the institution, the walls covered with the life-size paintings of its former presidents, I recently presented an international broadcast, the first such broadcast ever to go out to the world. Both Peruvian and American educators participated, including Doctor Alfredo Solf y Muro, the present rector of San Marcos and host, the Reverend Father John F. O'Hara, President of the University of Notre Dame, Father Jorge Dintilhac, rector of the Catholic University of Perú, which in prestige and historic service shares honors with San Marcos, Doctor Charles G. Fenwick, Professor of International Law at Bryn Mawr, and others. The program went off to perfection, except that Doctor Solf y Muro, the first speaker, arrived five minutes after the broadcast went on and the specially arranged glee club, which was to open and close the broadcast, did not arrive at all. I noticed among the symbolic gold and silver ornaments, which had been brought out for the occasion, a large silver bell. At the last moment, having no music, in desperation I seized the bell, rang it and in the manner of a town crier began my announcement by saying, "With the ringing of the historic bell which called students to their first classes in the year 1551, we bring you a special broadcast from the palatial Hall of Sessions of the oldest university in the New World."

I had not the slightest suspicion that such was really the case. Happily, however, it was not only the very same bell, but one which had been a gift to the university from the Spanish king himself and bore the date, 1550. One of Doctor Solf y

New Roads to Riches

Muro's assistants, a recent graduate of Harvard and with an appreciation of Yankee radio novelty, thought it was an inspired act that, in my frantic effort to save the day, I had caused "the silvery tones of one of the most treasured objects of all New World institutions of learning to be heard in Boston, Dallas, Denver and San Diego as well as in Lima." No less a novelty, I thought, than broadcasting the booming of Big Ben in London, whose tones are not nearly as musical as those of the San Marcos bell.

On every hand there is history, history that may be easily passed up because in Lima, as in no other city of the Americas, history has not been pushed aside by the new and modern. The two get along without ever clashing. The early colonial houses that still survive on the historic Plaza San Martin, the new movie theatres, the two great business blocks that face each other across it, the aristocratic Union Club, the Cerro de Pasco Copper Company's office building, seem to have enough suggestions of Spanish architecture to give at least the impression of conformity. From the outside the huge new and in many ways palatial Hotel Bolívar, the gathering, as well as the starting place of all foreigners visiting the city, is not out of harmony with its neighbors, at least insofar as the exterior is concerned.

I am compelled to observe that if it were possible, especially in the long foggy months of the year, to view the Bolívar only from the outside, it might prove much less taxing on the disposition of its patrons. What with its labyrinthian and draughty hallways, lobbies and public rooms, its enormous suites, and baths with cold water, no soap and a single towel as big as a counterpane—but never so soft—its imitation Swiss management, a French cuisine with a *cholo* tinge, the Bolívar all but prevents Lima from qualifying as a great metropolitan city. If it were not for the chief-porter-head-clerk, who speaks all languages, knows and remembers all things and never seems

Highway from the Sea to the Jungle

Modern Boulevard in the New Lima

to sleep or leave the registration desk, along with the potent Pisco sours served at the bar, I have no doubt there are times when guests would indulge in no little mayhem.

Without any intention of assuming permanently the rôle of tourist guide, but with no desire to linger in the Bolívar, I suggest that you turn to the left as you leave the front door of the Bolívar and proceed up the narrow Calle Union, the chief shopping street of the city. Along the way you will continue to find history and modernism dwelling quietly side by side. In the first block there are women's ready-to-wear stores filled with London and Fifth Avenue styles, radio and even television emporiums, newsstands carrying *Collier's*, *The Cosmopolitan* and *The London Times*, Eastman Kodak supply stores, Singer Sewing Machine stores and candy shops, all with attractive windows. Across the street flutter banners advertising Goodyear and Goodrich tires. Except for the Indian features of so many of the people that crowd the narrow sidewalks, it might be any downtown street in Boston. That is, until you look up at the old Moorish balconies of blackened mahogany and cedar.

The second block is similar to the first with the same kind of shops, but midway on the left-hand side is a great grilled doorway with a red carpet leading back through a long hallway and out into a *patio* where brilliantly liveried servants are darting about. This is the most exclusive of the military clubs. On the right-hand corner, flush with the sidewalk, is the carved and crumbling façade of the Church of La Merced, which also boasts a carved silver altar and a Virgin, whose crown of solid gold is decorated with precious stones.

A block to the right is the National City Bank of New York and a block farther on the headquarters of W. R. Grace & Company. Across the street is the home of one of the oldest newspapers in South America, *El Comercio*, *The New York Herald Tribune* of Perú. In the same neighborhood are other Anglo-

Saxon banks, stores and distributing houses—The Royal Bank of Canada, Duncan, Fox and Co., and so on. However, continue along the Calle Union from the Church of La Merced and you soon come to the Plaza de Armas, with the cathedral and the Bishop's residence. But the old adobe palace of Pizarro, which housed among his successors, forty-one viceroys, including the oratorical Father de la Gasca, and the romantic Don Manuel, scores of presidents, dictators, generals and others for four hundred years, has been replaced by an enormous new palace christened only in November, 1938. In spite of its glaring whiteness and carved ornateness, its great iron fence in the Versailles manner, and the fact that all the trees and tall sleepy palms that once shaded the plaza have been removed, it might have been there always.

Cross the plaza diagonally and take the Calle Junin four blocks to the Parque de la Inquisicion. In the center of the Parque is the famed bronze equestrian statue of Simón Bolívar, connected with which there is a tragic story. Upon reading the criticisms the morning following its dedication the artist who designed and sculptured it committed suicide. The statue it seemed was perfect in every detail, not only to the right number of buttons on the general's coat, but to the minute symbols upon them. Nothing had been overlooked except for one small detail. One critic thought it would be a little difficult for the general to stay on a fiery steed or in a saddle that had no belly band.

On the right of the plaza, and jammed in between other old buildings, is a simple columned portico. If you enter and follow winding narrow corridors, you will come to a series of offices, and some one will show you a large rectangular-shaped room with few windows, and two rows of desks facing each other on either side of the aisle, with a dais at one end. Nothing about the place seems unusual until you look up at one of the most gorgeously carved mahogany ceilings in all the world. You will then be told that this was the Hall of the Inquisition, that here men called heretics, because they did not happen to believe or were suspected or accused of not believing like other people, were condemned to die the most horrible deaths in all the annals of suffering. In the doors are the very same peepholes through which accusers could look upon without being seen by their victims. Within the surrounding rooms are cells, cellars and dungeons in which the sentences were meted out.

It seems a bit ironical that until recently this hall served as the meetingplace of the Peruvian Senate, when there has been a senate in Perú. At the time of my last visit the ballot boxes of the latest general elections, which were duly annulled, were neatly stacked up at one end of the room, in keeping, it may be said, with the traditions of the place.

Any new senate that may be elected and assembled in the future, however, will not sit in an inquisitorial atmosphere. The imposing Legislative Building at the upper end of the Parque with its marble entrance hall, like the Capitol in Washington, contains both a Congressional and Senate Chamber, and all the committee rooms and offices required. Somewhat unkempt since the days of Leguia, it was completely overhauled, refurbished and revarnished for the Pan-American Congress last December, and is now in good condition. Even in spite of its Yankee-State-Capitol exterior, the great grilled gate and the massive carved doors at the entrance, all in the Latin manner, serve to keep it within the Lima architectural pale.

From the Parque de la Inquisicion, go west two blocks and return to the Calle Union, by way of the balconied but shop-lined Calle Ucayali, named for one of those three great rivers of the country. Walk slowly, otherwise you may pass up some of the most interesting of the historical treasures. On this street is the national library with its 60,000 rare volumes and musty manuscripts. It was not only the first Peruvian library, but is one of the oldest libraries in all the continent. It was dedicated by General José de San Martin, who first drove the agents of the Spanish king out of Lima. Citizens take pride in the fact that on August 8, 1821, San Martin stood on the steps of this ancient institution and declared that "Ignorance was the Spanish government's pillar of strength in America, and therefore it avoided any activity that might further the cause of education."

Then there is the Torre Tagle mansion fronted by the most elaborately carved balconies of vice-regal times. Built by a Spanish merchant by the name of José Bernardo de Tagle, it is today the home of the nation's foreign ministry and is alone worth a trip to Lima. Señor de Tagle was making a trip with his ships to the Indies. On the way he captured a Dutch pirate ship, loaded with loot which he divided with the King to the extent of a million pieces of eight. His grateful Majesty in turn presented the merchant with the title of Marquis, and later made him Treasurer of the colony. Having decided to settle down permanently in Lima, the Marquis started his mansion in 1715. All the materials had to be imported, the wood for the panelling and balconies from Central America, the stones for the great arch doorway from Panamá, and part of the priceless floor tiles from Seville. The other tiles were made by a man who had been condemned to be hanged but whom the Marquis succeeded in having pardoned "because no other person in Perú could make tiles."

I saw the Torre Tagle palace last time in December, 1938, and at its best, on the occasion of the grand ball in honor of all the visiting diplomats the night before the opening of the Eighth International Conference of American States. Two thousand people jammed its great *patio*, ministers of foreign affairs, ambassadors, military officials and other dignitaries in glittering uniforms and gold braid, with medals and decorations hanging in clusters and festoons, ladies in colorful gowns and jewels, and the President of the republic surrounded by dozens of aides and flunkies. Full-blooded Indian soldiers, dressed in the picturesque uniforms of vice-regal days, stood stiff and motionless at the entrance, on the stairways and along the balconies, their faces perfect replicas of the ancient *huacos* in the Larco museum at Chiclin.

It took seventeen years to build this great house, at a cost which the Marquis himself did not wish to know. He kept accounts of the expenses up to a million pieces of eight and then tore them up saying, "Why should I report to myself?" His Marquesa was a very contrite lady, full of charity. When she was about to give birth to a child her physician prescribed a soup diet. So thereafter she made it a practice to supply soup to all the pregnant women in the neighborhood.

The fourth Marquis of Torre Tagle was the first to raise the cry for Perú's independence and the first to act as a president of Perú. The present head of the family, Don José Ortiz de Zevallos y Vidaurre, is the Peruvian minister to Sweden, while the friendly and jovial Emilio Ortiz de Zevallos y Vidaurre, the next in line, a graduate of Cornell University, is the Chief of Protocol, whose office is the first room to the right of the main stairway on the second floor, in which his father and grandfather took leave of Lima and this life. Further along the Ucayali you will not fail to notice the great columned Banco Italiano, the largest private banking institution in Perú with branches all the way from Piura to Arequipa.

And then before returning to the Bolívar, the country club in San Isidro, or wherever you happen to be in residence, stop at the Maury, the old hotel whose block of bars, restaurants and dining-rooms have served the nation's merchants, bankers, professionals, politicians, men about town, clerks, bookkeepers, and transients since time immemorial, and still do. It might be called "the house of mirrors," for every wall has on it two or three heroic old mirrors like those that used to adorn the walls of old European houses, hotels and public places. Whatever there is in the way of food in all Perú, the Maury will have it, and serve it in quantities sufficient to produce an embarrassing corpulence overnight. Eat little or much according to your likes, but don't fail to begin with a Cocktail de Fresas (or three or four), which, being interpreted, means strawberry cocktail. It is made of one part Old Tom Gin, for some reason the Gordon's Gin of Perú, two parts crushed fresh strawberry juice, not too carefully strained, poco syrup, and shaken into a foamy pink.

I repeat that in spite of its checkered political career, and the diversity of its rulers, as well as its tremendous growth and expansion in recent years, the old Spanish atmosphere of Lima has been maintained to a greater extent than in any other Spanish-American city. It is among the cleanest and, thanks to Doctor John D. Long, the experts of the Pan-American Sanitary Bureau, and the wholehearted co-operation of the local government, one of the most healthful of all South American capitals. Its water supply flows down in pipes from the mountains twenty-five miles away. The local Italian company which furnishes the water also supplies the power and light, and if there is a better lighted city between Canada and Cape Horn I have yet to see it.

Look far enough and there are slums of course, but far less obnoxious than in some of the newer cities of the continent. And it is unbelievably cosmopolitan. Not far from the Plaza de Armas is an enormous and typical Chinatown, with innumerable restaurants, laundries and opium dens. At one end of the Avenida Francisco Pizarro, there is also a Harlem. Although you seldom see an African in the downtown business section, or anywhere in the outlying districts, there are several thousand descendants of early African slaves. The Japanese are new-comers, and perhaps 15,000 of them have built their own subdivision with a school and spacious playgrounds. The Italian colony is large and important, but unusually assimilated. The Germans, with the exception of the younger set of steamship agents and representatives of the fatherland trading companies, are not nearly so swastikaized as in one or two other countries. But some of the Yankees, I fear, and not a few British stand out like sore thumbs.

Not only the flower but the great majority of the old Spanish element, who are only about fifteen to eighteen per cent of the entire Peruvian population, make their homes in Lima. They are the proudest, yet with few exceptions, about the most modest, unaffected people on the continent. Many of them still occupy their old mansions in the heart of historic Lima, but like the old families of Caracas, Venezuela, the majority are moving out into the suburbs and subdivisions.

On the five-mile-long Avenida Arequipa, first of the modern boulevards to be inaugurated, are many mansions set in enormous gardens. One of the largest and most imposing is the home of Señor Eulogio E. Fernandini, fabulously wealthy mine-owner who, Edison-like, loves to ride in a car of ancient vintage, sit in the gallery at the theatre, wear last year's suit, shoes and hat and appear thrifty.

It is said that years ago Señor Fernandini deposited several million dollars in cold cash in a New York bank and has not touched it since. Back in the boom days of the late twenties a vice-president travelled all the way to Lima to try to argue the old man into letting the bank invest this money for him. After about two weeks he left Lima with the word "No" ringing in his ears and a pretty definite idea in his mind that the old gentleman was not only a confirmed miser, but a little touched. To a bank vice-president in those days it could not be possible for a man in his right mind to have millions of dollars in cash and not want to speculate.

There are more grassy parks and plazas and tree-lined streets in Lima than all the other west-coast cities combined. This is remarkable when you consider that every tree, shrub, flower

New Roads to Riches

and hill of grass is watered by irrigation and that there are tiny canals and conduits leading to or crisscrossing every street, park, lawn, garden and playground and all the fields surrounding the city and the valley all so ingeniously constructed that the casual observer never notices them.

The Parque Exposicion occupies acres in the center of the city. In it stand the Italian art gallery presented by Lima's Italian citizens, and also the City Hall and scores of statues and fountains. Near by is the flower-lined Paseo Colón, not to be missed after the movies on Sundays and Thursdays at eight o'clock in the evening, when the town turns out to promenade. The broad Avenida Grau intersects the park and the paseo and practically cuts Lima in half. And then there is the Parque de la Reserva where the late Leguia allowed native architects, sculptors and landscape gardeners to revel in their art.

Five years ago miles of open fields and farms separated Lima from the sea south of Callao, but practically all of them have disappeared. A network of concrete boulevards and streets lined with new homes now occupy them, and golf courses, polo fields and a great new racecourse patterned after the one in Paris, have just been inaugurated; all the result of the most ambitious city planning on the continent.

North and east of the city are textile and woolen mills, breweries, shoe factories and other industrial plants, while on the south side of the city in the La Victoria district is Lima's newest innovation, the brand-new housing district for workmen. Several of these modern projects are already completed, while others are in process of completion. Each group of houses surrounds a central garden and recreational field, with a huge swimming pool, school, theatre and church. For each there is a model restaurant where the most carefully prepared food may be purchased for a song, at least the minutest part of a *sol*.

Everywhere there is growth and expansion, conceived,

[296]

planned and carried out with remarkable intelligence. And whether palaces, public buildings, private homes, play areas, or laboring men's houses, all is in reasonable keeping with what has gone before. Already a city of 750,000, Lima is not only a world metropolis, but a fit capital for a country more than 500,000 square miles in area and with a population of 6,500,000 people.

III

From the Sea to the Jungle

ON OUR way to the Country Club Pepe Matallana and I had stopped for a traffic light in the Avenida Grau. A huge truck with a cargo that resembled a miniature fruit and vegetable market drew alongside. Among other things I noticed green cabbages, carrots, Spanish melons, oranges, alligator pears and bananas.

"That truck," said Pepe, "has come all the way across the Andes from the Chanchamayo today."

"Why not from Venezuela or Mexico since yesterday morning?" I replied.

"So you are skeptical?"

"A bit," I said.

"Where're you from?" he called to the driver.

"La Chanchamayo y Tarma, Señor," was the response.

"And when did you leave?"

"At five o'clock this morning," was the reply.

For days Pepe had been telling me that if I really wished to know something about Perú I ought to make an automobile trip from Lima to the Chanchamayo country. Such a trip he had argued would convince me that, contrary to the belief of most foreigners, his country's material potentialities did not lie in the dusty coastal region alone, but that beyond the snowy cordillera was an empire whose riches were just now beginning to flow out to the world.

I was, of course, familiar with the vast Andean copper- and silver-mining activities at Oroya and Cerro de Pasco, and the remarkable railroad which had been built up the mountains to them. But it was hard to believe that fresh fruits and vegetables could be gathered in the early morning and transported by truck from the edge of the Amazonian valley and delivered in Lima before nightfall. To be convinced I would have to go and see.

Two days later we were on our way with Pepe as guide and in his car, on a leisurely excursion to the land beyond the mountains. We spent the first night at Chosica, twenty-four miles from Lima, where the valley begins to close in on the Rimac, which even this far down looks more like a brook than a river, and where, along its banks and clinging to the hillsides, people of climatic discernment flee on week ends from the capital's cold and clammy fog. If I were a Peruvian, or a foreigner compelled for business, professional or even plain economic reasons to keep an eye on affairs in the city, I would move out to Chosica, build a house, let geraniums and bougainvillea climb over it, enjoy the sun by day, the crystal clear sky by night and keep my lungs full of glorious dry air at all times.

We drove away from Mrs. Beach's delightful little inn at eight o'clock and were soon climbing up the ever narrowing valley. As we proceeded, the succession of barren cliffs, each leaning a little farther forward than the preceding one, suggested a long line of soldiers each trying to see the head of the column. An hour after we started climbing the mountains had encroached upon the road so closely that it seemed scarcely a hundred yards from wall to wall, and the sunshine reached the floor of the valley only at noontime. Wherever there is water there is cultivation and the narrow, carefully cultivated strip of green on the banks of the river averaged from a few feet to only a few yards wide. Forty-three miles from Lima, 5412 feet up, we passed under the famous Verrugas railroad bridge swinging between two cliffs 252 feet overhead, a bridge which got its name from one of the strangest and one of the deadliest diseases in history. Hundreds of workmen died of the ailment when the railroad was under construction. Some say the infection is due to the bite of an infinitesimal bug that seems to thrive only in about the altitude of the bridge. Others say the germ is in the water. No one seems to know, but those who contract it break out in sores that at first resemble the corns that most of us get on our feet from time to time. The sores grow steadily larger, and more inflamed, until a horrible death results.

The Verrugas scourge was but one of the difficulties encountered by the builder of the railroad, Henry Meiggs, another one of the select company of railway geniuses who some forty and fifty years ago strung iron rails from the shores of the Pacific up into the mountains along western South America. Meiggs arrived in Lima in 1869 and the following year began work on what was to be the highest standard gauge railway in the world. Old-timers, mostly Britons and Yankees, in Perú shook their heads, said the man was a foolish dreamer, or perhaps a little wild. "How," they asked, "could he build a railroad up the face of mountains so steep even a llama could hardly cling to them." To which he replied, "We'll suspend it by balloons if we can't get it up there any other way." Ten years passed and trains were already running from the edge of the Pacific out across the level delta lands around Lima and well up into the highest foothills.

A long and bloody war with Chile in 1879 caused the suspension of all constructive activities in the country for a time. But eventually work was resumed. Twenty years slipped by during which time Meiggs had passed on. By that time, due to his careful planning and the momentum he had given the project the road had climbed 111 miles from Callao up into the sky, along narrow gorges, around the faces of mile-high cliffs, through scores of tunnels to the very roof of the world.

Although conceived, planned and built by an American, unlike the Guayaquil and Quito line, this remarkable road is now owned by the British, whose general manager Jeffrey Morkill succeeds in making it one of the best and most efficiently operated anywhere along the coast. For forty-five years iron horses pulled supplies up the tortuous steeps and returned with fortunes in copper and other concentrates to be shipped out to the world. Meantime, isolated farmers and settlers on the eastern side of the mountains transported their coffee, sugar and rum from the Tarma and the Chanchamayo valleys by llama and mule trains to Oroya for shipment by rail down to the coast.

Now comes the remarkable highway making possible truck, bus and regular auto travel all the way from the sea to the jungle, as well as furnishing the stiffest of competition to the railroad. Two hours from Chosica by this new method of Andean travel Pepe and I were 8999 feet up. By eleven o'clock we had reached the 10,000-foot point, where the railroad tracks and the highway begin a continual wrestling match, twisting and turning over and under one another for miles without getting anywhere. The railroad zigzags and seesaws back and forth, backward for a hundred yards, then forward another hundred, and so on in order to progress up the almost perpendicular walls, while the highway literally spirals upward. Meantime the air becomes lighter, not to say the head.

Then the bridge at Quita, which means "take off hat," a fortunate reminder, since at this point a terrific wind always blows down the valley. By now agriculture has deserted the floor and taken to the walls of the canyon. Diminutive terraces, like endless stair-steps, rise sheer from the river bed to the tips of the mountains, all meticulously irrigated in the same manner and by the same methods as those employed by the ancients a thousand years ago. Every snowflake or raindrop is caught as it hits the crest of the mountain and is conveyed downward through ditches and tiny canals to every blade of grass and stalk of corn; all bearing eloquent testimony to the resourcefulness and skill of the old Incas.

Every few miles the mountains completely close in and the road squeezes through another bottleneck or tunnel and out into another narrow valley, every inch of whose walls are cultivated, and each more picturesque than the other. At fifty-one miles we came to the village of Matucana. Scores of natives were gathered at the railroad station for the arrival of the train. In striking contrast to the *cholos* farther down, these *Serraños*, or mountain people, all smiled and seemed friendly. But then this is a land of sunshine and bracing air, where each native has his tiny terraced farm, just as he did ages ago. His lot may not be far different from that which he has known ever since the Spanish conquest, but up here the yoke of the rulers rests less heavily upon his neck than it does upon those down in the lower valleys.

A little farther on and again the road squeezed through a perpendicular gorge to Tambo Viso, where one farmer had just planted corn on the steep walls as if by shooting the grains into the ground. At sixty-three miles we stopped at San Mateo to supply ourselves with several bottles of the famous Peruvian mineral water of the same name, only to find the place much excited over a group of gypsies. Dressed exactly as they are the world over, their immemorial costumes vied in gayety and color with the costumes of the Andean natives.

Appropriately supplied with plenty of *Agua San Mateo*, we soon reached the "Bridge of Little Hell," which in Peruvian is the Infiernillo Bridge, where the highway crosses a bottomless gorge in successive stages three different times. Here the railroad does no switchbacks, or climbing. A hundred feet up it rushes out of a tunnel on one side, darts across a swinging trestle and disappears into another tunnel on the opposite side. After this the highway, the railroad, the river and the ancient Inca llama trail all compete with one another for room in the valley.

At Casapalca, the seventy-seven-mile point, 11,600 feet up, there is a small copper mine and refinery of the Cerro de Pasco Company. From here snowy Mt. Ticlio rears its head above all the bleak crags on one side of the valley and the white-crowned Mt. Meiggs, 17,000 feet high, and named for the intrepid railroad builder, peers over the heights from another direction. By this time the car was jolting us terribly and we stopped to see about the tires. Naturally the air pressure without had become so much less than within that they were beginning to take the bumps like steel instead of rubber tires. After we let some of the air out of the inner tubes riding seemed more comfortable. But there was nothing to do about our own outer tubes. The skin on our bodies seemed to become tauter by the minute.

The backbone of the hemisphere, the crest of the western cordillera, is at Ticlio, eighty-three miles from Lima, where the railroad reaches 15,800 feet while the highway rises to nearly 16,000 feet. Without considering the effects the altitude might have on two lowlanders, we thought it would be a novelty to get out and pitch snowballs, "off the top of America's head," as Pepe put it. And we actually did it; that is, we threw approximately two handfuls of snow each, only to discover it was not such a bright idea. My heart pounded like a sledge-hammer and there weren't enough breathing exits in my body to accommodate all the air that insisted upon getting out. Pepe all but passed out and insisted he was threatened with *soroche*, the terrible mountain sickness. Latins or natives seem much more susceptible to the malady than Anglo-Saxon foreigners. But we both sat down on the running board of the car very quietly for half an hour before we felt equal to getting in and driving away.

It was already afternoon and the icy winds began to blow and prepare for the regular evening blizzard, when more snow would pile up on the brows of Meiggs and Ticlio. It was difficult to believe we were in the tropics, much nearer the Equator than Cuba, but where on June 8 it was perfectly natural to expect sleet, snow and a howling blizzard. But it was a thrilling scene. The marvels of nature were spectacular and awe-inspiring. The peaks and crags of the mountains suggested pieces of gargantuan sculpture left unfinished in the studios of the great World Maker. Spread out before us now was a broad valley surrounded on all sides by the high mountain walls, and in the center an indigo-blue lake and Mt. Meiggs sloping right down to the brink, like an aged giant about to bathe his feet in an old-time foot-tub.

After this we began to meet people, not *cholos,* or mixed breeds, but pure bloods. For now we were actually on the great plateau, the very homeland of the Incas who among themselves speak their ancient Quechua language. They still dress the same way, wear the same costumes and follow the same customs as in the days of the ancient Empire. The women were literally dressed in rainbows, each wearing half a dozen flowing, billowy skirts of different colors, a great scarlet or purple woolen *manta* or shawl with a baby peering out of the *manta;* and every one spinning yarn from alpaca wool. Whether sitting or walking their hands are never idle. They may travel a few hundred yards or twenty miles, but the spool of yarn will never miss a turn. Their lot is that of their sisters' from time immemorial. They bear the babies and the burdens.

In this plateau between two great central ranges there is much life and activity. Pale-green grass manages to grow naturally and herds of llamas and alpacas graze peacefully. All along the way we passed llama trains or *puntas,* as the

The Author Reviews a Llama Punta in the Cordillera

Yarn Spinners of the Andes

natives call them. As with a flock of sheep, there is always a leader with all the other members of the *punta* following in single file. This head llama usually wears a fancy headdress with red tassels and a string of small bells hung from his throat. It is also interesting that each *punta* not only has its keeper, but he is accompanied by his wife or his woman. The old Inca rulers, being realistic as well as mystically minded men, required a woman for every man travelling the lonely mountains with llamas. At first the early Spaniards, to their sorrow, failed to appreciate the custom until syphilis developed among the animals. But their descendants, who have gradually adopted so many other customs of the race, finally saw the wisdom of this one.

These fleet-footed animals are still valuable to the Peruvian highlanders. They are still the beasts of burden here in this age-old mountain country. Resembling a cross between a camel, mountain goat and a reindeer, the llama has the kindest but most penetrating eyes I ever saw. One *punta* of a hundred or more was halted by the roadside. Each carried a load strapped upon his back, exactly a hundred pounds, no more, so far as a llama is concerned, and no less if the owner can help it. It is absolutely true that if one more pound is added, the llama refuses to move—which proves that llama intelligence is no myth.

In Morococha we met a group of musicians, one of those minstrel bands that travel from village to village to play for *fiestas*, weddings and dances. Gay blades they were, dressed in special costumes, fancy jackets and the ancient varicolored knitted woolen *chullos*, or peaked caps with earmuffs, a little like the helmets worn by modern aviators. For a consideration they performed for us on instruments that were even stranger than the costumes they wore. The most ancient were the *queñas*, or native flutes, hollow pieces of wood or cane with holes in them. There were violins and a primitive species of clarinet, borrowed from the white man of course. But the harp was the wonder of all. If not ancient, it was certainly original. It seemed to be a sort of lyre, set upright on a giant bull fiddle with two legs protruding from the body. When being played upon, the legs stand on the ground while the neck rests upon the shoulder of the performer. From this assortment of instruments they conjure music which tends to enliven their *fiestas*, and to fill the stranger with a sense of mystery. Basically the music they play is as old as America, the same rhythms they played before white men ever saw the continent.

Also in Morococha we found a small llama *punta* carrying one of the strangest of cargoes—blocks of ice from the million-year-old glaciers on Mt. Meiggs for the Yankee and *gringo* foreigners in the mining camps to use in their cocktails and highballs.

We finally reached Oroya late in the afternoon and the wind was blowing ancient copper dust all over everything. Even so, crowds were still gathered in the main street. It was Sunday and market day. *Chola* women squatted on the curb-stones busily gossiping, spinning yarns and selling their products to whoever insisted upon buying them. No one in an Andean market place in Perú will ever ask you to buy anything. If you look, examine, handle, ask the price and pass on, there will be no hard feelings. It is your privilege. The customer is always right. They displayed an amazing variety of things: cheap shoes, pottery, woven blankets, sugar cane, vegetables and fruits. They had come from up and down the plateau, and the valleys below, some of them from as far as fifty miles away. Here and there entertainers were holding forth, mostly the carnival type of Italian, Syrian or Chinese impersonators, magicians or jugglers. A monkey show seemed to be taking the attention of all the men.

Oroya is the smelter town of the American-owned Cerro de Pasco. After oil, mining is the next most important industry, while the Cerro de Pasco is the largest copper company in Perú. Along with its large mine at Cerro de Pasco 93 miles up the central plateau, it owns several smaller mines. The company accounts for most of the entire Peruvian copper exports which last year amounted to nearly 45,000,000 soles or $7,-875,000. At some of the mines every shovelful of ore contains silver, zinc, and sometimes gold. In addition to its multi-mineral mines, it is also the leading company engaged in outright silver and gold mining. Nor is the mining industry in the Oroya vicinity new. The Incas mined gold here centuries ago and after the conquest the Spaniards continued doing so.

The mining interests in Perú, according to income, rank as follows: silver, copper, gold, lead, zinc, bismuth, and so on. Since it leads in the production of so many of these, the Cerro de Pasco becomes one of the two or three industrial giants of the nation. So again, as in Venezuela and Colombia, the British, who share in the oil and railroad enterprises, and the North Americans, who control so much of the metal mining industry, are the dominant foreign interests in one of the most important of the South American nations.

Oroya is a hub of transportation for the great central plateau. It is the terminus of the central railroad from Callao and Lima. From here the same company operates seventy-six miles of line southward to Huancayo, on the central plateau, from which a narrow-gauge line leads on to Huancavelica in the direction of Ayacucho and Cuzco. The copper company itself operates the line northward ninety-three miles to Cerro de Pasco.

In its road-building program the government plans eventually to connect up all the important towns and communities that lie between the two central mountain ranges, restoring something of civilization to the high country in the region where the civilization of the Incas flowered, where they built their cities and carried on their industries. Cajamarca in the north, where Pizarro captured the Inca, the Oroya mining country and the Cuzco region are all on the plateau. Pizarro's conquest was not made along the coast. He advanced southward down the mountains from Cajamarca all the way to Cuzco before he came down to the coast again. And even from Cuzco he had to return north to Oroya and down the Rimac valley. It was not preference that caused him to establish Lima on its present site but the fact that it was the center of a broad plain or delta region which could be easily irrigated, and where several pre-Inca cities had been built.

A highway has been laid down and roughly graded northward from Oroya to Huanuco, then across the eastern range and down into the Tingo Maria country in the valley of the Huallaga, which, like the Ucayali, flows northward into the Amazon. The Tingo Maria region is similar, although not as highly developed as the Chanchamayo. It is already possible to drive from Oroya, or Tarma, southward to Huancayo and on to Ayacucho, while work is also under way to continue the highway southward from Ayacucho to Cuzco and eventually to Arequipa, thus completely connecting up all the otherwise isolated but important Andean communities.

Pepe and I, however, were going to the Chanchamayo, and so we continued eastward. We began climbing immediately. The road upward is a continuation of the main street of Oroya. It makes just as many hairpin curves and spirals on its way over the eastern range, but the mountains are much less colorful and spectacular than the western range. They suggest the neglected graveyard of eternity. For hours it was a lonely world, until we came to the *Altiplano*, for the most part a more or less flat stretch of country which occasionally drops into unexpected bottomless caverns and which the road manages to get down into and out of with the greatest difficulty. Now and then we would hear llama bells faintly in the distance. Yet llamas were nowhere to be seen. Then suddenly they would begin popping up on the horizon as if out of the ground.

Perú

Finally we began to descend, and rather rapidly, down the eastern slopes. For an hour we descended so rapidly my ears clicked at regular intervals. Pepe assured me his clicked every thousand feet with the greatest precision.

Suddenly we entered a deep valley or gorge. On one side were tiny, terraced wheatfields clinging to the precipitous cliffs, the first terraced farms on the eastern slopes. On the opposite side Indian women watched flocks of sheep graze. At the foot of the valley we found grass-thatched *chozas*, houses of the old Inca type, square mud huts, with thatched roofs, and all surrounded by cactus-covered walls.

Late in the afternoon we emerged on another mountain shelf and looked out upon an inspiring scene. Like a landscape artist's model, the Tarma valley stretched out before us. There was green to break the brownish monotony. Suddenly I had a longing to emulate a Georgia friend of mine who had to spend two years in Arizona. He said, "If I ever get back where there is grass I shall get down on my all-fours and eat it like a cow."

Tall eucalyptus trees waved their feathery heads above the brown and cream-colored houses of the villages. The eucalyptus seems to grow taller and slimmer here than anywhere else in the world. But then it must constantly compete with the mountains for a place in the sun. On the hillsides were fields of corn and all manner of vegetable gardens beautifully kept, every inch of them, of course, irrigated. Old mud walls lined the roads and blood-red and pink geraniums climbed over them.

"This is Perú," said Pepe, with emotion in his voice. "This is one of the scenes I have been trying to tell you about."

Today the Tarma valley does much of the gardening for Lima. From Tarma had gone the cabbages, carrots, radishes, and melons I saw in the truck in the Avenida Grau a few evenings before. Last year 50,000 bags of Tarma carrots crossed the mountains to the coast. Here at 10,000 feet spring is perpetual and vegetables grow the year round. Four crops of alfalfa can be produced in twelve months. Land in the valley sells as high as $150 an acre, yet the farmers make money.

Tarma takes its name from the *taruma* tree, which is something in the nature of mountain ash. It is an old town and quaint, with a population almost wholly *cholo*, or Indian. There are not more than a dozen white Spanish families, including one lone Yankee, who is an institution, not only in the Tarma valley but all the way down to the Chanchamayo. He is Nathaniel Chalmers Whitten, owner and proprietor of a wondrous menagerie called a hotel, in which there are clean beds, home-made showers, wholesome food and, if you are a regular fellow, hours of conversation in the proprietor's cozy book-filled den behind the kitchen.

Having served his engineering apprenticeship in the Montana mining country, he migrated to Perú where he became engineer for the Cerro de Pasco Company. After a long service he retired, at something over sixty, and settled for the rest of life in the peaceful valley of eucalyptus trees, geraniums and gardens, where in quiet hours he reads history and philosophy, or indulges in amateur photography. He loves to play host to passing travellers, natives or others. In our case his hospitality went to the extent of offering himself to drive us to the Chanchamayo, an offer which Pepe accepted gladly, and for reasons which I was soon to appreciate.

While the road from Lima to Oroya and on down to Tarma reveals astounding feats of engineering, the road from Tarma to the jungle presents one with the experience of a lifetime. The original old Spanish mule trail from Tarma about twelve miles to Palca, later widened to accommodate vehicular traffic, was long the only stretch of highway eastward. Thirty-five years ago one Señor Capello, an Italian engineer, native of Perú, undertook the task of constructing a mule trail from Palca on down to San Ramon and La Merced, in the lower foothills, a task which called for all the road-building instinct and ingenuity of his Roman ancestors, as well as those of the ancient Incas who, from the standpoint of empire and road-building, were the Romans of the Andes.

The difficulties that confronted Meiggs in constructing his railroad were simple compared with those that presented themselves to Capello. For several miles it was necessary to carve a succession of descending half-tunnel switchbacks along the perpendicular solid rock face of a 3000-foot canyon. In some places the walls jut far out over the valley like overhanging balconies. Little did he realize that Peruvian engineers would come along later and blast out more rock, build stone and cement supporting walls, so that an automobile might, if the driver is endowed with iron nerves and a capacity for gauging space and distance in inches instead of feet and yards, get down it without disaster. Much of the road is actually supported and braced up with underpinnings of stone masonry typical of the old Inca builders, the work having been done by their descendants who still excel in the art.

Although originally built for pack trains, the old Italian charted his grades well. They have proven perfect for automobiles or even heavily loaded motor trucks. It is still a one-way road, however, the traffic going down one day and returning the next. Its width leaves little or nothing between the outer wheel of a car and eternity below. In some places the clearance is actually not more than six inches, and the running board always seems out over the edge. As Whitten expressed it, "shift your eyeballs too suddenly and the car might go over."

Frequently trucks plunge over and are lost; even buses have slid over, taking their passengers on a hurried trip to the hereafter. A few weeks before our trip an old padre, who had spent his life in the Andes, admitted when he arrived in San Ramon that he had said his prayers all the way down. I would not have missed it for anything, but I have no wish ever to repeat it. That same day Major Francisco Villanueva, an aviator hero and commander of the army air base at San Ramon, told me that he never allows himself to be driven over the road without first drinking himself numb.

Once down the face of the cliff, the road clings to narrow shelves just above the foamy yellow river. In several places the shelf has been chiselled out of the base of the overhanging and protruding cliffs resembling canopied theatre boxes. One is called El Balconcillo de San Lorenzo, while another bears the name of Perú's great naval hero, Miguel Grau. Farther down the canyon the road darts back and forth across the river over slender suspension bridges patterned after the old Inca bridges, some of which swing and sway up and down like a hammock as you pass over. Terrific floods sweep down the canyon in the rainy season and no wooden or even concrete bridge has ever withstood them. At one crossing a dozen such bridges were swept away in as many years.

Even before the road emerges from the canyon it enters another world. The dusty, brownish, lifeless Andes are only a memory. Here life and color riot together. All manner of *lianas*, vines, hundreds of feet long, swing down the cliffs. As one old writer expressed it, "The jungle hangs suspended over the road like velvety green portieres in a hallway." Once out, it is lined with colorful *achote* plants, loaded with red berries, and the giant *oropel* tree covered with scarlet blossoms. In one place the road was arbored with them. Here the honeysuckle plant becomes a tree instead of a vine. But the most glorious of all is the *campanailloc* tree, with its bell-shaped flower, six inches long, two inches in diameter and in many colors. A smaller species, which is called *kantuta*, the flower of the Inca, is the national flower of Bolivia.

"The best way to describe all this," Whitten suggested, "is just to copy all the unusual adjectives in Webster's *Unabridged*." But I am afraid even these would not adequately

A Chuncho Gives a Lesson in Amazonian Archery

Terraced Farms in the Tarma Valley

express the color, grandeur and beauty to be seen during a trip up, over and down.

In this region dwell the Chunchos, another type of Indian. The Incas and their predecessors were coastal or highland dwellers and highly civilized. Down here the lowlanders or jungle Indians are generally of a very low order of civilization who live by hunting, fishing and gathering the wild fruits of the jungle. Curiously enough the original natives of the mountains or coastal regions never refer to themselves as Indians. To them the word Indian denotes a member of the lower class, a semi-civilized inhabitant of Amazonia. Just outside of San Ramon we met several groups of them wandering aimlessly along the road as if there were no place in particular to go, and no reason to go if there were.

"Now," said Whitten, "you can meet the denizens of the jungle without having to go exploring for them. And they are just as primitive as those described by the majority of the brave and intrepid explorers, too. Make no mistake about that. Most of these fellows stop at my place on the way out of the jungle and I have to listen to their tall tales."

The Chunchos, except those who work on some of the plantations and have absorbed a little, very little, veneer are way down in the scale of civilization. They may be descendants of the Red Man, but their skin is almost black. They wear long and exceedingly dingy smocks made after the fashion of a Jesuit's cassock. In fact, the Jesuit missionaries introduced them to this most unbecoming dress. The moral-conscious padres could not bear to see the sleek bodies of the innocent-minded creatures glistening in the tropical sunshine. Besides robbing them of any grace or charm, it makes it almost impossible to distinguish between male and female. The only way to tell them apart is to examine the cut of the neck of the smock, which is sloping for the men and square for the women.

We met several families of them in the valley. The men,

like their ancestors for thousands of years, were equipped with bows that shoot the longest, slimmest arrows I ever saw even in a museum, and a *machete*, or long bush-knife, an instrument borrowed from the lower rung of the white man's civilization. The women carried a few pots and long slim gourds, or calabashes, filled with *masato*, or liquid lightning, made of the juice of the potatolike root of the *yuca* plant. The faces of all were streaked with what any one whose knowledge of jungle Indians had been gathered from story-books would think was war paint but which turned out to be red juice of *achote* seeds put on not for ornamental purposes, but to drive away insects. All had perfectly black teeth stained by the bark of the *chamairo* tree, which they chew as a preventive of fevers, as well as fatigue.

The country around San Ramon and La Merced consists of rolling hills, crowded with *haciendas*, which grow oranges, bananas, alligator pears, coffee and sugar. We visited Chalhuapuquio, one of the largest and oldest of the coffee *haciendas* where Señor José Signori, a friend of Whitten's, welcomed us with large glasses of fresh orange juice flavored with grated cinnamon. This was almost as tasty as the *Chilcano* cocktails served us at Demarini's gasoline store and bar when we reached La Merced. Made of Pisco rum, orange juice, bitters and ginger ale, three of them give the novice a feeling of having suddenly met head on with a moving truck.

At the Demarini's bar we met the fabled Deluduchi (whose name is spelled differently by every one of his acquaintances but this way by himself), the man who handles the Peruvian mail and any terrestrial travellers who wish to avoid as many difficulties as possible on the trip between Lima and the Amazonian city of Iquitos. A soft-voiced giant of a man, he succeeded his father who before him held the Lima-Iquitos overland mail contract. From La Merced it is a seven- to ten-day mule trip to Puerto Yessup on the Pichis River, from where it is one day by canoe with good paddling to Puerto Bermudez. Gradually rising in scale of transportation, a motor launch makes the remainder of the trip on down to Masisea on the river of the same name, then down the Ucayali to Iquitos. It usually takes about sixteen to eighteen days for mail to reach Iquitos from Lima by this route. By air from San Ramon it is only a six-hours' flight. Anyway, if you wish to travel from La Merced to Iquitos, you will find that Deluduchi is the king of the region.

"The Chanchamayo valley itself," says Whitten, "is one of Perú's treasure houses. In one year its plantations have produced coffee worth nearly $750,000, and over $500,000 worth of fruit. Its hardwood lumber is worth nearly $100,000 a year, rice and *achote* seeds another $10,000 and 50,000 *arobes* of *aguardiente*, common rum made out of sugar cane. Incidentally, this rum yielded $52,500 in taxes to the government last year. Enough excitement for every man, woman and child in the coastal cities."

This alone justifies the herculean task of building a road across the Andes. Due to this road making possible speedy truck haulage, it has reduced the cost of freight transportation from the Chanchamayo to Lima from seven soles to one and one-half soles per quintal, or from twelve dollars and a quarter a ton to two dollars and sixty-two and a half cents.

The forests of this vast hinterland containing every known hardwood on the continent, as many as 2000 different species, according to one authority, constitute potential fortunes. One of the most valuable of the hardwoods so far is black walnut or *nogal negro*.

Farther eastward in the Iquitos area hardwood lumbering has long been an important industry. One of the largest hardwood mills in the world, owned by the Astoria Importing and Manufacturing Company of New York, and under the management of Mr. José O'Neill, is located twenty miles from the

Peruvian metropolis on the Amazon. The mill has a capacity of 20,000 board feet per day. The products of this mill, which specializes in mahogany and cedar, are of course shipped to the United States. In 1937 some 2,500,000 square feet of cedar were shipped by steamer from Iquitos.

Before the present era of road-building, and the opening up of the Trans-Andean road, very little of any of the hardwoods from the Amazonian area could reach the coast of Perú except by way of the various rivers to Iquitos, then by boat down the Amazon to the Atlantic, around the north coast of South America, through the Caribbean Sea and the Panama Canal and down the Pacific coast. Oil prospectors are also frantically busy in these wild regions and reports are trickling out to the effect that there is black gold along the eastern Andean foothills.

On the return trip to Lima and the sea, I refreshed my memory on the unbelievable difficulties the engineers had overcome in the building of the central Trans-Andean highway and I realized that the material transformation of this age-old land of Mochicas and Chimus, of Incas and Spaniards is already under way. If automobiles can now cross the Andes at their highest point and the fruits of the jungle can be brought to the sea in one day, roads through the country are only a matter of time and money—and given time they produce the money with which to pay for themselves.

IV
Renaissance in the South

Harold Harris and John D. MacGregor, long the David and Jonathan of the Pan-American Grace Airways, were making one of their customary survey trips to southern Perú to look over landing fields and other facilities for the safety and comfort of Yankee bank vice-presidents, Peruvian commercial salesmen, lady tourists and Inca Indians now being flown in ever-increasing numbers up and down western South America. They invited me to go along. Since they were flying in a small "staff runabout plane" they didn't promise me all the comforts and conveniences of the regular passenger liners, but they could promise me new, and perhaps novel, glimpses of the Andes and their snowy peaks, the city of Arequipa, a few of the other interesting towns and cities, and a chance to inquire into southern agriculture and industry. Harris, a red-faced, big-shouldered war ace with a Fuller-Brush mustache would be the pilot. Meantime John D., with whom I have shared so many flying adventures around the continent, suggested a visit to one of Lima's oldest museums. "I want you to see something of the past as well as the present of Peruvian aviation," he said.

At first we looked at the usual dried corpses of ancient Indians, old pottery and *huacos* enough to fill three museums, and even drums, blow-guns and arrows from the primitive tribes of the Amazonian regions. Also there were such memen-

tos from colonial days as gilded coaches, guns and swords.
John D. led the way up and down aisle after aisle, chatting
with the curator in his suave Spanish. Finally we stopped and
he drew himself up to his loftiest dignity. Then I realized
what the museum trip was all about. There was the same battered old machine in which Jorge Chavez, a brave young flier
and Peruvian aviation hero, attempted without success the first
of all flights across the European Alps. "I wanted to show
you," he said, not unmindful, I am sure, of the critical ears of
the patriotic curator, "that our Peruvian friends need not feel
humble in the presence of all the modern flying activities in
their country. And I thought we would do well to come here
and pay our respects before we started south tomorrow."

A tall slender pyramid with figures in flight circling upward
around it, a symbolic and appropriate statue to Chavez, has
been erected in the place of honor on "The Field of Mars," one
of the newest parks and parade grounds of the city. Since
aviation came to play such an important part in Peruvian transportation, the statue has become a place of pilgrimage for flyers
and enthusiasts on the subject, as well as diplomats who wish
to court favor with the government in order that their nationals
may be able to increase their sales of aviation equipment in the
country. There is seldom a week that some visiting group
does not place a wreath at the foot of the Chavez monument.
At one time "propagandist firemen" from the land of the
Blackshirts kept a smooth path beaten to it.

As usual, on the morning of our departure southward when
we arrived at Limatambo, Panagra's new airport and flying
field on the outskirts of Lima, fog and mist shrouded the entire
countryside. But by the time we had breakfasted on ham and
eggs and coffee, black and potent enough to buoy us up even
without the aid of the plane, there was ample ceiling for a
take-off. With Harris in the pilot's seat and John D. and I
bringing up the rear, we pierced the fog and were soon high

up above the brown, seared coastal country, which in this section is even more dismal than that of the north, except for the rolling country immediately south of the city, the broad plains around Pisco and Ica and the occasional strips of green that follow the rivers and streams down to the sea.

After five hours of bleak and dusty brown with only an occasional verdant streak or splotch to relieve the monotony, the northern end of the Arequipa valley, resembling a green carpet spread out over the floor of the Andes, was a welcome sight. To me, it had been a tiring trip. John D. had slept all the way. A plane seems to have the same effect upon him as a rubber-tired cradle would have on a baby. But much as I have flown, I am always alert when in the air. The sky was clear, as is always the case when the coastal plain is foggy, and the three great peaks that look down upon the southern metropolis —Chachani, Pichupichu and the now silent and peaceful volcano, El Misti—were bathed in sunshine. El Misti, the grand, snowy-haired "old man of the Andes," is one of the tallest peaks in Perú, over 19,000 feet high. The city of Arequipa nestles at its very feet. About this mountain there are more legends, mysteries and tall stories than any other in all South America. Perfect in form, in the midday sun it looks exactly like an inverted ice-cream cone with the cream oozing down its tip, and dominates the city, the surrounding country, the people, their beliefs and lives.

"Sons and daughters of Misti," the Indians call themselves. "The old man" used to go on rampages and shake the city to pieces and send all his children hurrying to the church altars and shrines to beg his forgiveness. Even before the Spaniards came the ancient Indians worshipped Father Misti. The remains of their temples and altars are found at his feet. Even the early Spaniards stood in awe before him. A long cross stands near the summit, planted there by the good padres in 1677, when "they climbed up and exorcised him," at least implored him to stop his crazy spells and not shake them up any more. Along one of the roads from the city to Misti there are two piles of stones, half a mile apart. Since time immemorial Indians passing that way have carried a stone from one pile and placed it on the other. For what reason? Evidently Misti does not like idle hands.

As we approached the city in our little tin bird that day and swooped down onto the long, dusty field, I myself could not help feeling the powerful influence of the "old man." As we drove through the city I could not get away from him. He was always there, down every street, through every arch and towering above everything. No wonder Arequipa is a city of classic culture as well as everyday commerce. As the late Harry Foster, that observant and amiable tropical adventurer who wrote the best of all guide-books on South America, used to say, "a city of art, religion and endless oratory, a city whose people spend their time going to church, writing poems, making flowery speeches, going to church again, rewriting the speeches they have already made, and publishing the poems at their own expense, regardless of whether any one else reads them or not."

The second largest city in Perú, Arequipa is still much more Spanish colonial than Lima. Unlike the Plaza de Armas in the capital, its principal square is notable for its sidewalks under old Spanish arches, its overhanging balconies and the imposing cathedral that stands broadside to the square, a cathedral whose cornerstone was laid eight years before the Pilgrims got to Massachusetts. Leading off from the square are narrow streets lined with high, battered walls behind which are some of the finest old Spanish colonial houses and private clubs in all Perú.

The various foreign colonies, the Germans, Anglos, and others, as everywhere else in the world, have their own clubs. Some of them are cosy and accommodating. But the Arequipa Club is the "holy of holies" of high-toned Arequipanos. From its main entrance flush on the narrow sidewalk, just another

Newly Planted Andean Cornfield

Father Misti Over Arequipa

door in a wall, you would not suspect that inside there are palatial lobbies and ballrooms, tapestried banquet halls and private dining-rooms, gaming-rooms, as well as bars, barber and "hair dressing" shops respectively equipped with all the modern gear and gadgets to take care of the most fastidious tastes and requirements.

Unless he has had the good fortune to be invited to this club, the casual observer in Arequipa may easily assume that the city is a typical *cholo* and Indian community, with a good sprinkling of foreigners ranging all the way from slant-eyed Orientals to tall blonde Nordics. When the proud and cultured citizen of pure Spanish antecedents, a member of one of the old families, and usually a *hacendado* living on the income from his plantation in the surrounding valley, a lawyer, or more often a scholar, say an honorary professor at the University, leaves the luxury of his own *patio*, office or place of business, he lolls at the club, and in the late afternoon goes with his family to the cinema. Hollywood pictures are extremely popular in Arequipa. The last time I was there Deanna Durbin was packing them in. In the better-class houses, patronized by the upper strata, reserved seats are sold and the picture is run in two parts, giving the younger element an opportunity to meet and talk between times.

Shopkeeping and mere commerce are left largely to foreigners and *cholos*. At the present time Italians, Germans, Syrians and Japanese take the lead in the retailing of such things as European and Asiatic machinery, household utensils and textiles. But the native *cholos* dominate in the sale of American manufactures, radios, canned goods, automobiles, tires and local products. Arequipa is Perú's principal market for the highly popular products made from vicuña skins and alpaca wool. All articles made from vicuña skins, once so cheap, are now very expensive because of the diminishing vicuña family. The vicuña, a delicate animal resembling a small deer, with one of the softest silken furs in the world, like the original buffalo of our own West, has been the victim of greedy hunters who have tried to supply the ever-increasing demand for its downy coat. It is about the shyest of all creatures and until recently no one believed it could be domesticated. It would become a household pet, but would not cohabit in captivity. Its moral sense was very high. You could not take a female from one male and give it to another. Besides, the second male would not accept her. The old conquistadores may have succeeded in destroyng the high morals of many of the Incas, but they and their descendants tried for four hundred years without success to domesticate the love-life of the vicuña. At last one man thinks he has succeeded. And while it is to be regretted that the end of vicuña monogamy is in sight, the possibility of being able to purchase and export a vicuña blanket without risking jail, is a happy one. For in the words of the two old black crows, "they are so soft!"

The pure delight of sleeping under stacks of these glorious bedcovers is one of the innumerable reasons one never forgets a visit to Quinta Bates. The Quinta is the hotel, or inn where the immortal and inimitable gray-haired Tia Bates plays hostess to travellers from all over the earth. At this old colonial estate, with its gardens and parks, its roses and magnolia trees, surrounded by enormous walls, princes, premiers, explorers, adventurers and poets have enjoyed Tia's conversations, cocktails and courtesies for thirty years. Among them have been General Pershing, the former Prince of Wales, the ex-King of Bulgaria and the late Eleutherios Venizelos, the venerable old Greek statesman. In fact, Venizelos selected the Quinta for his last honeymoon. Once within the gates at the Quinta, aviation, air travel and going places are all forgotten. The world is on the outside. Within life becomes a garden of flowers and trees, swings and wicker rocking-chairs and a house with deep-cushioned divans, soft lights, relaxation, peace, good drinks, good food and servants who administer to your every want, the same kind who served Inca princes and emperors ages ago, and most important of all, Tia bubbling with humor, wit and kindness.

"Around the tables in her dining-room," says Blair Niles, "you hear many languages, while Tia herself drops from Spanish to English and English to Spanish unconsciously. The Quinta is the only place on earth where you have to beg for your bill. If you don't Tia will forget all about giving it to you. And when you do extract one from her, it seems miserably little in return for the favors, the hospitality and the happiness you have enjoyed."

If you ask Tia how she happened to go to Perú and start the Quinta Bates, she will ask you, "Who cares about that?" But insist and she will say, "If you really must know, when I was just a girl my father was superintendent of a railroad in northern Chile. I stayed there with the family until I was grown up and then decided I would like to find a job for myself. I always loved entertaining at home, or any place. Then I found this house which seemed to me the most beautiful place in the world, so here I am."

Every foreigner is curious about why she is called "Tia," which means Auntie. She doesn't remember who first called her by that endearing term, or when. But every one calls her Tia, including the policeman. She is more definite on the subject as to why her house is called "The Quinta." *Quinta* means a small villa. "I have always thought of it," she says, "not as a hotel or inn, but as a small villa or home for my friends."

The most worldly-wise of women, who knows personally and intimately most of the great who venture far from home, Tia is still as simple and unaffected as a child. "One evening," she recently told me, "my butler announced that two young men, one a Mr. Coward, were arriving that night from Mollendo, but they would be a bit late, as their train had broken down. I was playing bridge with friends that evening, so when the party broke up, knowing that the boys should be along fairly soon, I decided to wait up. Mr. Coward's first name was Noel. You will laugh, but until then I had never heard of him. I found him extremely interesting and we began to talk, and the first thing we knew it was six o'clock in the morning. We had talked all night."

If you are lonely, or if you have undergone a great sorrow, Tia will drink highballs with you, tell you stories until she cheers you up. If you so far forget yourself as to become a nuisance, she will also give you a good verbal kick in the pants, and a second one if you look as if you are worth it. Become ill and she will nurse you back to health, die and she will bury you in the proper manner, heap flowers on your grave, send pictures of your last resting place to your family—and maybe a bill, if the family insists. I visited Chicago with her recently when, on her way to Los Angeles, she stopped off just to pay a visit to a man she had never met but whose sister had died in her house and lies buried in an Arequipa cemetery.

If I were looking for an aviation enthusiast, one of the outstanding boosters of the industry in South America, I should go directly to the Quinta Bates to find her. Tia, at how near seventy, and on which side, I would not say even if I knew, has been commuting between Arequipa, Lima and New York for years. Recently she flew from Los Angeles via Mexico City and Panamá to Arequipa in four days.

But then the Peruvians themselves, all classes and conditions of them, both Indians as well as the members of the Spanish upper classes, are unusually air-minded, and their young men make good flyers. If their daring countryman Chavez could pioneer in the flying business, they must keep up the tradition. The Peruvian Army Air Corps, with some 150 airplanes, is one of the two or three crack air forces in South America. There are five regular commercial lines in the country, the

Perú

International Pan-American Grace Airways operating between the United States, Buenos Aires and Montevideo, Uruguay, one line going by way of Santiago, Chile, and the other by La Paz, Bolivia, and the Faucett Aviation Company, operating locally within the country. Both are American-owned. The Peruvian or National Air Line and the Aerovias Line, now merged with the Faucett Lines, both operate locally. Then there is the German-owned Condor Company, with one local line and a section which joins up with the International System operating across Bolivia, Brazil and the Atlantic to Berlin. All the locally operated companies do a great deal of charter work, making special trips for industrial and mining organizations. In 1936 the Condor Line transported nearly 1200 tons of gold-mining machinery from Trujillo to the new gold-mining developments of Parcoy on the Upper Marañon River.

Last year the five companies flew 2,135,456 miles within the country, carrying 34,571 passengers, nearly 1000 tons of cargo, almost fifty tons of first-class mail and seven and a half tons of parcels post. Significantly enough, two-thirds of the passengers, natives and foreigners, travelled by the American lines, while the National Line and the two American lines together transported most of the mail and parcels post. The German Condor Company handled nearly half the cargo.

The air bases, landing fields and terminals built by the Panagra in most of the towns and cities from Talara to Arequipa, especially those in Lima and Arequipa, are among the finest in South America. Limatambo in the capital city rivals many of the finest terminals in the United States. In view of rumors regarding air bases and terminals owned and operated by the Germans, it may well be pointed out that the German Condor line utilizes Panagra terminals both in Lima and Arequipa, paying adequate rentals for the service of course.

Arequipa is the hub of international air travel in southern Perú for the planes of both the Pan-American Grace and the

German lines. Planes bound to and from Chile, Bolivia, Brazil, Argentina and eastern points, check out of or into Perú at Arequipa, while from the southern metropolis local Peruvian planes make Cuzco to the north, Tacna and Mollendo in the south.

On the MacGregor-Harris tour of inspection, we made a special flight from Arequipa down to Tacna. Tacna is now the Peruvian portion of the Siamese Tacna-Arica combination that kept Chile and Perú fighting or glaring at one another for half a century. Along with the desperate and disastrous wrangle between Bolivia and Paraguay over the Chaco, and the still unsettled Ecuadorean-Peruvian dispute, the Tacna-Arica trouble was long down on the books as one of the three major international sore spots on the Continent. It will be remembered that, in the Warren G. Harding regime, General Pershing was sent to arbitrate the matter, but after months of arbitrating, during which time the more he arbitrated the matter the more unmanageable the Chileans and Peruvians became, the General finally developed such bad health, diplomatic or otherwise, that he sailed for home leaving the matter much more unsettled than when he arrived. It was not until the cool and calm days of Messrs. Coolidge and Kellogg that the Solomonian operation was performed definitely and finally giving Arica to Chile and Tacna to Perú.

Tacna is the last Peruvian center of habitation before you reach present-day Chile. It is another of those irrigated green valleys surrounding an old Spanish colonial town. A trucking and fruit-growing section, it produces oranges, grapefruit, peaches, and the largest, juiciest, best-flavored pears I have ever eaten. Due to lack of transportation, except by air, or railroad down to Arica, what might otherwise become a flourishing community awaits quietly the inauguration of a new highway to Arequipa, a highway already projected by the government.

Mollendo is the Pacific port for Arequipa and is 107 miles away by railway, or a half an hour straight down by air. Either route leads across the Islay Desert. The trip by air reveals a strange scene. Continuing my southern commuting with Harris and John D., we spent a day in Mollendo. As usual we were up as the first rays of light began shooting up from behind the Andes. It is always a bracing experience to get up at Arequipa. The cold of the high plateau sent shivers up and down my spine as we hurried off to the field, through trains of burros and llamas bringing in the produce of the countryside to the markets of the city. The moment the yellow beams of Old Sol glistened against the head of El Misti, we were in the heavens and out over the desert of glaring white sands across which mysterious *medanos,* or crescent-shaped sand dunes, move steadily from the sea to the mountains. A hundred feet from tip to tip and ten to fifteen feet high, these little sand hills start at the edge of the sea. Spanked by the prevailing winds from the south that follow or precede the Humboldt Current, they travel about sixty feet a year, always maintaining their perfect figures and graceful movements, one of the phenomena of nature.

Perched on the very edge of a high bluff overlooking the open Pacific, Mollendo as a port not only rivals but surpasses Salaverry and the ports of the north for the thrills and perils encountered by passengers leaving or boarding ships. At times the swells and rolls of the sea are so great that steamers do not attempt to discharge or take on passengers. And even lighters have been swamped in an attempt to take cargo ashore. Until the coming of airplanes there was no other way for citizens, officials, businessmen or others to travel between Lima and Arequipa.

This condition will not prevail much longer. The change is in process. When the magnificent port facilities and new extensions at Callao were completed, the Frederick Snare Corporation immediately began work on a $2,625,000 modern port and dock system for Mollendo. But not at Mollendo itself. The new port is to be on the Matarani Bay, twelve miles to the north of the old town proper. At Mollendo there isn't an indenture in the shore line where a breakwater could be built. For that matter Matarani Bay is not exactly a bay, but a bite into the precipitous coastline. But it has a small island a little way offshore to which one end of a breakwater can be successfully anchored. In any case the new port will give a new boost to the southern railway system and the southern metropolis of Arequipa. It is expected that tourist travel alone will grow by leaps and bounds, because this is the only land route to the historic Inca ruins in the Cuzco country.

Along Perú's extensive coastline numerous railroads make brave starts for the mountains, but usually give up after struggling twenty, thirty, and at the most thirty-five miles up river valleys. Only two lines actually reach the cordillera, the Central from Lima to Oroya and the Southern from Mollendo to Arequipa, then up to Juliaca, where branch lines lead southward to Lake Titicaca and the other northward to Cuzco. The 500 miles of narrow-gauge trackage operated by the Southern Railways is the longest single system in the country, and is one of the 1167 miles of British-owned lines operating in various sections of the republic. The state-operated lines, all of them short, amount to only 490 miles. In addition some 825 miles are operated by various industries, mines, large *haciendas* and oil fields, part of which are open to regular public traffic. In other words, in the entire country there are only 2792 miles of railroads, mostly narrow-gauge, hardly 300 miles of which even suggest a modern, up-to-date railroad.

Like the Talara-Chiclayo-Trujillo districts in the north, and the central regions around Oroya and Cerro de Pasco, the southern section of the country, that is, the Arequipa area, is becoming an important mining center. In fact, the gold-mining interests are shifting southward. Arequipa is headquarters for several of the new companies, some of which are American owned or financed. At Quinta Bates in the past year I have met numbers of officials of gold-mining companies, and numerous lone prospectors, solo geologists and adventurers, down from the mountains on vacation. One Scotsman had grown gray looking for the end of the rainbow high up among the peaks and crags, and had finally succeeded in finding it. Down to get supplies and finances to carry on, he could hardly wait to begin the perilous trip back. "It has been a long trail of hardship and disappointment through the years," he said philosophically, as he leaned back in one of Tia's easy chairs and the smoke floated lazily up from his pipe. "And now that the trail ends in success I can hardly believe it."

The Pan-American Grace Airways furnished the first spectacular example of the use of airplanes for transporting heavy mining machinery in South America. Three years ago it contracted to fly equipment for a mine in the eastern foothills of the mountains beyond Cuzco. In thirty minutes the plane made a trip which required three weeks by mule train even in dry weather.

South of Arequipa and up in the Lake Titicaca region are several mining properties. It is even expected that oil is to be found along the shores of the lake. Incidentally, most people are under the impression that Lake Titicaca is a Bolivian lake. The Bolivian-Peruvian border line practically cuts the lake in half at a northeasterly-southwesterly angle. Anyway, it is the dream of Peruvian officials that the Peruvian shores of the lake may soon be dotted with oil derricks. The government is already exploring and expects to begin experimental drilling within the next few months.

Returning northward to Lima after my visit to the south and the Arequipa country, I flew with my scouting friends as far as the city of Ica. I wanted to travel from this section north over the new highway which is steadily advancing from Lima to Arequipa, and which at that time had been paved as far as

Ica. Within the next twelve months, if all goes well politically in Perú, it will be possible for the first time in history to travel by automobile overland between the nation's two largest cities, cities which for four centuries, except by sea or air, have been as far apart as Moscow and Shanghai. "When that is possible," a Peruvian professor told me, "southern Perú will experience a new renaissance." Even the Ica-Pisco-Lima stretch inaugurated in June, 1938, brings into close contact with the markets and industries of Lima one of the most important regions of coastal Perú. Back in the mountains from Ica a third of the country's output of gold is mined, while the surrounding lowlands constitute a large farming section. Farther along in the Pisco section grapes are turned into a famed, potent and palatable rum of the same name.

At Pisco, history once again becomes hopelessly entangled with national economy. The near-by Paracas Peninsula has yielded some of the most priceless archæological finds in Perú. From the Mochica and Chimu country of the far north have been gathered valuable pottery, *huacos* and golden crowns. From an ancient burial ground for the priests and nobility of a pre-Incan race at Paracas, Doctor Julio Tello, Perú's most noted archæologist, has dug up mummies wrapped in the most gorgeous hand-woven *mantas* or tapestries five by seven feet in size. Many of them are of the texture of Gobelin tapestries. Some are even more delicate in texture. The figures on the finest of Gobelins show plainly on one side only. The figures on the Paracas *mantas* are equally distinct on both sides.

Incidentally it was interesting, not to say amusing, to see it announced in the New York papers recently that the Brooklyn Museum, on the requisition of Doctor Herbert J. Spinden, Curator of American Indian Art and Primitive Cultures, had acquired one of those *mantas*, calling it "the most famous textile of its kind . . . found in a pre-Inca tomb." Surely so eminent an archæologist as Doctor Spinden would know that this is

Perú

by no means the most famous and that Doctor Tello has dug up hundreds of them, many in a perfect state of preservation. It is only necessary to go to the National Museum in Lima or Doctor Tello's headquarters in the old Bolívar Museum at Magdalena Vieja to see them.

The people of the Pisco section expect the new highway to bring them tourists and sightseers as well as afford them new outlets for their products, especially their cotton. Interestingly enough, cotton is indigenous to the Pisco country. The ancients of this southern coastal region specialized in cotton, as well as woolen textiles, and cotton is today the most flourishing of its industries. Over half of Perú's hundred-thousand-ton production of cotton is grown in this region between Ica and Lima. What is more important, two crops are grown every year, one being picked or gathered from February to April, and the other from May to November.

Most of the cotton produced in Perú is literally Peruvian cotton. It is known as *tanguis,* a type developed in Perú by a Peruvian citizen, Fernando Tanguis. In this desert dry country ordinary cotton is subject to wilt. The *tanguis* variety resists wilt. There are types known as *alcala* and *pima,* the latter said to be a variation of that produced in the Yuma Arizona region. They do very well in the far north. But in the south *tanguis* predominates. It is only a medium staple cotton averaging a little more than one inch, but it said to be the whitest in the world, and is used in foreign countries principally for the manufacture of fine dress collars. Evidently the stiff-collar industry is looking up, for last year three quarters of the entire Peruvian crop was exported.

If you are travelling northward by water along the Peruvian coast nowadays, your steamer is always certain to anchor off several places between Pisco and Lima to take on cotton, while if you travel the highway you find yourself continually dodging trucks loaded with cotton for the mills of Lima, as well as grapes, rum and countless other products from these rich agricultural regions. Another indication of the progress that develops so quickly in the wake of new roads in these Other Americas.

Perú's road-building campaign is probably the most ambitious on the continent. Following the tendency in so many other countries which have adopted three-, five- or six-year public works plans, in 1936 the Peruvian Government decreed a three-year-highway plan, for which eight and three-quarter million dollars, approximately thirteen per cent of the entire national budget, was set aside.

By the end of 1938 the plans were already well under way and 35,000 men with two million dollars' worth of new road machinery were engaged in highway construction. At the beginning of 1939 nearly 15,500 miles had been surveyed or built throughout the country. Half of the completed roads had been paved with either macadam, concrete or crushed stone.

At the present rate Perú will be the first of all the large countries to complete its portion of the north and south Pan-American highway. Only a few sections of the grading from Lima northward remain to be done, while work on the Lima-Arequipa-Bolivian section is progressing rapidly. Since most of Perú's cities lie along the Pacific and the coastal region west of the Andes, the Pan-American highway is really a vital Peruvian trunk line, and its completion will serve Perú as well as international traffic. Meantime the government and the engineers are thinking of the importance of the high Andean valleys which, except for the Cerro de Pasco and Chanchamayo regions, have seen little development. So at the present time work is also proceeding at full speed on roads to connect the upper valleys with the main north-to-south road.

Not content with building roads, the government encourages the public to buy and use automobiles. Heretofore if you attempted to travel about on the few roads already built in the country, you were stopped every few miles to pay fees at toll gates. All toll gates have now been abolished. Along with the abolition of toll roads comes a new law providing for uniform license plates. The result is that within the past year Perú has become one of the leading world markets for American trucks, automobiles, tires and auto accessories, and the oldest of the countries of South America becomes the newest of all in transportation and communication facilities.

V

Death and Resurrection

JULIO TELLO was only a barefoot Indian boy when he came down from the mountains to look for an opportunity to go to school. The opportunity finally came, even if it was largely of his own making. Determination, perseverance and an apt mind enabled him within a very few years to complete his course in Lima and win a scholarship to Harvard University. To the banks of the Charles he brought the same mental and spiritual equipment that served him so well in the capital of his own country. In what to him at least was the extremely democratic atmosphere of Cambridge, he gained a new reverence for the great races whose blood and traditions he had inherited. Students and professors alike were not only interested in him, but admired him. Their expressions of admiration for the ancient and fabulous civilizations of his country inspired him with the idea of devoting his life to making them known to the world and to posterity. Archæology and anthropology became his favorite subjects.

In due time he returned to Perú with his degree, a broad outlook upon the world and the tools with which to ply his profession. In the years that followed he led expeditions to the north and to the south. He lived among the natives in remote mountain valleys. After hundreds of years of persecution, they offer the white man few confidences. But Julio Tello

[334]

is of their flesh and bone, and, although he is as reticent on the subject as they, there is little doubt that he gained from them knowledge which has enabled him to uncover cities, temples and ancient burial places full of archæological treasures that might have remained unknown. Anyway, from pottery and *huacos* from the hitherto unknown ruins of Chavin beyond the cordillera and north of Cerro de Pasco, the priceless textiles and tapestries from the Paracas Peninsula and the revelations from numerous other discoveries, he has pieced together much of the dramatic story of Perú in the days before Pizarro, a story as full of war and conquest as the years that have followed.

Lima is full of museums, most of them maintained by the government, at present under the administration of the scholarly and suave Doctor Luis E. Valcárcel. But Julio Tello, quiet, suspicious, and no doubt inwardly sharing the contempt of his race for politicians and white men, works unobtrusively and almost unnoticed in the Bolívar Museum, the rapidly crumbling old colonial house out in the suburb town of Magdalena Vieja between Lima and the sea, where Simón Bolívar lived with his inamorata, a remarkable Ecuadorean, while he was attempting to build an independent nation out of Pizarro's toppled Spanish province. I met Doctor Tello the first time in company with Doctor Wendell Bennett, the brilliant young American archæologist who has led many expeditions to South America for the American Museum of Natural History. It was just after Nelson Rockefeller had paid a visit to Magdalena Vieja. If any Indian could be on the brink of emotion he was, because young Rockefeller had been so impressed with the gorgeous Paracas tapestries that he had contributed several thousand dollars for their restoration and preservation. He showed me scores of them, and in room after room pointed out shelves stacked high with other articles that had been carefully studied and restored, great volumes filled with records and analyses of them, and tons of *huacos* and pottery, mounds of Paracas mummy bundles, some four hundred in all, still untouched and unopened. The hours slipped by like minutes, and just at nightfall we entered a great circular room where the mummies are unrolled as carefully and lovingly as if they were newly born infants, and the work of classification goes on. The entire floor, except a space in the center large enough for a desk and a chair, was covered with long row after long row of skulls of the priests and nobility of the ancient races, while the shelves which extended from the floor to the ceiling were jammed with their handiwork. As we stood with him in the almost semidarkness of that room, the thought came to me that here in the keeping of a man in whose veins flows the blood of all these ancient peoples reposed the mute but tragic record of old Perú before the coming of the white man, an age-old record of death and resurrection.

The story of Perú, both in the days of the red man's ascendancy and in the four hundred years that have followed, is the story of the rise of one tribe and its subjugation by a stronger, the story of the assumption of one viceroy, president or dictator and his violent overthrow by another. Perú's continual state of political change began with the Mochicas, who managed to dominate the north from about 200 to 600 A.D., when they crumbled and were succeeded by various races who descended upon them from every direction; one from Chavin up in the cordillera, another from Recuay, and still another from as far south as Tiahuanaco on the shores of Lake Titicaca. By 900 A.D. the Chimus had superseded these various races and built their great city of Chanchan near Trujillo. Meantime the last of the powerful Indian civilizations, the Incas, had risen to power in the south around Lake Titicaca and begun their steady march northward. About 1300 A.D. they got around to wiping out the Chimus and extending their domain all the way from the Pacific to the Amazonian lowlands and from the

Perú

Bogotá *Sabana* in Colombia to Cordoba and the edge of the great *pampa* of Argentina. But by the time the Spaniards arrived, the Inca empire had begun to show signs of decadence. It had been divided between two Incas or kings, one having established his capital in the northern city of Quito and the other in Cuzco in the south. Worst of all the two rulers had already fought among themselves and Atahualpa, the southern ruler, had taken the other prisoner, thus presenting a divided and depleted authority to the enemy. Some have even ascribed the ease and quickness with which Pizarro and his handful of tramps overcame the entire Inca armies, as much to a shaken allegiance, division and disloyalty in the Incas' own ranks as to the possession of horses, guns and cannon by the Spaniards.

But the rise and fall of races and governments before the conquest by white men cannot equal the succession of governments and rulers that have followed since. After the brief nine-year reign and tragic end of Pizarro, and a three-year rule by Governor Vaca de Castro, the Spanish crown for nearly three hundred years occupied itself with recalling and appointing its forty-one different viceroys, about one for each six or seven years, beginning with Blasco Nuñez Vala, and including the oratorical Father de la Gasca and the romantic Don Manuel de Amat y Junient. Besides these and two or three other notable exceptions, hardly any of them succeeded in ruling for any length of time without rude interruption, or having to leave under fire, both literally and figuratively.

In the early 1800s the Spanish-born Peruvians began a steady agitation and fight for separation from the motherland. These early Peruvian stirrings for independence were going on at about the time Napoleon was retreating from Moscow, and while we were having our second war with the British, as well as disagreements and fights about it among our own people, during the time, it may be remembered, when the English redcoats captured Detroit, incited their Indian allies to massacre the entire garrison at Fort Dearborn in Chicago, and finally invaded and burned Washington. The Peruvians finally declared independence on July 28, 1821. The next two years they spent mopping up the royalists, getting rid of the last viceroy who had fled up into the mountains to Cuzco, and debating and writing a constitution. The first elected President got under way September 28, 1823, a few months after the first steamboat sailed up the Mississippi and some two months before James Monroe announced to the world that it would be bad business, both for us and the European governments, if the latter should try to seize any more territory or attempt to transfer any of their political systems to this hemisphere.

When Don Jose de la Riva Aguero, the first President, took over in the old vice-regal palace on the Plaza de Armas in Lima, the government of Perú became a widely distributed if centrally directed affair. The country was divided into departments corresponding to our states, whose governors were and still are called *prefects*, provinces headed by *sub-prefects*, districts administered by *gobernadores*, cities ruled by *alcaldes*, and a congress, a judiciary and other governmental accessories, all roughly patterned after those of the United States.

From that time until now many periods in the republic's existence, like the greater portion of the life of the vice-royalty, have been characterized by forced presidential resignations, shotgun elections, assassinations, military *coups d'état*, and what might be called comic-opera revolutions. Few have been the number of elections or changes of government in the past fifty years that have not been accomplished by intrigue, force or even violence. Not only political but economic and social progress has been held back on this account, and few administrations, even those backed by force, have been able to remain in power long enough to carry out any lengthy constructive program. Until the present unprecedentedly busy regime of Oscar R. Benavides, the longest and most noteworthy in recent years was the administration of the dictatorship of Augusto B. Leguia, who came to power by a *coup d'état* in 1919 and ruled for eleven years.

Leguia's long reign was a combination of constructive and useful developments, unfortunate mistakes and intermittent dictatorial intolerances. Energetic, educated abroad, trained in the United States, where for years he was an insurance sales-man, and businesslike, Leguia had great ambitions for his country. He was a tiny man, five feet four inches tall, and weighed about 125 pounds. He was of pure Spanish blood, with fair skin and in later years wore a trim gray mustache and looked at you through clear, keen, gray eyes. If the late Andy Mellon had lived in Perú, he and Leguia might easily have served as doubles for each other.

Leguia possessed some of the Mellon financial ability too. At least he could raise money. He not only induced many foreign enterprises to come into the country, invest and develop resources, but in the boom days succeeded in borrowing from American bankers, that is, from widows, doctors and school teachers upon whom the bankers unloaded the bonds, a hundred million dollars. With this he made vast improvements in Lima and the surrounding country, as well as in other cities. He built the first paved highway between Lima and Callao and drew up elaborate plans for many other civic improvements and public works.

But he was what no dictator can afford to be, an indulgent father and friend who allowed some members of his family, as well as some of his own cronies, to have too much rein. His sons were not only extravagant, but behind the back of their father engineered deals and engaged in activities, or got the reputation for such things, which the public condemned. After his death it was proven before a United States Senate Investigation Committee that his oldest son got $415,000 in one lump sum out of United States bankers for helping to engineer one of the loans made to his father's government. The sons took advantage of the father's strong-armed government to lord it over the citizens and even officials in ways the father himself would not have thought of doing, but all of which was checked up against the dictator.

He maintained all the forms of a republic. The courts functioned, the Congress and Senate sat, although they took orders. He built up a strong army, a first-class, if small, navy trained by United States officers, and one of the finest national police forces in South America. Even today the national police function efficiently and courteously in every city and district of the country, in Talara and Tacna, in Lima and Arequipa, in Iquitos and the Chanchamayo. Under Leguia some effort was made to improve the lot of the Indians, and to compel property owners to pay living wages to their workmen. He brooked no interference with his government from any native or foreigner. He often shot Peruvians guilty of treason and usually jailed or banished his critics. The editor of *El Comercio,* a scion of one of one of the oldest Spanish families in the country, was banished, and the paper was not allowed to publish an editorial for ten years.

It is the consensus of opinion among responsible Peruvians that, although Leguia was always despotic, he was personally honest. But in his old days he became surrounded by some very dishonest ministers and secretaries, and he had to reap the fruits of his despotism and his unfortunate associates. When the depression struck, money ran low. Many activities had to be discontinued. It became more and more difficult to pay the armed forces, always the first nail in the coffin of a dictatorship. And then came that fatal night in August, 1930, when a diminutive, dreamy-eyed *cholo,* Lieutenant-Colonel Luis M. Sanchez Cerro, commander of the garrison in Arequipa, revolted and took the leadership of the already ripe revolution.

Perú

"I went aboard the cruiser Almirante Grau at 11 o'clock," the naval officer in charge of the fleet that night told me a few days later when I arrived in Perú. "Early in the evening I had called at the Presidential Palace in Lima and they had told me of the defection in the garrison at Arequipa. No doubt that the situation was well in hand, though. Anyhow, the strong man was at the helm. Many a disturbance such as this had been put down in the eleven years of his regime—so to sleep.

"I was hardly in bed when there was a knock at my door. A message from the President? Strange, I thought. Surprising, when I read it. I leaped into my uniform, sent orders to all the officers, dispatched a launch and waited. Finally the chug of the motor and the return of the launch. Up the ladder came the diminutive figure of a very old man. The crew stood at attention. Officers saluted. The President was aboard!

"Rumors spread. Nobody knew what it was all about. The President had said nothing. Was he still the President? And what was his mission on board a warship in the small hours of the morning?

"There was a hurried conference of officers. Each contributed the rumors he had collected and offered his suggestions. Finally we invited His Excellency himself to tell us the state of affairs.

"Haggard and nervous he came before us, a group of officers of the Peruvian navy, at 4:30 in the morning, and told us of the dramatic incidents of the last few hours—a haggard and nervous old man who until recently had been the most powerful figure of the Andean republics.

"His cabinet had been forced to resign. A group of army officers had urged a military cabinet in its place. Yielding, he appointed one and went to bed. Shortly they called him to his office and demanded changes. Inviting their suggestions, he appointed another and started to swear it in. Some one objected and said the colonel at Arequipa, Sanchez Cerro, who had started the revolt in the army, should be in the cabinet. The

New Roads to Riches

President acceded. But there were further objections on the grounds that some of the appointees were not present, notably the colonel from Arequipa. Several spoke in a disrespectful manner, some were even intoxicated. Suddenly a lieutenant pushed his way in and with a revolver drawn demanded the immediate resignation of the Chief Executive. The entire group then flopped and joined in the demand. The resignation was penned and the President fled to the cruiser in Callao harbor.

" 'But,' said the President, 'only the Congress has the right to accept my resignation. Until Congress meets and accepts it in the constitutional way, I am President of Perú!' And there was a momentary spark of the old Leguia. The group snapped to attention and saluted. The President returned the salute and went back to his quarters.

"Immediately he sent for me, and there, as the first streak of dawn crept over the mountains behind Callao and Lima, he complained that he was tired. He looked it—not only tired, but broken. His hands twitched. His eyes were sunken and blood-shot. What should he do? Imagine the Leguia of other days asking such a question—the Leguia who more than once had defied mobs and resisted assassins! The power of decision was gone. Nearly eighty years of a vigorous and eventful life had exacted their toll.

"The navy would have stood by him. He could have held the chief support and the key to the capital. One word and he would have been master of the situation and maybe still master of Perú. But the final punch was lacking. One word and the ship could have proceeded to a foreign port. But no word! Later the old man confessed he did not know what to do. He couldn't go away, for he hadn't a penny to his name. Besides, he wanted to leave Perú in the hands of a constitutional government.

"Later in the day orders came from the military junta which had taken over affairs at Lima, ordering the ship to proceed with the former President to Panamá. An hour later the colonel at Arequipa ordered it back. He did not recognize the group of senile and fat old generals. And so Leguia came back to be sent in disgrace first to the bleak island of San Lorenzo and later to the historic old prison in Lima, there to await the fate that has overtaken many another man in the stormy career of Perú, and, curiously enough, the fate he himself had meted out to scores of his enemies." And in the officer's own words, "Another period in Peruvian history is closed."

Leguia's successor, the little colonel from Arequipa, one of the first men of Indian blood to become the head of the nation, was a picturesque little man. I met him two days after he arrived in Lima. And he impressed me greatly. There was no show of importance, no attempt to impress a foreign writing man, but marked simplicity and unmistakable earnestness. I have had opportunities to meet many South American personalities—statesmen, generals and scholars. This little colonel, who had so suddenly, almost overnight, caused the overthrow and imprisonment of the most spectacular figure in modern Peruvian history, a feat eminently sufficient to warrant a feeling of importance, was about the most unassuming figure that I have ever met south of Panamá.

Born in 1889, Sanchez Cerro was graduated from military school in 1910 and thereafter served in various regiments until February 4, 1914. On that date came the revolution which overthrew President Guillermo Billinghurst. Sanchez Cerro played an active part in that revolt.

In 1919 Leguia became president by a *coup d'état*. A revolt was expected and in 1922 it came, with the dreamy-eyed Sanchez Cerro at its head. He took possession of the city of Cuzco, but was so seriously wounded that he lost whatever advantage he had obtained and the revolution ended. Sanchez Cerro succeeded in evading arrest and left for Morocco, where for fourteen months he fought in the Riffian war against Abd-el Krim.

Later he went to France, devoting several years to advanced military courses.

Back in Perú again, he obtained command of a battalion and was finally promoted to a lieutenant-colonelcy. But his bold career as a revolutionist was not ended. In his second revolt against Leguia, his fearlessness brought success. Following his bid for power in the south, and in the face of an uncertain state of affairs in the capital, he took a couple of aides with him, flew to Lima ahead of his forces, deposed the self-appointed junta, jailed them and proceeded to organize his own military government.

But Sanchez Cerro did not last. The old aristocratic families, who feel it their divine right to rule, many of whom had received scant recognition from Leguia, now saw a chance to recoup their lost power and prestige. Having the financial advantage, their bid for rule could not be easily put aside. Besides, Sanchez Cerro was not of the élite socially and traditionally. A little Spanish blood flowed in his veins, but he was actually more Indian than *cholo*. "His skin is too dark," said one prominent Peruvian at the time. "We can't have a *cholo* ruling over us."

Anyway, Sanchez Cerro was for the moment forced out, and followed in rapid succession by four provisional presidents and ad-interim executives until a genuine national election was planned and carried out in October, 1931. This election will long stand out in Peruvian history, not only as a marvel of democratic fairness, but as one of the most impressive dramas in modern South American politics. Responsible citizens able to read and write were finger-printed and registered in advance. What is more, they were required by law to finish the process. On election day approximately ninety per cent of them went to the polls and voted.

In every town and city, north and south—it was not only a quiet Sunday but a silent one. You could not buy a drink nor a cigarette. There were no masses, early or late. Churches were even closed. Not a bell rang out in all the devout land. Voters approached the polling places with an air of religious fervor. It was an election without an eruption, not a shot fired anywhere, not a broken head. It was more like a peaceful funeral than a political fight.

The moment the polls closed, ballot boxes, "urns of liberty," Peruvians called them, were locked, sealed and sent under military guard to the capital city where their secrets were revealed in the presence of the public and the press, a process which required several days. The successful candidate for the presidency was none other than the tiny Sanchez Cerro, hero of August, 1930, the first genuinely and freely elected constitutional President and Congress in a generation. Some say the first in a hundred years.

I talked with Sanchez Cerro in his own house while the ballots of the October election were being counted, but after it was quite certain he would be the winner. After ten o'clock at night, with secretaries, campaign managers, friends and curiosity-seekers filling the lower floors, the front yard and flowing out into the street, we went upstairs to his own apartment. It was a warm night and without ceremony he removed his coat and seated himself on a footstool. Sanchez Cerro was no longer the soldier, might never have fired a gun; and he certainly did not act the part of a Latin American about to become the first citizen of the nation. He was a plain Peruvian citizen ready to talk about the problems of his country.

"I wish to guarantee honest investments of foreign capital," was the very first remark he made, knowing, of course, that that was the question all foreigners were interested in. "But always with the protection of the just rights of Peruvians. Naturally, Americans will want to know my attitude in regard to bonds which they hold. Peruvians feel that money from the bonds sold by North American bankers for the old government was very badly invested by Leguia. In spite of this feeling, you will remember that when I came to power as provisional president one of the first things I did was to let it be known that it was the fault of Leguia, not the American capitalists, that the money was improperly spent.

"I made every effort to comply with the interest and amortization payments on Perú's foreign indebtedness while I was in power. I want to say I have always been a lover of justice without discrimination between foreigners and Peruvians, and did everything possible to meet our just obligations." And it is true that it was not until after his resignation as Provisional President of the military junta that payment of interest on Perú's foreign obligations ceased.

But, alas, on another Sunday, barely two years after he flew from Arequipa to take over the government following the resignation of Leguia, Sanchez Cerro himself was assassinated in cold blood just as he was driving away from a Sunday afternoon at the races. Congress immediately assembled, elected and called to the helm Oscar R. Benavides, who took office April 30, 1933.

Benavides, a regular army officer, had bobbed up several times before as a political figure. In 1914 he had led the military movement which overthrew President Billinghurst, and in which Sanchez Cerro had figured. Following this, he served briefly as the head of the provisional government. When elections were held in 1916 he handed over the government to the constitutional president, José Pardo, and returned to the army. Soon after this he was sent to France as a military observer and was assigned first to the staff of General Mangin and later on was with General Nivelle. He witnessed at close range one of the fiercest battles of the World War, the battle of Verdun. After the war he got into the diplomatic service and went as minister to Italy, but came back to Perú in 1921, only to be arrested and exiled by Leguia. Following the Sanchez

Perú

Cerro revolution of 1930, he again essayed diplomacy by accepting the appointment as minister to Spain, an appointment which he very soon gave up. He came back to Perú the last time in 1931, where he kept a close watch, not to say a close finger, on the course of events until Sanchez Cerro was assassinated and he took over.

Benavides is a short and paunchy little man, but stands straight as an arrow. He likes to wear uniforms and is proud of the fact he has always been a soldier, if not a hard fighter. He does not let people forget that he has observed much war and at close hand, even if he did not personally officiate in it. General Mangin had great respect and admiration for him and paid him a personal visit in Lima after he came to power the last time in Perú. His head is large physically, with little or no hair on top. He looks at you out of big, slightly starey eyes, wears a short stubby mustache, and when he talks seems to have difficulty keeping his false teeth in place.

Possessing a fiery or typically Latin temperament, he can fly into a rage if somebody fails to carry out an order, or makes a mistake. Otherwise, he is easy-going and loves good food and relaxation. On a warm afternoon he likes to put on pajamas and slippers and loll in his private garden, a good old tropical custom. Business people, both native and foreign, respect him and say they get a square deal from him. Even his enemies admit that he is personally honest. He is a good administrator who has surrounded himself with several of the keenest and ablest young men in the country, especially Hector Boza, Minister of Public Works, an energetic, quick-thinking and practical young engineer, under whose personal supervision most of the Benavides program of public works has been carried out. And it has been a formidable program.

When he came to office in 1933 Perú and Colombia were engaged in a serious dispute over a border question in the Amazonian region of Iquitos. In fact, the two countries were already on the verge of war. He immediately sent a cable to the President of Colombia saying, "Let's put our heads together and see if we can't settle this dispute like sensible men." The result was that within thirty days the two countries were again at peace with each other. He next tackled the financial situation of the government, and within a short time succeeded in bringing governmental expenditure into close company with governmental income. In fact, one of his proudest boasts is that the Peruvian budget has remained balanced, at least insofar as national affairs are concerned. No serious attempt has been made yet to take care of foreign obligations or bonds held by foreigners, but he has kept the internal budget balanced and carried on his program of public works without any restriction on exchange. Perú is one of the few countries in the world having an absolutely free exchange.

Benavides came into office with the promise that at the end of his term he would turn the presidency over to a duly elected successor and retire to private life when that time came. In 1936 elections were held, in which an old-line conservative and an extreme radical were the principal contenders. When it became apparent that the radical had won, the elections were annulled and Benavides became a dictator. He immediately instituted a tremendous plan for public works, chief among which has been his three-year road program. On the subject of roads he said in a statement to the public, "For many years the government should charge itself primarily with the highway problem because heretofore the exploitation of the wealth, the growth of commerce, the development of agriculture, and the proper feeding of the population, have been hindered by the immemorial barriers to industry and transportation. Remove these, open up the country so the people can travel and get their products out to market, and Perú will have made a tremendous advance toward her destiny as one of the most progressive countries of the Americas."

Perú

In this statement it is apparent that he and his advisers are not unmindful of the strength of the radical opposition. For, of course, Benavides is backed by the old-line conservatives. But if you get into the confidence of some of his ablest assistants, they will admit that their chief concern is the smoldering "communist ideas" held by the intellectuals, students and upper-class *cholos,* and that their programs of public works and social legislation are planned with the idea of counteracting these other influences. New irrigation projects have been instituted in various sections so as to bring more land into cultivation. Serious attention is being given the live-stock industry, but one of the principal innovations is the program of social welfare, one of the most advanced plans to be found anywhere on the continent. First of all, social insurance has been made obligatory for men and women workers and has already been put into effect in the larger industrial districts. This means, of course, that all foreign industries, such as the large oil and mining enterprises, were the first brought into the picture. The social insurance applies to sickness, maternity, incapacity, old age and death. The beneficiaries are hired men of not more than sixty years who draw annual pay of not more than 3000 *soles* or $525; apprentices even though they draw no pay; homeworkers and domestic employees in institutions and business houses. Insurance is paid by the worker, the employer and the state, three and five-tenths per cent by the employer, one and five-tenths per cent by the worker and one per cent by the state. To date 230,000 workers are on the rolls and it is planned to apply the system gradually throughout the nation.

Various services, which the insurance is to provide, include hospitals, clinics, recreational facilities, and so on. Already work has begun on one great hospital in the heart of Lima, and plans for another are being projected in other cities. Special plans are on paper to extend these hospitals and medical services to rural communities, as well as to cities and towns. The program is so elaborate that it will take some time to put it into effect. In fact, it is revolutionary in scope.

The new social and labor laws are designed to benefit, or are already benefiting, not only laborers employed by the large industries but those employed in agricultural pursuits as well. Some improvements are apparent on a few of the big *haciendas,* even if much of it is purely paternalistic, such as the system in vogue at Hacienda Chiclin in the Chicama valley. But it will be a long time, I fear, before these various benefits are made effective on behalf of the Indians of the far interior.

The Indians, who constitute more than half of the total population of the country, are the trying problem of Perú. There are idealists, some of them deeply sincere, but most of them impractical, ready to lead these children of the ancients in revolt against their rulers and "their betters." The outstanding and most intelligent among these leaders is Victor Raúl Haya de la Torre, founder and head of Alianza Popular Revolucionaria Americana, the Popular American Revolutionary Alliance, or the APRA movement. In fact, the APRA is so powerful that the government has not dared dispose of Haya de la Torre, although it has suceeeded in suppressing or at least driving the organization itself to cover. There are many who would like to do away with the founder but wiser heads have insisted that to make a martyr of him would be adding fuel to the flame, and their insistence has prevailed so far.

Interestingly enough, although his movement and its philosophy are both Indian, Haya de la Torre himself is not an Indian. He comes of an old aristocratic Spanish family of the north. Having studied abroad and travelled both in Europe and the United States, he is highly educated, sincere and amazingly convincing. He grieves over the historic injustice to the Indians and the less fortunate *cholos,* and the fact that so little has ever been done for them. He tries to be not only logical but practical in his program for the salvation of these unfortunates. He writes with great facility and speaks eloquently and honestly, even if some of his theories and arguments do not always stand up completely under strict analysis.

I talked to Haya de la Torre first in the heyday of the APRA movement, soon after Benavides came to office. He had a program. First of all, if and when his party came into power, he would give democracy to everybody. The fact that ninety-eight per cent of the people to whom he would give democracy could neither read nor write in Spanish, or any other language, and their ancient Quechua language was not a written language, did not seem to him a great handicap. There would be, along with democracy for all, education for all—although how people are to practice pure democracy successfully while waiting to climb the ladder from abysmal illiteracy to intellectuality was not explained. Large industry, which to a great extent means foreign industry, would be made to contribute more to the community and to the worker, even though he observed that in most cases foreign industry already paid the best wages, provided better living conditions, than any other enterprises in the nation. He was going to inaugurate great irrigation projects, more extensive than any that already existed, so there might be more farm lands for every one who wished to farm. Who would furnish the money for such projects and where the water would come from wasn't altogether clear. And as I have already pointed out in another chapter, the great problem in the country insofar as agriculture is concerned is the problem of water. In most sections not enough water comes down from the mountains to supply the acreage now under cultivation. He pointed out that a small number of Perú's 6,500,000 people, probably not more than 5000 families, own and control practically all of the irrigated land, a fact which nobody can deny of course.

Under *aprismo* there would be private estates, of course, but they would be rigidly regulated and operated for the equal benefit of the workers as well as the owner. Most of the land, however, would go back to the people, not necessarily individually, but under practically the same age-old "communistic" system that prevailed before the conquest. Nor is the word *communism* to be interpreted in the Russian sense. Haya de la Torre's communistic ideas were not derived from Russia. They are native Peruvian, not greatly different from those which prevailed in Mexico under the Aztecs. This system still prevails in some sections today, such as the *comunidades* of the Lambayeque department heretofore mentioned. The general idea seems to be that individuals would own the land in common, each working a certain tract and disposing of his crops, but all would share equally in the general responsibilities and obligations of the community from the standpoint of its economic and social welfare. The most amazing thing was the idea that all these things could be brought about without violent revolution. Haya de la Torre does not, or did not at that time, advocate or countenance violence. To me he even deplored it, and I believe he was sincere. Unfortunately, in the brief moments when his followers have gained the upper hand anywhere, as in the 1932 outbreak in Trujillo, they have carried violence to the limit. I have found numbers of foreigners who can elucidate and make perfectly logical the ideas of *aprismo*. But I have not found a disinterested Peruvian who can explain it satisfactorily. One Peruvian economist suggested that "unfortunately many foreigners, themselves familiar with Russian economy, read into *aprismo* their own ideas and their understanding of what Lenin tried to put into practice in Russia, instead of the teachings of Haya de la Torre himself."

It is certain that two forces are struggling for supremacy in Perú. The old conservative landowners are trying desperately to hold on to power, and maintain the economic system handed down from the conquest against the revolutionary idealism of *aprismo*. The present Benavides program is a desperate effort to effect a compromise and to make a capitalistic, and insofar as landholding is concerned, a feudalistic system liberal enough to benefit all the people so that *aprismo* or some other radical theory may be staved off. As in Mexico, although not to the same extent, something in the Indians of Perú is beginning to stir. They have seen flickerings before their eyes; they haven't seen them distinctly, but "only through a glass darkly."

Travel the Sierras. Cross the mountains as I have and on every cliff, the edge of every mountain wall, an Indian will be standing motionless and silent, looking out over the valleys below. He will see every stranger that passes. He may have his alpacas or llamas grazing near by, but while they graze he looks out upon the passing world. He sees all things but still regards what he sees in silence. He deals with the palefaces, works for them, but he does not trust them. He still regards all Spaniards and other whites with suspicion.

As one old Yankee, long resident in Perú, who made his stake and is now taking his ease back at home, told me recently, "The Indian will eventually rise up against the whites, against the foreigners, against the big *hacendados*. He probably won't win at first, but he will try again. He may be subdued for a time, but in the end he will triumph and possess his own country."

Which would mean another Peruvian death and resurrection.

VI

The World in Perú

STRANGE as it may seem, a young Irishman who began his career as a clerk for a trading company in the romantic land of the Incas, and who continued until death one of its tycoons of trade and industry, was twice Mayor of New York City.

In the eighteen-fifties and sixties Perú's Guano Islands were the rendezvous for a large portion of the world's windjammers and square riggers. Annually a formidable armada of these picturesque old ships sailed away from Peruvian waters with hundreds of thousands of tons of bird droppings with which to fertilize lands and crops throughout the world. Having arrived from the snakeless realm of St. Patrick in 1850, William Russell Grace, whom fate had selected to forage in many fields later on, very soon identified himself with the business of furnishing provisions for these ships. However, the high honors that came to him later might have passed him severely by except for a little incident of those adventurous days.

In the second year of our memorable mixup between North and South, a group of Yankee cruisers scouting the Pacific for Confederate raiders wandered into Callao minus food, supplies, or cold cash. At that time the South was having its innings and while Peruvian bankers and merchants graciously sympathized, they were not willing to take the checks of a losing government. Paymaster Eldridge tramped the streets of Lima

Perú

for days apparently at the end of his tether, his drafts un-
honored and unsung, when luckily he ran into young Grace.

"I am in frightful difficulty," he hastened to confide.

"You are in no difficulty at all," replied the young Irishman
with generous and characteristic impulse. "I'll get you all the
money you need."

Twenty years later W. R. Grace had established head offices
for his South American activities in the city of New York.
What was more he had ingratiated himself into the most exclusive of Democratic political circles, and flung his sombrero
into the ring as candidate for mayor, which "piece of presumption" caused some of the oldsters to raise their shaggy eyebrows.

"Foreigner," said some.

"Peruvian merchant," said others.

Whereupon Mr. Eldridge, by that time Chief Paymaster of
the entire United States Navy, unforgetful of the time when
the aspiring politician had snatched him from pinching circumstances, took his pen in hand and wrote to the newspapers.
Happily the New Yorkers were still near enough to the great
rebellion to be fervent in their love of the Union and its
saviors. So they rushed out and voted for the "noble and
patriotic" adopted son.

But a Peruvian business man he was and remained. From
that time until now his name has remained as much a fixture
in Lima as the name Pizarro or Calderon, and the House of
Grace as much an institution in Perú and the neighboring
republics as it is in Hanover Square in Manhattan.

From a one-gallused supply business for ships that called
at Callao and the Chincha Islands more than eighty years ago,
the Grace Company has grown to be one of the most ramified
business organizations in the northern and western regions of
the southern continent. Its merchant marine no longer consists
of a few old sailing ships that indolently skim the southern
waters around the Horn to Chile and Perú in eighty to a

hundred days. A dozen or more steam and motor liners, some of them among the finest and most modern in the world, keep fast schedules between United States harbors and the ports of the Caribbean, and Pacific South America. Airplanes which it operates and jointly owns take the mails twice a week through half a dozen countries between the Canal Zone and Montevideo, Uruguay. While its transportation activities are a formidable enterprise, its banks supply capital and credit in the va-ious cities of these regions. Importing and exporting houses, factories, general stores, plantations and even chain groceries up and down all the Andean countries, fly the Grace flag. It is not only one of the oldest American firms doing business in South America, but it is one of the few Yankee firms that operates on the old British trading company plan.

Without any attempt to weigh its operating faults or virtues, that is, its money-making aspects, if any foreign trade methods are likely to survive nationalism or expropriation in these days of nationalistic tendencies in most of the countries to the south of us, it will be those operated on the Grace plan, firms that buy as well as sell. Yankee business and industry are highly specialized. Therefore, most of our organizations doing business in the Other Americas are also highly specialized. They appoint agents to specialize in the products of one industry, or themselves operate branch houses for the same purpose. Moreover, most of them are interested only in selling. Occasionally some organization is set up for the purpose of buying one particular product, coffee, copper, hard woods, and so on. But the Grace Company buys and sells nearly everything, imports and exports, trades within the country in which it does business. In bad times and good it goes continuously on. If business falls off in one line it pushes something else. It buys and exports, helps the country and the people to dispose of their products. It identifies itself with the countries in which it operates. Many of its high officers, partners and managers are natives.

Perú

Anyway, these incidents and facts concerning the Irish-Peruvian Yankee, and the unique organization bearing his name appropriately serve up several subjects which just now excite the press, the commentators, business men and the inner circles of government. What is the outlook for United States business, industrial investments and trade in Perú? Are the totalitarian countries making commercial advances at our expense? What effects will the victory of Fascist arms in Spain have upon the country which was for so long the center of Spanish rule in South America, and the scene of the last battle between seekers of independence and soldiers of the motherland on the southern continent?

The importance of the first question is evident when it is realized that of the $300,000,000 worth of foreign investments in the country, two-thirds of them have been made by United States interests and firms. This amount is entirely aside from the $100,000,000 worth of defaulted Peruvian bonds held by United States citizens. Mention has already been made that American capital not only developed but is still prominent in airway transportation, in the copper and silver industries, and has shared with British interests in the development of the vast oil operations. The Lima telephone system and the All America Cables are operated by the International Telephone and Telegraph Company.

Britain's stake in Perú ranks second to that of Uncle Sam. Some of the oldest foreign trading companies in Perú, aside from W. R. Grace and Company, with ramifications in every city and town, are British-owned. In the field of transportation and communication she not only operates and controls the greater portion as well as the best and most important of the railroads, owns the West Coast Cable Company, and through the Marconi Company, also operates the Peruvian Postal System. The head of the Marconi Company, a Jewish gentleman bearing the Irish name of McNulty, directs Peruvian radio broadcasting. For those concerned about Fascist and Nazi propaganda, it should be reassuring that whenever a citizen or outsider in Lima wants to make a telephone call, send a cable, write a letter or postal card, broadcast or put on a radio program, he has to resort to facilities which are under the vigilant eyes of Uncle Sam and John Bull, as well as the national government.

The two English-speaking countries are all-powerful in the fields of industry and investments. Their capital not only controls the large basic resources, the means of transportation and communication, but they are and have long been predominant in the trade and commerce of the country. Last year we sold Perú more than thirty-eight per cent of all the goods she bought in the outside world, while Britain bought from her a little less than twenty per cent of everything she exported.

Three and four years ago cursory observers were excited about Japanese influences in Perú. Next to California, Perú has received more Japanese and other Oriental immigrants than any other region of the Americas bordering on the Pacific. About 30,000 Japanese have settled in the country. For a time the Nipponese waged a lively trade campaign, the net effect of which was to frighten and discourage many Yankee salesmen and business men. In 1935 and 1936 if Japanese products had sold as successfully in Perú as Japanese propaganda sold in the United States, there would now be little use for this or any other country to attempt to sell its goods in that country. We are told so often that merchants of the Mikado had taken the markets of all South America that few people took the trouble to investigate the matter.

I studied the Peruvian situation carefully at the time. On the surface all the evidence indicated that the Japs were making great inroads. Japanese goods were on display in every city, while every day the Bolívar Hotel dining room had a large round table "Reserved for the Japanese Trade Mission." There

Perú

was even a Japanese Chamber of Commerce, with a smiling little secretary who reeled off Spanish with the same grace and ease as any other Oriental diplomat. Local newspapers were full of advertisements, stories and pictures concerning Nipponese officials, visitors and activities.

American salesmen returning from Perú, Chile or Colombia at that time were full of despair. After a trip to the leading west coast cities the foreign manager of one of our largest cotton-goods concerns told me there was no longer any use to try to compete with low-priced Japanese fabrics in these markets. Indeed, according to many commercial salesmen, it was almost useless to compete in any other line, for no matter what the product, the Japanese could offer it for less.

Of course some Japanese goods were being sold. They were being sold not merely because of low prices, but as the result of high-pressure salesmanship and diplomatic ingenuity. However, none of the important local merchants made any large purchases. The Peruvians, like most Latin American merchants, are not only conservative, slow to respond to high-pressure salesmanship, as American business men have learned only too well, but they are more suspicious than most other people of propaganda, whether commercial or otherwise. In order to introduce their goods into the country, it was necessary for the Japanese to own their own shops. Even then, to induce customers to forsake other stores, ingenious sales methods were resorted to. Invariably they displayed prominently German, English and American products along with Japanese products, and the Occidental goods were always offered at lower prices than they could be bought elsewhere. A tube of American tooth paste which sold, say, for forty cents in regular stores, could be bought for twenty-five cents in the Japanese stores. A cake of extra-fine, sweet-smelling American soap, which cost fifteen cents in the native stores, was on display in the Japanese shops for ten cents a cake.

[359]

New Roads to Riches

Naturally most of these products were sold below cost, the idea being that once a customer got the habit of buying articles cheaper in Japanese stores than elsewhere, it would be easy to switch him to Japanese products, which cost even less than the ones to which he had become accustomed. Indeed, the Japanese product often resembled the European or American product. Because of the lack of up-to-date trademark laws in most of the Latin American countries, it is possible for Japanese manufacturers to prepare their wares in similar packages, if not to duplicate altogether the products of other countries.

For a time these stores prospered. Japanese imports into Perú increased. Interestingly enough, these imports consisted not only of cotton textiles, rayons, silks, cosmetics, electrical bulbs and other fixtures which might be described as Japanese staples, but there were also all manner of heavier manufactures and radio receiving sets. At one time Peruvians were buying Japanese cement, sheet iron, nails, iron and other steel products, and buying them for 25 per cent less than superior American products.

About that time Japanese manufacturers startled the motor-car world with the announcement that they proposed to offer in the South American markets a small, entirely new type automobile called the Datsun, which would sell for more than thirty per cent less than any other small car in the world. This story was broadcast throughout the United States, headlined in every important newspaper from Maine to California. Magazines and rotogravure sections of the great Sunday papers even carried pictures of it. That was more than three years ago. To date some five low-priced Japanese passenger cars have been imported into Perú, and all by Japanese citizens resident in the country. Nor are there any on display.

Peruvians not only learned that Japanese electrical bulbs and cosmetics were of inferior quality, but the government has raised barriers against cotton goods and other Japanese manu-

Perú

factures, because they were competing with their own textile mills and young growing industries. The cold fact is that Japan's share in Perú's trade for the last two years has averaged less than two per cent of the whole.

At the moment the number of Japanese in the country is actually decreasing at the rate of 1000 a year. Many have gone home to join the fight against the Chinese, while the failure of the trade campaign and the growing restrictions raised by the Peruvian government have brought such discouragements they have moved on elsewhere. Even the suicide rate among them has been increasing of late.

Following the Japanese came the Italian and Nazi scare, which is still prominently played up in the newspapers in this country and by dozens of writers whose principal acquaintance with Perú and western South America was gained from the trip to the Eighth International Conference of American States held at Lima in December, 1938. To any one going to Lima for the first time there are many conspicuous evidences of Italian influences on every hand, including the famous Italian school on the picturesque Avenida Arequipa, Italian hospitals, the Italian Art Gallery and many palatial homes of Italians.

Descendants of Romulus and Remus give light to Pizarro's old capital from plants powered by waters which flow down through pipes and aqueducts from the icy peaks of the Andes. Last year the Italians erected an airplane factory near the government flying field of Las Palmas where Caproni planes were to be manufactured for the Peruvian armed forces. Perú, like Venezuela and Ecuador, has engaged an Italian aviation as well as a police commission to instruct its army flyers and to train its already efficient and splendidly equipped national police force. California has its Italian banking wizard, A. P. Giannini. Perú has its Gino Salocchi, whose Banco Italiano is not only the largest private financial institution in the nation, but finances a goodly portion of local Peruvian industry and agriculture.

Impressive as these activities may seem, it should be noted that for the most part the Italians in Perú are old settlers, and most of their financial interests are of long standing. Gino Salocchi's Italian bank was established exactly half a century ago. It was already a purely business and money-making Peruvian concern just about the time Mussolini was emerging from the diaper age. As for Italy's trade with Perú, she stands in about the same position as the merchants of the Mikado. Her total Peruvian imports and exports in 1937 were on a par with those of the Japanese, slightly more than two per cent of the country's total trade.

In spite of their factory, very few Italian planes have been added to the Peruvian army, while several orders for military aircraft have been placed in this country in the past few months. Recently when the government-sponsored commercial line wanted planes suitable for flying from the national capital to the Amazonian metropolis of Iquitos, it bought them in this country. In fact, four large eight-passenger, twin-motored amphibians have just been flown from Long Island to Lima.

The pretentious Italian school in Lima was founded forty years ago, and the Art Gallery was presented by the 13,000 Italian citizens of the country in 1921 on the occasion of the nation's one hundredth anniversary of independence. At that time dozens of other countries including Great Britain, the United States, and even China presented similar gifts, monuments and memorials. And while Peruvian military flyers and policemen are under the tutelage of Italian aviators, a United States Naval Mission has been on duty with the Peruvian navy for more than twenty years. American naval officers even established and organized the system of instruction in the National Naval Academy. And speaking of schools, the most popular foreign educational institution in the country, the one patronized by the most prominent Peruvian families, is the Villa Maria School, maintained by Philadelphian nuns.

German investment in Perú is represented by a few small factories, a branch bank or two, the recently established Condor Airline, several trading companies and a few *haciendas*, including the Casa Grande properties in the northern Chicama valley owned by the Gildemeisters. It is in the field of buying and selling that Hitler's subjects are conspicuous. Japanese trade methods are not only less successful but, compared with those of the Germans, positively conservative.

The Germans go out into the commercial byways and hedges and cultivate the ancient art of barter, exchanging Nazi-manufactured goods for Peruvian sugar, cotton, hides and other raw materials. The largest, shiniest and newest omnibuses that swish up and down the broad boulevards of the city are made in Germany. But in order to sell them they had to agree to establish a shop and provide trained mechanics to maintain and keep them in perfect repair for two years.

The Peruvian foreign office was in the market for a hundred new typewriters for use at the recent Pan-American Congress. Although the gathering was called to deliberate on purely American matters, this delicate fact did not deter German manufacturers from offering to better any proposition or quotation made by any competitor, Yankee or European. They offered the use of the machines absolutely free of charge during the entire conference. Afterward the government could buy them at second-hand rates, and what is more, pay for them in Peruvian exports instead of cold cash. However, the typewriters were finally bought in the United States.

When it comes to trading the Germans are just as happy to compete with their fellow Fascists as they are with any other foreigners. In 1937 while the small group of Italian Fascist sympathizers, mostly those with connections in Italy, steamship agents, members of the air and police missions, were going in heavily for ceremony, receptions and placing wreaths on the tomb of Jorge Chavez, the Germans were busy buying exactly five times more products from the Peruvians, and selling them twelve times more machinery, household utensils and trinkets than their colleagues were able to do.

In view of the comment which has been made upon the fact that Enrique Gildemeister, member of the Case Grande Gildemeister family, has recently served as Peruvian minister to Berlin, the comment of a Nazi diplomat in Lima made to me recently is rather interesting.

"Of course," he said, "it may seem significant that a man with a German name should represent the country in Berlin, even though he comes of an old family and was born in Perú. On the other hand the preponderance of Peruvian officials trained in United States colleges and universities is very significant.

"Don't forget," he went on a little bitterly, "that the foreign minister who presided over the Eighth Pan-American Conference was formerly on the staff of Harvard University. The Chief of Procotol, Doctor Ortiz de Zevallos, who presents all ambassadors, ministers and other callers to the President, is a graduate of Cornell. Santiago Bedoya, another important attaché, spent more than fifteen years in this country, and is married to an American wife, while the chief of the Propaganda Section of the Foreign Office is also a graduate of an American university. Why, you can't call on any department of the government hardly without meeting Yankee influence."

It is also significant that while in recent years the Germans have been able to make some trade gains in Perú, they have made them at the expense of Great Britain and not of the United States. United States trade with Perú has been continually increasing in recent years. Besides, it should be remembered that before the World War Germany occupied second

Perú

place to Great Britain in the commerce of all South America.
The gains she has made in recent years have been in regions
and sections whose trade she once controlled or shared with
Great Britain. Even so, her share of trade in Perú today is still
much less than it was prior to 1914.

The newest worry about totalitarian influence in our neighboring countries is the effect that the Franco victories in Spain
may have upon governments and peoples. Already there are
rumors that the little Spanish Generalissimo is preparing a
tremendous propaganda campaign not only for the purpose
of regaining lost Spanish favor in the various countries, but
to assist Italy and Germany in furthering totalitarian doctrines.

If this were true, it would, in the first place, be an admission
upon the part of Hitler and Mussolini that their own efforts in
this direction have failed. In the second place if, with superior
organization—long and highly trained propaganda experts, powerful short-wave radio facilities and the desperate necessity for
trade expansion—they could not make any headway, what can
Franco do with a shattered country, a demoralized population
and a chaotic economic machinery? And since the first necessity of a dictator is to maintain himself, all these home problems
are going to keep little Franco more than occupied in Spain
for some time to come.

Incidentally, the Spanish Loyalists themselves, hoping, of
course, to further their own ends, were the authors of this idea.
They were the first to embark upon a campaign to spread prejudice and confusion in Latin America and to create misunderstandings between the peoples of those republics and the United
States. Long before the collapse of the Madrid government,
the Spanish Loyalist Ambassador in Washington said, "There
can be no doubt of the influence of race, thought and ideals
exercised by Spain over all South American countries. Should
they see Spain influenced by such dictatorial countries as Ger-

many and Italy, the ideologies and political influences of those two European nations will enter South America by way of Spain and have a negative effect on the democratic spirit which the United States has always sought and maintained in the New World."

There are people in the other Americas, and especially in Perú, who cherish their Spanish traditions, their Spanish culture, the language, literature and music handed down by the Motherland, just as many old families in the United States treasure their British tradition. At the Plaza Theatre in New York, frequented by the reactionaries of the Park Avenue district, many members of the audience are always ready to greet with wild applause a news picture of the King of England and remain silent when one of the President of the United States appears. In the case of President Roosevelt they hiss of course. This class in Perú is a very small minority of the population, but unlike Anglophile reactionary North Americans, they would be quick to resent Spanish interference in the political affairs of their country. They would be the first to condemn any meddling upon the part of Franco. It should also be borne in mind that these old Spanish families in Perú and all the other countries from Venezuela to Bolivia, were the people who led the fight against Spain, who chased the viceroys out. It was not the Indians or the *Mestizos* who led the fight for independence. The Bolívars, the Sucres, the San Martins, the Torre Tagles and most of the other famous leaders of the wars of independence, were Spanish aristocrats. As well expect the descendants of the Adamses in Massachusetts or the Byrds in Virginia to welcome British influence at Washington as to think that old Spanish families in Perú would countenance Franco's interference with their affairs.

Naturally all of the Latin American countries were interested in the outcome of the Spanish War, just as were the people of the United States. They sympathized with the grief-stricken women and children. They looked with horror upon men of the same flesh and blood tearing one another to pieces. They mourned the destruction of Spanish culture and civilization. They gave aid and comfort to the homeless and suffering wherever and whenever possible. Their embassies and legations in Madrid furnished asylum for many Republicans, and with one accord afterward defied Franco's efforts to have them turned over to his firing-squad courts-martial. But no one country of theirs became in any way involved in the conflict.

Individual citizens or officials favored one side or the other. In the last year of the war Colombian sympathies swung heavily toward the Republicans. In most of the other countries, including Perú, sentiment among Conservatives was on the side of the Rebels. But no government anywhere between Panamá and Patagonia gave any material assistance to either side. Not one of the governments would have lasted overnight if it had tried to compel a single one of its soldiers or citizens to shoulder a gun and cross the Atlantic to fight.

And any Spanish politician, statesman or diplomat, who does not know this, is either kidding himself or has never set foot on the soil of the Other Americas. Nor has the outcome of the war had one iota of effect upon the relationship between these countries and the United States. Neither Venezuelans, nor Colombians, nor Peruvians are more pro-Yankee, or less pro-Yankee.

It is true that pro-Nazi Germans and pro-Fascist Italians, and, I repeat, mostly diplomatic representatives and agents of Italian and German steamship companies or commercial houses, with headquarters back home, tried to exploit the Franco angle of Spanish South American relations. In May, 1938, I arrived in Lima at about the same time Captain Eugenio Montes, Franco's special good-will scout, arrived to give a series of lectures and otherwise drum up sympathy for the cause of his master. Wherever he went, appeared or spoke, Italian and

German diplomats were present. In many cases the events or occasions were of the latter's making.

Forty-eight hours after Captain Montes arrived he joined the Italian and German ministers with their staffs, as well as the Papal Nuncio, in a gala *fiesta* in commemoration of Italian Empire Day, which incidentally coincided with the anniversary of Mussolini's march on Rome. On the 21st of May, the Peruvian-Italian Cultural Institute celebrated the founding of Rome, the ceremonies taking place in the presence of the Papal Nuncio, the ministers of Germany and Italy and Captain Montes. Next day the same dignitaries gave a formal reception in honor of the Spanish captain.

Curiously enough, on all of these occasions Peruvian officials were conspicuous by their absence. For the most part only routine officials were in attendance so that each of the ceremonies took on the aspect of a purely private gathering. It is significant that with the exception of the recent United States Ambassador to Perú, the Honorable Laurence A. Steinhardt, now our ambassador to Moscow, not a single prominent North American, diplomat or business man, with more than two years' experience in the country, has been in the slightest worried about the permanent effects of Hitler's, Mussolini's or Franco's propaganda. The ambassador, new to Latin America, as well as to official diplomacy, and plainly possessed of a Nazi-Fascist phobia, was outspoken in his suspicions of most Italians and Germans or of any Peruvian who had dealings with Italians or Germans. Yet members of his own official household, most of them men with long experience in Latin American posts, thought his suspicions exaggerated, if not wholly without foundation.

The substance of what I heard from the lips of Americans, business men and officials, as well as from natives and foreigners everywhere, was best summed up by one of the oldest and most important Americans in Perú. "Worried about the

Francoistas, the Black Shirts and the Brown Shirts?" he said. "Why, all we need do is to keep them talking and saluting. Peruvians already realize what their line is. Since they started talking the Peruvian newspapers have been publishing head-lines in praise of Pan-Americanism. I have even lived to see the day when a leading Peruvian newspaper says: 'The American navy is the shield of our institutions.'

"Yes," he went on, "let them tell the Peruvians how won-derful they are. If we keep quiet, and attend to our business, the Peruvians will continue to speak and think well of us.

"Besides," he concluded, with a stunner, "isn't it a little naïve, not to say childish, for a mere tourist, or a round-tripper, to suppose that any South American government or citizen wants to be taken over by a foreigner, any more than you or I want anybody with a protruding chin, or trick mus-tache, to take over the United States?"

Some of our people here at home who entertain grave sus-picions about various European isms penetrating South Amer-ica have fallen into several unfortunate habits. One is the tendency to apply Russian communistic, Fascist or Nazi termi-nologies to South American social or political movements that have long existed and which, except for a few individuals, have always been appraised by the people themselves as merely radical, liberal or conservative. Naturally some of the political and social theories existing among various groups in these coun-tries are similar to some of the theories of Russian communism, Italian Fascism or German Nazism. But then some of the theories of communism are found in the teachings of Jesus, while here and there, in *Mein Kampf*, as well as in some of the phrases of Il Duce's eloquent efforts, is phraseology not far different from some of that in the Declaration of Inde-pendence and the writings of Thomas Jefferson.

It is also the invariable habit of the itinerant traveller or observer fresh-from-Europe, or fresh-from-reading-all-the-jargon-and-catch-phrases that have emanated from Europe, to be unusually impressed with the fact that there are great numbers of people of Italian or German birth in these countries, or people with German or Italian names holding high positions in various governments. He allows himself to draw false conclusions from these facts, forgetting that there are little Italys in New York and Detroit, little Germanys in Chicago, Newark or Milwaukee, and that there are federal judges with Italian and German names, that the great cities of New York and San Francisco have mayors of Italian ancestry. He does not realize that there are more people of German birth in New York and Chicago than there are in all of South America.

When he hears some one in Lima listening to a German or Italian short-wave radio broadcast from Berlin or Rome, he jumps to the conclusion that people are swallowing, without chewing, European totalitarian propaganda. He passes up the fact that the speeches of Hitler and Mussolini are usually rebroadcast verbatim throughout the entire United States. A little investigation would reveal that in the city of Chicago commercial broadcasts go out many hours of the day and night over local stations in German and Italian, as well as several other European languages. Most such observers have recently commented at length about Italian and German clubs, newspapers and magazines published in the Italian and German languages in the South American countries. But they overlooked the fact that in Lima, as well as other cities south of Panamá, there are American and English clubs and newspapers and magazines published in English. As for Panamá, mention has been made earlier about the two leading newspapers of the republic being published in English as well as in Spanish. The American and Anglo-Saxon clubs in most of these cities are the most exclusive among such organizations. The imposing country club in Lima, the finest of the city and perhaps the finest in South America, was founded, built and is maintained by Americans. And if any one present at the reception given there by the American Society of Perú in honor of Secretary Cordell Hull and the American delegation to the last Pan-American Conference still doubts the tendency of Yankees to stick together and remain Yankee, he was blind, deaf and dumb.

"You Yankees amuse me," one of the highest officials of the Peruvian Government told me recently. "You read so much and listen to so much radio comment about European affairs, about Fascism and Nazism, and become so imbued with the jargon and catch phrases emanating from the totalitarian countries of the Old World, that every German and Italian you find down here is wearing horns. Just because you see an Italian flag on an Italian business house, or a swastika on a German trading company, or hear people in the streets talking Italian or German, is no reason to believe we are threatened with Nazism or Fascism. Have you never travelled in the big cities of your own country, and can't you understand that we think of our country just as you do of the United States? To a Peruvian his country is the greatest country in the world and he isn't sitting down holding his hands waiting for anybody to come in from the outside and try to rule him."

BOLIVIA

I

The Lake in the Sky

A Spanish traveller to the Andes once called Bolivia the Switzerland of South America, "a landlocked country, cut off from the outside world, with jagged mountains etched against the sky, lakes as blue as indigo, and people who dress as colorfully as the Tyrolean Highlanders."

Except that it is geographically hemmed in from tidewater and has no use for a navy, I find little similarity between the third largest country on the southern continent and the tiny Old World republic. If you multiplied Switzerland by forty, made its tallest mountains a third higher and ten times as bleak and rugged, poured down among them crystal-clear ice water enough to make one lake 3220 square miles in area, over a fifth the size of Switzerland itself, and another of over a thousand square miles, put in half a dozen old Spanish colonial cities and towns, scores of primitive villages, and peopled them with a mere sprinkling of Spanish aristocrats, a half million *cholos* and two and a half million descendants of almost legendary races, you might have something slightly resembling a Switzerland of South America.

No two authorities or officials, foreign or native, agree on Bolivian statistics of populations and areas. But more accurate comparisons, along with more logical contrasts, could be found closer home. Spread Bolivia out over the middle Rocky Mountain and southwestern plains section of our own country and it would cover roughly the states of Wyoming, Utah, Colorado, Arizona, New Mexico and a portion of Texas. The great Bolivian *altiplano*, or plateau, averaging twelve and thirteen thousand feet above the sea, would be almost as high as Utah's loftiest mountains, and the flat, hot Texas plains, with their mesquite and sage brush, would be a highland heaven compared with the tropical Chaco lowlands. Titicaca would occupy about the same position, except that it is much larger than Great Salt Lake, and the Bolivian metropolis of La Paz would be in about the same location as the Utah capital.

Bolivia has its deep valleys and canyons, deeper and wider than those of the Colorado. Its immensely rich mining towns of Oruro, Potosí and others are no less active than those of Wyoming and Utah. The oil wells in its eastern foothills correspond in location with those of Amarillo and the Panhandle. The Pilcomayo River rising in central Bolivia and flowing southeastward eventually becomes the frontier with neighboring Argentina, as the Rio Grande marks the border between Texas and Mexico. The principal rivers of Wyoming and Colorado flow northward and eastward into the Missouri and then the Mississippi. Likewise Bolivia's leading rivers, the Madre de Dios, the Beni and the Mamoré flow northeastward into the Madeira, which eventually joins the Amazon.

Shut in from the sea on all sides by much more highly developed nations, all the avenues of transportation and communication, both land and air, into or out of Bolivia, lead through alien territory. It is impossible to ship a sack of flour, or a case of condensed milk directly into the country from any part of the world beyond the Continent. Every piece of freight must be consigned to an agent at a port in a neighboring country who receives and transships it to its Bolivian destination.

Even so, in the matter of transportation to the outside world, it is more fortunate than any of the other Andean republics.

Bolivia

With only 1399 miles of railroads within its own borders, it is the only one of the five countries with complete rail connection both to the Pacific and the Atlantic. It is possible to leave a ship at Mollendo, travel up to Arequipa and Puno at the Peruvian end of Lake Titicaca, cross the hundred-mile-long body of water by steamer, take a train to La Paz, 525 miles, and then another train southward across the country into Argentina and to Buenos Aires, a total distance of 2000 miles. Another railroad begins at the city of Antofagasta, Chile, runs northeastward across the western cordillera to a point on the Mollendo-Argentine line and thence to La Paz, 719 miles. The most direct route from the Pacific is the line from the Chilean port of Arica eastward straight up the mountains 274 miles to the capital.

By air there are connections from Chile, Perú and Argentina by the Pan-American Grace Lines and from Brazil over the German lines. The sparsely inhabited northeastern lowland regions may be reached by water and rail from the Atlantic. Small ocean steamers sail up the Amazon and the Madeira Rivers to Porto Velho in western Brazil, the beginning of the great rapids. From Porto Velho the famed Madeira-Mamoré Railroad, built in the days of the Amazonian rubber boom, operates, as a Brazilian friend says, "with uncertain frequency," as far as Villa Bella on the Bolivian border, from which launches make their way on up the Beni and the Mamoré to the very heart of the interior. Considerable rubber is still produced in the Mamoré Valley and this is the route by which the product goes out to the world markets.

I have travelled to Bolivia both by railroad and by plane. Each has its advantages and attractions. One is a slow, laborious journey. The other, for the seasoned air traveller, is quick, convenient and comfortable. If altitude is not a problem, I would suggest flying from Perú—from Lima to Arequipa and then up to La Paz. There are volcanoes to gaze down into and

New Roads to Riches

Titicaca to feast the eyes upon from above, and from very much above, too. Often it is necessary to fly at eighteen and nineteen thousand feet to get over the cordillera. Those with weak hearts, and lungs, and especially those with susceptible natures, minds, innards, or whatever controls or permits *soroche*, as well as those who care for the spectacular, odd or unusual experiences, or have a mind for history, will do well to travel more leisurely.

My most interesting trip was by railroad from Mollendo and Arequipa, Perú. During an interlude at Arequipa, at 7500 feet, I trained my lungs for the 13,000 *altiplano* of Central Bolivia. In the meantime I revelled in the hospitality of Tia Bates' Quinta, and met interesting people, Bolivians and foreigners, on their way to La Paz. Prominent citizens, diplomats, leaders in government and politics from the City of Peace are usually travelling up from Arequipa and all are eager to talk, tell about their country, its attractions and activities. In the warm atmosphere of the Quinta, and under the democratic spell of Tia, they often reveal inside affairs of Bolivia that they would not think of hinting to an outsider in La Paz.

It was here that I heard from a Peruvian diplomat of the acceptance of the peace terms ending the war between Bolivia and Paraguay in the Chaco before they were ever made public in the Bolivian capital. He had rushed to Arequipa by the first plane, after the Peruvian representative on the Peace Commission sitting in Buenos Aires had reported the agreement to Lima, and was flying on the following day in order to deliver a special message to the La Paz government.

It was also here that I met Father Velarde, a venerable Peruvian priest, who loves history, tradition and the folklore of the Andes. Father Velarde often travels up to Bolivia to spend his vacations at Tiahuanaco and the villages of Lake Titicaca, where he wanders among the ancient ruins and talks to the old *Aymara* Indians about them. This time he was going up in July both for his vacation and to be present at the Festival, or the Coronation of Our Lady of Copacabana, which takes place every August 6 at the Shrine of Copacabana on one of the Peninsulas of the lake.

But for Father Velarde, I, like many another traveller, would have found the trip over the mountains and across the lake woefully prosaic. With only the naked eye through which to see, the bleak mountain gorges soon become monotonous and Titicaca only another lake dotted with islands and swept by the iciest of winds. Naturally I would have planned to cross the lake by daylight so as to see whatever sights there were. But by day there are few sights, only water and the distant mountain ranges. "It is by night when there is a full moon," said the good Father, "that the lake is at its best."

So we left Arequipa at night for the rail junction at Juliaca on the central plateau from where one branch of the Peruvian Southern Railway turns north to Cuzco and the other southward to the lake port of Puno. The following evening we sailed, appropriately enough, on the S.S. *Inca* for Guaqui, Bolivia, the port of La Paz. The *Inca* is one of two sister ships of about 1000 tons that ply between the two ends of this highest navigable body of water in the world. We were given two of the best staterooms, which could have been much less comfortable than they were, although we didn't stay in them very much. Titicaca may lie in the heart of the tropics but the cold winds are not merely penetrating, they are piercing. "Because of the altitude," according to Padre Velarde, "the kind of cold that is particularly dangerous to lowlanders whose lungs are not accustomed to it."

When dinner was over, dressed in all we had—in sweaters, mufflers, heavy coats, and I in two pairs of pants—we went on deck, shivered and waited for the moon. Meantime the old Padre reminded me of the stock joke about the steamers having been built in Scotland, sailed across the Atlantic, then brought up the mountains piece by piece, set up on the shores of the lake and launched for a second time, long before the day of Sears & Roebuck mail-order-prefabricated-houses. Hour after hour he related the fables and the actual history, although it was difficult to distinguish between the two, and commented on the philosophies and religions that surround the lake and its peoples. "For," as he said, "on the islands and around this lake most of the great cultures that have flourished and faded in the Andean regions had their origin."

It was July, the dry season in the mountains, when the sky is clearer, it seems, than any other sky in the universe. Just before midnight there was a pale glow in the east, then a rim of burnished metal appeared from behind the snowy peaks which was presently a silvery shield suspended in the eastern sky. As it poured its pale light down on the waters it seemed so incredibly close, just beyond the railing of the boat.

I have travelled in the moonlight on the Texas plains, once in a dilapidated Ford from Boulder to Denver, Colorado, in the early morning hours, and another time, on a frozen December night, in an open wagon on sleds from Carnarvon to a neighboring town in Saskatchewan, when the northern lights were engaged in one of their most glamorous displays. But even a clear wintry moonlight night in Canada with the Aurora Borealis thrown in cannot compare with a moonlight night on Lake Titicaca nearly two and a half miles above the sea.

"Even I," Father Velarde admitted, "could not find fault with those ancients of the Andes who worshipped the moon. No sight such as this could be other than divine."

"Nor do I wonder," I replied, "that the sun god became romantic, fell in love with the moon goddess and took her as a wife. Even a god of the primitives could hardly resist such a sight."

"And when you see the sunrise in the morning," Father Velarde came back, "you will also understand why the fable

Bolivia

Indeed, I did not learn about it until I had already experienced the inspiring sunrise, compared with which the rising moon, magnificent enough, was more than pale. Here was color, all the shades. First the yellow glow behind the mountains, then the peaks glistening like molten gold, and as it splashed down on the lake the water was streaked with blue, purple and vermillion. The sailboats and *balsas*, that were by now on their way between the islands and villages of the mainland, looked like giant waterfowl with brilliant plumage.

The Indians themselves still travel Titicaca in the unique *balsas* made of the twisted *totora* reeds that grow in profusion in the shallow waters. Picturesque as they are, they are of very simple construction. Four bundles of dried reeds, two large bundles for the bottom, and two smaller ones for the sides, are lashed together and bent upward at the ends, forming the body of the boat. Power is furnished by a single sail, also made of reeds plaited together and raised or lowered like a Venetian blind. Occasionally water soaks into the reeds, but drydocking becomes a very simple matter. The craft is merely pulled up on shore and the sun does the balance.

Most of the freight of the lake, supplies for the villages and plantations and the products being shipped out, is handled by small sailboats. The lake flats and islands constitute one of the principal agricultural regions of northern Bolivia. Very few trees grow even around the farmhouses and in the villages, unless they are sheltered. But this is the homeland of the potato. Here it originated, and from here it was carried up and down the continent and throughout the Americas, long before it got to Ireland. It should be called the Inca potato instead of the Irish potato.

Other hardy plants, such as barley, wheat and corn grow very well but usually entire plantations are devoted to the growing of potatoes. At harvest time the fields are dotted with great potato mounds surrounded by flocks of chattering natives who clean and sort them for the market. Although the potato is the most important product, fish and game are also plentiful around Titicaca. Ducks and other waterfowl thrive in the thick cane brakes, especially around the islands, while fishing furnishes a livelihood for many of the natives.

At Guaqui I said goodbye to Padre Velarde who was going for a visit and to study some ruins on one of the islands before he went up to Copacabana for the festival. I had wished that he might have been with me at Tiahuanaco, the most famous and most imposing of all the ancient ruins of the region. Tiahuanaco is twelve miles from Guaqui on the railroad, and now the highway, to La Paz. The Inca ruins on the Islands of Titicaca and Coati are of a new civilization compared with those of Tiahuanaco. The mainland city was the center of a civilization and culture, as powerful and as rich as that of the Incas, which had already perished before the first Inca was born. It extended northward along the high plateau and the coast country of Perú and Ecuador, and southward far down into Argentina and Chile.

If the Incas were the Romans of the South American Andes, then the Tiahuanacos were the Egyptians. Their buildings and temples, besides being on an heroic scale and constructed of enormous blocks of sandstone brought from the northern shores of the lake, were decorated with exquisite carvings. Some of its great monoliths, covered with delicate figures, are still standing. Others representing giant figures of men and animals have rested for ages under mountainous sand heaps, some of which have recently been dug up.

One of the most talked of was uncovered by my friend, Wendell Bennett, formerly of the American Museum of Natural History, in 1932, and now stands on the Prado in the city of La Paz. The eighteen-ton figure of a man is profusely carved and decorated, and there are long braids of hair down his back, signifying a personage of high office.

Travel by Balsa on Lake Titicaca

Sorting Potatoes on a Titicaca Farm

Bolivia

The Indians who inhabit this region and most of the highlands of Bolivia today are called the *Aymaras*, probably a mixture of all the ancient races who have gone before, although more of a Mongolian type than those of Perú and the north. They even speak a language all their own. And while they are not nearly as industrious as the *Quechua*-speaking Incans of Perú and other parts of Bolivia, they are much less given to servility. About the ancient ruins they are particularly superstitious and especially so when it comes to digging among them. An incident which occurred at the time Bennett discovered the monolith in 1932 reveals the hold of the ancients upon them and the fact that the four centuries influence of the Spaniards, more particularly the influence of the Spanish religion, has not penetrated very deeply. In fact, it forms a very thin outer coating.

When the digging had proceeded sufficiently to begin the careful uncovering of the stone, the foreman, or majordomo, informed Bennett that the men wanted to put on a special ceremony before they continued any further. He admitted that they were actually frightened, and wanted to propitiate the ancient gods. Naturally the request was granted, and what followed was a mysterious and almost voodooish proceeding.

At nightfall they assembled in a near-by stone hut with a medicine man, or fortune teller, to conduct the ceremony and prepare the special concoction for the ritual. Such things as peanuts, ground cocoanut, fœtus of llama, Pisco rum, *coca* leaves, from which cocaine is made and which all the Indians of Bolivia and most of Perú chew, candles and silver and gold tinsel had been provided. A woolen cloth, twelve by fifteen feet, was spread out on the floor. The medicine man wrapped the fœtus of llama in the tinsel and placed it in the center of the cloth. Then every one present placed three *coca* leaves in each corner. The ground cocoanut, peanuts and more *coca* leaves were placed on the llama fœtus and rum was poured on the whole. This done, the corners of the cloth were folded in, or rolled in, after which for hours, until midnight, the medicine man told the fortunes of every one with *coca* leaves.

At twelve o'clock the cloth containing the mysterious preparation was taken to the scene of the excavation, followed by the entire party. A fire was built near the head of the monolith and a prayer or hokus-pokus was said. Finally the bundle was thrown into the pit by the medicine man and all hurried away without looking back. Next day the digging continued as usual, but every morning thereafter *coca* leaves were put into the pit and rum poured over them. What it all meant they never explained, and Bennett can only surmise.

The mysterious attitude of the Indian excavators was dignified, sincere and logical compared with the behavior of the La Paz journalists, poets, professors and politicians afterward. For a year and a half, even though the country was in the throes of a terrible war, speeches were made, poems were written and 500 newspaper articles published on the subject of the discovery. At first the argument centered around the significance of the monolith, and the integrity of the discoverer. The charge was made that Bolivian archæologists, if any, already knew about the great piece of stone long before the *gringo* ran onto it. Later they debated the propriety of allowing foreigners to dig in the ancient ruins, and whether it would be proper to remove the ancient piece of sculpture to the capital city. It actually became a hot political question. But then, as we shall see, almost anything may become a political question in La Paz.

It is a pleasant ride by automobile from Tiahuanaco southward to the Bolivian metropolis, now that the old trail across the *altiplano* has been turned into a modern highway. The government has just announced that this is the first completed link in Bolivia's portion of the Pan-American Highway, which it expects to extend on northward along the shores of the lake to the frontier where it will connect up with Perú's new north and

Bolivia

south trunk line, now nearing completion. Meantime, it makes
it possible for citizens and visitors to La Paz to drive with the
greatest convenience to some of the most notable and attractive
of all the ancient ruins in South America. More important still it
is a great boost for the Titicaca farmers and fishermen in that it
affords them easy and economical access to the La Paz markets.

La Paz is forty miles from Tiahuanaco and only fifty from
Guaqui. As you speed toward it across the perfectly flat country
you wonder at first what has happened to it. Even two miles
away no trace of it appears on the horizon. Then suddenly you
come to the rim of a U-shaped canyon, three miles wide and
ten miles long, and there it is, 1500 feet below, but still 12,000
feet above the sea. Having gazed upon a continual succession
of mountains from Venezuela to Perú, each taller and more
spectacular than the preceding, by the time one has reached
Bolivia, lofty peaks and snowy diadems should no longer be
impressive. But even from this city, "in a hole in the ground,"
21,030 feet Mt. Illimani and others seem to dwarf all those
that have gone before. Although wisely located so that it is
shielded from the wind and weather above, La Paz is so cold at
night that I have never been completely warm either in bed or
out. Streets have been laid out and houses built so that the
sun may hit them broadside. Heat is a problem because Bolivia
has no coal and the cost of importing it makes each piece as
expensive as a nugget of precious metal. Only the rich can
afford enough heat to break the perpetual chill and they must
use electricity.

Not even Peggy Hopkins Joyce has changed her name more
times than La Paz. The fourth Inca called it Chuquiago. A later
one changed the name to Choqueyapu, the present name of the
little river that courses down the canyon, and the earliest
Spaniards christened it La Ciudad de Nuestra Señora de la Paz.
Through colonial times it was popularly known as Gold
Orchard, not because there were many, if any trees in it, but

[387]

because gold was found in the river and on the sides of the steep hills. Finally, when General Sucre defeated the last group of Spanish loyalists in Perú, it was re-christened La Paz de Ayacucho, after the place of the decisive battle.

But by whatever name it may be called, it is still architecturally the least attractive, but its people the most colorful of all the large Andean cities. Important buildings, old and new, are neither Spanish colonial nor Indianesque. The City Hall is distinctly Versailles French. The Capitol Building is a combination of Greek, Syrian and Moorish influences, while the cathedral, after fifty years still unfinished, is entirely Greek. Most of the new houses are Italian modernistic. Only in Socabaya, the now deserted old house of the blue-blooded Spanish Diez de Medinas, and the church of San Francisco, are there any suggestions of the picturesque Spanish colonial architecture that characterizes most of the Peruvian towns and cities. San Francisco was decorated by the same artist who carved the choir stalls of the cathedrals in Cuzco and Lima. But even San Francisco is now crowded on all sides by the glamorous market stalls and bazaars of the *chola* women, who, in spite of its unprepossessing architecture, furnish the city with a distinctive, as well as distinguished atmosphere found nowhere else in South America. To me these half-breed women are La Paz. They are upstanding and superior, with more business ability than any half dozen men of their particular class. This is not Perú where the Incan man dominates. This is Bolivia where the *Aymara-Spanish-chola* runs and bosses the business and where her man must go and find a job.

They wear short skirts, sometimes six and eight of them, too, each of a different color and all billowing out like old-time hoopskirts. Around their shoulders they wear gleaming red, yellow, blue or purple *ponchos*, or shawls, with a high-crowned, narrow-brimmed felt hat to top them off. The higher the crown of the hat the more prominent and wealthy the woman who wears it. Their shoes are usually pumps and, if the wearer is young, with very high heels. The way they can sling a big shawl around their shoulders so that it makes a bag in the back, in which can be carried anything from a baby to a hundred pounds of merchandise, is simply amazing.

In their market stalls these female merchants sell everything, pottery in interesting designs and lavish colors, rugs, richly woven, knitted goods, rag dolls dressed in the native costumes, bead necklaces, even the exotic blooms from the eastern valleys. And to buy a single item is an adventure in commercial diplomacy. When they were still plentiful, I bargained with a good-natured old *chola* for a vicuña blanket. The verbal encounter ran something like this:

Chola: "A beautiful blanket, Señor, so soft. The vicuña skin is so very light, but warm for the coldest nights—it is so beautiful."

Tomlinson: "So beautiful, Señora, but how much?"

Chola: "The beautiful vicuña—it is—200 *bolivianos.*"

Tomlinson: "Two hundred *bolivianos.* Señora, I could buy one down the street for half that much, but it would grieve me greatly to have to do so."

Chola: "Ah, well for the Señor—he is so gracious—175 *bolivianos.*"

Tomlinson: "Ah, the Señora is very gracious—but I am so very poor."

Chola: "Oh, I am so sorry. Well then, I will make it 160 *bolivianos.*"

Tomlinson: "The Señora's generosity is touching, but it is not yet sufficient."

Chola: "But Señor, the poor little vicuñas—they are so lovely —so delicate——"

Tomlinson: "But, Señora, I am so poor—so——"

Chola: "I am so sorry, Señor,—then maybe—150 *bolivianos.*"

Tomlinson: "Now the Señora is beginning to be generous to a poor *gringo.*"

[389]

Chola: "Ah, Señor, the beautiful vicuñas, the noble little animals——"

Tomlinson: "One hundred *bolivianos*, Señora."

Chola: "One hundred and thirty *bolivianos*, Señor."

Tomlinson: "Ah, but I have only 100 *bolivianos*, Señora."

Chola: "But I could not let it go for less than 125, Señor— my poor little vicuñas."

Tomlinson: "But Señora, I too will be generous—110 *bolivianos*."

Chola: "The Señor is so gracious—111, Señor."

La Paz may be the City of Peace, but it is as volatile as Quito. In the last five or six years only Ecuador has surpassed or equalled Bolivia in the number of revolutions and *coups d'etat*, or the frequency with which governments have waxed and waned. "Of the 175,000 inhabitants of La Paz," says one expatriate Bolivian journalist with a sense of humor, and residing at a safe distance from his native land, "there are 100,000 Indians engaged in common labor or various forms of servitude, who have nothing to say about public affairs. The other 75,000 are white and *cholo* politicians. No matter what they do for a living, whether bankers, lawyers, doctors, writers, salesmen, soldiers, shopkeepers or taxi drivers, they are politicians. They will argue on or about any subject, question or state of affairs until it becomes a political matter. La Paz is truly the political, if not the national capital."

Herein is suggested an anomalous situation, theoretically at least. La Paz is the seat of government, but it is not the capital of the nation. The Bolivian capital is the old colonial town of Sucre, 300 miles southward, the city which was named for the first President, General Antonio José de Sucre, who lies buried in Quito, Ecuador. Although General Sucre was the first President, and it was through his efforts that independence had actually been effected, the republic took its name from Sucre's

Bolivia

great chief, Simón Bolívar. Later, even the unit of money was called the *Boliviano*, after the Liberator.

On the other hand, while there is one capitol building in Sucre, the functioning capitol building of the country is not located in the capital of the nation, but in La Paz. The President, the Congress, upon those rare occasions when there is a Congress, all the executive and administrative branches of the government, function in La Paz. Only the Supreme Court keeps vigil in Sucre.

This would be a novel and fitting state of affairs, if the Bolivian government were an uninterrupted democracy, instead of a military dictatorship. To have the politicians and politically-minded officials do their trading and wrangling in one place, and the Supreme Tribunal, oracle-like, hand down its decisions in a quiet, detached, uncorrupted atmosphere, where the early flame of democracy flowered genuinely if briefly, would be just about ideal.

To give the merest details concerning the usually brief administrations of the various presidents and dictators who have been elected, led revolutions or otherwise acquired office in Bolivia since Spain gave up the ghost in the Andean nations would fill a volume. As in the case of Bolívar himself, who was politically lashed and driven from office in Colombia and the north to die in disgrace at Santa Marta, General Sucre was overthrown within two years after he had established independence, and the revolutionary game, except for a few lulls now and then, has gone merrily on ever since.

Although a country rich in minerals, oil and other sub-soil products, its political instability has kept it backward and economically hamstrung. During the late golden age of borrowing and lending, Bolivia, like most of her neighbors, joined the international bankers, mostly Americans, in a bond-floating spree. This spree, which was at its height eleven and twelve years ago, touched off what might be called the latest period

[391]

of pronounced revolution in Bolivia. The trade and traffic in money which went on between the gentlemen of La Paz and the gentlemen of Manhattan not only relieved thousands of our people of millions of dollars in savings and hard-earned money, but it shouldered upon the unfortunate and unwilling inhabitants of Bolivia, a debt which in all probability will never be repaid.

Besides the $61,619,000 of stocks and "securities" in Bolivian industry and resources held in this country, there were in 1934 $61,104,000 in government loans which Bolivian politicians pledged their people to pay. This fact would be much less odious if the Bolivian people themselves had received any great benefit from these loans. But if the revelations before a United States Senate Investigating Committee in Washington at the time were any indication, a great portion of it went to further the pet projects of ambitious officials if not into their personal pockets.

In a single transaction in 1928, Dillon Read and Company of New York sponsored the flotation of $23,000,000 worth of bonds, a goodly portion of which were bought by private individuals. Although the people who bought them were led to believe that they were investing in sound securities, the money for which was to go into needed public works which would greatly enhance the welfare and progress of the southern republic, it was brought out in the testimony at Washington that $5,000,000 of the amount, with the knowledge of both the sponsors and officials of our own State Department, went to a London company for military supplies, while another million and a half was retained by the War Ministry itself for military purposes.

Mr. Lawrence Dennis, former Foreign Service officer of the United States government, and wartime employee of the then flourishing New York banking house of J. & W. Seligman & Company, was quoted as having told the Senate Banking Com-

Bolivia

mittee that probably not more than two and a quarter million dollars of the twenty-three million actually was spent for public works and public enterprises.

The officials and politicians party to and responsible for all these deals were long since driven from office and most of them from the country itself. In spite of all of the money borrowed they left the treasury absolutely empty, and every ruler that followed found himself without cash to carry on the government and at the same time keep the local army paid, and if he could not keep the local army paid he could not stay in power very long, in a country that has always depended upon the army for stability. So governments came and went with clocklike regularity from the overthrow in 1930 of the arch-borrower, President Hernando Siles, to July 17, 1937.

For the most part each upset merely meant a change of personnel and not a change in political philosophy until May 17, 1936. At that time a group of leftist army officers turned out President Tejada Sorzano and put in Colonel David Toro, who had agreed to transform Bolivia into a Socialist state. Although Toro hesitated for nearly a year, on March 13, 1937, he began keeping his promise with a vengeance. On that date he issued a decree cancelling the forty-year oil concession of the Standard Oil Company and confiscating all of its property, an act which precipitated world-wide discussion and speculation. For weeks it was figured that the giant American-controlled tin industry would be next.

But before Colonel Toro could go any further, if indeed he intended to, he was overthrown by the same group of army officers that put him in office, headed by Lieutenant-Colonel German Busch.* Busch was elected Constitutional President in 1938, constitutionally elected in the Bolivian sense, of course. Then, offering evidence that he himself was not altogether sold

*The news of his death on August 23d was received just as this book was going to press.

on the socialistic performances of his predecessor, he suspended the constitution and made himself supreme dictator on April 24, 1938. His new regime is called National Socialism, which many observers insist smacks more of Fascism than of Socialism.

During the greater portion of all this long period of political change at home the country was either fighting or trying to settle the disastrous war with Paraguay over the Gran Chaco. President Busch himself was a veteran and hero of that war, having been decorated several times for bravery. Busch is thirty-six years old and the son of a German-born father and a Spanish Bolivian mother. As a young man he spent a good deal of time abroad, lived and went to school in the British Island of Trinidad in the West Indies. Later on he studied at the Military College in La Paz and became an officer in the army. Following the World War the Bolivian government invited the Prussian general, Hans Kundt, a former member of the Kaiser's general staff, to reorganize and instruct the Bolivian army according to modern military methods. Captain Ernst Roehm, later the victim of Hitler's famous blood purge, was Kundt's chief assistant. While in Bolivia Roehm had as one of his brightest pupils the then Lieutenant Busch.

President Busch is a handsome fellow, with black curly hair, worn pompadour style, and dark eyes. He is more a Latin than a Nordic type. Although soldierly and smart he is not the stern and severe militarist you would expect to find in a dictator. In conversation he commands respect, although he does not give the impression that he has thought everything through. It is evident that he has relied upon others to do some of his thinking for him. Neither is he, as some have referred to him, a starry-eyed dreamer. He is really a very practical and straightforward person, who is convinced that what Bolivia needs is discipline and absolute direction. In a country of three and a half million people, the overwhelming majority of whom are

Bolivia

illiterate Indians speaking only their ancient dialects and having no knowledge, much less interest in public affairs, what other kind of government could maintain itself, even for a brief period of time, is more than I know.

It is all well enough to deplore dictatorship, or government by a group or class. But to expect democracy as we know it, and sometimes practice it badly, to function for all the people in a nation like Bolivia is something else. Yet it is a failing of us Yankees to insist that it should. Nor is it fair to hold Busch responsible for dictatorship in Bolivia. He inherited the system, a system which he could not change in a day, even if he wanted to. If there is any other way to bring about a permanent democratic social order except through the laborious and perhaps old-fashioned method of education, a higher standard of living and better economic conditions for the masses, no one has found it so far.

But if the young colonel, or any other man, should make a start in this direction, and at the same time administer the government honestly and efficiently, he might eventually place himself among the immortals. Knowing the material with which he has to work, the tightly knit group of old land-owning families, and especially the well-to-do *cholos*, who, with few exceptions, would rather have their throats cut than see the Indians rise from serfdom, and the few powerful industrial groups who would view any broad policy of social betterment as a threat to their existence, I cannot be very optimistic. Without regard for what should or should not be, dictatorship has been, in practice, the prevailing form of government in Bolivia for a hundred years, and is likely to continue for some time to come.

Because of his German antecedents and early influences, Busch has been charged with being pro-Nazi, if not actually under Nazi direction. This he has openly denied, saying, "There is no place in Bolivia for either Nazi or radical ideas."

New Roads to Riches

Again, it should be borne in mind that no ruler or head of a government, whether in Italy, Perú or Bolivia, wants to play second fiddle to anybody else. Busch very definitely does not wish to do this. Besides if he seriously subscribes to Nazism it is rather strange than his is one of the few governments in South America or the world, that has been consistently accepting large groups of German Jewish refugees right along.

Upon close analysis, the Busch regime appears to me to be an old-fashioned South American dictatorship dressed up in the modern streamlined manner, that is, a dictatorship more social than political. He expresses two new impulses that permeate the younger Bolivians since the Chaco war: intolerance toward the old political cliques and ultra-nationalism.

As a soldier who, along with the flower of Bolivian youth, fought and suffered in a war which was the culmination of political prejudices and hatreds enkindled by the old professional politicians, he wants a new deal in the country. He, like the other young men, realizes that the welfare of the nation has been sacrificed in the hundred-year scramble by a handful of people, to feather their own nests at the expense of the country's general welfare.

He has contemplated the fact that in spite of the enormous riches—the gold, silver and tin that have been dug out of Bolivia's mountains, the nation is still as backward socially and politically as it was a century ago, while the overwhelming portion of the population lives in the most abject poverty. He knows something is fundamentally wrong, and he wants to correct it. How this is to be done, what methods should be used, he and the other young men around him do not quite know. They intend to try to find out. Meantime grievous mistakes will be and are being made. The result naturally will be either of two things: His dictatorship will go on the rocks, as have so many others, or through trial, error and travail, a new order will be born.

II
Land of the Tin Kings

As ELSEWHERE in the Andes, it was gold that led the Spaniards to Upper Perú, the name by which the Bolivian *altiplano* was known in those days. Gold they found and took, first from the temples and palaces of the Incas around Titicaca. Then they compelled the newly conquered natives to work overtime, under pressure and the lash, in the already discovered mines, to dig out more.

Yet silver and not gold was to become the great bonanza of the country. Silver, tin and most of the other metals destined to play such an important part in the economy, and poverty, of the country later on, were mined by the Incas in several regions. But thanks to the superstitions of the red men it remained for the palefaces to exploit the mines of Potosí.

Ancient lore has it that the Inca, Huayna Ccapac, was travelling across the country. At the end of a day's journey he stopped for the night at one of the government *tambos*, or inns, near the foot of a great black mountain. Officials in that region informed him that the soil of this mountain was laden with metal "white like the moonlight on Titicaca."

"Tomorrow," said the Inca, "I shall go to the foot of the black mountain to see with my own eyes this metal 'white like the moonlight.' "

Next day, seated in his golden palanquin, he was being borne toward the mountain when a voice thundered out, "Huayna Ccapac!"

The procession was halted and the frightened soldiers and attendants fell upon their faces, while the Inca responded in solemn dignity, "It is I, Huayna Ccapac, the Inca. I await thy sacred utterance."

"Turn your back upon this mountain," said the voice. "Touch not the white metal, it is destined for other men."

The Inca was warned away by the mysterious voice, so the legend runs, and the great silver mountain of Potosí awaited the conquerors, who descended upon it in frenzied greediness in the early sixteen hundreds. Within a few years Potosí became the richest and gayest mining center in the world, a city of 150,000 people with fortunes flowing through their hands every day.

The mines hummed with the activity of the countless enslaved Indians, who endured such cruelty as has seldom been recorded in history. Sharp trading foreigners milled about in the clubs and exchanges. Here, in a remote and almost inaccessible high Andean valley, a great aristocracy developed and lived in undreamed of splendor. They lavished millions upon satin and silk, lace and pearls, the finest tapestries of France and furniture of ebony and ivory from the Orient. Two billion dollars' worth of the pale metal was taken out of the great black mountain. At one time Bolivia supplied silver for the coinage of half the civilized world.

But eventually the seemingly inexhaustible veins reached the point of diminishing returns. The mountain, honeycombed with tunnels and caverns, became an empty shell, while the city itself became a mere ghost of what it once had been. Two-thirds of the population drifted away. The doors of most of the great houses were closed, and their occupants, those who had not squandered their fortunes, took up residence in Paris, Barcelona and other European cities, while the non-thrifty ones moved out into cottages or hovels.

Then the tin can, perhaps the outstanding symbol of Yankee civilization, was invented, and the days of glory came back to Potosí. New fortunes were made from tin, not only in Potosí, Oruro and the regions of Lake Poopó, but even around La Paz. Tin is still Bolivia's chief product and export, accounting for seventy per cent of the national wealth. Tin exports in 1937 amounted to 81,885,657 *bolivianos*, the *boliviano* being worth nearly five cents at that time. The country is said to possess three-quarters of the world's supply of tin ore.

And here we must consider the Crœsus of the Andes. A young *cholo*, of *Quechua*, or Incan and Spanish mixture, born in the mountains near Cochabamba, had already risen so high in the world that he had been put in charge of a large metal store in Oruro. A native Indian from far up in the mountains came into the establishment one day and the young manager engaged him in conversation, speaking in *Quechua*. The visitor was so overjoyed to be addressed in his own ancient tongue, instead of *Aymara*, that he became very confidential and showed the storekeeper a bag full of high-grade tin ore which he had gathered near his own village.

Immediately the young man, Simón I. Patiño, future tin king of the world, resigned his storekeeping job, took his family back into the mountains and began building one of the greatest fortunes of our time, along with an industry whose ramifications reach around the world.

At first Patiño and his wife dug out the ore with their own hands, rolled it down the hill in wheelbarrows, transported it across the country by mule and llama and sold it to another company. With their first returns helpers were hired, more ore was sold and more equipment bought, until the first Patiño mine was a going concern. Afterward he borrowed money from

an English bank and bought another mine. Later on he amal-
gamated the two into one company. Next he decided to build
a railroad sixty-five miles long to connect his mines at Uncía
and Catavi with the main-line railroad, and thus with the sea.
The contract for its construction was awarded to a German
company. But suddenly the World War exploded and the construction company went broke, or its members went home to
fight for the fatherland. A British company finally completed
the project. Eventually Patiño journeyed to New York to
interest American firms in his properties. The National Lead
Company joined with him, put in more money and an industrial
colossus was formed—the Patiño Mine and Enterprises, Con-
solidated, which also owns properties in Malay, the East Indies
and elsewhere.

Meantime the Andean Rockefeller, first citizen of Bolivia,
and now cosmopolite, became a philanthropist, a patron of the
arts and a connoisseur of European aristocratic and noble
daughters-in-law and sons-in-law. One of his two daughters is
married to a Spanish Marquis of long and important lineage.
He built palaces on the Riviera, in Paris, and Bolivia. He owns
several mansions in and around his own home town of Cochabamba. A town apartment contains a Persian room, a Louis XVI
room, one in the Spanish Renaissance style and another of
ultramodernistic design, a room to suit every mood and disposition.

One enormous Bolivian house, most of its walls covered
with Gobelin tapestries and many priceless paintings, he has
never even seen, because he has not visited his native land
since 1922. The high altitude, due no doubt to the easy living
of late years, as well as the ravages of time, in which he once
could dig and roll wheelbarrows full of ore for miles without
puffing or blowing a single time, is now too much for him. He
oscillates between Paris, New York, London, Deauville, the
Riviera and the exclusive Florida resorts, but without forget-

ting or neglecting, for a single moment, his many white-hot irons.

A personal fortune variously estimated at from three to four hundred million dollars, aside from shares in a dozen firms, cannot be kept secure and profitable without the most careful overseeing and ingenious planning. And no Rockefeller or Mellon was ever more far-seeing and gifted in financial matters.

But he does not forget Bolivia. He was long its minister in Paris, engineered, at least helped to orient its foreign affairs, while, through his mines, furnishing the major portion of its income. He has tried to introduce new industries and induce the people of the fertile Cochabamba valley to engage more and more in agriculture. He spent hundreds of thousands of dollars in blooded cows and fancy bulls in an effort to increase and improve the cattle industry in that section. On a model farm he offers to train free of charge any young man who wishes to study and follow the livestock business. But so far beef is still scarce, tough and expensive in Bolivia, at least in La Paz and the highland towns. Nor is the Cochabamba valley crowded with herds of cattle.

Patiño's fellow countrymen have not taken enthusiastically to his suggestions, but his government, not to say innumerable governments, has and have never hesitated to call upon him for loans and hand-outs. He has prevented the spiders from weaving their webs across the doorway of the treasury more than once. Sometimes when he has balked or hesitated, the wily ones of La Paz have applied the squeezers—added another tax, another fine for some supposed infraction of a mining law, or simply demanded cash in no uncertain terms. And now, in his late years, come decrees from the Busch government which, as we shall see, put the entire industry under strict government control.

The Aramayo firm, headed by Carlos Victor Aramayo, member of one of the wealthiest of the old Spanish families, whose

New Roads to Riches

first fortunes were made during the silver boom, has long been an important operator in the tin industry. The Aramayo group, now heavily interested in gold mining, is also financed by American capital, most of it furnished by the American Smelting and Refining Company.

Meantime, while Simón Patiño and the Aramayos carry on, and the combines and companies which they organized continue to function, more recently another spectacular character, in this instance a foreigner, has arisen to challenge the supremacy of the old-timers, particularly the supremacy of Patiño. His name is Mauricio Hochschild, an Argentine-born gentleman of German-Jewish parentage. He is a giant of a man, nearly six and a half feet tall, with a bristling black mustache, and a circle of unruly coarse hair draped just beneath an enormous bald pate. He fairly bores holes in you with eyes that are widely separated by a nose only a little less impressive than Jimmy Durante's. He has an amazing command of the Spanish, French, English and German languages, as well as a startling facility for the picturesque profanity peculiar to each.

The Hochschild activities and enterprises in Bolivia have also had an interesting history. In the beginning they were financed by German bankers. In turn Señor Hochschild hired German managers, lawyers, accountants and engineers. In the early days a meeting of his entourage in the big conference room in the Hochschild Building in La Paz, sounded like a German Tower of Babel. All of which gave the Germans reason to believe they actually controlled his holdings, but proved how little they knew about the Señor.

With Hitler's first blast against the Jews, Hochschild left La Paz and went on a quiet visit to several world capitals, Buenos Aires, Paris, London and New York. Upon his return, having provided himself with new and ample financing, principally from the Phelps Dodge Company of New York, he dismissed his German bankers, fired his German employees, from engineers to office boys. Today at a meeting of his staff in Edificio Hochschild, only English and Spanish are spoken. All of his engineers, managers and office force now are either Americans or Bolivians. And thus ended the Nazi bid for participation in Bolivia's principal industry.

But no sooner had he freed himself from the German bankers and embarked upon a great program of expansion, than he, along with the Patiños, the Aramayos, and all the other mining titans, came face to face with the military and economic dictatorship of President German Busch. In spite of taxes, fines and other demands, the tin kings had usually had their way in the matter of the sale of their products. Locally all tin transactions had been handled through the Mining Bank in La Paz. Since they sold the ore in the outside world and received their pay in foreign exchange in foreign countries, they really controlled their own finances.

This will no longer be possible. For all practical purposes the mining industry is now under the complete control of the Federal dictatorship. By government decree the Mining Bank has been taken over bodily by the Bolivian Central Bank, which will handle all transactions under the vigilant eye of the Minister of Mines. Even though the tin is sold and paid for outside the country, there will be no waiting for the checks to arrive, and no chance for a diversion of any of the receipts, before the government can intervene. The companies must themselves deposit in the Central Bank the gold value of the total exports, after which the government itself will decide what amounts shall be paid out for various expenses, obligations abroad and dividends, when and if any.

Permission for the importation of all necessities, machinery and equipment for carrying on the industry, even the food supplies for the personnel in camps and mills, must be secured from the Ministry of Mines.

Bolivian citizens will receive no foreign currency for their labors or their services, and foreign employees, technicians and engineers, whether Yankee or otherwise, will be paid only a part of their salaries in foreign money. Not only must all surplus earnings be invested in the country within two years, but any reserves held by the companies abroad must be returned to Bolivia, or an additional tax of twenty per cent will have to be paid.

If any one doesn't like these regulations, of course, he is at liberty to sell out, if he can. But he may not choose his buyer. Eighty per cent of the properties must be sold to the government, and only twenty per cent of the receipts for that may be taken out of the country. Moreover, if any one should be so thoughtless as to resist these decrees, by such methods as sabotage, lock-outs, restrictions of work, et cetera, he will be guilty of high treason, for which the punishment is death.

Along with these manipulations and changes in the management and operation of the mining industry, labor is also to be regulated, and probably to its own benefit. Labor will not be given a free hand through union leaders as, for instance, is the case in Mexico. Labor in Bolivia will be subjected to the same discipline as management. So far codes and rules have not been thoroughly worked out. But evidently the government takes the full responsibility for seeing that reasonable wages are paid. The present average wage in the mines seems pitiably little. It ranges from nine to twelve *bolivianos,* about thirty to forty American cents a day.

"But the Bolivian Indian and *cholo* laborer," according to one important Bolivian engineer in the Oruro district, "is the most inefficient and indifferent workman in the world. He chews and has chewed *coca* leaves until he does not get hungry. Left to himself he will not eat wholesome food. So he is about thirty per cent efficient as a laborer."

To remedy this condition some of the companies have installed kitchens and mess halls at their mines where good nutri-

Bolivia

tious food is served for less than cost, hoping in this way to build up the strength and efficiency of their workmen.

The government, through the Ministry of Mines, will also settle any disputes or difficulties that may arise between the laborers and the companies. That is to say, it will probably look the situation over and tell both parties exactly what must be done. In answer to a question which I recently asked on this point, the Ministry of Foreign Affairs has this to say:

"Social legislation is being planned which takes into consideration experience in the application of labor laws abroad as well as within the country. Recent conflicts arising between laborers and employers have been settled through the conciliatory intervention of the Ministry of Labor, and this experience makes us hopeful for the future. As President Busch himself has said, 'It demonstrates with reality that it is possible to coordinate the rights and interests of employers with those of laborers, to the general benefit of the country, when the laws, regulations and the government are situated on a superior plane of impartiality as regulators of social relations.'"

Although the interests of regular workers, that is to say employees of the mines and corporations, as well as other large business concerns in the more populous centers, who of themselves constitute a class apart, and who have been to some extent organized, are to be safeguarded and looked after, little is said about the Indians, the peasants, the submerged or neglected, who constitute at least two thirds of the entire Bolivian population. There are only about 35,000 miners in the country, some 4000 of whom are in the La Paz district while the others are concentrated in the Oruro-Potosí and other mining communities.

Thus the lot of the ancient inhabitants of the *altiplano* and the high mountain valleys, which ever since the conquest has been only a little better than that of the common animals, will probably not change rapidly. Their interests will probably be the last to receive consideration, so that they will continue to eke out a miserable existence, chew *coca* leaves, debauch themselves, and drown their sufferings in *chicha*, the native rum, now and then, until their ancient gods call them to a happier realm.

Some of the young Bolivian officials, and intellectuals, insist that the Yankees ought to do more to help the Bolivian tin industry, which may seem a bit strange under the circumstances. First they bear down on the mine owners and operators, scare them, and in effect threaten them with nationalization. At the same time they insist that the mine owners should not only like it but spend more money in expansion.

One Bolivian official suggested to me in a recent conversation that he saw no reason why those in the United States with such large interests in the Bolivian mining industry should not begin to develop their own tin refineries, either in Bolivia or their own country, so that the tin ore could be imported directly from Bolivia.

"Since American capital practically controls the Bolivian tin-mining industry," he said, "and since the United States is the world's principal consumer of tin, it seems a little silly that it should continue to depend upon Great Britain for practically all of its tin plate.

"The tin in your tin pans and buckets," he went on, "the cans in which your tomatoes and asparagus come, the tin roofing for your house, the tin toys with which your children play, the tinfoil around candy boxes and even the tin compound on the backs of your mirrors is, without doubt, a British product which may come from the British-controlled Malay states. Even if it should be Bolivian tin, it reaches your country by way of the Old World.

"Here's a statement from the Pan-American Union, that great inter-American agency of information located right in Washington," he continued picking up a pamphlet from his

Bolivia

desk. "This official document states, 'Although the United States is the world's largest tin-consuming nation, ailthough tin is not produced in the United States, and although Bolivia among Latin American nations is the great tin-producing country, nevertheless the United States does not import tin from Bolivia. Bolivian tin which enters the United States comes by way of Great Britain after the ore has been refined in British plants. On the other hand the United States obtains the greatest portion of its tin supply from British Malaya in the form of bars, ingots, et cetera.'

"You see," he said, "this forces Bolivia into the world tin cartel. Because England controls most of the tin ore outside of Bolivia, and because she also has a monopoly on the refining of ore into tin plate, mind you through the voluntary consent of other countries, principally yours, Bolivian ore can be marketed only in Great Britain, and only in such quantities as she, with United States consent, chooses to buy. In reality, the Americans who control the mines in Bolivia join with the British refinery owners to handicap and restrict Bolivian tin production and exports, all to protect the owners of British tin mines in the Far East."

Before I could put in a word, he hurried on, saying, "How inconsistent! Great Britain and her dominions are trying to get closer together, which means that in the end they must enter more and more into ironclad trade contracts among themselves to keep business within the family, if not discriminate against outsiders. Yet the United States chooses to buy one of its most essential commodities from England, rather than import it directly from the mines financed by its own people in a country which owes them millions of dollars.

"If here is not a splendid field for reciprocal trade bargaining," he said, with evident bitterness, "one which would greatly benefit both parties, there is no such thing as a promising reciprocal trade opportunity. And yet languishing Bolivia, with millions of dollars of stagnant North American investments, has not, up to this moment, even been invited to discuss such a possibility.

"For the life of me," he rambled on, "I don't understand you Yankees. You are the most industrious and resourceful people on earth. You have most of the money in the world. The people of your great cities live out of tin cans. Millions in American capital are invested in the tin mines of this country, yet you are wholly dependent upon England for your refined product. Suppose England gets into a desperate war? Suppose the Fascist powers suddenly bomb her industrial centers into Kingdom Come? What would you do for tin?

"Why not," he concluded, with a grand flourish, "invest some of your moulding gold in tin refineries, build new plants, new industries, create hundreds of thousands of new jobs and new opportunities for your young chemists and engineers now being turned out in regiments by your colleges and universities? Why, it would put millions more dollars into circulation. Besides, buying Bolivian tin direct would help to make better customers of the Bolivians. If they could get more American dollars they might spend them for Massachusetts and St. Louis shoes, New England and Carolina cloths, Missouri flour, Iowa lard and innumerable things which you have and they do not possess. Incidentally, it would help to stabilize industry and the country." Then as an afterthought he added, "It might also enable Bolivia to pay off some of its defaulted bonds held by your people."

There is much logic behind, if not very clearly expressed in, the young man's statement. But the reluctance of American financiers of Bolivian tin mines to follow any such suggestions can be understood. Suppose they laid out millions for large refineries, and became wholly dependent upon Bolivia for the raw product? Then suppose the rulers at La Paz should no longer be content to control the industry as they practically do

New Road East to the Orient

now, but decided to confiscate the mines, as they have already done in the case of American-discovered and -developed oil fields? Even if they should not decide to confiscate the properties, continual new regulations, taxes and demands placed upon the mining companies might eventually force the industry to the wall. In either case the refineries in the States would be in a helpless situation, and would probably have to close down.

I am inclined to think Americans will probably still prefer to depend upon or to tie up with the British refineries, for their supply of tin plate. This situation spreads the responsibilities to say the least. England controls enough tin resources outside of Bolivia to influence world prices and perhaps to keep the brakes on the Andean dictator politicians.

Naturally if Germany and Italy should get hold of the Bolivian industry, a different situation would present itself. But Bolivia wants money, cash, real exchange. The totalitarian countries do not have it. Besides, the United States is the great world consumer of tin. President Busch and his associates are wise enough to realize, in fact they have already indicated, that they will be better off to accept a steady income as long as they can get away with the present rigid control than to attempt to run the mines themselves.

Much has been said on the subject of German or European totalitarian activities in Bolivia. There is a general impression that both the Nazis and the Fascists are heavily interested financially in the country. This is not the case. United States capital is not only predominant in the tin industry, but in several other lines. The new Aramayo gold mines, the largest such development in the country—some call it the new Bolivian Eldorado— are in the hands of a syndicate which is backed principally by North American capital.

The newest operations of this outfit are centered in a deep valley behind a snowy mountain wall only sixty-five miles by air northeast of the city of La Paz, in the Sipiapu district, the rivers of whose valley flow into the Rio Beni. When I was in the Bolivian capital recently, a crack pilot of the Pan-American Grace System had already made a hundred trips in a cargo plane transporting heavy machinery and other equipment to one of these mines, one of the most perilous of flights. To get through a narrow pass down into the valley it was necessary for him to career the heavily laden plane at an angle of forty-five degrees until it was practically on the ground. If he had ever been a few seconds slow in levelling off all would have been finished. Incidentally, gold production has been steadily increasing in recent years, in weight from 5385 ounces in 1932 to 15,636 ounces in 1937.

The largest importing and trading firm in Bolivia is the W. R. Grace Company which, as in Perú, engages in many lines of business, such as the manufacture of cement and flour milling.

Britons and Canadians are extensively interested in the hydro-electric enterprise and railroads. Britons own the line operating between La Paz and Lake Titicaca, the north-and-south line from La Paz to the Argentine border which connects the Bolivian capital with Buenos Aires, as well as the Antofagasta line as far as the Chilean border. They also own the two spurs that extend eastward from their north-and-south main line, one from Uroro to Cochabamba and the other from Rio Mulato to Potosí, 806 miles in all. The Bolivian government itself owns and operates 497 miles, including the all-important La Paz and Arica railroad, the country's most direct outlet to the sea, and a number of feeder lines here and there, such as the one from Potosí to the old capital of Sucre, and the spur from La Paz to the near-by Yungas Valley, which furnishes the capital with most of its fresh vegetables and fruits. The other 96 miles are operated by various private mining companies.

German and Italian interests are more apparent than real. Neither country has ever controlled any of the important mineral resources such as gold, silver, tin or oil, except for the brief period when Hochschild was being financed by German bankers. As a matter of fact, except when German officers were employed to train the *cholo* and Indian soldiers, and later when General Hans Kundt helped to plan the early Bolivian-Chaco campaigns in the war with Paraguay, the Germans have never even been influential in Bolivia.

Interestingly enough, Italians outnumber Germans in Bolivia and, as in other countries on the western side of the continent, pro-Fascist Italians attempted for a time to carry on a propaganda campaign. But it received so little attention from the Bolivians, as well as from the old Italian settlers, that the campaign soon subsided. On one of the main residential streets of La Paz, they started out two years ago to erect a commodious building to house the Bolivian-Italian cultural institute, but for months now no work has been done on it and nobody seems to know when construction will be resumed, if ever. As in Ecuador and Perú Italian aviators were brought in to train Bolivian flyers, but their mission proved fruitless. Italian material interests are confined largely to a few stores and shops, a spaghetti factory and the only two woollen mills in the country. Italian exports and imports are negligible.

The Germans are engaged in the manufacture of a few canned goods and the beef butchering business. They own a number of important stores and trading companies. And while German manufacturers in the old country have increased their exports to other parts of the world in the last two years, their trade with Bolivia has fallen off sharply. In 1937 Bolivia imported $3,524,160 worth of German products. In 1938 her imports from Germany amounted to only $2,660,800. Our sales to Bolivia in 1938 amounted to $5,395,000.

As suggested in another place, the shrewd and industrious native *chola* women, together with the large colony of Near-Easterners—Armenians, Greeks, Syrians and others, all of whom the Bolivians call Turkos—with their shops, bazaars and fruit stores, dominate the field of small business in the cities.

At the same time the Germans in La Paz maintain their own beer halls and clubs. The original German club, by the way, has been split wide open because of the rise of Nazism. The older and substantial element of Germans have no use for Hitler. Consequently the younger set who sympathized with the Nazi regime found it too uncomfortable to remain under the same roof with their unfaithful fellows, and have organized a separate club of their own. The Colegio Alemán, or German college, has an excellent record and was for a time a haven of Nazism, supported, until recently at least, by the German government. At one time its instructors even received their appointments directly from Berlin.

However, the most popular foreign school in the entire country for the past forty years, and one of the best of its few colleges, is the American Institute, which was established and is still run by American missionaries. Its graduates are found in most of the American business firms and industries in the country. All of them not only speak excellent English, often with a Yankee accent, but find rapid promotion because of their efficiency and industriousness.

Only in commercial aviation do the Germans cut any great figure in Bolivia. They were the pioneers in this field. They established, and continue to operate, the extensive Lloyd Aéreo Boliviano Air System which connects all the widely separated and otherwise completely isolated Bolivian cities and towns. It also connects with the German Condor, or Lufthansa combine, now operating a line from Lima, Perú, through Bolivia and Brazil and across the Atlantic to Berlin. On the other hand, the latest aviation development, which has put Bolivia on the main highway of world travel, is the Pan-American Grace Line direct from Panamá to Buenos Aires by way of Lima and La Paz.

Bolivia

Pro-Nazis, among the newcomers, and especially those in the diplomatic and consular service, have put forth desperate efforts, and waged a terrific campaign of propaganda for the purpose of keeping their natives loyal to the home country. They even resorted to desperate methods. There was the case of Fritz. He was a handsome fellow, six feet tall, slim and twenty-seven years of age. His blonde hair, clear complexion and baby blue eyes made him look about twenty. He had come out to Bolivia as bookkeeper for a German trading company four years before and was about to return home on what he thought was to be a quiet vacation, but which came dangerously near resulting in the tortures of a Nazi concentration camp. Within a few hours his fate would have been sealed if at that moment the Bolivians and Paraguayans had not been trying to hack each other to pieces in the pitiable slaughter of the Chaco War.

Fritz came of an old Bavarian Catholic family, whose somewhat laconic letters, vaguely describing activities in the homeland, and appropriately interspersed with phrases about the New Day and the brilliant statesmanship of Der Fuehrer, had long filled him with forebodings—these and the stories about purges and persecutions which he had gleaned from Bolivian and occasional American and English papers. On one or two occasions he had expressed to close friends his concern for conditions in the fatherland. He was glad to be going home so that he might see for himself what the real situation was.

The German Consul, who had been in Bolivia for only a short time, but who had always seemed friendly, was unusually pleasant the day Fritz called to say good-by. In fact the Consul entrusted to him a very important letter for delivery to the Foreign Office in Berlin.

"The war censorship and the Bolivian suspicion of all foreigners," the Consul had told him, "make it necessary for us to be very careful with our communications."

New Roads to Riches

Sure enough, as he was about to cross the border on the way out of the country, the Bolivian customs and Immigration inspectors not only searched his baggage, but asked him to reveal the contents of his pockets as well. Naturally the official-looking letter to the Berlin authorities whetted their curiosity. They rudely opened it and began reading it aloud. As Fritz listened he learned to his amazement that at various times he had spoken disparagingly of the new regime in Germany, to friends at the club, at beer parties and on numerous other occasions. According to the dutiful agent of Herr Hitler there could be no doubt as to the heresy and disloyalty of the homeward bound lad.

Needless to say, the vacation was immediately postponed, and indefinitely. Since then Fritz has secured employment with another firm and applied for Bolivian citizenship.

This incident may not have been true, but it was one of a number of stock stories current in Bolivia during 1937 and 1938. It suggests the length to which the enthusiastic young Hitlerites have gone in an effort to convert or keep their fellow countrymen faithful to the Brown Shirt doctrines. But it also illustrates that what they actually accomplished was the determination upon the part of most of the Nationals to stay away from the country of their birth, so long as Nazism flourishes.

Of late, and in spite of all of Hitler's efforts to preserve the Teutonic racial strains in his nationals at home, many aspiring German lads in Bolivia have been following the example set by the father of Dictator Busch. They have been studiously cultivating and marrying into the best families; not, it seems with the idea of subduing Bolivia for Hitlerism, but to make permanent places for themselves in the New World. And since there are so few whites among all the Bolivians, these marriage ties almost guarantee entree to all exclusive circles, social, political and financial.

III

East to the Orient

"ToDAY there are two Bolivias," a young engineer said to me in La Paz recently, "the very old and the very new. The old Bolivia is Andean, high up in the sky. The other is in the Eastern lowlands or, as we call it, the Orient."

The old Bolivia, which had its origin on the shores of Lake Titicaca, and the lineage of whose native inhabitants goes back unbroken to prehistoric times, is for the most part confined to the dusty wind-swept *altiplano*, and only now and then ventures over into the adjacent valleys.

Politically the entire country is divided into eight departments, or states, and three vast territories. Yet, except for two or three large mining towns, there are but five important urban centers. When you have named La Paz, Cochabamba, Oruro, Potosí and Sucre, you have called the roll of upper Bolivian cities. Among them La Paz is the only one bearing any resemblance to a metropolis.

The new, or Oriental Bolivia, comprises two thirds of the country's area. It begins in the green far eastern foothills and fertile valleys of the Andes, sprawls eastward into the Gran Chaco and northwestward into the Amazonian jungle. The only town of any size in all this limitless region is Santa Cruz de la Sierra, capital of the department of the same name.

Santa Cruz is the center of a potentially rich agricultural

and stock-raising section, and lies just north of the famed region of black gold, the magnetic influence which has attracted
the attention of the world to what the younger Bolivians insist will eventually overshadow the highland region.

"As in the days when you Yankees looked to the West as
your new empire," said a young intellectual, "our slogan today
is, 'Go East young man, to the Orient.' To establish ourselves
in this vast territory we have undergone much the same experience you did in winning your great West. The people of the
United States fought war after war with the Indians and the
Spaniards of Mexico, in their efforts to establish themselves
and open up the Western empire that stretched from the Mississippi to the Pacific. In the same way we Bolivians have engaged the Paraguayans in a hundred years of disputes, clashes
and finally a great conflict in the effort, first to gain undisputed
right to exploit the Eastern lowland country and to call it our
own; second, the outlets for the fruits of that exploitation."

I might have pointed out that we fought our way westward
step by step, claiming and settling only a portion of the land
at a time. On the other hand, the Bolivians were more ambitious. They claimed and fought for the entire Chaco Boreal, a
triangular piece of territory, larger than Illinois, Iowa, New
Jersey and Massachusetts combined, lying between the Bolivian
foothills on the west, Argentina on the southwest, and the
Paraguay River and Brazil on the northeast, much of which is
a desolate, unusable, uncultivatable no man's land.

To go back a little, when the Spanish Viceroys and soldiers
reluctantly took leave of South America a hundred years ago
and independence reigned, completely if stormily, from the
Caribbean to Patagonia, all the various republics agreed that
the old administrative boundaries of colonial times should form
the frontiers between them. This in effect gave the Chaco to
Bolivia, since, for administrative purposes, it had been under
the jurisdiction of the officials of upper Perú. But what with

the gold mines of the cordillera, and later the silver of Potosí, the unhealthy and unexplored Orient had been neglected, if not forgotten. Meantime the Indians of Paraguay gradually penetrated far into it, made settlements, so that later on Paraguay, by virtue of having occupied it, claimed it as her own.

Eventually Chile began biting off chunks of territory along the Pacific side of South America, until Bolivia was completely cut off from the sea. It then occurred to the Bolivians that, if access to the Amazon and the Atlantic from their northeastern rubber country was possible by way of the Beni, the Mamoré, and the Madeira of Brazil, transportation from the southeast could be effected by building a railroad across the Chaco wastes to the Paraguay River from which steamers would connect with Buenos Aires and the South Atlantic. That is, if they could get control of the Chaco which lay between the foothill region and the river. But to this the Paraguayans strenuously and successfully objected.

After this the Chaco became a sort of whipping boy for the politicians in Bolivia, and in Paraguay, too, for that matter. Whenever a president or a dictator found himself being forced to the wall, he diverted attention from himself by charging, or having it reported, that the Paraguayans were marching against the country. Usually a few weeks of patriotic debating, flag waving, investigation and diplomatic maneuvering furnished the needed respite during which political fences could be mended sufficiently to keep the opposition off the executive neck. Now and then of course it became necessary to send soldiers on the long and laborious trek over the mountains, and down into the unknown, so that months would elapse before public attention was again directed to home affairs. Since Paraguayan officials were also resorting to such stratagems to protect themselves from their critical populace, these forays occasionally coincided and real clashes occurred.

New Roads to Riches

As time passed, suspicion, bitterness and hatred grew in both countries. Even people in adjacent territories across the borders began to take sides. Eventually the Chaco question became a menacing disease in the heart of South America, the virus of which threatened to spread to all the surrounding nations. Through the years overtures came from many sources urging a solution of the question. Several attempts at arbitration, one by a President of the United States, Rutherford B. Hayes, were made. All of which failed largely because the politicians in both countries did not want a final solution.

Then in 1912 oil was discovered along the edge of the Andean foothills, in a strip of territory about one hundred miles wide and apparently extending from the Argentine border all the way up to Perú. This of course furnished a legitimate excuse for a genuine rivalry between the Bolivians and Paraguayans. Although the new riches lay in territory never even claimed by the Paraguayans, they now looked with covetous eyes upon it. Bolivians knowing that oil could not be siphoned a thousand miles across the Andes to the Pacific in order to get it to world markets, were now completely convinced that they must have at least enough of the Chaco through which to build roads to where the Paraguay River is navigable by ocean-going tankers and ships.

In 1922 a concession which amounted to 689,839 acres, had been awarded to the Standard Oil Company for exploitation, the company to develop the industry and dispose of the oil under a forty-year lease, paying the Bolivian Government eleven per cent royalty and, in addition, a rental of approximately one-fifth of a *boliviano* per acre per year. No doubt it was thought that so powerful a concern would itself find ways of getting the oil out to the world. And there was no reason why the company should not have felt that it could manage the situation without much difficulty. Fields which it operated in northern Argentina were in reality only an extension of the

Bolivian deposits. From here it would be comparatively easy to construct pipe lines and even roads on up into Bolivia.

Unfortunately developments in Argentina made this impossible. At one time the Argentine Government tried to force the foreign oil companies out of business, but since Argentina is a country in which the judicial machinery functions with independence, she could find no legal way of doing it. There being nothing to prohibit it, the government itself entered the petroleum industry in competition with the foreign companies. Sky-high tariffs were raised against private importation of oil, which served to block any plans to bring the Bolivian product out through Argentine territory. A pipe line across the Chaco was impossible because it would not only have been necessary to make many concessions to Paraguay, but to admit her ownership to the Chaco proper, to which Bolivia would not agree.

Before all this, however, an overly confident, not to say foolhardy Bolivian Government, with a dramatic bravado akin to that of Balboa taking over the Pacific, decided to send down an army sufficient to appropriate the Chaco bodily. Little did they, or any one else, realize this was to be the beginning of one of the longest and most disastrous struggles in South American history. Although the members of the administration which conceived and ordered these desperate measures soon found themselves walking the plank into political limbo, and their successors remaining in power hardly long enough to warm their official chairs, desultory warfare prevailed for years. There were a few lulls, but soldiers continued to roam the desolate wastes. One day there would be a serious clash in one section, a few weeks later on somewhere else, enough to keep the diplomats wrangling and the war spirit kindled both at the front and back home.

But in 1932 intermittent fighting gave way to protracted conflict, to large-scale bloodshed and suffering. Poor Bolivian

Indians, whose hearts and lungs were accustomed only to the cold, rarefied atmosphere of the high mountain country were suddenly plunged into the suffocating tropical lowlands. They died by the hundreds before they ever faced the enemy. Even after a period of relaxation and a certain amount of acclimatization they were in no fit condition to fight. Besides, having been subjected for hundreds of years to such oppression and mistreatment that all the fighting spirit had been taken out of them, they were never equal to the tough and fearless Paraguayans, who were not only at home in the Chaco, but are conceded to be the great fighters of the Southern Continent.

In addition to these human handicaps, the Bolivians labored against superhuman difficulties in getting supplies, ammunition and war materials, as well as themselves, to the battle front, not to mention the indescribable conditions under which they had to fight. "No matter what the stakes," a captain who succeeded in living through four years of it told me in La Paz a year ago, "they could never be worth one single day of the suffering we endured.

"To reach the front from La Paz in the early days," he said, "it was first necessary to travel 1200 miles by train and truck, then 450 more on muleback and on foot, over rugged mountains, down bottomless canyons to the edge of the Chaco. The Chaco itself is a vast sandy desert with intermittent patches, sometimes 12 to 18 miles wide, of thorny, impenetrable desert plants five and ten feet high. The sand is so fine that trucks had to be especially constructed to prevent the motors from completely choking every few minutes. Guns would become so clogged they would not even fire.

"In the wet season," he continued, "it rains in spots so that in one section the desert becomes an open sea, through which no truck, mule or man could pass. Dry gullies and valleys became surging rivers of mud, and it would be necessary to put all men and equipment on rafts built of gasoline barrels. And yet thirty miles away men would be dying of thirst and dust strangulation. Water had to be carried for hundreds of miles. Usually each man was issued a quart a day, and that had to answer for all purposes, cooking, drinking and bathing. The heat is stifling. Flies and insects of every variety travel over the land in swarms like bees."

While men endured all this, politicians in La Paz and Asuncion wrangled among themselves. Presidents and dictators schemed, revolted, took control and were overthrown, one after another. Neighboring countries pleaded and brought pressure to bear for peace. Members of the Seventh International Conference of American States meeting in Montevideo, Uruguay, in December, 1933, succeeded in bringing about an armistice during the Christmas period. Following this the League of Nations, of which both Bolivia and Paraguay were then members, tried its hand at a solution, only to find some South Americans lukewarm towards its efforts and others openly critical of its methods. So that neither party to the dispute would agree to anything. Finally the League, having completely failed in its mission, retired from the scene.

The war was resumed and bloodshed became more terrible than ever. For a long time the Paraguayans were easily the victors. They fought, so to speak, on their own ground, in a climate and under conditions to which they were accustomed. Besides they were nearer their home base, and the source of supplies and materials. In the end they drove their adversaries out of the Chaco proper and right up against the Bolivian foothills. But by this time the advantages were with the Bolivians. They were nearer their home base. Most of their soldiers had become veterans, practically acclimated to the lowlands. Besides that they had learned something about fighting and therefore were able to offer serious resistance. Neither side was able to make any great headway after this.

During the Economic Conference in Buenos Aires in 1935,

another armistice was effected, and a peace conference called, in which Argentina, Brazil, Chile, Perú, Uruguay and the United States were represented. Emissaries continued in session almost uninterruptedly for nearly three years until an agreement was finally reached in August, 1938. By that time Bolivia could count the cost in some 80,000 casualties, and a $50,000,000 piled-up debt.

In the treaty of peace Paraguay of course received the lion's share of the southern Chaco. While Bolivia was awarded only a mere strip of it in the south, she was given a rather large section, more than 14,000 square miles in the north, adjacent to Brazil. In addition she was granted the right to use a port on the Paraguay River, Puerto Casado, and by a treaty she has secured from Brazil, a piece of territory with a thirty-mile front on the Paraguay River in the north.

But while the peace conference was struggling to bring about the final settlement between the two countries, La Paz officials were devoting their attention once more to oil. They had developed many grievances about the matter. First of all they were disappointed over the fact that the oil company had neither provided nor found any way to get oil to the markets, and that after seventeen years the industry was still undeveloped and they were receiving no royalties.

Partly because of their own suspicions, and partly because of propaganda, and perhaps some maneuvers upon the part of the oil company itself, they convinced themselves that the Standard had never intended to develop the industry in Bolivia, that it merely intended to explore, drill a few wells, enough to furnish oil locally and hold the concession in reserve for use when other sources had been exhausted.

Incidentally the propaganda had originated from many sources, principally, some believe, from Argentina. Informed people suggest that Argentina, having little oil of her own, is ambitious to share in the exploitation of the Bolivian fields.

Bolivia

Also Germans and Italians, it was said, had vague hopes of greasing their fingers with Bolivian oil. Meanwhile enemies of the Standard at home were active, and threw fuel on the fire. To even scores with his old enemy, whose operations he had fought in Louisiana, the then very much alive leather-lunged Kingfish arose in the august United States Senate and charged the company with playing both ends against the middle.

Because of all this, and more, coupled with their growing nationalistic and socialistic tendencies, the young La Paz officials decided to take over the industry and carve a new economic future for the country. How they did it, and how they justified themselves—the legal hair-splitting and the court procedure in which they engaged—is a long and complicated story, and it is past history. The fact is they have scrapped the concession, confiscated the properties and have their oil fields to do with as they please. And I am not here concerned with the details, nor the justification, but merely with the fact.

How they are to develop, exploit and otherwise make the properties profitable to the country is now the big question. They cannot do it without assistance from the outside. That they will be willing to co-operate in any way with American companies is doubtful, since they have already developed such an anti-Standard, or anti-American-oil phobia. It has been reported that various agreements have been made with the Germans. According to one such report a railroad is to be built across the Chaco in Paraguay, a refinery set up on the Paraguay River and gasoline supplied to that country and peddled to the outside world. Bolivia might be willing to agree to some such plan, although she has denied it. For that matter I can see no reason why she should refuse, or why any reasonably minded person should think she should refuse to sell oil to the Germans, or anybody else in Europe for that matter, who can pay for it. But again Bolivia wants cash and needs it, and where Germany is to get it has not been explained.

New Roads to Riches

But no matter what the difficulties to be confronted, Dictator German Busch believes that the Bolivian Orient, with its various resources, has a bright future. Oil, of course, is number one on the list of its products. Northward in the Basins of the Beni, the Mamoré and the other important rivers is the center of what was once the richest rubber-producing section in all the Amazonian Basin. This industry, it is believed, can be restored to importance. *Coca* is already a source of considerable income for the country. In fact, Bolivia is the largest producer of this drug in South America. Coffee may also become a major crop and all manner of tropical fruits and nuts have been waiting for transportation to world markets. No section of the world, say experts, is more suitable for cattle raising than the grassy valleys in the region of Santa Cruz.

All these possibilities loom large in the mind of German Busch. He is not a highlander, but an Oriental, a native of the Santa Cruz section. In far-away La Paz I have no doubt he looks out upon the bleak surroundings, the snow-capped mountains, and longs for the green valleys below. At night he probably shivers in the biting atmosphere of the *altiplano* and thinks of his home country and its equable climate, where almost everything grows, trees, flowers, all forms of agriculture, and where more white people have settled in recent times than anywhere else in the country. He wants to see this region developed. Besides, if this can be done, he feels it will offset the economic stranglehold which the tin industry, not to say the tin kings, had on the country.

Immigration to the Orient has been and is being encouraged. Italians, Germans and Jugoslavs have settled around Santa Cruz in former years and they have gone on the land and become substantial citizens. In the past year and a half Bolivia has received large numbers of German-Jewish refugees, hoping to settle them in the new eastern empire. For a while she was admitting as many as 800 a month, so many that a serious passport scandal developed over the question. In spite of this she has continued to accept substantial numbers.

But already the plan is faced with great difficulties. Most of the newcomers want to remain in the upland cities, which is creating a serious problem. In old communities, whose populations have remained more or less static for years, and in which every available job or professional position has been handed down from generation to generation in the same families, a sudden influx of hundreds of foreigners of a different race, with different customs, causes considerable reaction.

Not only is the slogan, "Go east to the Orient," but plans are under way to provide means of getting there. Several railroads to the lowlands are already projected. The first and most important is the one from Sucre down to Camiri in the oil fields, "of great importance," says an official statement, "for the extraction of petroleum destined for the domestic markets." Another is to connect Cochabamba with Santa Cruz. "This one," to quote from the government's rhetorical outpourings once more, "will signify the material and spiritual tying together of the east and the west." Besides these two key lines, which would link the Chaco with La Paz and the old cities of the *altiplano* as well as the Pacific Ocean, there are to be two or three short lines connecting certain of the more populous communities of the region.

Only a few highways to the east have been planned so far. First-class motor roads already constructed in Bolivia aside from those in and through the suburban districts of the cities, may be counted on the fingers of one hand, leaving more than one finger to spare. The new fifty-mile strip between La Paz and Lake Titicaca is about the longest. Another, passable only in dry weather, extends northward from the capital over into the near-by Yungas Valley. These and two others built by the mining companies, connecting certain camps with railroads, are about all.

[425]

New Roads to Riches

One rough military road was built across the southern mountains from the Bolivian-Argentine railroad to the edge of the Chaco in the early days of the war, which is to be improved. Of the new roads under consideration, but by no means under construction, one from Cochabamba to Chimore in the Valley of the Mamoré River, will make possible transportation from the highlands all the way to the Amazon, as the Mamoré is navigable to that point by shallow-draught river boats. Another in the Santa Cruz region, one in the far south, and short stretches here and there are on the program.

Bolivia is the only one of the Andean countries in which railroad building takes precedence over highway construction today, although the physical difficulties to be overcome in the building of railways are even greater than those encountered in the laying of highways. While in either case, it is necessary to span countless canyons and gorges, and to bore tunnels through mountains and chisel ledges out of solid rock, all at tremendous cost, highways are certainly much less expensive.

But of all the plans for transportation to the oil country and the lowlands, the projected plans from Yacuiba on the Argentine frontier to Santa Cruz, paralleling the oil strip, is probably the most significant. This line naturally extends on down to the main-line Argentine roads with direct connections to Buenos Aires. It suggests that the statesmen on the Rio de la Plata were thinking far ahead when they put high tariffs on the importation into or transit of Bolivian oil through Argentine territory. Now that Bolivia has taken over her oil resources, and the industry is no longer in private hands, she is to enjoy complete Argentine co-operation.

Brazil, not to be outdone by Argentina, is also bidding for a share in the conquest of the Bolivian Orient. In co-operation with the La Paz Government, she is to construct a railroad across the northern Chaco, between Santa Cruz and Corumbá on the Paraguay River, to connect with her long transcontinental line to the Brazilian cities of São Paulo, Santos and the Atlantic coast.

And herein lies the reason why the Nazis will hardly be likely to gain control of any portion of the Bolivian oil deposits. They may be able eventually to purchase or bargain for oil, but not for any wells. Brazil and Argentina are the two largest, richest and most populous countries on the Continent. Brazil so far has found no petroleum deposits anywhere within her vast territory, while the Argentine fields supply only a small portion of that country's needs. Both nations are extremely nationalistic and without the slightest sympathy for Nazi doctrines or interference in South American affairs. Brazil is openly and violently opposed to totalitarian penetration.

If the lowland region is to become the stage for a revived Bolivian economy, if there is to be a new Bolivia in the Orient, Brazil and Argentina will not only help to bring it about, but will undoubtedly share in the results. Anyway, they are already building new roads to its riches.

Index

Index

Index

Index

Index

Index

412; history, 387-8, 390; house of Diez de Medina, 388; Military College, 394; names for city (obsolete), 387; native dress, 388-9; public buildings, 388

La Perla, 278, 279

La Posada, Juan de, 138, 139, 140, 150

La Silla, Mount, 4

Latacunga, 242

Latham, Edward, 191

La Vela, 63

La Victoria, 37

lead, 243, 307, 400

League of Nations, 421

Lecuna, Juan, 36

Leguia, Augusto B., 283, 296, 339-44, 346

Lesseps, Ferdinand de, 177

lianas, 312

licenciado, 82

Lima, 112, 274, 275, 309, 310, 324, 325, 328, 388; air mail, 314-15; air terminal, 318; American shops, 289; architecture, 279, 289, 291; Banco Italiano, 293; Bolivar monument, 290; British firms, 290; buildings, modern, 288, 295; buildings, public, 296; cathedral, 282-3, 388; churches, 282-3, 289; climate, 276; Country Club, 371; foreign sections, 294-5; Hall of the Inquisition, 290-91; history, 263, 279, 281, 283, 292, 338, 341, 342; hospitals, 349; hotels, 288-9, 293; industrial plants, 296; Italians, 293, 361; legations and embassies, 279; Legislative Building, 291; Library, National, 291-2; light and power, 294; mills, cotton, 331; museums, 317, 318, 331, 335; newspapers, 267, 289; old city, 279; palaces, 283, 290; parks, 290, 295-6; Paseo de Aguas, 284, 286; Pizarro's tomb, 283; Plaza San Martin, 288; police, 340; population, 297; prison, old, 343; race course, 296; sanitation, 294; San Marcos University, 286-8; suburbs, 278-9; Torre Tagle mansion, 292; Union Club, 288

Limatambo, air port, 318

Little America, 256

llamas, 245, 246

Llamozas, Manuel V. Rodriguez, 33

Long, Huey, 423

Long, John S., 224, 294

Lopez, Alfonso, 94, 117-18

Los Teques, town of, 36

MacGregor John D., 210, 317, 326

Machu Pïchu, 265

Macuto, 6

Madeira River, 376, 377, 417

Madre de Dios River, 376

Magdalena Nueva, 278-9; Magdalena Vieja, 278-9; Bolivar Museum, 331, 335

Magdalena River, 85, 95, 96, 106, 123, 125, 128, 132, 137, 150; valley of, 100, 101, 102, 112, 125, 128, 132, 134, 135

malecon, 211

Mama Occllo, Inca Queen, 381

Mamore River, 376, 377, 417, 424; valley of, 377

Manamo River, 28

Mangin, General, 346, 347

Manglares, Cape, 211

Manizales, city of, 100, 125; Colombian state of, 125

Manta, 111, 212, 213, 214, 215

Maracaibo, Lake, 5, 28, 47, 52, 56, 103, 128; Bowl, 44, 48, 50; city of, 44, 45, 46. See Oil

Maracay, 34, 35, 39, 40, 41, 57, 59, 60, 62, 71, 72

Marañon River, 239, 255, 325

Marinera, 268

Marquez, Amalia Madriñan de, 143, 147-8

masamorra, 144-5

masato, 314

Masisea River, 315; town, 315

Matarani Bay, 328

Matucana, 302

McGinnis, Theodore, 168-70

McGrath, Anna May, 46

Means, Philip Ainsworth, 110

medanos, 327

Medellin, 125, 134, 135, 150, 151, 152; business and professional men, 141; Jews, 138; mint, 141-2; native customs, 138; San Pedro Cemetery, 138; travel to, 134

medianeiro, 33

Meiggs, Henry, 300, 311

Meiggs, Mount, 303, 304

Mejia, Gonzalo, 135-6, 147, 149-51, 152, 166

Mellon, Andrew, 130

mestizos, 46

Milne, Alexander, 259

Miraflores, suburb of Lima, 279; presidential palace of Venezuela, 59

Mirand Venezuelan state of, 36

Mochica country, 330; Mochicas, 336

Mollendo, port of, 326, 327, 328, 377; dock system, 327; Frederick Snare Corp., 327; railway terminus, 328

Monagas, Venezuelan state of, 29

Monroe Doctrine, 272, 338

Monroe, James, 338

Montalvo, Juan, 249-51

Index

Index

Index

Index